Los *Duendes*

A NOSTALGIC JOURNEY THROUGH SPAIN

TERRY RUSCIN

PublishAmerica
Baltimore

First printing

ISBN: 1-4137-1435-8
PUBLISHED BY PUBLISHAMERICA, LLLP
www.publishamerica.com
Baltimore

Printed in the United States of America

ALSO BY TERRY RUSCIN

Taste for Travel

Mission Memoirs

FOR TÍO CARLOS
My trusty squire

Menciones

To my unstinting editors Sandra DeVonish and Dr. Carlos Vallbona and to my diligent reader-consultants Diego Corriente, Sue Diaz, Beverly Halvorson, "Annie" (Alice) Jue, Tom Lozano, Rima Montoya, I extend *muchas gracias, mis amigos!*

Design and Maps
Terry Ruscin and Sandi Whitaker

Photography
Terry Ruscin

Front cover, clockwise, from upper left: "Catedrales y Río Tormes," Salamanca; "King Tut," Las Ramblas, Barcelona; "Torre de Oro," Seville; "Stomping at Los Gallos," Seville

11:    "Not Giants but Windmills"

15:    "Lady in Red," Tablao Flamenco El Cardenal, Córdoba

21:    "Hunger is the Best Sauce in the World," Bar Concepción, Segovia

49:    "Pazo de Oca"

67:    "Cave Dweller," Cuevas de Altamira

85:    "El Cid's Mausoleum," Catedral de Burgos

89:    "Fuente de Neptuno y Plaza Cánovas del Castillo," Madrid

119:    "Plaza de las Cortes," Madrid

Indice de Materias

prefacio

The *duende*…. Where is the *duende*? Through the empty arch comes a wind, a mental wind blowing relentlessly over the heads of the dead, in search of new landscapes and unknown accents; a wind that smells of baby's spittle, crushed grass, and jellyfish veil, announcing the constant baptism of newly created things….

…there are neither maps nor exercises to help us find the *duende*. We only know that he burns the blood like a poultice of broken glass, that he exhausts, that he rejects all the sweet geometry we have learned, that he smashes styles, that he leans on human pain with no consolation and makes Goya work with his fists and knees in horrible bitumens….

—Federico García Lorca,
"Play and Theory of the *Duende*," 1922

PREFACIO

Does a savvy traveler sense more clearly the nation he explores than does its own citizenry? Does the cleareyed visitor look deeper?

Through the centuries, non-Spaniards have written of Spain, a broad range of authors addressing the country's history, geography, or culture; others allowing fictional characters to express the sentiments of the Spanish people in a variety of novelistic settings. Many of these books, however, no matter how factually descriptive, failed to capture the spirit and soul of Spain or what we Spaniards call the *"duende."*

Duende defines inadequately in dictionaries because it is expressed through nuances of looks, voice inflections, or other intangibles more accurately interpreted as "energy." Some have compared *duende* to a demon of inspiration. Short of an understandable description, Spain's *duende* cannot be noticed, seen, or even sensed by the ordinary person. *Duende* must be seized through an elated immersion by only those uncommon individuals who embody an unorthodox sensitivity, beyond that which is required to understand art in its myriad forms.

Spain no longer pretends to be one country, with only one culture, one language, one faction of folklore, or one soul. Spain comprises a mosaic of seventeen independent regions (*comunidades autónomas*), fifty provinces, four official languages (*Castellano, Català, Euskera, Gallego*) and rich literatures. Even where *Castellano* (Castilian Spanish) is spoken, local accents and dialects establish recognizable distinctions between Spain's regions. Each region manifests its own soul and deep down, a sensitive person will find its unique *duende*.

I spent my childhood and early adulthood in a Spain intended to be one and one only, but the differences between regions remained as in the past. Four languages continued to be spoken, although not officially recognized. Only a handful of foreign writers noticed these phenomena of life in Spain. Others concentrated on analyzing what they understood to be Spain's rich history, its diverse culture, architecture, literature and cuisine. Such manifestations of Spanish culture have been described in numberless books, but in my opinion, precious few of those, which I have read, perceived and savored Spain's characteristic *duende* or *duendes*.

I detected a *duende* in Ernest Hemingway's acclaimed novels, *The Sun Also Rises* and *For Whom the Bell Tolls*. *Duende* was also evident in the classic *Homage to Catalonia* by George Orwell, in the magnificent opus *Iberia* by James A. Michener. I sensed *duende* in the short but delightfully illustrated entry of Spain included in a diary of the Bouvier sisters—Jacqueline Kennedy Onassis and Lee Radziwill—which they wrote during their travels in Europe in the early 1950s.

The book you hold furnishes another example. Moreover, as Ruscin's experiential account provides valuable information concerning residences and key sites, his musings far exceed the parameters of a travel book. Terry's prose about Spain is attractive as well as addictive, an Hispanophile's delight. One cannot pick up a chapter and not be interested in all others. Terry uses a fascinating technique. As an impulsive navigator, he describes his impressions relative to his travels throughout Spain and perhaps without realizing it, weights them against those of his inseparable companion. The striking contrast is there for anyone to notice. Imbued with a Don Quixote spirit and driven by his own *duende*, Ruscin's lyrical narrative sounds like a chant to the Spanish soul, be this reflected in persons with whom he speaks, in stones he touches, or in food he savors. You need not have *duende* to find the love story—the romance is all between the lines.

Ruscin's companion, Uncle Chuck, a true "Sancho Panza," occurs less interested in the soul of the Spanish people. Whereas Terry takes Spain by storm in his quest to grasp the *duende*, his pragmatic companion's introspection drifts to succulent meals, siestas, or other enticements. On the other hand, Terry's sensitivity goes beyond the five common senses of vision, smell, hearing, touch, or taste. His quixotic thresholds of perception differ vastly from those of his down-to-earth Sancho. Enriched by this collision of personalities, Terry's panoramic words demonstrate an uncanny ability to capture the souls and the *duendes* that surround him.

Does the savvy traveler sense more clearly? Terry Ruscin does, in Spain.

I hope for a sequel, looking forward to more piercing observations by Terry Ruscin. Through them, I shall learn more about the soul or souls of a country I love: a country destined to play a major role in the history of the new Europe in decades to come.

—Dr. Carlos Vallbona

Los Duendes

A NOSTALGIC JOURNEY THROUGH SPAIN

TERRY RUSCIN

Presentación

It is not the hand but the understanding of a man that may be said to write.
—Miguel de Cervantes, *Hidalgo Don Quixote de La Mancha*

A Gypsy cried. Her harrowing rasp impaled my heart. Spiked a belly-drop surge of adrenaline as her eyes brimmed with crimson droplets. When the black-eyed Muse locked her gaze with mine, a chill tore down my spine, hurtling me across the ages over saw-toothed mountains through Aragón and Galicia and wind-swept vegas of Castilla, then pulled me back to the tablao in Andalucía....
  "¡Por Dios!" *I cried.* "¡Eso es!"

Each language yields idioms barely graspable. Spanish proposes *duende*. *Webster's New World Spanish Dictionary* defines *duende* as "imp," "ghost" or "having a certain magic." About *duende*, there is so much more.

Time was, I wondered if *duende* bore semblance to "mojo"—the Creole notion of magic. Though, as *duende,* mojo waxes more complex, impossible to describe.

Duende led me to Spain. I first heard the word after a keynote speech I made to a conference for Los Californianos—descendants of the Spanish colonists of San Francisco, California—a settlement they called *Yerba Buena* in 1775. Los Californianos's lineage counts among its cognomens Alisea to Martínez, Peña to Valdés.

Since arriving in the Golden State in 1980, I was pulled by Spain's indisputable influence. Though marketing was my vocation, history became my ambition. I became fascinated with Spanish explorers, *conquistadores* and Franciscan priests. I wrote of the California missions and lectured dozens of times on the subject, yet questioned why Los Californianos chose a Wisconsin emigrant to speak to them of their origins in California.

"Sir," the event planner explained on the phone, "you know California's early history. We want to hear your perspective."

To Los Californianos I spoke of Spain's early exploration of Alta California, through the epoch of missions and secularization to the Mexican period. My audience of more than one hundred, transfixed Los Californianos wanted the unabridged version, then asked spirited questions for more than an hour.

Afterward I was offered membership in Los Californianos, a coterie that includes only those descended from colonists who came to California in 1775 from Sonora Mexico—then, a part of *Nueva España*—under *Capitán* Juan Bautista de Anza.

"Madame," I apologized. "I'm a 'Heinz 57,' but the mix doesn't include Spanish."

"Oh," she said with a big smile, "but you have the Spanish heart. And *duende.*"

"Duende?"

"Well, this cannot be explained, especially in English," she said, then, breathed deeply. "The *afición* (passion) was here in this room when you spoke tonight."

Seduced, I joined Los Californianos, became a proud, card-carrying historian-member and shortly after, embarked on my first trip to Spain to seek my Spanish heart. How could I have known this would become an annual rite?

As all lovers, I am crazy—in my case, for Spain's moods and character, flavors and textures. Though incurably romantic, I question why this Anglo-American falls under the sway of all things Spanish—with exception of *la corrida* (the bullfight). Admittedly, I am addicted to Spain's irresistible charms. Moreover, as addictions do, this one began innocently, and the habit has lasted for more than a decade. I hope to never shake it. How does one explain this addiction? What do I find so remarkably familiar in Spain's intricate amalgamation of cultures and strikingly familiar in her poetic *Mudéjar*[1] architecture? In her dramatic contrasts, in her *sol y sombra* (sun and shade) that renders me helpless?

Spain's pageantry intoxicates me, as do her undying walled villages, flaxen fields of sunflowers, boundless hillsides a-march with silvery olive trees. I come alive in her landscapes spared from World War II bombing, within her ethos that reluctantly resists globalization. She moves me deeply with the earnest pastiche on canvases of her native sons: Picasso, Velázquez and Goya. And shakes me to the marrow with indelible verses of Federico García Lorca and organic-architectural feats of Antoni Gaudí.

I favor the sonorous roll of the *r*, better still, the double-register of two.

Moreover, why does *cante jondo*—the deep song of flamenco *puro*—enkindle my spirit fervently, compelling my heart to beat faster, whenever I lose myself in it?

The answer: I come alive in Spain and discover myself there.

Now, come along and savor the mysterious virtue known as *duende*. Brace yourself for haunting scenery, riveting sites and notable cuisine in a seductive land called *España*.

In Spain, one finds old memories at unexpected places.

—James A. Michener, *Iberia*

---

[1] *Mudéjar* (from the Arabic *mudajjan*, domesticated subject): 1. Muslims who remained in Spain after the Christian *Reconquista*, paying tribute to the Christian rulers. 2. *Ibero*-Islamic forms produced under Christian rule.

1. Benavente
2. Salamanca
3. Segovia
4. Coca
5. Pedraza de la Sierra
6. Ávila
7. San Ildefonso y La Granja
8. Cuéllar
9. Buen Amor

Castilla y León

Throughout my life, I mostly worked backwards. Fumbled with a newfound passion, then took the course. Messed up as I endeavored to grasp a new software application or VCR functions and afterward studied the tutorial. Same principles applied to my obsession with Spain. Enamored of California's Spanish missions, I researched those outposts with reckless abandon then went to their source.

Persuading my crusty Anglophile companion Uncle Chuck that a future adventure must include Spain rather than his beloved British Isles proved no easy feat. Uncle Chuck toured England more than a dozen times and his addiction increased with each visit.

I appealed to Uncle Chuck's sense of history. And I whined, pouted, cajoled. Spain, after all, spawned our home state California. Worn down, the old boy concurred that a bit of diversion was in order and we were off one autumn at daybreak, eastbound in direction of the Iberian Peninsula.

It was easy for comfortably retired Uncle Chuck to get away. And I seriously needed a break from the hectic advertising and marketing grind. Furthermore, I was on a pilgrimage.

Castilian Heads and Tales

The moment Customs set us free, we drove our miniature rental car from Madrid's Aeropuerto de Barajas to the medieval village of Segovia.

I am exhilarated in this land of tangible pride and passion. *Why has it taken me so long to visit Spain, the second largest country in Europe?*

From the airport terminal, serious-looking guards herd us American passengers, as so many suspect terrorists, through a gauntlet, then into a bus that whisks us across the tarmac to another section of the airport. Oh, Customs.

With forms filled out and passports inspected, uniformed personnel turn us loose. Officials in Spain are so official.

Airport behind us, we negotiate ring roads of *La Villa de Madrid*, passing clusters of grimy brick-and-stucco row housing. From balcony clotheslines, socks and sheets flap in the wind. Just beyond this high-rise-congested landscape, we see a blight of *marginados*—cardboard shanties, corrugated aluminum lean-tos: homes of hapless residents on the margin of society. Finally, traffic eases and scenery gives way to open fields under impossibly blue sky. We spot the random home swathed in bone-white plaster, capped with red roof-tiles.

Worlds apart from other countries we have visited, Spain comes forth ponderous. There is a feeling in the air and I cannot put my finger on it.

Unlike the rest of Europe, we recognize straightaway in Spain a semblance to our home state in climate, flora and topography. Surely, Spain's *conquistadores* noted these similarities when they penetrated California in 1769.

We note the genesis of our Southern California architectural themes in color, arches, roof tiles. But California is an infant compared to ancient Spain.

Forty minutes northwest, a southern slope of Sierra de Guadarrama rises up to a village girdled with eroded ramparts. We gaze upon Segovia crowned with its stealthy *alcázar*,[1] a classic Spanish citadel sprouting from the brink of a cliff. Breaching a sapphire sky, cathedral towers glimmer in hues from yellow-ochre to mesmerizing mauve to cinnamon.

Suffering dry swollen eyes and Segovia's twisty roads, we head up the hill, pursuing Los Linajes, a medieval mansion transformed into a hotel.

We press through tight passageways crammed with cars and double-park in front of our hotel. Inside, a desk clerk points us to a lower level of the terraced hillside, to a garage. We are happy to leave our car, reasoning days ahead will engage us mainly on foot as we delve into the soul of a fine old village.

The half-timbered, plaster-and-brick façade of Los Linajes dates to the eleventh century. Inside we find handsomely restored, masculine décor, clean and comfortable. From our modest room's private balcony, we gaze upon glorious prospects. Miles of parched landscape fling beyond our fortified hillock. Under melodramatic sky, gone-to-seed sunflowers bow their heads amidst plats of golden-ripe grain.

Settled in, refreshed, we mosey to the *plaza mayor* (main square) where we see villagers voluptuously unhurried. Air smells delicious, the climate pleasant, and Uncle Chuck needs to relax.

Windows beckon with spinning glass tiers artistically plotted with bottles of wine, creamy-white piglets, frothing blue-shelled mussels, deep coral-hued *pulpo* (octopus). We eye fleshy brown mushrooms; convoluted, larger-than-life bell peppers; slippery, speckled squids and glossy whole fish dressed with citrus. One of these bucolic marketing ploys lures us into a bar called La Concepción.

Putting into service our pidgin Spanish, we manage to order sweet red peppers stuffed with succulent crabmeat, tender fried *chipirones* (whole baby squid) and mushroom *croquetas* (croquettes). Pleasurable, this first experience with *tapas* and we savor each delectable morsel with glasses of refreshing Rioja *blanca seca* (dry white wine from the region of La Rioja). As we munch, we overhear effusive villagers indulging in siesta-time *charlatanería* (café chatter).

LAS TAPAS

Snacks known as *tapas* or *tapitas* (small *tapas*) originated in Spain in the Middle Ages when physicians instructed an ailing Alfonso X El Sabio (Alfonso The Wise, 1221-1284) to take small bites of food with wine between meals. Alfonso recovered and imposed a dictum: *inns of Castile were not to serve wine without food.*

Years later, the custom of small bites persevered in Spanish *tabernas* (taverns). Royal mandate notwithstanding, barmen found it prudent to place slices of cheese or meat (*tapas* or "lids") over wine jugs, on rims of glasses—a means of keeping flies and airborne impurities from beverages. In those days, barkeeps did not charge for the *bocadillos* (snacks).

As the custom evolved, bars vied for customers, varying their *tapas*. Delectables they arranged on saucer-sized plates, makeshift lids for jugs and goblets. Each bar served up its own interpretation ranging from olives to meatballs—and a tariff was charged for this tasting menu.

Tapas bars abound in Spain and in Latin America where consumption of the snacks has become a ritual. Metropolitan areas in other parts of the world also adopted this popular tenor.

Tapas range in portions from *raciones* (small) to *gordales* (large). The limitless arrayal varies regionally, running the gamut from olives, nuts and meatballs to anchovies, whitebait, sardines, clams, snails, prawn, crabmeat and *calamares*. Some morsels are deep-fried, others more complex, such as stews of potatoes, mushrooms, tripe, lamb or chorizo (sausage). And *rellenas* (stuffed vegetables or seafood), pâtés, terrines. Croquettes and fritters of minced fish or meat we often find on *tapas* menus, together with sherry-

25

doused chicken livers, steamed gooseneck barnacles, hard and soft cheeses. A favorite is a wedge of classic *tortilla a la española*: casserole of layered potatoes, onions and egg, generally served air-temperature. Even the humble egg ranks among sacred *tapas*, from hardboiled to *brava, a la flamenco* (spicy), *revueltos* (scrambled). Artichokes, asparagus, peppers, aubergine and flavored string beans—even melon—are commonly seen on *tapas* lists. An inventory of *tapas* ranges from a single sheet of paper to more than a dozen pages.

In Spain, where dinner is taken much later than in other parts of the world—nine to eleven P.M.—*tapas* are seen as a means to bridge the lengthy span between meals, providing a *merienda* (light, late-afternoon or early-morning meal). *Tapas* are the fast food of Spain, though the custom has taken on sacramental proportions. Generally, one eats *tapas* with one hand while standing, leaving the other hand free for conduction of conversation. On the other hand, when taken with salad and the staff of life, *tapas* may replace lunch or dinner.

"Here we are," Uncle Chuck intones behind a travel brochure, "in the belly of an old military town named *Segovia*[2] by Roman conquerors." He clears his throat and continues, "Later an Arab textile center, Spain proclaimed Isabel Queen of Castile at Segovia in 1474.... Segovia is an historical treasure trove!"

I need a nap. Uncle Chuck persuades me to carry on,

"Best way to deal with jet lag," he says. "Let's explore; wear ourselves out, so we'll sleep well tonight."

Segovia's sixteenth-century cathedral stands near-at-hand, flanking one side of the square, the heart of Segovia's old Jewish quarter. The honey-colored edifice appears Gothic in style, but Renaissance domes and a pinnacled apse float above, imparting a palace-like character to this mammoth temple.

Inside the cathedral, we wrench our necks, gazing in wonder at stone-ribbed vaulting, at extravagant details awash in kaleidoscopic spectrum cast from panes of Flemish stained glass. We study masterful life-sized polychrome statues of the corpse of Christ surrounded by mourners, sculpted by Gregorio Fernández. In the ambulatory, we discover tombs of this cathedral's architects, Juan Gil de Hontañón and his son Rodrigo.

My Catalan-American colleague, Dr. Vallbona, lauded a local Mesón de Cándido as one of the top restaurants in Europe, second oldest in Spain. We follow our city plan, strolling in the direction of the *mesón*.

Soon we stand face to face with a muscular conduit, El Acueducto Romano, a monumental construction dominating Azoguejo Plaza. The span stretches twenty-five hundred feet long and soars one-hundred-and-two feet to the top of two arched tiers of granite. In Roman times, Segovia's water supply from Río Acebeda ten miles distant coursed through this aqueduct. Poignant remnants tally eighty-eight arches supporting seventy-five above and four more incorporated into the city walls—totaling 167 arches. Dating from the era of Trajan (A.D. 53-117), bound together with only the forces of gravity, El Acueducto Romano dwarfs all that huddle in its shadows, but we are too hungry to be humbled for more than a moment. Uncle Chuck spots Mesón de Cándido across the plaza, a public square of rustic stone arcades carrying second-story façades plastered in cantaloupe. The district buzzes, analogous to time-lapsed photography. Patiently, we wait to cross the plaza.

We find the *mesón* dark. Scanning a menu posted on the door, we see *cochinillo asado*, a dish so tender—say the international accolades—it can be easily carved with the edge of a plate. We will have to wait for the illustrious roasted piglets.

Uncle Chuck snoozes; I take to Segovia's cobbled lanes. Slender alleys lean between thick wooden doors studded with time-weathered hasps. Overhead, buildings intersperse a series of terrace-bridges at their second or third levels, open spaces proffering glimpses of shrines and altars bearing *santos* (statues of saints) together with floral offerings. Simplistic beauty of redbrick Romanesque Iglesia de San Esteban soars high above these humble residences.

Around each corner, ruined fortifications sigh with the destruction of age. Beyond moldered city walls, a windblown cemetery of leaning cracked stones list pitifully forgotten from matted yellow grass.

Again on the alleyways, I duck into doorway crevices a breath away from vehicles that pinch by. Spirited *niños* scramble dangerously between cars and mopeds, squealing with glee. Bright-eyed teens and young adults exude enchantment. These people are handsome, even older folk who shuffle along slowly, one on a cane, many women in kerchiefs.

Distinct from her European neighbors, Spain radiates poignancy, in the sky, in formidable landscapes, in the eyes of her people. Before aerospace, Spain hunkered beyond two of Nature's stalwart barricades, the daunting Pyrenees to the north and the enormity of the sea. Though Phoenicians,

Greeks, Carthaginians, Romans and Berbers invaded Spain through the Straits of Gibraltar, she retains her natural dignity and unequivocal sense of mystery.

Where I grew up in northwest Wisconsin, exoticism manifested only in old-timers who spoke broken though musical English, languidly drawing out their vowels—Scandinavian immigrants, fair-skinned or ruddy with blue eyes and blond or red hair. I recall no sense of *duende* in those people. In Segovia, faces do not belie Roman and Moorish pollination. Complexions of olive-brown, eyes dark and primarily hair jet-black—except the elderly and the occasional women with henna-rinsed dos.

Back at the hotel, I stop at the desk to reserve a table at Mesón de Cándido.

"At which hour, *señor?*" asks the deskman.

"Eight, please."

The man's eyes smile.

"Too early, *señor*. Let us try nine o'clock. Even better at ten."

When in Segovia, I reason, concurring with the clerk's suggestion; but the popular restaurant is fully booked for the evening.

"Nothing available until tomorrow. Tonight, try Mesón de José María," the clerk proposes. "Very good and open at eight o'clock."

I deliver the news to Uncle Chuck.

"Just as well," he yawns. "We should turn in early."

We return to Plaza Mayor and sip manzanilla *seca* (dry sherry) at a sidewalk café, watching as spirited crowds congregate in their outdoor living room. Energy spikes this plaza. Older folk thick-of-middle and reed-thin youth celebrate the evening, exchanging gossip, laughing and people-watching. These villagers have substance, more than likely, the arcane virtue of *duende*. Beyond this exotic look, there is an irrefutable demeanor, a nobility of spirit. Segovians are engaging, remarkably attractive.

No city in Europe would be complete without the jarring *Eee-er–Eee-er–Eee-er* from sirens, with tonight no exception.

We cross the square to Mesón de José María where our *comedor* (dining room) awaits. At eight o'clock, we are the only customers. Other Americans, then a German-speaking party arrive, perplexed as we at the paucity of patrons.

Vino de la casa (house wine) pairs supremely with sumptuous, airy *croquetas* enfolded with pâté. I have an appetite for fresh fish, but only roasted meats are offered. I want to hold out for Cándido's *cochinillo*; Uncle Chuck will not.

"Can I manage an entire piglet?" he gambles.

"Split one?" I volunteer.

On my platter rest a tiny head and trotters; on Uncle Chuck's, the rear, with curly little tail. Neither potato, nor vegetable and nary a sprig of parsley garnish our plates.

In Wisconsin, our food lacked exoticism, attributable, likely to stoic personalities of Swedes and Norwegians who settled there. Pot roast, ham or baked chicken was the mainstay of our meals. Always astride: potatoes—usually mashed, with gravy—one or two vegetables—generally peas, carrots or corn—sometimes canned versions. In those days, Midwestern restaurants did not serve à la carte. Furthermore, heads and tails never found their way to my family's table, so I find tackling this piglet a real adventure.

To our satisfaction, the meat tastes delectable, done to a turn, exquisitely offset in crackly caramel-colored skin. We share on the side a piping-hot dish of broad white beans dotted with cubes of bacon. Our meal weighs against more healthful, less meaty California diets, yet, when the *mozo* (waiter) retrieves our plates, he finds only bones—plus the head and the tail.

[1] *Alcázar:* From the Arabic *al-qâsr* (the castle) and Spanish for citadel or fortified castle

[2] Segovia: From the root of the Roman word *sego*, or victory

From Stones and Saints to Fortresses and Palaces, and *Yemas de Almas* to *Tragadores*[1]

Teresa de Ávila (1515-1582) was a nun and prioress of her reformed Carmelite (Discalced) order. Born to an aristocratic Castilian family, Teresa Sánchez de Cepeda y Ahumada left her home in Ávila at age fourteen to live at the local Augustinian convent. She later took her vows at Ávila's Carmelite convent, where she was visited by the image of Christ.

The Church canonized Teresa in 1622 and Pope Paul VI declared her a Doctor of the Church—the first woman to receive this honor—in 1970. Devotees deemed Teresa de Ávila patron saint of contemplative prayer.

"Tang?" I ask, peering through a glass of thin, limpid orange juice. With Spain's reputation for abundant citrus, it is a wonder our hotel serves such a cliché. Coffee tastes mediocre, the food, blasé. Guests of Los Linajes face an identical repertory each day: zwieback toast, hard rolls, one sweet bun and *conserva de membrillo* (quince preserves).

Damp air chills and the sky looks anemic as we hike northeast to the outermost cliff of Segovia, to the *alcázar*. At one time, more than ten thousand castles existed in Spain; now fewer than twenty-five hundred stand. On the horizon looms one of the finest.

Segovia's *alcázar*, commissioned by Alfonso VI in 1075, was built on the site of a Roman fortress. The overall shape of this citadel resembles the prow of a grand old ship; from other angles, a storybook castle, but its pristine, Disneyesque lines came long after Segovia's Roman occupation. In the mid-eighteenth century, the *alcázar* was revitalized after fire gutted and rendered it roofless. Since then, a new roof and slate-capped towers were appended with conical rooftops resembling candlesticks with snuffers.

A thick-planked drawbridge takes us into museum rooms, beginning with Sala de Reyes (Hall of Kings), a cavernous space occupied by life-sized wooden statues of early Spanish monarchy. We take in Sala de Chimeneas (Fireplace Hall), Sala de Solio (Throne Hall), Sala de Piña (Pine cone Hall), a royal bedroom and chapel. We explore chambers dedicated by Carlos III to the Royal Artillery Academy—former tenant here, the one allegedly responsible for the fire. An intricate dado of incised stone, a Franciscan cincture (*cordón*), embroiders Sala de Cordón (Hall of Rope), a braided motif symbolizing the blasphemy of Alfonso X, the king who ventured to suggest Earth revolved around the sun. *How long did Alfonso languish in this dungeon for such a crime?*

Throughout the *alcázar,* intricate *Mudéjar* touches decorate *artesonado*[2] ceilings, hatchways, skirting boards, entablatures and friezes. Unlike many of Europe's barren or sparsely furnished castles, Segovia's scintillates with sumptuous stained windows, Flemish tapestries, inlaid Islamic-styled furniture and a regiment of armor.

We move on to La Torre de Juan II, a massive dungeon and lookout configured with corbels and crenellated turrets, calling to mind a movie-set for medieval chivalry. This dungeon stirs with allure of medieval prisoner of literary fame, Gil Blas: the folkloric hero in the eighteenth-century tome *Gil Blas de Santillana* by Alain René Lesage. Next week we will lodge on Spain's northern coast in a *parador* (roadhouse)[3] named for Blas.

When Uncle Chuck wonders out loud about the number of steps within the keep, a docent replies, "One-hundred-fifty-two, with no landings."

"You go ahead, young man," Uncle Chuck says to me. "I don't know about this...."

Nevertheless, he joins me. Ten minutes in the ascent, we have covered only one-third of a challenging spiral staircase. Each of the tiny stone steps has been worn to concave smoothness under centuries of footfall, adding hazard to our precipitous trek. Cursed with vertigo, I thank God my sense of adventure transcends this affliction.

Stopping intermittently, Uncle Chuck catches his breath long enough to lob accusations of murderous intent at me. At the top, we venture outside to Segovia's highest mirador. Up here, we behold an eyeful of steepled village, a sprawl of Valle de Eresma far below and the snow-peaked Sierra de Guadarrama beyond. Immeasurable vistas define breathtaking, notably for Uncle Chuck, who wonders how many seventy-year-olds have made the treacherous climb. While he stalls to gain his wind, we soak up scenery, and I give my camera a workout.

Descending the tower more easily than our climb up, we discuss the day's options. Ávila is nearby; we will drive out to explore.

Beyond fields of megalithic boulders, Ávila (*Avela* to the Romans) occupies a mesa behind a ring of fortifications (1088-99). This city's *murallas* (curtain walls) stand intact, including eighty-eight D-shaped towers and two bastions. Experts cite these defensive walls as Europe's finest, for size and state of preservation. Ávila, within, once the highest provincial capital in Spain, was home to *Celtiberians* (Roman appellation for Iberian Celts), Romans, Germanic Visigoths, Muslims, Jews, Christians.

Chaos awes as we pass through one of Ávila's nine gates. The circuit of medieval walls embraces a thriving village and, unlike Segovia's tiered hilltop arrangement, Ávila appears flat.

Earnestly in need of intelligently brewed coffee, we duck into inviting La Posada de la Fruta. With cups of *cortado* (espresso infused with a splash of hot milk), we sample *yemas*: made with egg yolks, rolled with sugar into yolk-sized balls. Santa Teresa contrived this treat, in the sixteenth century, to give as *almas* to the poor.

"Ready to tour, Uncle Chuck?"

We down our coffee, spoon up vestigial wisps of mocha-colored froth, then set forth to discover treasures of *Ciudad de Cantos, Ciudad de Santos,* "City of Stones, City of Saints." We have viewed windblown, treeless fields of boulders outside the city's fortifications. Now, where are the saints— Teresa and one of her confessors and fellow mystic San Juan de la Cruz— who brought fame to this important Castilian center?

31

Ávila's Parador Raimundo de Borgoña, a converted palace, gives access to the *murallas*. Uncle Chuck sputters and plods behind me. Above, we tramp the sentry-path against blustery wind, observing the city from bird's-eye perspective. Dawn's pallor brightens to cobalt blue and frail clouds streak the horizon—bracing, behind a backdrop of red-tile-roofed, dun-colored stone buildings. And up here, we are able to gain our bearings.

At an extremity of the *murallas* stands a rustic cathedral, the oldest Gothic church in Spain, its massive apse forming the eastern terminus of city walls. At the western end courses Río Adaja, a virtual moat nearly encircling Ávila.

Santa Teresa de Jesús was born and did her life's work in Ávila de los Caballeros (of the Knights). What's more, here Teresa had conversations with Christ. Uncle Chuck reluctantly helps me find her shrines.

"I don't understand your fascination with dead saints," he says.

I am Roman Catholic and he, Anglican....

Our mute tour includes the convent of Encarnación—Teresa's spiritual home for thirty years—and another named simply "Santa Teresa," built over her birthplace. We find earthly reminders of Teresa at Convento de San José, including one of her mummified fingers on display.

"Look at that," exclaims Uncle Chuck, wincing at the sight of a withered digit. "I just don't understand Catholics. No wonder the Anglicans split off."

While Uncle Chuck remains stubbornly blasé, I shiver, walking upon the same tiles as had Teresa and her *Descalzas* (discalced, or barefoot) order of Carmelite nuns. We study stained-glass panels depicting the *Transverberation* (miracle of the Holy Spirit piercing Teresa's heart), and a re-creation of her humble cell. Teresa's body rests not here in Ávila, but where she embarked on the afterlife, at Alba de Tormes near Salamanca. Displayed at Alba de Tormes, too, is her incorrupt heart with the marks of her *Transverberation*.

Outdoors stands a fine white statue of Teresa de Jesús commemorating her rank as Doctor of the Church.

> There is more value in a little study of humility and in a single act
> of it than in all the knowledge in the world.
>
> —Santa Teresa de Ávila

We pass a quiet moment at a bridge-gate called La Puerta del Puente, savoring distant Sierra de Gredos silhouetted against a transfiguring sky.

Betting and praying against rain, we drive southward in pursuit of Palacio Real de la Granja in a town called San Ildefonso de la Granja.

"Hungry?" I hint.

"Dear boy, if we plan to adhere to Spanish protocol and dine near bedtime, I suggest we take our lunches late."

Palace grounds are closed for siesta, so, thank goodness, we will first have lunch. Sophisticated shops and restaurants fringe a regal chestnut-lined *alameda* that verges upon the grand palace-estate. Nearby Restaurante Segovia draws us upstairs to a cozy, second-level *comedor*, a beamed-ceiling chamber, snug against brisk weather we escaped.

Sopa de fideo (pasta in broth), a warm, hearty elixir, comforts. We follow with *ensaladas variadas* and mountain-stream-fresh *truchas* (trout) stuffed with smoky slab bacon. *Vino blanco* (white wine) accompanies.

Sky lets loose as we tread up a pine- and chestnut-lined boulevard fronting Puerta de Segovia. Just ahead looms the late-baroque palace dedicated to Saint Ildephonsus of Toledo that was built in 1450 as a country home with chapel for Enrique IV. In centuries following, the estate's development included a monastery-hospice, a hunting lodge for the Royal Court and subsequently a grand palace-residence. Though smaller and more severe, the architecture speaks of Versailles in august domes, finials, columns, carved portrait medallions, and fan-topped windows. Pale mauve-gray walls hail from the same quarries as the stony fabric of Segovia, and spires and domes capped with steel-colored slate are tantamount to those of the *alcázar* we toured this morning.

Inside, we marvel at incomparable luxury: sumptuous appointments in marble, velvet and gilding. King-sized chandeliers blaze against intricately carved and frescoed plaster ceilings. Recessed murals propose glimpses of heaven. Red-gold-and-green-embroidered Flemish tapestries plus silk carpets and ancestral oil paintings brighten the walls. From the extravagant, crimson throne room to sophisticated, monochromatic tapestry halls, this environment bespeaks regal opulence.

Salons gleam with fine porcelains, Chinese lacquer, urns, French furniture, clocks, marble pilasters and busts. We admire galleries of fine art: sensuous sculpture, etchings by Goya, paintings by Van Dyck, Poussin, Correggio, Thierry and Dürer. Painted and chiseled depictions of the *Five Senses*, *The Virtues*, the *Life of Christ*, *The Ethics* count among the treasures.

Not at all cozy, this palace seems more a museum than a residence. *Where did the dwellers get comfortable?*

We move on to the somber *capilla* (chapel), a collegiate church sporting an impressive dome with cupola, and final resting place of Felipe V (Philip de Anjou) and his Queen, Isabel Farnese.

When rain lets up, we adjourn outside and visit a celebrated park of gardens, bridges and lake. Ruefully, the season precludes operation of the palace's renowned waterworks, though we take pleasure in viewing complex forms and carvings amidst shocks of fall color blanketing our path. Bronze and stone sculptures: equestrian tableaux, gladiators, deer, a bear, cavorting frogs and a virile Neptune enliven acres of intricately wrought fountains.

Above moist grounds the *Four Seasons* in marble gaze from the portico, alongside urns topped with chiseled pine cone motifs. A party of English women obliges to photograph us with our cameras and we return the favor. Uncle Chuck engages in lively conversation with these ladies from Lancaster, reminiscing of the English Costwolds. Uncle Chuck would rather be there than in Spain.

Uncle Chuck asks me, "Enough for one day?"

Only a tourist between naps, "siesta" defines his expression.

Near dusk, we strike out for world-famous Mesón de Cándido. Segovia simmers with youthful *fashionistas*. Glib elders hunker on benches, teens buzz by on mopeds and sirens blare incessantly. We stroll in direction of a dramatic spectacle, the floodlit aqueduct.

Glowing dining halls of El Mesón Cándido resemble movie sets for medieval banquets, propped with prodigious mantels, glowing hearths, stone archways, trussed ceilings, placards inscribed with Old-World-style lettering.

Granted National Monument status in 1941, Mesón de Cándido has served as an inn since 1760 when it was known as El Mesón de Azoguejo, when diners included Enrique IV. Internationally renowned Mesonero Cándido Mayor de Castilla, mayor of Castile and author of *La Cocina Española*, assumed direction in 1931. Cándido, with his talented wife Patro, carried on the tradition of serving excellent roasted meats with utmost hospitality. Here, the guest book reads as a *Who's Who* of aristocracy, royalty, Nobel Prize winners, diplomats, artists. Cándido's son sustains the tradition with the grace and skill of his parents.

The restaurant cadre includes lovely "mayoresses" donned in traditional fifteenth-century dresses and *monteras*: jewel-encrusted headgear fashioned as miters, worn over embroidered veils. We watch these lovelies in the soft glow cast from ancient fireplaces as they carve roasted pigs with the edges of plates.

"When will we learn," Uncle Chuck sighs, "that we specify *gin* and forget the *martini*?" If he stares long enough, will the sweet vermouth magically evaporate from his beloved gin?

This version of martini we encounter far too frequently in Europe. We must find another way to order our favorite cocktail.

A waiter, not a mayoress, delivers sensuous soup of puréed crayfish, ambrosial nectar dotted with toothsome crustaceans. We follow with *ensaladas del tiempo*, buttery seasonal greens tossed with olive oil and hints of earthy vinegar.

By ten o'clock, Spanish patrons overwhelm our restaurant. As we nurse vigorous Rioja *tinta*, anticipating entrées, other tourists finish dessert.

Spaniards are loquacious, conversation ranking high in their dining experience, a custom contrasting my Scandinavian-American ancestors who ate in silence. This evening, I recall my Norwegian grandparents. As a child, when I was being seen and not heard at the dining room table, my grandmother broke the silence, chiding my grandfather. "You never say that you like my cooking," she sniffed. Resolutely, Grandpa responded, "I would tell you if I did not like it."

Glazed pottery casseroles arrive. Uncle Chuck's brims with flavorous, bubbling beef ragout and mine, with morsels of hare. These masterpieces make up for the pink martinis! The beef is roasted, with potatoes; the hare with *granja* beans the size of half-dollars. Sauces are hearty, vinous, the meat, inconceivably tender.

Entrées, though unctuous with olive oil, we find irresistible, savoring each vibrant mouthful, sopping up juicy vestiges with bread. Generally, even when sated, we make room for dessert. Breaking tradition, we will settle instead for *digestivos* at the plaza near our hotel. Meanwhile, heady memories of ancient fare linger on our appreciative tongues.

Eleven P.M. finds us sipping cognac at La Concepción. We watch Segovians who have just begun their evening. As for us, we will dream of the castle circuit north of Segovia.

---

[1] *Tragadores*: gluttons

[2] *Artesonado:* coffered wood with geometric incisions

[3] *Paradores:* from *waradah* (Arabic for halting place, and the Spanish *parar*, to stop), these are government-run lodging places throughout Spain (initiated in 1928). Of the eighty-six, some are modern, though all stand within convenient reach of ancient or otherwise intriguing sites. *Paradores* are converted convents, castles,

fortresses and other historically significant structures. The author has always found these emblematic hotels comfortably clean. Each has an excellent restaurant specializing in regional cuisine.

CASTLES GLOOMY TO GLOWING
FOR FROLIC AND FORTIFICATION

Uncle Chuck and I had taken in our shares of castles and fortresses, a broad range of them mere gaunt shells or extensively restored. We understood that Spain's castillos and alcázares stood reasonably intact. One of us was raring to explore them.

Morning dawned wintry, the sky acerbic, with lavender- and pewter-tinged clouds. These skies one sees in paintings, but never had I dreamed they were real, imagining the artists were given to exaggeration or were under the influence of alcohol, maybe something stronger.

With maps and guidebooks spread on our breakfast table at La Concepción, we plot our foray. Circling castle icons with a pen, cross-referencing sites in our books, the resulting highlighted route takes shape as an oblong swirl north of Segovia.

"This plan will make a full day," suggests Uncle Chuck, who has irrefutably factored in his siesta.

I finish my third cup of coffee and we set off to find the village of Coca.

Advancing northward toward our first conquest, we pause at diminutive Santa María la Real de Nieva. In this village, we photograph a church with *campanario* (pierced bell tower or wall) girded with an enormous stork's nest. The grand birds reputedly bring good fortune to villages where they build their twiggy incubators.

Ahead, on Avenida de José Antonio, Coca's main street, we face a massive brick gate and adjacent fragments of medieval *murallas*. Beyond, we see the castle, notably intact and purest *Mudéjar* in two-toned brick, interlacing arches and a proliferation of ornate turrets. The late-fifteenth-century castle's strategic position was not intended for fortification. Alonso de Fonseca I, Archbishop of Seville commissioned this *castillo* as a setting for his lavish banquets.

We pass through the old city gate and park near the castle. A deep moat seems inappropriate considering the bishop's commission. *Did the daunting trench inhibit party crashers?* Now this twenty-foot-deep moat flows only with waves of tall grass.

Each of multiple turrets bristles with crenellations, the embrasures pierced through with cross-and-orb loopholes. We step across the drawbridge to a claustrophobic stairwell and climb to the ramparts. Up here, we peer through a leitmotif of globes and crosses—ancient sentry windows, narrow slits allowing archers to shoot at a range between 180 degrees, but a moot point for this party castle. We cast our view across the tiny village and see not a sign of its Roman past when Coca was called *Cauca*. Moreover, Coca volunteers scant interest beyond this imposing folly where we stand. Many of the quarters within this pink fortress are off-limits to tourists, as a forestry commission school occupies the core. We move on.

Up the road, our map shows the town of Cuéllar, a walled town called *Colenda* by its Roman settlers a century before Christ. As most of Europe's defensive towns, Cuéllar mushroomed beyond its ramparts.

We spot the battle-scarred castle on a hill and breeze up for a look. Unlike Coca's splendid state of preservation, this fifteenth-century *castillo* stands ruined, though it presents a spectacle in four towers, each of disparate design. While pink bricks compose Coca's castle, this one rises in chalky gray stone, a ghostly vision against a transmuting, sullen sky.

Of Cuéllar, we know little but that Leonor, Princess of Castilla y León, was born here in 1382. And British sea captain Francis Percy died of natural causes at Cuéllar in 1812.

We shuffle along a rock-strewn pathway to the entrance of a crumbling pile. Intact sections of this castle document splendid fretwork, though even these remnants sigh with the passing of time. Beyond the crude exterior, a splendid Renaissance courtyard draws us into a forest of Corinthian-style columns. A bitter wind moans between. We try the doors, but find no access to a nuclear palace designed by Don Beltrán de la Cueva. Uninspired, cold and hungry, we retreat.

Below us lies the dismal, rundown town of Cuéllar, a blight of spiritless architecture sheathed in deep gray, no doubt attributed to coal heat and diesel fumes from a surfeit of lorries. Uncle Chuck approaches a workman and asks for a good family restaurant. The stranger points down the way.

Inside the dour restaurant, a grizzled old woman shivers in the draft. Toothlessly she smiles and rattles off a list of comestibles.

"Let's get out of here," Uncle Chuck barks, as he notices the establishment falls short of *A* status.

As we turn to leave, the woman clutches at our coat sleeves.

"I really struggled to free myself from her grip!" my exasperated travel mate complains on the way to our car. "And that fellow who recommended the place...was he a shill? Evidently, business stinks and our pesetas would have made the old woman's day; yet, I was not about to risk my health!"

Feeling sorry for the old woman, I slipped her some bills.

Beyond the outskirts of Cuéllar, we wend through systematically planted pine forests of time-honored trees tapped and girdled with buckets, for turpentine, Uncle Chuck guesses.

Back on the motor route, we discover a modern building emblazoned with the words *Restaurante Florida*.

"Ah...more like it," breathes Uncle Chuck.

The room caters tempting aromas and, unlike the restaurant we escaped fifteen minutes earlier, this is spick-and-span, cozy and the waitress, young and pretty—with teeth.

The food is tasty, if impossibly rich with olive oil. *Agua mineral con gas* (fizzy water) should relieve our swollen stomachs.

If I have my way, we shall add a half-dozen or more towns along the route. Next, Pedraza de la Sierra,[1] a compact village of singular charm. After our experience at Cuéllar, we are pleasantly surprised with the inviolate medieval character of this legendary birthplace of Emperor Trajan—though speculation suggests he was born in Seville.

Access to this lightly visited, sixteenth-century village greets us in blanched redbrick. We roll through an arched entryway below a niche cradling a crucifix, believing we have landed in a ghost town. Or, has siesta-time rendered these streets entirely drained of people?

Uncle Chuck champions the afternoon nap. In Spain, however, siesta supplies more than that. Yes, one may rest. After all, options are negligible as all generally shuts down from noon to two P.M. in large municipalities, noon until three or later in smaller towns. Even the younger working class partakes of this interval for long lunches, shopping, conversation and reading. I am envious, though the Age of Technology gains on Spain where commerce abates prolonged lunch breaks. Tellingly, this change has not caught up with medieval Pedraza.

Wind buffs away clouds and sunshine gilds plastered sixteenth-century stone dwellings in radiant amber tones. Afoot, we drift leisurely, communing with antiquity. The plaza encompasses hard-tramped earth bounded by sagging seigniorial mansions. Baronial escutcheons enlighten of Pedraza's medieval glory. And, decidedly, this is not a ghost town after all. Two friendly dogs greet us. Healthy, red geraniums bloom on multiple wrought-iron balconies and a smattering of buildings bearing mercantile signs.

A worm-eaten timbered arcade shades our way along one quarter of the plaza. Pitted stone columns support the other three sides of ivory-colored stone walls dominated by a Romanesque bell tower, leaning in and out from age. Above thick wooden doors, seigniorial crests boast of foregone glory.

Beyond this plaza stand a good number of structures fashioned of the same blanched stone in their lower stories with old coaching lamps clinging to the walls, upper levels fashioned from brick and mortar crosscut with darkened timbers. All these hoary buildings are wired for electricity and plumbed on the outside, utilities housed in long galvanized pipes. And while Pedraza's plaza sports balconies, humbler buildings beyond do not. This must be the residential area, but still we see no people.

"If we return to Spain one day," Uncle Chuck opines, "we will stay right here. So peaceful."

Upon a sandy crag at an extremity of this village stands a supple, golden-toned *castillo*. In the early-twentieth century, Basque painter Ignacio Zuloaga restored this castle, now part-time residence of his heirs. Not in the least does this fourteenth-century fortress resemble the gingerbread affair we saw at Coca, nor the ghostly castle at Cuéllar. Pedraza's castle appears a thoughtful arrangement of enormous rectangular stones. We tromp over for a closer look.

Crudely hewn stone turrets straddle a double postern more metallic than wooden. We face two doors that bristle with hundreds of five- to six-inch pyramidal spikes.

"Formidable salutation," Uncle Chuck remarks.

I read a weathered wooden sign that cautions, *Hoy no se visita.* ("No visits today.") Damn! The castle harbors an illustrious collection of political documents. And here, two sons of the French king Francis I were imprisoned after the Battle of Pavia.[2]

"Just as well," says Uncle Chuck. "We're doing a lot of walking and climbing, and we can't even get inside these old piles."

Navigating around this immeasurable castle, we hear a menacing growl. Overhead, a russet cocker spaniel watches us from the sentry walk. He reminds me of my own cocker and, as my dog, this one above us forewarns intrepidly, his wagging rump belying feigned ferocity.

As we pull away from Pedraza, I wish to check in on neighboring Sepúlveda and Riofrío. Uncle Chuck has but one venue in mind: naptime.

39

Back at Segovia, I pace byways in the company of one, rejoicing in ever-changing light. Haunting strains issue faintly from the cathedral's stout doors. Light filters through the western firmament, a tapestry of rainbow hues against resplendent patina of aging monuments. Banks of deep purplish clouds lazily course behind the stalwart *alcázar*. Randomly, street lanterns and apartment windows add specks of luminance to the village under a burgeoning cloak of twilight.

Carnal senses cycle my absorptive reverie to dinnertime.

Rich, roasted food taxes our systems. When I reach my compadre, we agree on a *merienda* in the square. We select Mesón Mayor, where sit only two other patrons: Don and Sara, a middle-aged couple from Phoenix. After an exchange of greetings, they tell us Segovia has been their base for a week. Sara seems pleasant, a 1960s Earth-mother type. She is a kindred southpaw, her husband Don, characteristic of his trade as salesman, a braggart.

"Can you recommend a light dish?" Uncle Chuck asks.

The Arizonians laud this restaurant's *huevos revueltos*, describing the dish as sensuous, fluffy omelets. We commiserate on rich Castilian food and gab throughout dinner, the Earth mother and I exchanging tales of left-handed woes.

"I believe we're the only minority group without a sort of coalition to protect us against discrimination," Sara laments. "With few exceptions, everything's made for right-handers. How often have you numbed the edge of your hand on the coil binding of a tablet or ledger? Or dragged your left hand through ink?"

"They say we don't live as long as right-handers," I add. "And some believe we're inclined toward certain perversions."

"Nonsense," says Sara with a smirk. "Righties are envious because we're in control of our right brains. We're creative, sensitive."

"I'm often mistaken for European," I tell her, "because I use the fork in my left hand."

Gazpacho arrives.

"For that matter, I use the spoon in my left, as well," I add.

We relish the cold, refreshing soup with honest bread, continuing with exquisite *revueltos* punctuated with *camarones* (shrimp), tender asparagus, savory onions. After thanking Sara and Don for their recommendations, Uncle Chuck and I splurge with a bottle of quality Rioja *blanca*, then split dessert of luscious caramel-drizzled flan. Perhaps tomorrow, we will dine again in the manner of macho Castilians, but this lighter fare was a treat.

As we bid our compatriots *adiós*, they ask where our travels will take us next.

"Far and wide, he hopes," Uncle Chuck says, his eyes laughing.

I wave goodbye with my southpaw.

As we stroll through cool twilight, Uncle Chuck remarks, "Generally, we don't do that in California."

"What's that?"

"Strike up a conversation with people we don't know."

"Natural, in Europe, isn't it, to speak freely with fellow countrymen? Barriers come down."

"Funny. I know more about those people back at the restaurant than I know of my neighbors."

[1] The *plaza mayor* in Pedraza de la Sierra was the set for a Super Bowl XXXV television commercial *Running with the Squirrels*, a parody of the annual Running of the Bulls at Fiesta de San Fermín at Pamplona. In the television spot, instead of bulls and steers, squirrels chased the dauntless runners. At the close of the sixty-second spot, an old man reflects, "I have lost many friends to the squirrels."

[2] Battle of Pavia: One of the last battles of the Italian Wars of 1525 (23-24 February) when the Spanish Imperial army attempted to relieve a French siege of the Italian city Pavia.

Good Love discovered at Castilla y León

I must have forgotten—or did not take seriously—what I read of Spain's fortified wine. Recollections from my youth included the seldom hangover, though it took more than one of those lessons to learn my limits. I was unprepared for the wallop of Spain's fortified Rioja, particularly when taken after a cocktail or two.

Next stop: Benavente. Uncle Chuck always bends on making the subsequent leg of a journey in record time. Enchantments tempt beyond the beaten path. With this in mind, I do my homework months ahead of a trip and while in the country at hand, scour maps for historic edifices and villages of intrigue. This is elementary; the poser, convincing Uncle Chuck to detour, even to pull over.

After an early café breakfast, we wend down Segovia's slope toward N-110 to access N-501. Mist, stark white as cotton blankets rolling fields outlying the university seat of Salamanca.

"Remind you of Segovia?" Uncle Chuck muses.

He notices from the outskirts of Salamanca familiarity in lines of the double cathedral. With my insistence, we pull in. Given the off-season and a workday in progress, we easily find parking near the city's illustrious square.

Far-reaching Plaza Mayor mesmerizes with medieval gingerbread, myriad arches and balconies traced in yellow sandstone.

"I love this setting," Uncle Chuck concurs. "But there's not much time to explore."

We settle for a brief tour, beginning with flagged arcades of the grand plaza. Here we admire intricate architecture of Alberto and Nicolás de Churriguera. A focal point in the three-storied square, the *ayuntamiento* (town hall) carries a three-bell-*campanario* clock tower. With our eyes, we follow lacy balustrades, rhythmic pinnacles and commemorative medallions. In the thick of these flourishes, busts of monarchs, warriors, explorers, artists and saints pose stoically. The books commend Salamanca's plaza mayor as the most beautiful square in all of Europe. We agree.

Within this city of churches, convents, halls of learning, towers and palaces, we pause at an ocherous stone mansion called Casa de las Conchas. Walls of this 1490 structure bristle with four hundred carved scallop shells. During Spain's Golden Age, this town mansion belonged to a doctor-professor, a knight of the Order of Santiago named Rodrigo Arias Maldonado de Talavera. Arias's time-honored *casa* incorporates deep-set *Isabeline* windows with elaborate *rejas* (wrought-iron grilles). The leitmotif of shells has to do with the Order of Santiago, symbolizing St. James. Along the roads of Spain trudge pilgrims with scallop shells dangling from broad-brimmed hats.

Intrigued with the cathedral's duality, we wander in the direction of majestic towers and spires. The younger (sixteenth-century) component dwarfs Catedral Vieja, a Romanesque cathedral constructed in the twelfth century. One of three apses incorporates La Torre del Gallo (The Cock Tower), a fetching characteristic overlaid with scalloped tiles. While the two cathedrals share a common wall, the *plateresque* (Spanish-baroque)[1] style of the old gives way to juxtaposition of Gothic and Renaissance motifs in Catedral Nueva (1513-1560). The new cathedral's architect, Juan Gil de Hontañón, also designed Segovia's cathedral.

"Hence, the similarities," I tell Uncle Chuck.

We step across ample flagstones to the plaza's arcade in pursuit of a coffee bar. Just up the way, a smart café beckons and we duck inside. Sipping *cafés solo* (espressos) at the bar, we pore over a map for our sortie north. I notice an icon that symbolizes *castillo* along the N-630 route from Salamanca to Benavente.

"Can we stop for a look?"

"I'll bet it's just an old ruin. And we've seen plenty of castles. Besides, the *parador* where we'll stay this evening is—or was—a castle."

Only one other customer graces the bar, a tall, well-groomed man with movie-star looks and perfectly tailored suit. He introduces himself as Ángel Hernández Román. Under the name engraved on his calling card: the words *Abogado, Administrador de Fincas* (Lawyer, Administrator of Ranches). The charming hidalgo apologizes for overhearing our conversation, but wants to recommend the monument I referenced.

With chest puffed out, he tells us, "If you like castles, you will love Castillo del Buen Amor."

Señor Hernández's black eyes sparkle with ethnocentric pride as he shares historical nuggets concerning his beloved Salamanca. He explains its provenance, the region's settlement by Iberians, then its vanquish by Carthaginian commander Hannibal in the third century before Christ, called *Salmantica* by Romans, conquered again by Muslim warriors in the eighth century. Alfonso IX de León founded this city as La Universidad in 1218, "though some say 1230," the gentleman mentions. In the seventeenth century, the French came to town. During the War of Independence (1808-12), Napoleón's troops occupied Salamanca, and one-third of the city fell during French occupation. But *Señor* Hernández's hometown flourishes, in spite of incursions.

Our new friend recommends a tour of the university, noting chiefly its Patio de las Escuelas. "And you must tour the *ayuntamiento,*" he beams, "El Pabellón Real (The Royal Pavilion), and Puente Romano (Roman Bridge) spanning adjacent Río Tormes...."

Uncle Chuck thanks the kind man for his suggestions, but we'll have to save those sites for a future holiday.

"Can you recommend a place for lunch?" Uncle Chuck asks *Señor* Hernández.

The affable lawyer steps outside and aims his finger toward Casino de Salamanca, a restaurant known for the most tender of *calamares*. Swiftly, we're on our way with taste buds on alert.

The steady din of jam-packed Casino de Salamanca drowns any attempt at conversation. Patrons lean on a long bar chattering, ordering *para picares* (nibbles). Crumpled *tapas* tissues, toothpicks, olive pits and shrimps' heads and tails litter the floor, particularly along the bar. We pull up to a table, order *cañas* (draft beer), *raciones de huevos flamencos* (*tapas* of spicy eggs) and *calamares* that exceed the lawyer's accolades. Between bites, we discuss the kind gentleman, wondering if he characterizes the average Spaniard.

Uncle Chuck insists we make headway to our next post. As we speed up the road, my eyes jump between map and road signs. *We simply have to locate the castle of Buen Amor.*

Uncle Chuck does not believe in U-turns, or even left or right turns when he guns for a destination. I have often heard, "Whoops, we've missed the turnoff. Too bad! Maybe another time."

I spot my junction, and we pull off the motor-way where asphalt gives way to an unpaved, deeply pocked track. Irrefutably, the wrong road, or a fair stretch from the castle, with zilch ahead but miles of fields. We dodge potholes along our deliberately slow trek as I survey between craggy holm oaks that dot a sweep of pasture-land. Glossy black bulls eye us from grazing lands as we bump along the earthen road between split-rail fences.

"Where in the hell are we going?" Uncle Chuck huffs. "I don't see a castle...."

Afield, beyond the bulls, the *castillo* looms: music in stone exquisitely poised on a wind-swept plateau. No modern encroachment whatsoever, only lush meadows midway skeletal orchards encompass a lovely configuration of nougat-colored castle. As we draw near, Uncle Chuck's love for classical architecture piques. With a look of reverence, his eyes trace the remarkable structure.

"I'm glad we turned off," he admits.

Parked in an empty lot, we're doubtful of finding the monument open. But there's a sign on the massive portal. *Timbre* (call bell), it says. We engage the button. Minutes pass. No one answers. We walk above a dry moat, admiring the castle's details.

This architecture looks gentle, not fortress-like in the least. *Señor* Hernández explained to us its soft, curvilinear design. In 1476, Alfonso II, Archbishop of Toledo, converted the 1227 castle into a lovely palace for his mistress, his *buen amor*. The Catholic Monarchs (Fernando II de Aragón and Isabel I de Castilla) resided here while they jostled for power with Isabel's rival niece Juana la Beltraneja, daughter of Enrique IV. Queen Isabel won the battle in 1479.

Sensing someone inside, I again ply the bell. To my complacency, a voice calls out. Gazing upward, we see a shadowy woman framed in the lancet arch of a window.

"I am eating my lunch," an aged voice calls out, in Spanish. "I will meet you in ten minutes."

Uncle Chuck mutters, "Must be the chatelaine; we've interrupted her siesta."

After ten minutes of Uncle Chuck's champing to leave, a massive door groans and swings in. A white-maned woman in cotton apron about her thick hips greets us and asks for three hundred pesetas each. The woman's eyes disappear behind foggy spectacles. She toddles down corridors, recapitulating tales of the precursory resident-mistress, then giggles as she points out a chastity belt. Gazing at the golden girdle, she asks in Spanish, "You know what this was for?"

Practical Uncle Chuck asks how the wearer of the device used the bathroom. Good thing the old woman understands and speaks not a word of English.

We follow the woman through the dining hall, a stately ballroom with *artesonado* ceiling and *Mudéjar* fireplace. Next, we peruse a gallery of jewel-toned tapestries and blistered, faded frescoes of hunting scenes. Antlers festoon walls of a great hall, along with dusty, old, stuffed animals' heads. Glinting suits of armor hold court from the corners. Massive wooden trusses sag overhead.

The *castellan* again takes amusement as she describes an odd piece of furniture. With long seat and inclined back carved in the form of a woman, this chair—eloquently suggesting childbirth, a grimacing face incised at the top—could have been a medieval delivery table.

"I'd like to buy that birthing chair," Uncle Chuck says to me. "It would make quite a conversation piece."

Exotic flora graces a centrally set Renaissance atrium where overhead panels yield natural luminance into the womb of this enchanted palace, a lushly planted patio hemmed with sleek piers looking more like the milky smooth limbs of a damsel than traditional Renaissance pilasters.

A network of corridors blazes with sconces, modernized with electric bulbs. Our guide engages each in turn, as we pass through, then she douses them as we depart each individual wing.

Our tour lasts for only thirty minutes. We bid the lady *hasta la vista*. Now, off for our one-night lodging halfway between Segovia and a staging point at La Coruña.

We selected Benavente in the region of Zamora strictly for its highly praised *parador*. Besides this comfortable place to overnight, Benavente gives no reason for pause.

Parador Nacional Rey Fernando II de León, formerly the seat of King Fernando's court, hunkers on a prominent cliff above boundless rural fields and a dilapidated flour mill. All that remains of the twelfth-century bruiser of a castle-fortress is its keep, a *Mudéjar* tower known as La Torre del Caracol (The Tower of the Snail). The "snail" moniker stems from a spiral design in the plinths of its turrets.

We drive through Benavente unimpressed, finding it bleak, commercial, concurring with its doleful descriptions. In a tiny grocery store, where we ask for directions, a pleasant shopkeeper points beyond the village, toward the *parador*.

As we near the *parador*, homely Benavente gives way to rolling agricultural plains painted in broad strokes of verdure. We glimpse a golden tower rising high above its hillside perch, plus an architecturally consistent, though contemporary, wing of guest rooms. Fashioned of comparable beige sandstone as the *torre,* and fenestrated with brick-arched *terrazas,* the modern wing complements the contiguous, extant keep.

Splendid accommodations: roomy, loungy, sparkling clean and our terrace framing the epic tower rising above a virginal forest of pine trees. The grounds encompass formal walled gardens and beyond, sprawling farmland.

"Let's explore the old keep," I urge after we've unpacked.

"Not another keep," Uncle Chuck moans.

I tuck my toes out of the way, hold the door and let him pass before me.

Within the tower, a restored gallery presents a coffered *Mudéjar* ceiling aloft an atmospheric lounge. Niches harbor gray, pitted stone benches. Groups of oversized, period-reproduction furniture beckon in dark wooden tones thoughtfully arranged with brocaded cushions. All of this, plus cozy balconies with views far beyond the balustrades propose pleasant retreats for reflection. Accessed by a skinny staircase of stone, a bar below glows in rousing mosaics of medieval scenes crafted of ceramic shards excavated from the grounds. One of the walls heralds the royal crest of Fernando II, another, richly hued tapestries lending warmth to the stony chamber. An enormous, black, wrought-iron chandelier dangles above our heads. Save a wide-screen television, this cavernous chamber suggests a medieval time warp. Uncle Chuck relaxes, relieved to discover the steps leading to other levels are off-limits.

As we admire an etching, the concierge informs us the bulk of this castle fell under siege during an Anglo-Franco battle in 1808. The artwork enlightens us of the castle's antecedent grandeur.

"Shall we have a drink?" Uncle Chuck suggests.

My travel mate makes it clear to our waitress that we want gin with only faint parentheses of dry vermouth. Uncle Chuck gestures with four inches of space between thumb and forefinger when he mentions "gin."

Soon we're tackling the largest straight-up gin martinis imaginable.

"Now this is a martini," Uncle Chuck beams.

With our majestic martinis, we enjoy complimentary sausages and olives.

Sizing up the menu, we reminisce of Salamanca and Buen Amor.

"I'm happy to see we may take dinner before the wee hours," Uncle Chuck says. He wilts.

Having cast decisions, we change for dinner, then return downstairs to the *comedor*.

Our waitress proffers *copitas* (small glasses) of dry *jerez* (sherry). We carry on with seafood salads—nests of delicate greens dotted with ocean-sweet littleneck clams (*almejas*), tiny poached mussels, smoked fish. With a bottle of Rueda Cantosan *blanca*, we follow with superb entrées. Uncle Chuck's delectable grilled fish are *salmonetes*, described on the menu, "baby salmons," but we believe these fish are red mullet.

I enjoy a half-bottle of spicy, leathery Rioja *tinta* with fork-tender wood pigeon, a succulent bird baked in its own juices with wild mushrooms, a dish fit for royalty.

As I ponder dessert, the entire room lists. Could be the wine, a king-sized martini, or a combination of the two.

After we finish the last moist crumbs of sumptuous dense cake soaked in amontillado, we stagger to our room for the night.

---

[1] The style of *plateresque* (Spanish baroque) comes from the Spanish for silver (*plata*), denoting the decorative architectural characteristic's resemblance to silver filigree.

galicia

N

Costa da Morte

Rías Altas

Bay of Biscay

France

Pyrenees

★MADRID

Spain

Balearic Islands

Portugal

Atlantic Ocean

Mediterranean Sea

Africa

1. A Coruña
2. Santiago de Compostela
3. Oca
4. Sada

GALICIA

On Uncle Chuck's seventieth birthday, we journeyed northwest to a wilder region of Spain unfamiliar to many of our compatriots: Galicia, with its unforgiving Costa da Morte, the Coast of Death. How appropriate....

A HARD NIGHT'S DAY
FROM *RESACAS*[1] TO SEAFOOD HEAVEN

Utter agony best described my discomfiture. Patently, Uncle Chuck had more fortitude-of-libation than I did, since he experienced "only a mild hangover," or so he claimed. Recalling the previous evening's spinning bed, I resolved forevermore to drink nothing heavier than spring water.

Eager to commence his special day, Uncle Chuck urges me to the breakfast room. A pageant of food, enticing under other circumstances, frankly renews my queasiness. At our command stand bright-faced sous-chefs behind braziers and pyramids of brown-shelled eggs, equipped to prepare eggs to order from *revueltos* to *fritos*, any manner. Baskets overflow with gooey sweet rolls, platters with mild and ripe cheese, cold meats and cured fish. An array of just-plucked fruit and beakers of fresh juice spring from ice floes. At one station, a display of sardines assaults. Aargh! Suddenly the zwieback we admonished at Segovia seems appetizing. Yet, I find none, and cannot even stomach coffee. What a waste.

My travel mate returns from a second trip to the buffet, his plate stacked with what looks to be unappetizing portions.

"I'm going up to the room, Uncle Chuck. See you later, if I survive."

Miserably, I tuck clothes into my suitcase. What a way to spend a precious vacation day.

As I sit bent forward on the edge of my bed with face in hands, Uncle Chuck steps in with a napkin of pastries and a cup of coffee.

"Feel better? I brought these for you."

51

I moan.

We tool toward Galicia. I nurse a bottle of *agua gaseosa*. Two hours from Benavente, my symptoms subside, auspiciously so, for the unfolding scenery strikes magnificent.

The course of our journey meanders from golden ranch-lands to freshly harvested fields to gently rising foothills of Sierra de la Cabrera, Montes de León and Sierras de Cantabria, ranges cascading with verdant forests, with vineyards terraced as a Roman amphitheater, and the landscape dots randomly with gray granite dwellings. Between swipes of wiper blades, greenery sparkles silver through droplets of rain, a pleasant contrast from the harsh, thirsty plains of Castilla behind.

Ascending slick, black mountain roads, we overtake stocky trucks coughing billows of diesel smoke. As occasional cloudbursts force burgeoning traffic to a conservative pace, we crawl in the thick gauntlet of transports. Four hours from Benavente, the brawny port city of La Coruña crystallizes where horizon meets sky.

Pedantic graffiti mars directional signs along our route. In "La Coruña," *La* is stricken over with paint and supplanted with *A*. Overtly, *la* (female "the") is a Castilian corruption of the Galician *a*. Proud inhabitants have rebuked the offense. In these parts, "plaza" is *praza* among other variations on Castilian Spanish. The Galician vernacular traces its origins to the early-eleventh century. Thus and so, we believe we've crossed a border into another era, into a proud country.

Galicia differs strikingly from Castilla, more verdant, forested, untamed. Local natives descended from *Celtiberian* tribes who called their wild habitat *Gallaeci*. Yet, this northwest corner of Spain shares in common with neighboring regions a legacy of invasion from Roman legions, Muslim corsairs, intrepid Englishmen.

We may have guessed what we would discover when, finally, we reach the isthmus of A or La Coruña, Galicia's seminal city and capital (population 240,000). One of the largest fisheries and commercial ports in Spain, A Coruña fails to mirror the placid, village atmosphere we prefer. Nevertheless, there are points of interest here and we will use A Coruña as our base, as we found no vacancies in Santiago, our chief objective in Galicia.

Here, in the heart of a bustling port, my eyes focus on decayed ramparts and a brooding fortress. Fringing La Marina, a harbor lilts with ships, tankers, assorted pleasure craft. Atlantic-facing buildings stand densely packed, each of them multistoried and overlaid with glass-paned porches known as *galerías* or *miradores*. These walls of glass earned A Coruña her handle *Ciudad do Cristal* (City of Crystal).

We inch amongst commuter traffic through A Pescadería, the fishing district, in a northwesterly direction along the coastline until density unwinds to wilder scenery. We see far afield the Roman-period lighthouse A Torre do Hércules perched on a bluff. According to our map, we'll find the hotel within striking distance of the lighthouse.

Our accommodations at the high-rise Hotel Ciudad de la Coruña afford outlooks to the rugged Coast of Death.

Exhausted, famished, we seek the hotel's restaurant. Alas, no menu service; just *bocadillos* this time of day. Uncle Chuck doesn't mind. He'd polished off an entire banquet for breakfast. And he expects me to take him to A Coruña's finest restaurant to celebrate his birthday this evening.

Settled in, with dinner reservations confirmed, we take to local roads. Intrigued with the old lighthouse, we drive a short track to the isthmus where it stands. Bus-loads of tourists teem at the foot of the oldest operating lighthouse in the world, an angular tower originating from Celtic times, rebuilt by Romans in the second century A.D. and massively restored in the eighteenth century. Carlos III had the tower modified then, when engineers moved the formerly exterior case of 245 steps inside. Judging the prospect below us, at least one ship's captain failed to mind the beacon. Just beneath lies a man-made reef, the rusting hull of the corpse of oil tanker *Mar Egeo* engulfed in thundering waves. Uncle Chuck contemplates the wreck and distant islands from the bluff while I hike a precipitous switchback route down to the ocean.

Refreshed with ocean air and absorptive vistas, we roll back toward Ciudad Viejo, the old city center to Castillo do San Antón, a sixteenth-century palace converted in the eighteenth century into a fortress. Here, we make out remains of A Coruña's thirteenth-century Antiguas Murallas y Puertas del Mar, ramparts and gates dating from the thirteenth century.

Castillo do San Antón, a turreted fortress, hunkers on a spit of land northeast of the city. Before our tour, the ticket vendor catches us off guard when he refuses to believe Uncle Chuck qualifies for the senior rate. Uncle Chuck brandishes his passport. Even with evidence in hand, the young man says he does not understand how a seventy-year-old looks *"muy bueno, muy juvenil."*

"Must be all of that Castilian oil," I tease. "Keeps you well-preserved."

Within boundaries of the old *castillo*, we peruse galleries of an archaeological museum, inspecting fragments and dioramas of prehistoric Celtic dwellings, Roman statuary, potsherds, armaments and intricate silver artifacts. And here, we learn that Julius Caesar entered A Coruña from Gaul in A.D. 60.

From sentry posts outside, we eye expansive nautical scenery—the same as *Gallegos* (residents of Galicia) undoubtedly gazed upon when the invincible armada of Felipe II de Habsburgo set sail for England in 1588, and again when England's Sir Francis Drake attacked this city in 1589.

> Full seven long hours in all men's sight
> This fight endured sore,
> Until our men so feeble grew,
> That they could fight no more.
> And then upon dead horses
> Full savoury they fed,
> And drank the puddle water,
> They could no better get.
>
> When they had fed so freely
> They kneeled on the ground,
> And gave God thanks devoutly for
> The favour they had found;
> Then beating up their colours,
> The fight they did renew;
> And turning to the Spaniards,
> A thousand more they slew.
>
> —Lord Willoughby

"Small wonder," I mention, "Spaniards are so complex, so mysterious, given they've been leavened by one and all."

About Spanish ethos I have much to learn, though I appreciate the average Spaniard's vivacity, indelible pride and ethnocentricity. I sense deep religious devotion—the wearing of crosses on the outside, a church on practically every corner and I detect no affectation as I do in Uncle Chuck's beloved Britons. Spaniards project strong wills and compassion. I feel a kinship as I sink my teeth into Spain.

Rather than hunt after dark, we take a spin into A Coruña to seek a temple to seafood called El Coral. We can't spot the restaurant from our car, so we park, taking to sidewalks and alleys. Though friendly, people we approach look confused as we quiz them in pidgin Spanish. Eventually, we strike up an acquaintance with a shopkeeper who speaks little English and abides our Spanish. Our question takes us to the street. Outside, she says, "Yes, yes. El Coral is good. I show you."

The pleasant, middle-aged woman takes us each by an elbow. Chit-chatting in singsong *Gallego*, she escorts us three blocks from her yardage shop to the front door of the highly touted though obscure seafood restaurant. We'd passed it by three times in our car! We survey the surrounds to gain our bearings, thank the kindhearted lady, and we're off.

The shopkeeper and others we encounter in this remote sector of Spain propose the Portuguese persona of humble, sociable, willing to please. Not a surprise, as Portugal, bordering this part of Spain, has been autonomous only since 1668.

We enjoyed all of the meals behind us, yet frankly look forward to purportedly lighter *Galicana* seafood fare. We practically drool during the drive back toward town for our nine o'clock appointment.

There are people within, but El Coral's front door does not give way. Those inside are employees, eating. One of them quickly advises, through a door opened but a crack, this *comedor* opens at nine o'clock. We glance to our watches, now, to one another in disbelief. Three minutes till nine; guess all runs like clockwork in Spain.

Restaurante El Coral glows in candlelight, a cozy retreat from the heavy night air. In strict contrast to industrial gloom of the city, this *comedor* portrays elegance from bleached wooden hues to pastel napery and twinkling crystal chandeliers. Our host obliges graciously, tendering the best from among a dozen tables.

We open menus. Serendipitously, we are out of the oily-casserole zone. On the contrary, a panoply of sea creatures teases: wriggling *percebes* (gooseneck barnacles), just-harvested razor clams and scallops, live lobster and crabs, fish from *A* to *Z* and turtle soup. But even with our Spanish phrase-finder, we cannot interpret all from a raft of seafood items listed.

"One of each," Uncle Chuck says. "Seriously, though, I see dishes we must try and share, if that's all right with you?"

An army of servers fusses over us with wine list, luscious breads, trolleys of live menus and a bottle of *cava* (sparkling wine). The captain suggests lobster on our salads, but this will take thirty minutes to prepare. We must first choose our victims; these will be boiled then chilled.

While the ill-fated crustaceans are executed and conducted to suitable temperature, we sup on exquisite *sopa de tortuga* (turtle soup) with champagne. Next, we sample silky *navajas*. These delicacies are supple razor clams broiled with garlic and parsley. *Doesn't get any better than this*, I imagine as beautiful salads come forth with much ado. Two waiters dress greens prudently with rémoulade according to our taste, slice lobster tails into medallions of white, then artfully arrange them on beds of lacy greens. On the sides: whole perfect coral-hued claw meat. We savor each sea-sweet bite with more *cava*.

Our dinner includes a parochial specialty of pilgrim food. These are saucer-sized scallop shells laden with a fusion of chopped *vieiras* (scallop meat) under cloying vegetable sauce topped with breadcrumbs, all baked to bubbly eminence. Next come enormous broiled *cigalas* (mantis shrimp), savorous, toothsome. We selected these unusual *cigalas* from the live bar as they snapped and leapt upon their icy altar.

"I've died and gone to heaven," Uncle Chuck manages between bites. "Absolutely sublime. I'd like to savor the memory of it, so you go ahead with dessert if you'd care for some. I'll pass."

"But it's your birthday."

We each order rich, dark chocolate mousse crowned with slim, crispy chocolate meringues.

"I enjoy the cuisine of the *Gallegos*," Uncle Chuck sighs.

"Happiest of birthdays to you, old chap."

[1] *Resacas:* Hangovers

SANTIAGO'S PILGRIMS, THE SEA'S BOUNTY, AND A NOBLEMAN'S RANCH

Before switching off my reading lamp, I boned up on Santiago de Compostela—"St. James of the Starry Field," also known also as "St. James of the Burial Ground." Then, drifting off, I imagined the etheric figure of James the Apostle on his white horse.

In A.D. 844, pending imminent defeat to the Muslims, Spanish Christian soldiers espied on the battlefield an apparition of the sainted apostle on his steed, armed with shield, brandishing a sword. The desperate troops obeyed their spectral commander's orders and were led with faith and aplomb to victory against the enemy at Clavija. Following that pivotal battle, Spain expelled the infidels. Thereafter, St. James, ordained Matamoros *(Slayer of Muslims) by the populace, became the proud country's patron.*

Purportedly, devotees had smuggled St. James's headless remains (King Herod had him decapitated) to Spain where a hermit discovered the tomb one starry night in the 800s. A celestial body led the hermit to a field near present-day Santiago de Compostela where he unearthed an ossuary. Zealots reinterred the hallowed remains of St. James behind the silver and gold, Romanesque high altar of Santiago's cathedral. Since, the shrine entices thousands of pilgrims, among them, Francis of Assisi in 1214.

Strident laughter of sea gulls stirs us at an early hour; the tumultuous Atlantic crashes against the *ría* (inlet) below our top-floor room. In utter bliss, I listen to the rhythmic *swoooooshhh* of waves. I part draperies and open windows, admitting a briny tang.

"Breakfast this morning?" Uncle Chuck teases.

Though not as sumptuous as yesterday's *parador* breakfast, this hotel presents a respectable buffet. Strong, yet silky-smooth *cafés con leche* (half, rich coffee or espresso and half, steamed milk) taste superb.

Lured by the architectural and spiritual repute of Santiago de Compostela, I am eager to experience it, suggesting to Uncle Chuck that we walk as true *romeros* (pilgrims) from A Coruña. Uncle Chuck arbitrates, reminding me he has twenty-six years on me.

"In this century, we pilgrimage by car," he insists.

Three-odd miles from Santiago, I ask to be dropped off.

"Meet you on the steps of the cathedral," Uncle Chuck suggests, as I climb out of the car to embark upon my mini-pilgrimage.

Along the way, I encounter trudging pilgrims. I feel underdressed in sneakers, cotton trousers and shirt with sweater tied around my waist. But I carry in my pocket *recuerdos* (mementos), three cockleshells I collected on the shore of a *ría* this morning. Some of the homage-seekers wear substantial, brimmed hats; each decorated with a shell. Each of these pilgrims, in Bohemian clothing tinged with dust from serious hiking, carries a staff bearing a drinking gourd. Near Santiago's expansive Praza del Obradoiro file pilgrims bedecked with the same paraphernalia and even more attired as simply as I am.

Give me my scallop shell of quiet,
My staff of faith to walk upon,
My scrip of joy, immortal diet,
My bottle of salvation,
My gown of glory, hope's true gage
And thus I'll take my pilgrimage.
   —Sir Walter Raleigh, Diaphantus, *The Passionate Man's Pilgrimage*

The concept of pilgrimage is inherently Spanish. Though sticky-hot today, an impetus beyond my meager comprehension drives these compulsively spiritual people to journey hundreds of miles on foot. Yet, the pilgrims are composed, peaceful and soulful.

From a distance, the façade of the grand *seo* (cathedral) comes into view, a brown-sugar castle under attack by an army of ants. Closer up, the "ants" are hundreds of people skittering nonstop through a *praza* shut off to vehicular traffic. Hundreds more line up athwart the massive, twin-towered Iglesia Metropolitana. I audit the steps, the assemblage below, and spot Uncle Chuck's distinctively tall figure in the crowd.

"We should have parked where I dropped you off," he gasps. "Not one place to park. I drove round and round and finally discovered an underground lot. I waited...." He points to a faraway spot. "They let one car in as another one left. And would you look at this flock!"

We take our places in a snaking queue and patiently shuffle behind throngs, noting rich details of the façade—a plethora of three-dimensional carvings of saints, and ensconced high above, St. James in the garb of pilgrims he attracts. Eventually, we scale the steps of the bewitching cathedral, a Gothic-baroque edifice that traces its origins to the eleventh century.

A hive of activity, the opulent interior buzzes with a cross section of humanity. No queues here, only a mass of humid pilgrims sparring their way to the sanctuary. To fulfill our pilgrimage will take time, we reason, as we watch hundreds of awe-stricken devotees, some carrying flowers, a rosary or statue. We inch along and, following protocol, trace with our fingers the sculpted Tree of Jesse, an ornate column, in the same spot as have countless hundreds of thousands. Upon this stone shaft, eight centuries of tradition fashioned a deep, hand-shaped impression.

We reach the steps to the crypt and witness an elderly woman swoon from spiritual elation or from standing for so long.

Behind the high altar, we kiss a shell on the alb of St. James's statue, then patiently wait our turn to view a silver-*repoussé* urn of the saint's relics. We struggle to see between heads and shoulders of the throng, but manage a glimpse.

Goal accomplished, we turn to leave, squashing our way through the conflux of perpetual mob. Escaped, we refresh with ice-cold *cerveza* (beer) in the bar of the plush Hostal de los Reyes Católicos across the *praza*.

"Those pilgrims," I tell Uncle Chuck, "evoked *duende*. You could feel it. Reverence hung on the air."

"I felt claustrophobic," Uncle Chuck answers. "And now I'm hungry."

The bartender recommends Restaurante Mesón Compostela, mere paces away, near Praza do Quintana.

A spectacle of fish, crustaceans, bivalves, *pulpo* banked on mountains of shaved ice greets us as we enter the *mesón*. Tablecloths dazzle in crisply starch white. Blond wood with black accents sparkle clean, modern, in contrast to this city of weathered stone.

When Uncle Chuck sought a car park, he saw long lineups at the *taperías* and no-frills restaurants. We are pleased with this fancy *mesón*, ours, alone, for lunch.

We order a bottle of Ribeira (white Galician wine) and *mariscado de la casa* (mixed shellfish of the house). We're wide-eyed when a platter the size of our tabletop appears. Atop, a colossal spider crab's legs stretch like spokes of a wagon wheel between *langostinos*, prawns, shrimp, cockles, oysters, mussels and another variety of crab—all steamed, presented cold save, and on the side, gigantic scallop shells brimming with the *Gallego* specialty of baked scallops.

The memory of Castilian oil fades as we pick up sweet ocean flavors with squirts of lemon juice and the kick of pepper sauce. Even the bread tastes delicious and we use chunks of it to mop up the savory scallop-vegetable mixture. Uncle Chuck suddenly looks startled.

"Look over there," he says, bending his head west.

There stands our *mozo* in a corner, picking his nose!

Uncle Chuck calls for the maître d' and requests another waiter. Our new *mozo* offers complimentary dessert, but we have lost our appetites. Retreating, we worm our way through choked *paseos* to Uncle Chuck's underground parking place.

"Back to A Coruña?" he asks.

"We're not far from a *pazo*; may we have a look?"

"What's a *pazo*, dear boy?"

He will soon get a primer on the sublimity of northwest Spain's feudal mansions: country estates (*pazos rurales Gallego*) held by *caciques* (wealthy land barons) that lorded over vassals in Galicia's Golden Age. Pazo de Oca is but a moderate drive to the east.

We soak up unspoiled milieu of Galicia, occasionally spotting farmers leading mule- or goat-drawn carts spilling over with green hay.

As we disembark at Oca, a photographer wraps up his session with a black-eyed beauty floating in tiers of gossamer white, her groom bedecked in *traje de luces* and *montera* (satin "suit of lights") and hat of torero.

Passing the country manor's twin-towered, private chapel, we cross under an old, stony porte-cochere carved with a three-dimensional crown between two elliptical escutcheons. One of these heraldic badges frames two chiseled sheep, the other, three trout. We guess at the symbolism, surmising a king granted this land to a feudal lord who raised sheep and fish.

Before us lie impeccably manicured gardens of velvety lawns and raked gravel pathways meandering between sculpted hedges. Camellias, avocado, yew, blue hydrangea, marching rows of autumnal flowers in yellow to rust brighten our path. Beyond, emerald pastures stretch to a lavender horizon.

Lavish grounds encompass marshy gardens, a silken pond mirroring images of arched footbridges aloft with stone balustrades, graceful swans gliding through an artificial lake in the shape of a ship. At the pond's center stands a granite fisherman in a boat. Contemplating this peculiar sculpture brings to mind a parable about the corpse of St. James conveyed to Galicia on a ship carved from stone.

"The baron had a terrific spread," wide-eyed Uncle Chuck remarks. "Now, I'd suggest you hurry up and take your pictures so we can head back."

On return to A Coruña, we approach an astounding vista. Far afield, spanning languid Río Ulla, we spot a bridge borne on stone arches, riverbanks stepped with rustic dwellings and an ancient church under a sky blazing in Technicolor.

Uncle Chuck stands on the brakes. Fine gravel jettisons from the shoulder. We scramble for cameras, fearing light will reinterpret the scene. *Sol y sombra*, I silently chant. Beautiful scenery in southern Europe is elusive. With a telephoto lens, I capture the splendid scene.

We drink ice-cold beer and play cards in our hotel's salon before driving into the city to find an eatery.

As in Segovia, restaurant windows tempt with seafood so fresh it seems alive. As all looks the same, we let prices dictate decisions. At cozy, bustling Balsa II, we begin with a bottle of fizzy *vino* Pazo *blanco,* and bowls of delectable *caldo Gallego*: a stew with pork, minimal broth and much cabbage known as *couve.* We follow with a platter of crispy *morralla* (deep-fried whitebait), *navajas* and *pulpo.* I expect the octopus to be chewy, as in American sushi bars. Instead, this *pulpo* defines tenderness. Plates of velvety flan round out another sterling meal in this obscure corner of Spain.

Pazos Cerrados, Hórreos, y Paella con Langosta

The sea's percussive symphony again lulled us to blissful sleep. When sunlight danced upon the walls, I determined to luxuriate in the morning's glow and have breakfast sent up.

"This is the life," boasts Uncle Chuck from behind sunglasses.

We sip luscious *cafés con leche* and nibble continentals. Above our heads, sassy birds call, likely expecting a share of our breakfast. *El Océano Atlántico* roars below us and the climate is mild.

"What's the program for today?" I ask.

"Besides the fort and lighthouse, we haven't seen this burgh. Why not explore A Coruña? And it's Sunday; let's find a church."

We dress and make for town.

Clarion tones resound from quaint squares of A Coruña and the faithful file into churches. One, Iglesia do San Jorge, allures with its rustic stone *fachada* (façade) cut with an oculus designed as a snowflake. In A Coruña, we find only Catholic churches, so Uncle Chuck will have to forego an Episcopal experience. We follow a trail of worshipers through a pointed-arch portal for Mass.

The service transports me back to a pre-Vatican II childhood. I'm familiar with all of the cursory rituals, but do not comprehend a word of ancient Latin. We sit amidst families new and old, the ladies and girls in veils and hats. After the closing hymn, we trail the stoic flock back into the street.

Just around the corner, we enter A Coruña's main square, A Praza do María Pita. The *ayuntamiento,* El Palacio Municipal (1908), bewitches. This smartly proportioned town hall capped with three finely wrought Italianate domes of red tile flanks one quarter of the square. Stately, though lacking the *plateresque* gingerbread we saw in Salamanca, A Coruña's town hall is more functional than it is a museum.

The other sides of this *praza* carry *miradores* above a pillared arcade. Not a soul stirs in the square.

The *praza* was named for María Pita, a plucky housewife who, in 1589, fired a cannon to warn fellow citizens of an English attack. England's first Elizabeth deployed Sir Francis Drake and his troops to assault the Iberian coast. *Señora* Pita heroically saved A Coruña with her selfless act. Furthermore, she used her slain husband's lance to fend off a Briton who essayed to plant his native standard in her native soil. María then rallied other *Gallega* women to join in the battle. María Pita's effigy, bearing a lance, rises triumphantly from the deserted *praza*.

We tour the town hall, enjoying within chilly vastness, resplendent tapestries and stained-glass skylights. Three stories up, one of these windows, garlanded with jewel-toned designs, keynotes a bearded man with shield and club, likely St. James the Apostle. We also make out a stained-glass depiction of A Coruña's Roman lighthouse.

All but one shop in the plaza is closed, but soon we have company. We pause, listening to mournful strains of a *gaitero* (bagpiper), drop pesetas into his humble repository—a hat—then duck into Bar Río Tinto for espressos and *bizcochos*.

"Okay, we've seen the town," I say. "Now, let's stake out more *pazos*."

My suggestion elicits a groan from Uncle Chuck. More than likely, he anticipates a leisurely day sans crowds and curious roads. Sunday is, after all, a day of rest. Yet, there is so much more to see.

"Let's drive out and explore the eastern environs," I propose. "If there's nothing momentous, then we'll head back and you can nap all day long."

Spain feels earthier than other countries I have explored, rougher around the edges, particularly in Galicia. Medieval residue hangs in the air, a dynamic robustness. In Spain's people, I sense off-the-cuff frankness, imparted, however, in a respectful manner. The French, particularly Parisians, I have found to be insolent, and Germans, in my experience, downright robotic and coarse. Though I hold the Italian persona in high esteem, the average Spaniard's passion surpasses the Italian counterpart.

I liken my experiences in Europe to the ultimate spa treatment— luxurious, stimulating. In Spain, the therapy exhilarates even more so, as an unexpected slap on the back. Here, the notion of pleasure elevates to art form. The spa treatment works. Decompressed, with sated soul, I am swept away in this rousing, hardy land of *España*.

As we coast along, we take in captivating scenery, deeply cut *rías* and crashing surf. We drop into the hamlet of Sada for an intimate survey. Rugged coastline supports only waving marshland grasses amongst rock-strewn, sandy islet shores. The Atlantic stretches forever under a wind-whipped shimmer of churning, white-capped surface. From a salt-scented beach, we spot on the horizon A Coruña in a new light, more engaging from afar.

The *pazos* of Mariñan and Meiras lie within range. I appeal to Uncle Chuck for a car trip to each.

Finding the gates of Mariñan bolted, we regard the estate from outside. Meiras also closes on Sundays, yet the mansion stands in clear view beyond a public road. Twin granite towers of gray span an ivy-clad wing and arched doorway, and vivid carmine-tinged vines cling to stone veneer. Golden rows of autumnal vineyard superbly highlight this feudal estate. In an adjacent field, we spot an *hórreo*.

Hórreos are antique granaries unique to Galicia and Asturias. Those found in Asturias are fashioned from wood, in Galicia, constructed of granite, measuring about twenty feet long by four wide, six high and three or four feet above the ground on stone pillars. Farmers built these structures to protect grain from vermin and moisture. Modulating in style from pithy to elaborate, common aspects among *hórreos* include a cross atop one end of their rooflines, an ornate finial on opposing peaks. Dozens more such architectural gems dot Galicia and I want to photograph each of them, but give in to Uncle Chuck's remonstrance.

"Exactly what will you do with all the pictures you take?"

"Just one more and we'll return to A Coruña."

Clouds yield a spritz of rain. We revert for Uncle Chuck's siesta and for what promises to be a bang-up sunset background for A Coruña's Roman lighthouse.

Abandoning an elated Uncle Chuck to naptime, I hike up a muddy lane to the *torre*. In the drizzle, I make photographs, balancing camera and umbrella. The Romans called this city *Ardobirum Coronium*, when vanquished Iberians resigned to the Pax Romana (Peace on Roman Terms). Drenched, I stand admiring a vestige of an ancient civilization's contribution to the townscape, a classically styled lighthouse silhouetted against brooding sky adrift with clouds tinged in tangerine and violet.

Back in the room, Uncle Chuck invites me to join him for a drink and game of cards in the lounge.

"*Dos* vodkas," Uncle Chuck tells the bartender.

"*¿Qué? ¿Bode-ka, señor?*"

"Vod-ka," Uncle Chuck articulates.

"*Sí, bode-ka.*"

After futile repetitions, Uncle Chuck finally exclaims, "*Dos* Coca-Colas, *por favor.*"

This, the man understands.

When I return to California, I have mind to buy stock in Coca-Cola®. In Europe, this beverage is ubiquitous.

Later, with taste buds piqued for Balsa II cuisine and a real drink, we inch our way through foggy drizzle into the city's core. Sunday night life in A Coruña approximates a Saturday evening in an American city.

"Where did all of these people come from?" Uncle Chuck asks.

"Question is, where did they all hide before? This is a huge metropolis."

We find not a place to park near Balsa II. Nor does our scouting yield a space as we cruise through clogged, wet streets and alleys. Hundreds of people under umbrellas and awnings line up outside cinemas and clubs; thousands more roam sidewalks and pack glowing restaurants and bars to busting.

"Looks as though we'll have to eat at our hotel," says Uncle Chuck.

We head back, resigned to a dinner of lesser fare.

On the hotel's menu, we discover paella. As we have not yet sampled this dish on our holiday, we decide to try the hotel's version. Following hors d'œuvres of potato *tortillas*, we sip vivid *caldo Gallego* with *vino* Ribeiro Anciño. When the waiter places between us a huge shallow pan of golden rice, our spirits pick up. The chef plotted our paella with great chunks of *langosta* (lobster).

"Must have added lobster at the end," Uncle Chuck remarks. "Otherwise it wouldn't be so tender. This paella is outstanding."

We eat each grain of our saffron-tinted rice. Besides generous portions of lobster meat, we discover succulent morsels of chicken and cockles. Amazingly, we have room for *postres* (dessert). We sample smooth *natillas* (vanilla custard), and *fillaos:* sautéed apples between crêpes heaped with mounds of whipped cream. With the end of our wine, we toast the discovery of another meal that far exceeded expectations.

Further congratulations are in order. Outside, an angry storm pummels rain against our windows. We tuck away warm and dry, dreaming of our next day's trek along the northern coast to Cantabria.

Paella, Spain's National Dish

In Spanish, *pala* means shovel or spade. Paella takes its name from this word, if we subscribe to folkloric interpretations—tales of peasant-farmers who hundreds of years ago worked rice paddies in the region just west of Valencia. Legend tells us it was in Valencia that the dish called *arroz a la paella* originated. The Moors introduced *arroz* (rice) to Spain. Spanish laborers used shovels to cook up meals of rice, adding vegetables at hand plus morsels of rabbit or chicken and sometimes snails. They placed shovels-full of these ingredients over fast-burning fires of wood or dry vine clippings.

The standard recipe takes its roots from one of Spain's signature dishes. Rice (unwashed medium to short grains), saffron (*azafrán*) and olive oil still figure into the mix. To these staples, cooks add vegetables and rabbit or chicken, broad beans and tomatoes, nothing more. True Valencian paella includes no garlic, nor does it incorporate seafood or sausage.

Modern paella consists of any combination of sweet paprika, lemon, rosemary, lima or string beans, pork, fish, shellfish. This mixture cooks prepare in two-handled, shallow pans twelve to eighteen inches in diameter. Meat or seafood—or both—plus vegetables they arrange on top of the rice, but do not blend in, then cook over high flame or electric heat. Paella simmers uncovered, not stirred, and must be served before sticky or overcooked, particularly when ingredients include seafood. The desired effect is dry, preferably crusty on the bottom.

Paella's distinctive characteristic: the unwashed rice retains flavors of meat, olive oil, vegetables and elegantly subtle saffron.

They had best not stir the rice, though it sticks to the pot.
—Miguel de Cervantes Saavedra, *Hidalgo Don Quixote de La Mancha*

Asturias y Cantabria

1. San Vicente de la Barquera
2. Santillana Del Mar
3. Cuevas de Altamira
4. Comillas
5. Suances
6. Santander
7. Picos de Europa

Asturias y Cantabria

Our drive along Costa Verde from A Coruña to Santillana Del Mar would take "about four hours," said Ana González, our Spanish-born travel agent in California. Ana overlooked the gauntlet of congested commuter traffic in a city such as A Coruña. Had we not paused for lunch, photography and fuel, "there's still no way in the world," Uncle Chuck remarked, "we could have made that kind of time." Added to that, two eastbound lanes snaking through fierce granite cliffs along the north Atlantic coast held our speed to a pace more gradual than Ana's assuredly lead-footed method of driving.

Sol y Sombra along La Costa Verde to a Village Lost in Time

The journey to our staging post in Cantabria endured more than eight hours, yet the drive was enchanting, despite a schizophrenic sky and sporadic storms. And poor Uncle Chuck caught cold.

We creep along Costa Verde on a coastline-snuggled highway between panoramas of Mar Cantábrico and the awing Cantabrian Cordillera range tufted with forests, cloaked in veils of mist. Couched within the valley's depths are rustic *fincas* (ranches, farms). Occasionally, we spot a farmer leading a burro and *carreta* (wooden hay cart). Precipitation, narrow switchback roads with hairpin curves, transport trucks and the random passing of cattle hold us at a deliberate pace.

Midway to our destination, I suggest we pull into Gijón, but Uncle Chuck doesn't want to "get mixed up," as he puts it, "in big city traffic." We persevere through a sifting of fine mist to gusty showers, torrential downpours, through mist again. Illimitable measures of rain keep this coast leafy. As we glide along, we survey the glory of endless miles of lush growth glistening like emeralds whenever sun manages to penetrate cloud-cover.

Longing for a café, we exit the motor-way near Llanes, drawn to a quaint restaurant called El Horno de Buelna. The two-storied building looks like a converted farmhouse, rustic, inviting. A stocky paisano greets us affably, then escorts us up creaking flights of stairs to an open-beamed loft vibrating with spirited Spaniards. Uncle Chuck, having had his fill of seafood in Galicia, hankers for steak. Finding *bistec de buey* on the menu, he orders one broiled medium rare, with fried potatoes and salad on the side. I opt for *menú del día* (menu of the day): two kinds of fish delicately fried. My sides: a hearty casserole of peas, turnip, beans and carrots dotted generously with cubed bacon. This fare takes the edge off the autumn chill.

With a pitcher of *vino de la casa* and crunchy rolls, we relish lovingly prepared fare in a cozy environment with pungent aromas of smoldering wood wafting up from the kitchen. Rain pelts resoundingly and wind whistles through roof tiles. Behind lacy curtains, steamy windows document a nippy world outside. We prolong our stay, dawdling over *cafés con leche*, munching almond cake.

Hoping to arrive at Santillana before nightfall, we brave the weather, advancing our journey eastward. Splendid scenery resumes in pine forests unfolding to deciduous woodlands drenched with impetuous outbursts of crimson and ochre. The sun, at last, is victorious, obliging us with views beyond compare. Near San Vicente de la Barquera, sunlight wraps a vista in a golden cloak. We stop to soak up staggering vistas of a time-honored peninsular village defined on either side by forks of Río Escudo. Perched on one end of the isthmus stands thirteenth-century Iglesia de Nuestra Señora de Los Angeles, at the other, a fortress all but extinguished by the elements. Even the more modern buildings within plaster coats under persimmon-colored rooftops are in rapport with their vintage correlatives.

"A view from heaven," notes Uncle Chuck. "One day I'd fancy lodging down there."

We make photographs, then press on.

"I will discuss with Ana her 'four-hour journey,'" Uncle Chuck admonishes, as we roll into Santillana to locate our *parador*. "Yet we're here at last and it is stunning. Look at Santillana...."

Late-afternoon sun works its alchemy on the radiant sandstone-spun fabric of Spain's best-preserved, ancient village. I can hardly wait to hit the cobbles, though we will first check into Parador Nacional Gil Blas.

"Your keys, *señores*," says a young man at the desk. "You will find your room across the plaza, in our annex."

"The annex," answers Uncle Chuck, sniffling and blotting his nose with a tissue. "I specified 'original *casa*' when I booked."

The annex of local stone reflects the character of its medieval neighbors, yet we looked forward to aged ambiance. From chiseled and molded escutcheons on the eighteenth-century mansion's austere façade to baronial appurtenances within, the germinal *parador* imbues a chivalrous past as a roadhouse, ancestral home of the Blas de Barreda family, celebrated in literature. French novelist Lesage ascribed this residence to his folkloric character, a knight named Gil Blas.

The man, sensing our frustration, disappears into an office behind the desk. *Does he think Uncle Chuck is upset because of his teary eyes brought on by a cold?*

Soon, behind a porter, we pass alongside glinting suits of armor and heraldic banners to the mezzanine level, to the medieval mansion's superior suite of baronial-style rooms generously sized. Genealogical stitchery in wall hangings, expanses of seasoned plank floors, plus weaponry above a fireplace add up to pleasant décor. Our ample veranda gazes out on autumnal gardens. I make a note to make Uncle Chuck cry on check-in in the future.

The village teems with sightseers. We will wait until their coaches depart before we explore. Meanwhile, siesta-time calls from our luxurious digs.

Paradores are notorious for fine dining rooms, with Gil Blas no exception. Rootsy flavor of the old mansion's restored dining hall documents a haven of medieval ambiance.

At dinnertime, a crew of French geology students sit with their professor-guide, a cadre of twenty at a refectory-style table. As they discuss their tour of caves at Altamira, we sup on silky crab bisque and *ensaladas variadas*. Uncle Chuck squirms as our waiter presents my plate of *anguilas* (whole, baby eels). Avoiding eye contact with them, I attest the eels are delicious, prepared as they are in lemon juice and olive oil. Conventional Uncle Chuck declines my offer to sample, and relishes his lamb ragout. Having read favorable reports on northern Spain's Txacolí, we order this young, tart, spritzy white wine to accompany our tasty dinner.

My eagerness arouses as I overhear the French students abuzz about regional caves with stalactites or paleolithic paintings.

From the dessert menu we choose creamy rice pudding and tangy *tarta de naranja* (orange cake) and savor the confections with herbal tea. We will sleep well tonight in this village that escaped time's passage.

SEVENTEEN CENTURIES IN THREE DIMENSIONS

Granted national monument status in 1889, the pristine village of Santillana Del Mar warrants its praiseworthy designation. Santillana *(a contraction of the Latin words* Sancta Juliana*) Del Mar (Spanish for "of the sea") was a town built around the relics of a saint: Juliana, an Italian virgin and martyr, tortured then beheaded in Nicomedia in* A.D. *308. In the latter half of that century, devotees translated Juliana's incorrupt corpse to Spain from its depository in Purol, Italy, for safekeeping from the Lombards. Juliana's rescuers carried her reliquary to what became known as "Santillana Del Mar"—a hamlet named* Planes *in earlier times—and erected a shrine above her new tomb. Dominican monks appended Monasterium de Sancta Juliana in the ninth century, and transfigured the chapel in the early twelfth to a Romanesque church, the cornerstone of the village. Oldest portions of the collegiate church and cloisters date from the 1100s, with additions fashioned in the seventeenth through eighteenth centuries.*

Santillana Del Mar was a see of abbots from the ninth century until 1439, but ceded after a struggle in 1512 to royal sanction under Don Íñigo López de Mendoza, first Marqués *of Santillana. Protected by a new Asturian monarchy and kings of Castile, the town thereafter became a political center with battlements, and home to lords and knights who foiled the advancement of Berber armies.*

Much of the village was abandoned to elegant decay during the sixteenth century after its nobility migrated to South America to mine silver and gold. When their descendants, called Los Indianos, *returned to northern Spain with tremendous wealth in the late 1700s, they deemed the comeliness and religious-historical significance of Santillana reason to preserve their ancestors' faded village. In that era, a town hall, additions to the church, the* mansion*-parador and other villas sprang up. Many of the* casonas *(seigniorial mansions) survive as remarkable legacies in golden stone.*

We step from Gil Blas into a tiny square and pause to admire a bison sculpted in stone, tribute to extinct subjects of the high paleolithic paintings at Altamira. A dissonant clang calls to us from the north end of town.

We follow the tolling, up one of Santillana's two main cobbled, sloped roads in direction of a time-honored church, wanting to take this in before annoying coach tours infest.

The morning sky yawns exceptionally clear. On Santillana's streets, tourists are few. Onward, we study noble *casa* façades, each badged with a unique escutcheon: flying pennants with lions, fleurs de lis and wolves, dragons and eagles. Others are traced with stars, crosses, bulls, plumed helmets, horses and crowns. The random building sports comical gargoyles as rain spouts.

We halt at fifteenth-century Torre de Merino, Santillana's medieval keep. Vague merlons and crenels are blocked in, capped over with russet *tejas* (fired-clay barrel tiles). Just beyond looms Casa de Velarde, a massive, austere palace crowned with chessman-style finials. A black dog trots across a stone footbridge spanning the mere dribble of a spring. Nearby, we detect a well where this town's main roads converge. We imagine inhabitants dipping from it in bygone days. Yet, the showpiece of this village is its collegiate church.

We amble over the rugged, uneven flagstones of Plaza de la Iglesia. The Romanesque church before us presents a magnum opus in golden stone, appearing to grow from the earth, and the spread of its wings engulfs us in welcoming arms. Crumbled fabric and faceless statues embroider a measurably eroded pediment with mellowed patina. This spectacle in stone draws us in. Above, intersected by its pediment, a loggia delineates with squat steles and primitive statues principally headless. Above these decapitated subjects, an intact Saint Juliana tucks into a niche. The dauntless saint reins in Lucifer with a chain, standing victorious upon his writhing back. To her right soars a cylindrical tower, the church's original campanile.

We move under a tympanum-arch, into the church's stony depths. Throughout the three-aisle interior, hollow ribbed vaulting reverberates with our steps. Wherever the eye comes to rest lies a treasure, from a massive baptismal font inscribed with Kufic (Arabic inscription) to a high relief of Daniel with lions, to the centerpiece: the tomb of Juliana, a stone sarcophagus overlaid with Juliana's carved likeness, and under her feet, Lucifer himself.

Atop steep columns skirting the nave, capitals enliven a scene with the lives of Christ and saints. A four-tiered *retablo* fills the entire space of the apse with brilliant color in three-dimensional statuary including a *Cristo* and *Pasos de la Cruz* (Stations of the Way of the Cross) in polychrome, plus silver-relief panels in rich detail.

At a side altar, we light votive candles in remembrance of dearly departed, then feed pesetas into a metal box. Passing through the nave, we note mostly expressionless tourists not as intrigued as we are with this church's complexities.

Behind the church squats a rustic *claustro* (cloister). We survey this rugged patio encompassed by rows of stocky, double pillars. Tufts of turf supplant mortar between the paving, and weeds have taken root in the rooftops. Throughout the richly carved arcade, we view a virtual gallery of capital motifs: animal, vegetal, military, monster, geometric intertwines. Irregular, sienna-colored *tejas* in wavy, mossy rows cap the ambulatory. Ingenuously simple, triangular corbels support the fragile roofline. *How many mysteries were resolved here? How many prayers answered?*

Around the back of old monastery, fieldstone walls sequester a herd of black-and-white cattle. The rude corrals escaped time's passage, as have the surrounding buildings.

Just outside our clustered village stand two convents. One of them, Regina Coeli, housing Santillana's Diocesan Museum in sixteenth-century architecture, seems austere as its Claritian order; yet, we appreciate methodic gardens and an elegant *campanario*. Inside, we explore remarkable galleries of devotional art that includes a Romanesque carving of the *Pantocrator* (Christ, the King of the Universe). We take especial pleasure in the timeless atmosphere of upper galleries as we navigate across creaking, wide-planked floors under tilted beam ceilings to discover the fourteenth-century tomb of a count named Agüero.

Beyond the historical purity of Santillana's convents, church, historic town hall and *parador*, we see seigniorial homes outfitted as shops, restaurants, art studios and galleries. We duck into ateliers for a serious browse, on a mission to buy tchotchkes—namely, boxes of saffron for friends in California. This deep-orange powder, from stigmas of crocus, is priced at a fraction of the cost back home. We chance upon a puny *banco* (bank) in this ancient setting, and use our ATM cards to replenish our stash of peseta notes.

"Where does time go?" asks Uncle Chuck. "I feel like lunch."

Outside of town, in pursuit of a restaurant, we debark at the posh resort town of Comillas. We have heard of this town's distinguished Restaurante El Capricho de Gaudí, designed by the illustrious Catalan architect of its namesake. We hunt for the restaurant in tiny Comillas just east of Santillana. This neurotic-*Mudéjar* folly sports cylindrical bays, green-glazed window casements, a Fabulist tower borne on classical-style colonettes. The entire building Gaudí emblazoned with hundreds of sunflowers in glazed tiles. We peer inside to a formal, ultra-modern setting, imagining ourselves partaking of *alta cocina*. El Capricho de Gaudí is closed, but we take the telephone number.

Up the road perches mauve-colored Palacio de Sobrelleno by Modernista architect Joan Martorell, 1881, in Neo-Gothic lines more organic than angular. Alongside rises a chapel steeped in antiquity.

Ahead, we spot a lively restaurant called Gravalosa. Spotting *navajas* on the menu, we pull up to an outdoor table. Among garrulous locals, we look forward to devouring a platter of delectable razor clams, heavenly supple in garlicky oil, flurried with minced parsley. We cannot resist sweet pink *gambas* served in their jackets. From bowls of steamed mussels, we dredge savory broth from bowls with mops of bread, then chase it all with dry *vino de la casa*.

Contented, we move on, discovering the village of Suances that overlooks the Costa de Cantabria. Unlike deep-cut islets of Galicia or rocky cliffs of Cantabria, this region tames with a posh greensward shifting gently to sandy beaches. Dense marine layer palls the daylight, obscuring architecture in this seaside resort where most buildings are modern. But we see also a winsome lighthouse and gray rubble of what appears to have been a fortress. We make photographs, then drive back in the direction of our *parador*, gliding past farmers with mule-drawn carts—some with an added advantage of rubber tires.

We identify Santillana Del Mar gracing an escarpment in the mid-ground, a sweep of burnt-orange rooftops ensconced within patchwork quilts of fields and meadows. In the foreground, the patches are brilliant in shades of viridian and ochre, yielding to understated hues of chartreuse and beige, then misty lavender afar.

Coaches have again invaded the outskirts of our bewitching village. We eschew the mobs to the sanctum of our suite.

His Nibs luxuriates in siesta-time. I sit on our private balcony with journal and coffee. Autumn turns, foliage dazzles and a stiff breeze refreshes. Endless ribbons of sienna rooftops unfold before me, dotted with velvety moss and pale green lichens.

After exploring the Diocesan Museum earlier today, we noticed Hotel Los Infantes, formerly Casa de Oreñas. At one time an aristocratic residence, this hotel's restaurant offers sea urchins among its *aperitivos*.

At a quarter till nine, Los Infantes's *comedor* stands packed to waiting. We conclude that the outlying villages of Spain regard earlier dining hours, suiting us to a T.

We commence our meal with sensuous *oricios* (sea urchins) steamed in wine and lemon juice, together with a bottle of Monopole Rioja *blanca seca*. Next, house salads of sparse leaves and copious toppings of tuna, sardines, anchovies, glossy purple olives, supple white asparagus, briny pickles. Uncle Chuck savors a ramekin of vegetables with generous cubes of *cordero* (lamb) and I, *rape* (monkfish), lobster-textured, grill-hatched, rubbed with olive oil and lemon juice. Astride: crisp *patatas fritas* (fried potatoes).

Unlike the more formal dining room at our *parador*, this restaurant buzzes with casual conversation. Tables are arranged such that fellow diners' discussions merge. Youthful clientele, speaking Dutch, German and French, dress in uniforms of blue jeans, turtleneck sweaters and leather jackets. In English, these European tourists generously share travel tips with us. One of them at the next table recommends that we not leave the region before experiencing the Picos de Europa.

"Oh! The Picos are Spain's most unblemished range of mountains," the Dutch fellow yields with musical accent. "And only a short drive from Santillana," a young lady chimes in.

With creamy *cafés con leche*, we conclude our luscious meal with just-ripe figs and *queso* Valdéon (blue cheese, sweet and salty). We discuss prospects of mountain scenery, plus the prospect of dinner at one of Europe's top restaurants, our venues for tomorrow.

FROM NATURE TO GAUDÍ TO GHOSTLY REFRAINS

I have always been enamored of fine old churches, solemn temples replete with artistic treasures steeped with mystery. In them, I have often heard ghosts of yesteryears' worshipers at prayer, in song, celebrating the sacraments. For me, churches are for not only worship, but also for reflection, places to find oneself. Uncle Chuck did not consider churches and convents as fascinating. But I usually convinced him to join in my spiritual expeditions.

We have our personal preferences, but Uncle Chuck and I share interests in good restaurants, in mountain scenery. Today we will revel in the finest of each.

"Wonder if they'll pack a box lunch," Uncle Chuck muses over his continental breakfast. "Let's take a picnic on the off-chance we don't find a restaurant along those mountain roads."

Raring to explore the highly touted Picos de Europa, we pore through brochures given to us by the concierge. Spain's tourist bureau bills the range as highest in the Cordillera Cantabria. The entire zone of 257 square miles is protected as a national park and wild-game reserve described as unspoiled, wild. Skeptical of travel writers' tendency toward the euphemistic, we're not sold on the *unparalleled, natural beauty awaiting your exploration of the eastern massif known as the Liébana.*

We set off with white cardboard lunch boxes, cameras and map. We duck into one of Santillana's grocery shops for water, wine and a corkscrew. Daylight struggles against graying firmament, yet we determine to tour. We pilot in the direction of Potes, a foothill village and point of entry to the Picos's eastern extremity.

As the sea and far-flung pasture-lands of Cantabria disappear behind us, we find ourselves in the midst of deeply etched limestone hills. As we wind our way up, we watch these hills taper steeply to neck-wrenching heights serrated with ridges and spires soaring more than 8,600 feet.

For miles we follow the highway through gauzy mist, our eyes feasting on peeks of sylvan panoramas. From time to time, sunlight penetrates smoky-gray clouds, granting adrenaline-inducing prospects of glistening alpine meadows and fierce stone massifs.

"The weather keeps tourists away," Uncle Chuck notes mirthfully as we enjoy an easy trek, observing scenery through our rain-splattered windshield.

Extraordinary vistas are ubiquitous: stands of trembling golden alders, silvery waterfalls tumbling hundreds of feet from sheer rock walls, quaint farmsteads dotting the Liébana Valley floor.

Passing the occasional car, one towing a tiny caravan, we pull over whenever a photogenic scene presents, though we reason our film supply will not hold out unless we discriminate. This national park embraces 120 villages, though we spot only a dozen. We note now and then a hamlet of humble guile nestled into a path-hatched mountainside. And occasionally, a shepherd in black rubber boots drives lumbering cattle or frolicking goats across our snaking course.

"Time for a picnic," Uncle Chuck says after an hour of sightseeing.

We pull off near a bridge. Considering climatic uncertainty, we picnic in our car. We find inside our boxes spicy sausages and two varieties of cheese, one veined in blue and the other ivory and firm. Mmm...with grainy brown bread. We make rustic sandwiches and enjoy our wine, with a window on nature exceeding art. For dessert, we slurp juicy plums and munch bars of dark chocolate. Accordions and banjos entertain us from a Basque radio program. Above, saw-toothed ridges wear a dusting of snow; just below us, muddy Río Cares rages through a deep canyon.

Breaking from lunch, I read aloud passages from our brochures, *"This pristine range remained unmapped until the nineteenth century. The snowy mountains sustain the Deva and Ebro Rivers."*

We pursue our scenic tour along hairpin bends, past boundless wilderness and fields dotted with sheep, goats and skeletal nut trees. On slopes planted with neat vineyard rows, fall foliage dazzles. Lavender-gray peaks jut all the way to a point called Fuente Dé. The geography at this boundary comes forth even more untamed with formidable pinnacles and clefts. But for a smiling valley of mossy green, scenery stretches barren of larger vegetation for miles. Stoic, resort-style buildings—a modern *parador*—back up against a sheer rock face crisscrossed with wires suspended with red *teleférico* (cableway) cars. Above this *parador*, eagles glide between jagged heights.

I'm eager to augment our wondrous adventure through the range's western side, home to Covadonga—described as the birthplace of Spain. But to travel there from this point requires a lengthy detour.

Shrouds of mist hang between gorges and the sky weeps as we tool back to Santillana. Pushing along, we imagine heartening cups of tea back at the inn.

Warmed and refreshed, we drive to Comillas at dusk. The sky strikes deep indigo as we arrive at El Capricho de Gaudí. Floodlights bathe the fanciful restaurant in white luminance, a whimsy of ceramic sunflowers in yellow and green.

Only one other vehicle occupies the lot.

"Looks to me as though we'll have another of our private dining experiences," Uncle Chuck points out.

Traveling off-season, coupled with a propensity for top dining rooms in back-road locales, finds only the pair of us in more than a number of restaurants. The reward: a kitchen focused and service obliging.

Only four others share this beautiful room accoutered with napkins folded into "swans," effusive pastel flowers and wall-coverings tastefully mute.

First comes cold, nutty *jerez,* and nibble airy puffs larded with pâté mousse. We sip extraordinary *sopa de pescados y mariscos:* delicate bouillon with morsels of fish, clams, mussels, garlic and saffron. With warm, husky rolls, we dredge the remaining drops of this ephemerally delicious soup from wide shallow bowls, and I nearly cry out with pleasure.

A broad expanse of windows volunteers a twinkle-light panorama of Comillas below. We toast with Rioja *blanca*, turning our attention to the vista as we parley of tomorrow's plans for cave tours. Meanwhile, a staff of servers and busboys attend to the details of our dinner.

For main plates, we each selected *solomillo estrogonoff:* veal cubes with mushrooms enrobed in creamy sauce of tomato and blue cheese on a nest of broad noodles—a masterful combination of textures, focused flavors, a beautifully crafted interpretation of the Russian classic. A bottle of Ramón Bilbao 1985 *tinto* and casseroles of autumn vegetables round out the superb course.

"Dessert?" asks Uncle Chuck.

"I believe I can handle it."

To top off our celestial meal, we order *postres* El Capricho, each of the restaurant's desserts capriciously constructed, a jarring architectural melange of glazed apple tart, tangy sorbets, slivers of cheesecake, chocolate *pot du crème*, impeccable berries, all drizzled artistically with raspberry sauce. I relish each morsel with espresso; Uncle Chuck sips herbal tea with his.

"We've sampled delicious food on this holiday," Uncle Chuck breathes. "Yet this meal was hands-down superlative."

I agree, though what we tasted was categorically Basque or Basque-inspired. Unlike the Castilian and Galician fare we've sampled, El Capricho's cuisine is fancier, French-influenced. Castile and Galicia offer heartier victuals of Old Spain, while Galicia serves up a munificence of freshly caught seafood. Cuisine of Castile we consider macho, full-bodied with earthy flavors, unctuous with olive oil or animal fat or both. Castile's food has not evolved from the diet of medieval warlords. Throughout Spain, we discover an array of ethnic tastes in French, Moroccan, Saharan and Persian innuendoes. Even the ancient Romans influenced Spanish taste buds. And evening meals, regardless of region, are taken late.

We drive back to Santillana through inky nighttide. Wearing extra pounds, we agree life is indeed *muy buena.*

Red digits on my bedside clock radio indicate half-past two. I lie wide-eyed, restless. *Shall I walk off the insomnia? Imagine, having this ancient setting all to myself....* I pull on warm clothes and silently venture from the room. I inch cautiously down a sighing staircase, and step into the bracing night.

Deathly quiet.... The moon's silvery visage filters through corrugated layers of steely-gray clouds. This frail light guides my steps.

Only one other soul roams the gaunt alleys of Santillana, a mostly-Labrador dog. We saw him yesterday near the community well. Seems friendly enough, so I saunter alongside him, wading through steamy cobbles up Calle del Río.

My furry escort ambles across the moonlit plaza and pads up the church steps. *Funny, doors ajar at this hour....* I sense crunching underfoot and look down to a host of razor clamshells.

Stranger still, an eerie dirge resonates from the old church, echoing in sepulchral, off-key pitch. The chanting sounds like, "Wendy, Wendy, Wendy." Above the portal, the tympanum glows gently, fluttering as though from candles. A whiff of mustiness piques my nostrils.

From night's crisp air, I tread over the threshold into mustiness. Stale air spikes with melting wax and pungent incense. I espy a shadowy congregation of monks encircling the tomb of Santa Juliana. Each of the monks carries a long-stemmed sunflower. As I shuffle forward, bass voices grow larger, the incantations more off-key. *"Duende, duende, duende,"* the hollow voices intone. Suddenly I realize the monks' capuches are vacuous.

Ca-THUNK! Massive doors slam behind me, the dull clamor reverberating against stone. Now the grisly assemblage of hollow cassocks floats toward me. Spinning round, I flee, jostling doors, rattling handles. Chanting escalates to sinister wails and groans; outside, the Lab howls maniacally. In vain I push at the doors, my heart pounding violently, hot perspiration streaming down my forehead, then....

"Wake up, boy!"

Uncle Chuck stands over my bed.

"You're dreaming. Too much rich food?"

I blot my forehead with the back of my forearm. "You have no idea...."

I stop mid-sentence. Details would elicit disparaging comments; possibly, too, arguments concerning further exploration of ecclesial antiquities.

Relieved, I take a sip of water, then turn over to sleep.

Now...do I hear a dog howling in the distance?

LOOKING BACK, CIRCA FIFTEEN-THOUSAND YEARS

It was a day we long anticipated, having requested permission a year earlier to visit Las Cuevas de Altamira. Officials restricted even the occasional tour of the significant caves after conservators discovered the Ice Age murals' vulnerability to light and dampness—including moisture from human breath. These prehistoric paintings, amongst the oldest art on the planet, I viewed before only between covers of art history books.

"Look. Santillana," Uncle Chuck remarks.

He points northeast as we wait for the office to open at Altamira. We distinguish through drizzle red rooftops of Santillana nestled into a fold of landscape. Just beyond rolls the shimmering Bay of Biscay.

Inside the administration office, we tender a copy of the letter we sent together with our passports to an *oficiala* named Magdalena. In her khaki uniform, this woman looks seriously official, and her appointment book shows not a trace of our names.

"*Pero*," she consoles, "sometimes we have cancellations."

A Japanese family arrives. They exchange paperwork without a hitch and move on; a docent will meet them at the foot of the hill. Fifteen minutes pass. No one else shows. Magdalena tells Uncle Chuck and me that one of us may join the coterie. Graciously, I am allowed to go, Uncle Chuck insisting that he will prowl through facsimile dioramas in the adjacent museum while I tour.

"Besides," he says, "with my head cold, in a dank cave...."

Though grateful, I will spend the half-hour expedition immersed in guilty pleasure. Impressed as we are with Santillana, one day we will return. Then Uncle Chuck will enjoy the Altamira caves.

They say a dog discovered Las Cuevas de Altamira in 1868, when a hunter named Modesto Cubillas followed his pet in pursuit of a fox to an aperture at the foot of a hill. As Cubillas pulled away growth and loose stones, he unsealed the entrance to a cave. At that moment, he hadn't a notion that he uncovered a millennia-old repository of art. Cubillas notified a scientist from Santander named Marcelino Sanz de Sautuola. In 1875, Sanz entered the cave for the first time, breathing air left chaste for millennia, and noted a meandering series of caverns and random black pictographs. Sanz considered these unimportant. Later, aroused by prehistoric displays he'd viewed at the 1878 World Fair in Paris, he returned to Altamira. In 1879, with his young daughter, Sanz probed deeper inside the cave and surveyed by lantern light an arresting gallery of primeval paintings.

Our animated guide unbolts the gate and swings open the thick door behind it. Deep inside a stale abyss, the five of us plus our expedition leader will soon behold the same phenomenon as had *Señor* Sanz and his daughter, vaguely illumined with sunbeams that leaked into the mouth of this cave. The guide's eyebrows dance as he points out a dozen or so bison rendered in black and red with static technique.

Cool blackness envelops us. Only the beacon of a lantern guides our way. Our heels echo hollowly throughout the dank limestone tunnel into a recess ascribed as the Sistine Chapel of Quaternary Art. We shuffle mindfully round a bend, crouching to elude hazards of a low ceiling. Our guide instructs us to sit on boulder-shaped stones that rise from the chamber floor, and waves his light at these stones. Once we're seated, he tells us to lean back and cast our eyes upward. He aims his lantern toward the ceiling.

We gasp. Overhead thunders an energetic herd of bison, some rendered expressionistically, others realistically, life-sized, including a pregnant cow—emphatic forms outlined in spontaneous strokes of black, filled in with reddish-orange pigment. A dozen-or-so of these animals ripple with natural contours and fissures, the ceiling's irregularities imparting a plastic quality to illustrated fauna.

Hair bristling on the back of my neck, I stare in wonder, imagining a paleolithic hunter-artist as he noticed organic shapes in this stony ceiling, then creating over them these fazing images with only the flicker of a torch or oil lamp to guide him. Did that ancient man believe his art worked a kind of magic regarding the hunt? Concluded that he enslaved the animals in this cave? Moreover, did he consider that others would see his indelible messages thousands of years later?

The vault where we sit, called Salón de las Pinturas Policromas, darkens again. Instructed to mind our heads, our guide leads us deeper into subterranean chambers. Here we inspect hundreds more sketches, polychrome renderings echoing clues of prehistory: deer splendidly rendered, a boar and a herd of bison lowing, galloping or resting.

Carbon tests calculated these friezes' age between thirteen and fifteen thousand years. The medium, charcoal, natural red- and yellow-ochre-based minerals, was feasibly chewed, mixed with the artisans' saliva, then spit-blown in frenetic spurts through reeds—a primitive airbrush technique. Still other configurations the aboriginal artists created with sticks of carbon or mineral used as pencils.

Exactly what inspired these suspensive murals? Historians suggest inventories of tribal hunting grounds. Others imply components of a primitive religious ritual. By any means, the abrupt *sumi-e* manner—a disciplined brushstroke technique, a comparison pointed out by my Japanese tour-mates—stuns, even by modern standards. Realistically depicted, the ephemeral poses surpass modern technology only in fast film.

My head filled with wonder, I locate Uncle Chuck, who browses the museum's bookshop. Having reviewed the slide presentation and dioramas, he expects I enjoyed the originals even more so.

"There's another cavern in this vicinity, with stalactites," he tells me, "accessible without special permission. Yet, I've seen my share of cave formations in the States. This museum is more engaging than a forest of calcified formations."

We return to Santillana, following our noses to Restaurante Casa Cossio just up the road from our inn. The rustic second-floor dining room overlooks the village.

With great difficulty, I spare Uncle Chuck details of my cave tour. He nevertheless realizes I experienced one of the aesthetic thrills of a lifetime.

"What now?" I inquire, folding my napkin.

After succoring fare, Uncle Chuck suggests a drive to Santander, Cantabria's capital, just up the road.

"British friends of mine take summer holidays there," he says. "Shall we head over to have a look-see?"

Coastal Santander, called *Puerto de San Emeterio* in 1068, fills our windshield. We look to each other in dismay. Before us stands an overgrown, vapid expanse of post-modern structures. Does the contrast of delightful Santillana spoil our impressions of Santander? On the other hand, is Santander as surly as it appears?

"I don't want to get embroiled in big-city traffic. I hope you don't mind if we forego a tour," Uncle Chuck says.

"I agree, let's get out of here."

There's no love lost with Santander and us. Since his British friends last visited, Santander had lost its sheen. Uncle Chuck makes a surprising U-turn, then we hightail it back to Santillana.

With daylight favoring the urbanscape, we peruse alleyways for photo opportunities, lolling about Santillana for the balance of the afternoon.

Tomorrow, we depart for Madrid. Given a long drive ahead, we plan to dine early this evening at the *parador* restaurant.

Having packed our luggage, we settle downstairs for cocktails and a browse of the dinner menu.

"Ever tried skate, Uncle Chuck?"

"Where do you see that?"

"Second item under *pescados*. *Raya en salsa de pimentón*, skate in paprika sauce."

"You ask for more bad dreams, boy. I would suggest a less exotic dish."

Resolving to go lightly on wine as well, we order a demi-bottle of *tinto* to accompany our meal, *solamente*. We each sample a ramekin of *fabada:* gutsy bean-and-sausage stew, followed by salads dotted with tart olives of glossy purple and green.

Uncle Chuck's *costillas de cordero a la parrilla* (grilled lamb chops) are quintessentially pink in the middle, bursting with woody fragrance, and my *perdiz* (partridge) baked en casserole with figs in wine is superb, until....

"You know that bird came from the wild," Uncle Chuck muses when I show him a piece of buckshot that nearly cracked a tooth. "I suggest you chew more cautiously," he says.

We top our meal with the chef's signature rice pudding, passing on coffee. Instead, we savor *porto* and clink our glasses to a corner of heaven known as Santillana Del Mar.

mas castilla y león

85

Más Castilla y León

El Cid, legendary hero of the Reconquest,[1] rests beneath the cathedral at Burgos. Rodrigo Díaz de Vivar (El Cid Campeador, 1040-99) was a vassal of Alfonso VI in the late-eleventh century. He earned his place as national hero after he rallied troops against Berber invaders, thus redeeming his cherished Castile. Following the victory, Spaniards dubbed El Cid "Eminent Medieval Warrior of Spain." (Cid, a corruption of the Arabic Sidi, meant Lord.) Poets greatly exaggerate El Cid's chivalrous deeds in song and rhyme, yet historians concur with his ostensible tour de force.

A fourth coffee refill? We've lost count, lingering over breakfast, neither of us wild about leaving our secluded enclave at Santillana Del Mar. I suggest a parting look up and down spellbinding streets, though all lies somber under a seething sky. We amble along, wondering when we may again call this village home.

"On our way?" Uncle Chuck asks after fifteen minutes of scenic reverie. "I'd prefer to drop our car at the airport and cab into Madrid before nightfall."

Gray-bottomed clouds muddle vast landscape in shades of smoky-violet as Santillana fades into the distance, but its glories shall remain etched in my memory.

Neither of us has visited Madrid, so we haven't a notion what lies beyond, nor have we experienced Burgos, The Crucible of Castile, Castile's old capital founded in 884 as a military town.

Mist-fringed Cordillera Cantábrica flattens to mesas, then to topography even more uniform as we travel southward along silvery-slick N-623. A caravan of low-hanging clouds courses swiftly through an aluminum sky; our pint-sized car lists with the gales. Scenery underwhelms until Catedral de Burgos proposes above the banks of Río Arlanzón. Above inextricable cityscape rise 275-foot-high spires, elongated pyramids penetrating somber atmosphere. Our way in to Burgos stifles with dingy industrial parks and a warren of dismal tenements.

Wending through swarming *paseos* in direction of the massive cathedral, we pass through Arco de Santa María, an old city gate, and park outside Plaza del Rey San Fernando. A chilly squall nearly sweeps us off our feet as we cross streets following a gaggle of black-and-white nuns doing their best to sustain respectability, their habits and veils billowing on the wind.

Before lunch, we explore the soot-smudged cathedral. To regard the exterior of this thirteenth-century colossus from confines of the square proves a neck-wrenching matter. Uncle Chuck points out lacy openwork spires relieving the mass of enormity both aesthetically and practically. The spires remind me of twin Eiffel Towers hewn from stone.

Inclement weather accelerates our tour of the exterior as we scurry up ramps and short flights of steps to view the entire structure. I wonder at Judaic symbolism. *Why the Star of David on this Catholic temple?* The six-point star embroiders an oculus cradled within a niche above the portal. Other designs, trefoils and lacy pinnacles undulate alongside dozens of three-dimensional saints, archbishops and popes.

Inside the cathedral, we welcome its shelter, though the cavernous space sweeps over us, shuddery cold. Pacing beneath rib-framed vaulting, we discover an epigraph in the transept floor: tomb of El Cid and his spouse Ximena.

Third largest in Spain, this cathedral of Burgos was founded in 1221 by Fernando III. The vast structure embodies thirteen chapels and a grand, gilded double-staircase, dozens of choir stalls intricately carved, lavish paintings and royal escutcheons.

From a bay in the nave's ceiling, a grotesque, mechanical-mannequin-clock chimes twelve times. We return to the fierceness of the square, and duck into the warm haven of Mesón del Cid. A klatch of businessmen in trench coats stand at a marble bar smoking and tippling. We shake off the cold and retreat to a cozy nook in the near-empty, smoke-free *comedor*. A young, doe-eyed waitress jots down our order. Within moments, she brings *cervezas* with still-simmering bowls of savory *lechón con nabos:* stew of pork hocks and turnip tops. For the ride ahead, we down a couple cups of *cafés con leche*.

We return to the streets under drizzle. I already miss Santillana.

---

[1] Reconquest (*Reconquista*): The Christian conquest of those parts of Spain occupied by the Moors.

MADRID

As we journeyed southward, plains rose up to the smoky Guadarrama range,
then dipped and leveled to fields sprawling flatly under a turbulent sky.
Occasionally, we regarded gigantic black toro *cutouts poised along the*
motor-way. I attributed these icons to popularity of the national spectacle of
bullfighting, though I had heard these once served as billboards for cognac.
Another hour passed when the rough edges of Madrid palled with
marginados, *industrial tracts and clustered high-rise dwellings. When we*
reached the airport, the storm had blown over.

MAJESTIC MADRID

Until the sixteenth century, *Madrit* (Madrid) was a peaceful, negligible
farming community fringed by a wooded *meseta* (plain). Though we read of
Roman occupation[1] in Castilla y León's Segovia and Castilla-La Mancha's
Soria, scant citations propose Roman occupation of Madrid. Beyond
indigenous farmers, Madrid's history began with Moslems. In the eighth
century, Emir Mohammed I called this region *Majerit* (Arabic for water
source) and built here a fortress in the foothills of Sierra de Guadarrama, on
a rise above Río Manzanares. Under Alfonso VI, Christians captured the
Moorish *medina* (city) between 1083 and 1086 and renamed it *Madrit*. The
Moors were not expelled, and the two religions coexisted peacefully.

In 1085, Alfonso VI purportedly discovered near the Moorish bastion a
statue of the Virgin in an *al mudin* (granary). King Alfonso ordered the
mosque converted to church and dedicated this to Nuestra Señora de la
Almudena (Our Lady of the Granary), who was declared patroness of the city.

Late-eleventh- and early-twelfth-century Madrid was home to a local
farmer, Isidro, who was sainted in 1622, and became the city's patron.
Madrid's first cathedral was named for him.

In the fourteenth century, Pedro I El Cruel (Peter the Cruel, 1334-69)
ordered Madrid's first castle constructed on the site of the Moorish *alcázar*.

In the fifteenth century, Isabel La Católica commissioned *Madrit's* monastery, San Jerónimo El Real, about a mile from the palace.

The Habsburg's (House of Austria) Felipe II proclaimed Madrid capital of Spain, moving the seat of Spanish kings from Toledo in 1561. Henceforth, seigniorial mansions, churches, monasteries and convents dotted the mushrooming urbanscape of Madrid de los Austrias. Of merit, and still thriving: the Habsburg dynasty's Plaza Mayor, the largest square in Spain and Puerta del Sol (Gate of the Sun). Carlos V refined the crude castle of Pedro I El Cruel, though what we see today is a reconstruction, the Palacio Real (Royal Palace).

As Madrid developed, the uncontrolled cutting of surrounding forests led to erosion, drought and extremes in temperature. Eighteenth-century Bourbons—who were said to civilize Spain—found their capital an overrun, squalid, crime-ridden city. Though Madrid had grown from a population of twenty thousand to 175,000 in its first one hundred years as capital—and fifth largest capital in Europe—officials of the new Bourbon dynasty set about to correct the squalor by constructing fine parks and baroque monuments and palaces. The Bourbons' finest accomplishment stands on foundations of the old Moorish *alcázar*: the enhanced Palacio Real designed under command of Felipe V. Combined legacies of Habsburgs and Bourbons include Madrid's wealth of paintings harbored in museums such as the Prado. Talented artists beautified eighteenth-century Madrid with *Isabeline* (Romantic) architecture. In that century, a dispute over royal succession led to the Carlist Wars (1833-1876)—liberal revolts, and the short-lived First Republic.

French troops occupied Madrid at the dawn of the nineteenth century, followed by rebellions and reprisals, then a vast expansion of the city.

Until 1900, Madrid remained almost entirely an administrative city, its few industries producing goods for local consumers. The city's great cathedral, Nuestra Señora de la Almudena, was begun in the nineteenth century, though not completed until the late twentieth.

The twentieth century ushered in urban renewal and French-inspired architecture—including Banco Central Hispanoamericano, Edificio Metrópolis, Hotel Palace and Hotel Ritz—and Madrid's growth as a major center of finance, stock exchange, universities, administrative bodies, private cultural institutions and political organizations.

Near the geographical center of Spain, Madrid thrives as the highest laying capital in Europe at 2,165 feet above sea level. A population of nearly four million occupies its 194,885 square miles. The government is a parliamentary monarchy, a hereditary title. Madrid is Spain's chief transportation and administrative hub, with a flourishing economy of industry, tourism and service enterprises. Major industrial products include motor vehicles, aircraft, electronics, chemicals, pharmaceuticals, processed food, printed materials, tobacco, paper, leather goods and furniture. The service sector involves banking, publishing, insurance, hotels and restaurants.

Tourists many times overlook Madrid, chalking it up to a big administrative and financial seat. After all, the beguilement of Seville and Granada, the mysteries of Santiago de Composetela and natural wonders of the northern coast all vie for tourists' sense of discovery and adventure. Nevertheless, Madrid furnishes a trove of history and monuments. Witness the reasons to visit Madrid.

NOTEWORTHY SITES OF MADRID

Ayuntamiento: Madrid's baroque town hall at Plaza de la Villa, designed by Gómez de Mora in 1617.

Banco de España y Central Hispanoamericano: Fine examples of Madrid's early-twentieth-century re-urbanization.

Basílica de San Francisco El Grande: By Francisco Cabezas; Neo-Classical façade by Francesco Sabatini. Treasures include eighteenth-century frescoes and a masterpiece by Goya.

Campo del Moro (Moors' Field): A greensward of shade trees, winding paths and a lawn leading up to Palacio Real.

Capilla de San Antonio de la Florida: A chapel built in 1798 under Carlos IV; painted by Goya and containing his bodily remains.

Casón del Buen Retiro: A gallery annex—once a ballroom, a fragment of the former Palacio de Buen Retiro—of Museo del Prado housing an incomparable collection of nineteenth-century Spanish art.

Catedral de la Almudena: Madrid's cathedral, adjacent to Palacio Real. Begun 1883, the cathedral was completed in 1993 and consecrated by John

Paul II. Fernando Chueca Goltia designed this classic though simplified Gothic temple. A wall of an original Moorish granary appends the cathedral's foundation.

Catedral de San Isidro: Designed by Jesuits Pedro Sánchez and Francisco Bautista, this church harbors the mortal remains of Madrid's patron Saint Isidore. Formerly the church of the Imperial College of the Company of Jesus (1622), this served as Madrid's cathedral from 1885 to 1993.

Congreso de los Diputados: Built in the mid-nineteenth century on the site of a former convent, this Roman-classical building is home to the Spanish parliament, the Cortes.

Convento de la Encarnación: At one time adjoining Palacio Real, the cloister now houses royal portraits. Ventura Rodríguez designed the eighteenth-century church.

Convento de las Descalzas Reales: Royal Convent of the Discalced (Barefoot) Sisters, an order founded by Teresa de Ávila. This convent founded by Juana of Austria (youngest daughter of Carlos V) houses a trove of art treasures.

Emir Mohammed I (park): A pleasant greensward near ruins of Madrid's old Arab walls, south of the Royal Palace and cathedral.

Fuente/Plaza de la Cibeles: Madrid's symbolic and famous fountain of Cybele, the Roman goddess of fertility, driving her chariot with two lions.

Fuente de Neptuno/Plaza Cánovas del Castillo: Named for leading statesman Antonio Cánovas del Castillo, who was assassinated in 1897, this is a stunning plaza with a fulminating Neptune fountain designed by Ventura Rodríguez in 1780, and situated at the juncture of Paseo del Prado and Paseo de Recoletos.

Gran Vía: A main traffic artery inaugurated in 1910, flanked with architectural showpieces and upscale shopping.

Hemeroteca Municipal: Beyond its *Mudéjar* portal are harbored more than

70,000 bound volumes of newspapers printed in the eighteenth and nineteenth centuries.

Iglesia de San Jerónimo El Real: Only the church remains of this fifteenth-century Hieronymite monastery used by the Catholic Monarchs as a *retiro* (place of meditation), the monastic cells and cloisters reduced to rubble in the Napoleonic Wars. The church was rebuilt in the nineteenth century and the coronation of Carlos I took place here in 1975.

Iglesia de San Nicolás de los Servitas: The oldest church in Madrid (1202). The *Mudéjar* tower may have originally served as minaret for a mosque.

Iglesia de San Pedro Real: A fine old church trimmed with a fourteenth-century *Mudéjar* tower.

Jardines Sabatini: Formal gardens north of Palacio Real.

Jardines de las Vistillas: Splendid gardens at a high point above Río Manzanares offering views of the Sierra de Guadarrama, Casa del Campo, Catedral de la Almudena and the viaduct.

Murallas Árabes: Vestiges of Madrid's Moorish walls just south of Palacio Real and the cathedral.

Museo Arqueológico/Biblioteca Nacional: Collections from prehistoric Spain, Roman and Visigothic treasures, plus a wealth of manuscripts dating from the tenth century.

Museo de Carruajes Reales: A pavilion built in 1967 in the middle of Campo del Moro winter garden, this Royal Carriage Museum features vehicles dating from the seventeenth century.

Museo de Cera: The waxworks museum.

Museo Cerralbo: Nineteenth-century palace rigged with artworks, furnishings and weaponry.

Museo de la Ciudad: Displays of Madrid's prehistory to the present time.

Museo del Ejército: Army Museum in a remnant of the former Palacio de Buen Retiro.

Casa de Lope de Vega, Museo de América: Former home of playwright Felix Lope de Vega, this somber home now showcases an overview of European ties with America.

Museo del Prado: Considered the greatest gallery of classical paintings (more than 8,000) in the world. At one time intended to house the Natural Science Museum, this Neo-Classical building is located across the Paseo del Prado from Parque del Buen Retiro.

Museo Lázaro Gaidiano: Early-twentieth-century Italianate palace and gardens, once the private residence of publisher Lázaro Gaidiano who bequeathed his art collection to the Spanish government in 1948.

Museo-Palacio de Liria: Once the eighteenth-century residence of the Alba family and still belonging to the Duchess of Alba, this palace designed by Ventura Rodríguez in 1780 may be visited by appointment only. The palace houses an outstanding collection of art and Flemish tapestries.

Museo Municipal: Historical exhibits from Madrid's Paleocene Epoch to the present time.

Museo Nacional de Artes Decorativas: Founded in 1912 as a showplace for Spanish ceramics and interior design.

Museo Nacional Centro de Arte Reina Sofía: Former Hospital de San Carlos founded by Carlos III, now housing examples of leading avant-garde art movements including works of Picasso, Miró and Dalí.

Museo Sorolla: Former home of Joaquín Sorolla, featuring his artwork.

Museo Thyseen-Bornemisza: Late-eighteenth- to early-nineteenth-century Neo-Classical Palacio de Villahermosa, magnificently rejuvenated by architect Rafael Moneo to house the collection of eight hundred works, mainly paintings, owned by Baron Hans Heinrich Thyssen-Bornemisza.

Palacio Real: Twice the size of Buckingham Palace, this opulent Neo-Classical construction of Guadarrama granite and Colmenar limestone was begun on the site of Madrid's Moorish and Habsburg *alcázares* after a fire on Christmas Eve, 1734. Alfonso XIII last occupied this sumptuous palace; today it is but a museum.

Parque del Oeste/Templo de Debod: Western Madrid's answer to Parque del Buen Retiro, though smaller and more informal. This park's attractions include a zoo, a swimming pool and the spectacular Templo de Debod, the reconstruction of an Egyptian temple from the fourth century A.D.

Parque del Buen Retiro: Originally the grounds of a seventeenth-century palace of Felipe IV, developed into a park by the Duke of Olivares. Formal gardens, water features including a small boating lake, fountains, temples and monuments grace this 321-acre oasis.

Paseo de la Castellana: A delightful tree-lined stretch of open-air *terrazas* bisecting the city between the train stations of Estación Atocha and Estación Chamartín.

Paseo del Prado: An elegant, shaded avenue interspersed with fountains and plazas. Based on Rome's Piazza Navona, this stretch was part of a plan of Carlos III to dedicate a sector of Madrid to the arts and sciences.

Plaza de Colón: Graced by a statue of Christopher Columbus in celebration of the discovery of America, erected in 1885.

Plaza de las Cortes: A tiny square approximate Congreso de Diputados, shaded by cypress trees and graced with a fine bronze of Cervantes.

Plaza de España: A sophisticated esplanade dominated by a monument to Cervantes, at one time the largest, freestanding concrete structure in the world.

Plaza de la Lealtad: A beautiful square in the Paseo del Prado harboring the Monumento del Dos de Mayo, commemorating Spain's War of Independence against the French.

Plaza Mayor: The largest square in Spain, sanctioned by Felipe III in 1617, designed by Juan Gómez de Mora, raised on the site of the Arabic marketplace *El Arrabal.* Over the centuries, this square hosted a theater for tragedy and celebration. Here, up to fifty thousand spectators ogled from four hundred and seventy six balconies the persecution of heretics: *autos da fe,* public punishments imposed by the Inquisition, plus events ranging from royal weddings to bullfights to canonization ceremonies of Saints Teresa de Ávila, Ignacio, Francisco Javier, Isidro and Felipe Neri. In this illustrious plaza, Felipe V, Fernando VI and Carlos IV were each proclaimed King.

Plaza de la Moncloa/Arco de Triunfo: A monumental archway from where the Velázquez landscape of Casa de Campo may be admired.

Plaza Monumental de Toros de Las Ventas: Known as Madrid's cathedral of bullfighting, this early-twentieth-century *Mudéjar*-style bullring yields seating capacity for 22,300 spectators.

Plaza de Oriente: A sculpture garden hosting Gothic kings in marble and a pedestrian square laying between the east façade of Palacio Real and the main façade of Teatro Real. In the midst stands an equestrian statue of Felipe IV by Pietro Tacca (1577-1640, Florence) after a painting by Diego Velázquez. Tacca consulted Galileo to ensure proper balance for his nine-ton statue. From this square, mobs of Franco supporters listened to their dictator speak from the roof of adjacent Palacio Real.

Plaza de la Paja: The commercial center and most important square of medieval Madrid, featuring Capilla del Obispo (1520-1530) by Gutiérrez Carvajal, a part of domed Iglesia de San Andrés, where peasants of old Madrid tithed. Palacio del Vargas defines another side of this square.

Plaza Santa Ana: Hub of Madrid's seventeenth-century theater district, now a throbbing sector of nightclubs.

Plaza de la Villa: A pedestrian square flanked by architecture from the fifteenth to seventeenth centuries. Here stand three of Madrid's rare examples of medieval civil architecture: the fifteenth-century baroque Casa del Cisneros, the *ayuntamiento* and Torre de los Lujanes. In the *torre,* Francis I of France languished as prisoner following the Battle of Pavia.

Pontificia de San Miguel: Exquisite example of eighteenth-century Italian baroque, this basilica sports sculptures of the Roman child-martyrs Pastor and Justus to whom the church was previously dedicated.

Puente de Toledo: A splendid bridge over Río Manzanares, built by Pedro de Ribera and finished by Francisco Moradillo.

Puerta de Alcalá at Plaza de la Independencia: A ceremonial arch built by Francesco Sabatini between 1769 and 1778 to commemorate the triumphant entrance of Carlos III into Madrid.

Puerta del Sol: In the heart of Madrid, a fan-shaped district of jam-packed pedestrian ways, eighteenth-century buildings, shops, department stores and restaurants. This is Spain's *Kilometre Cero* (Zero) and the hub of most of Madrid's metro and bus lines. Here stands Gobernación (Ministry of the Interior), originally Madrid's central post office, with a nineteenth-century bell tower to *Madrileños* what Big Ben is to Londoners. A bronze sculpture of a bear eating from a strawberry tree in the Puerta serves a popular meeting place for *Madrileños*.

Puerta de Toledo: A ceremonial gate erected for Fernando VII in Plaza de la Marina Española.

El Rastro: Northeast of Puerta de Toledo, in the south of the city, this illustrious flea market—thronged each Sunday from 10:00 A.M. to 2:00 P.M—dates back to Moorish market tradition.

Real Academia de Bellas Artes: Eighteenth-century building by Churriguera housing magnificent works by Spanish masters including El Greco and Murillo. Famous, former students of this art academy included Salvador Dalí and Pablo Picasso.

Real Jardín Botánico: Inspired by Carlos III, these Royal Botanical Gardens were designed in 1781 by botanist Gómez Ortega and by Juan de Villanueva, the architect of Museo del Prado.

Teatro Real: Opened as an opera house in 1850, this royal theater ranks among the most technically advanced opera houses in Europe, seating 1,800 spectators.

[1] Roman corsairs met with marginal resistance in the south and north of Spain. The inhabitants of *Numancia* (region of Soria, northeast of Madrid) vigorously resisted the Romans. Sixty thousand Roman troops battled for nearly two years to subdue the four thousand inhabitants of *Numancia* who finally chose death rather than surrender. Ancient inhabitants of Madrid with similar mettle give further reason to consider their resistance, and a landlocked inland position set high on a vast *meseta*, left untouched by Roman invasion.

According to Leonard Curchin, historian-scholar of central Spain: "There was definitely Roman settlement on the site of Madrid, but no actual town. Roman pottery (*terra sigillata*) has been found in several places under the modern city, and there are ruins of Roman villas in the suburbs of Madrid known as *Carabanchel* and *Villaverde Bajo*. The foundation of a town on the site of Madrid still dates to the ninth century."

TASTING SPAIN'S CAPITAL

Sunshine obliged as we rolled our luggage to the taxi queue at Barajas airport.

"Hotel Gran Victoria Reina," I tell the driver.

He shrugs. *"¿Qué?"*

I roll my *rs* more distinctly. Now he knows where we want to go.

"¡Ah, sí, R-eina Victo-r-ia!"

We open our windows to survive effects of second-hand smoke as the wee Mercedes inches deliberately amongst a traffic jam. Reaching Madrid's hub, we see sweeping parks and boulevards lined with yellow trees, stately monuments, ebullient fountains, fashionable shops and natty pedestrians. The legacy of Habsburgs and Bourbons lives. When we ultimately reach the vicinity of our hotel, we are pleased with the tidy milieu.

I am excited to be in Madrid where, under Carlos III in the eighteenth century, the decisive step was taken in founding my hometown of San Diego, and eventually, the colonizing by Spain of Alta California. Furthermore, expatriate guests such as Ernest Hemingway immortalized our grand hotel.

Before registering, we exchange large bills for smaller denominations, for a garrison of open-palmed staff that greeted us the moment we stepped from our cab.

Smart and masculine, the lobby passes our critical inspection, and a bar papered in carmine looks inviting.

We requested a quiet room, so our view does not afford splendors of Madrid's pulsing streets and verdant parks. Instead, our room faces the hotel's core of air-conditioning units and other guests' windows.

"I suppose you can't have it all," Uncle Chuck breathes, as he draws the heavy draperies. "Let's explore."

Evidently, he feels better, and decided his cold was an allergy.

We walk in direction of Plaza Mayor with the help of a city map. Along the way, Uncle Chuck makes mental notes of antique emporiums. The best of them are shut for the day.

The hoi polloi thickens as we near the enormous city square. Principally, natives comprise the crowd. Buskers perform on the sidewalks, some with garishly costumed animals. Other hucksters sustain air-shows of juggling pins.

"At least they earn their keep," Uncle Chuck points out, as blank-eyed beggars vex with outstretched hands.

We cross under an archway, into the heart of Plaza Mayor, a vast arena of history. I listen for the wails of heretics, the cheers of spectators, but hear only the haggling of shoppers, the clinking of plates and cocktail glasses.

Late afternoon's sun dapples one end of the arcade with a play of golden light. Another side, named Casa de la Panadería (House of the Baker), hails as the oldest section of this plaza. Here, frescos of fanciful scenes engage in splashes of vivid hues. Trompe l'œil spectators watch us from their balconies. Clustered upon the flagstones under bright red umbrellas, white café tables beckon. We nab a table at the shadowy side, then feast our eyes from sun-drenched arcades to stalls abounding with bric-a-brac, engravings, watercolors.

"¿Señores?"

A black-haired *mozo* in black trousers and white smock emerges from the shadows. We order *cervezas*, then resume our optical tour. Artists make caricatures or render portraits with pastels or charcoal. A mounted, bronze Rey Felipe III holds court from his lofty pedestal in the plaza's center, a stone monarch, and target for photographers and pigeons.

Uncle Chuck tastes his beer, then excuses himself from the table. He returns with fried *calamares* and *patatas bravas* (spicy potatoes). Grateful the weather did not follow us from Cantabria, we munch and drink as we people-watch in the cool air. Tourists finagle with vendors. Others pose for artists. Beggars—pigeons, sparrows, Gypsies—make gambles on handouts.

Generally, beggars annoy me. Nevertheless, my heart sinks when I spot a man who smacks of the ideal image of Christ, if not for a horrendous physical aberration. This dark-haired, bearded man with sweet countenance has no arms. Hands spring directly from his shoulders, open, for *almas*. I fidget in my seat and clear my throat.

"What's wrong?" Uncle Chuck asks.

"Never mind," I say.

"No. Something's amiss. What is it?"

"Don't be obvious, but look at that man near the statue of Felipe."

I push my chair back, fish for my wallet, pull out a note and shuffle over to the misbegotten fellow. I deposit the bill in his McDonald's cup. With his lips and eyes, he smiles ardently, then blesses me in Spanish. His haunting image will forever remain with me.

Cristo	Christ,
tenía un espejo	a mirror
en cada mano.	in each hand.
Multiplicaba	He multiplies
su propio espectro.	His shadow.
Proyectaba su corazón,	He projects his heart,
en las miradas	through his black
negras.	visions.
¡Creo!	I believe!

—Federico García Lorca, "*Símbolo*" ("Symbol")

Heading out of the plaza, we prowl through displays of hats, fans, *castañuelas* (castanets) and statues of saints and Don Quixote. Other shops purvey matador dolls in silk costumes and papier-mâché bulls upholstered with real hair, bristling with *banderillas*, suggesting *toro* pincushions.

We move on to La Puerta del Sol where a solid wave of humanity flows against us with the fervor of hot lava. Uncle Chuck and I dodge the mass, worming our way into the puerta.

Why are they all here?—Madrileños cramming this precinct where ten streets converge. Surveyors regard La Puerta del Sol as Spain's geographical center. Kilometer Zero originates in this sector, a compass from which all distances are measured in Spain.

Claustrophobia gets the better of us. We return to the hotel, on a mission to reserve seats for an evening of flamenco.

EL ARTE FLAMENCO
SPAIN'S SINGULAR, MYSTERIOUS FOLK MUSIC

Flamenco evolved over hundreds of years to its present status as seductive art form and popular, complex style of voice and dance. Much more than a musical style, flamenco defines a philosophy, a way of life. Many of us know flamenco as performed on spotlit stages in nightclubs, in television studios or on movie sets, but its origins are earthier and more intimate. *Puristas* prefer flamenco's primordial characteristics, where dancing is incidental. The stark spirit of flamenco extricates itself, even on the modern stage, providing the mood is right.

Contemplative mood establishes the operative virtue in flamenco, as do elements of arrogance, exuberance, spontaneity and pathos. As with so many of Spain's riddles, so, too, go flamenco's ancient roots.

Considering nomenclature, there are those who incorrectly speculate the idiom flamenco took its etymology from "Flemish courtiers," because of the flamboyant mode of dress and courtly dances acculturated by Gypsies who passed through Flanders. In Spanish, *flamear* means to flame, a palpable etymological root of "flamenco," suggesting the fiery performances. But musicologists dispute these theories, and likewise any suggestion of "flamingo" as the word's origin. More accurately, the phrase in Arabic, *felag-mengu* or *felah men encûn,* means "singing fugitives" or "you the peasants." This phrase corrupted became "flamenco."

Musicologists believe flamenco as we know it achieved its zenith centuries ago in Andalucía where its roots run deep. Roots run even deeper in Arabic, Jewish and Castilian cultures. Musical styles influencing today's flamenco originated from Arabic religious chants and poems, that were sung, developed three or four centuries before Islam. Since those ancient times, the tradition has been learned by ear and assimilated from one generation to another.

Just as very ancient oriental elements are found in the music of the *siguiriya* and its derivatives, so in many poems of deep song, there is an affinity to the oldest oriental verse.

When our songs reach the very heights of pain and love, they become expressive sisters of the magnificent verses of Arabian and Persian poets.

—Federico García Lorca, "Deep Song"

Under the heel of Islam for eight hundred years, it's a small wonder folk music of Andalucía was shaped by aural styles of the Muslim and pre-Muslim world. We detect also in repertoires of virtuosic flamenco cantors the haunting liturgical solo of the Jewish hazan. Moreover, Turkish and Hindu characteristics come forth together with Kurdish and Armenian musical techniques.

So, did flamenco originate in the Middle East? In Egypt, Persia or India, as analysts infer? One can trace flamenco's Muse, a fusion of cultural styles, to musical forms from each of these Eastern regions. But experts agree on flamenco's Arabic genesis popularized by Spanish Gypsies. Through time and cultural influences, the art form became hybrid.

Gypsies (*gitanos*, or *romanís*) were outcasts, thus transients, assimilating along their way cultural attributes of lands they roamed—Persia, Egypt, India. Speculation suggests Gypsies came from India. Others believe they hailed from the Lost Tribes of Israel, fugitive people who worked odd tasks—harvesting, forging and mining. At day's end, these dejected, exhausted subsistence laborers sang for freedom by glowing campfires—as a means of easing suffering and disgrace. Influenced by Arabic chants, *coplas* (verses) took root with Gypsy field-worker, blacksmith and prison inmate. A style known as *tonadas* (naked voice) of the *cante jondo* (profound or deep song), Gypsies ultimately cultivated to chromatic acumen.

> If we do not relate the music to brutality, repression, hunger, fear, menace, infirmity, resistance and secrecy, then we shall not find the reality of flamenco.
>
> —Felix Grande

Over time, musical assemblages added rapid, rhythmic hand-clapping (*palmas,* a Moorish custom), finger snapping (*pitos*), heel-work (*zapateado*), castanets (*palillos*), the flamenco guitar (*guitarra flamenca*), steel anvil or whatever method of percussion was at hand. Perchance, flamenco dance originated when a spirited onlooker, seized by Dionysian force, gamboled impulsively. The performance as we know it began that simply, though today, non-*aficiones* consider flamenco a choreographed performance set to the tunes of *guitarras flamencas, palmas* and *jaleos*. Nevertheless, flamenco artists, particularly Gypsies, typically achieve flamenco pared to its essence with bodies and voices, spontaneously.

The *duende* does not repeat himself, any more than do the forms of
the sea during a squall.

—Federico García Lorca

Gypsies were familiar to Andalucía as early as the 1400s. At that time,
their music did not include accompaniment of guitar as we know it.
Performers may have used *la ud*, the Persian lute, to which Gypsies added a
fifth string, but it was not until circa 1856 when Antonio Torres created the
guitarra. Though flamenco's roots are ancient, the nineteenth century
ushered in the powerful art form known for its level of spectacle.

Gypsies popularized flamenco in public forums such as *cafés cantantes*
(singing clubs) from the 1860s to the dawn of the twentieth century, a
phenomenon that crested in 1920. The art stagnated during the earlier years
of the repressive Franco regime, but flamenco flourished internationally by
the 1950s. Franco, by then, realized flamenco's touristic appeal.

Flamenco may be sentimentally delicious. Performers incorporate
beguiling movement and emotive gestures—an unleashed evisceration of
energy conjured from emotional depth, an energy that builds in an exemplary
production to wildest abandon. For performers, flamenco sanctions cathartic
release of artistic expression, a means to enact pain, hope and joy. For a savvy
audience, flamenco may be magical, even hypnotic and sexy. Flamenco, after
all, becomes a performance of shared feelings, effecting the crescendo of
Spanish *afición*. For outsiders, the art form proposes a glimpse into the soul
of Spain.

Flamenco is the soul of Andalucía transformed into music.

—Pepe Romero

Flamenco consists of *cante* (song), *baile* (dance), *toque* (guitar playing)
and *jaleo* (rhythmic accentuation and spontaneous verbal comments). And
three categories: *jondo* (profound or deep flamenco), *intermedio*
(intermediate flamenco), *chico* (light flamenco). The complex *jondo*
embodies primitive chant styles including lyrics without accompaniment of
guitar: *tonás, deblas, martinetes* and *carceleras*. Another style is the *soleá*, a
long, contemplative solo considered by Andalusians *la reina del cante* (the
queen of song).

Just as Andalucían deep song surpasses in complexity, intelligence and musical wealth the old oriental songs, dark and full of monotony, Spanish dance brings us both the perfume of the ancient religious dances of the East and the culture, serenity and measure of the West, the world of criticism. The marvelous thing about Spanish dance is that here, as in *cante jondo*, there is room for personality and thus for the contribution of the individual. There is room for modernity and for personal genius. A modern dancer from India, aside from her personal, human grace, dances as they have always danced and…follows eternal norms. A Spanish dancer or singer or torero does not simply resuscitate, he invents and creates a unique, inimitable art, which disappears after his death.
—Federico García Lorca, "In Praise of Antonia Mercé, La Argentina"

Flamenco's complex syncopation builds against *compás* (the beat) with voice offbeat and musical instruments—for more than one hundred years, the guitar—setting the rhythm, furthering the syncopation.

Regardless of methods used, *puro* (genuine) flamenco conjures spontaneous contraction and release. The music seduces, swelling and soaring to dizzying heights, an unbridled human inferno as dancers or singers—or both—catch the spirit, tilting their voices, their emotions to the limits. For keen listeners, the spine-tingling pitch of a cantor's voice resembles a primal scream. Understandable, when we consider the musical style's reflection of Gypsies' hardships and exile over the centuries.

Steeped in mystery, flamenco—when worthy—is hot-blooded, arresting, spellbinding. The pure art of singing, *el cante,* remains the centerpiece of flamenco. The oldest known manifestation of this deep song, or *cante jondo,* comes from the Arabic *Gannia,* a prayer of the *Almohades.*[1] And when an accomplished *cantaor* or *cantaora* belts out one of these tunes from the depths of his or her soul—when you're moved, losing yourself in the moment, connecting with the singer, then you've experienced *el arte flamenco puro.*

¡Qué maravilla!

Selected Flamenco Terminology

aficionado: fan, ardent connoisseur

así se canta: "way to sing" (a *jaleo*)

bailaor/a: dancer

bulería: lively vocal style

cantador/a: singer

cantar: to sing

cante chico: light flamenco

cante jondo: deep song

castañuelas: castanets

compás: the beat

cuadro: troupe

escobilla: sweep-step

farruca: A strutting, stomping dance from Galicia

fin de fiesta: end of the performance

Gitano/a: Spanish Gypsy

intermedio: intermediate flamenco

jaleos: accentuation; verbal comments of encouragement between members of troupe

palmas: rhythmic clapping

preparación: introductory song

rajo: hoarse voice

rasgueado: striking guitar strings with the fingernails

remate: final guitar phrase; finale

siguiriya: sad song; the most poignant of the *cantes jondos*; the theme: a setback, such as unrequited love, or even a stillbirth

tocaor: flamenco guitarist

tonás: music sung, not accompanied by instruments

toque: flamenco song performed in spontaneous guitar-work

voz afilá: raspy vocal style

zapateado: rhythmic heel-work

The concierge at Reina Victoria confesses that many of Madrid's *tablaos de los flamencos* are tourist traps. She will arrange for us reservations at a reliable club. She rings up one; now, another; each, fully booked. She can get us into Corral de la Moreria tomorrow. For entertainment this evening, we'll shop Calles Velázquez, Goya and Serrano.

Though fancy, Madrid's department stores remind us of earlier decades but for futuristic displays. We know colors and styles that surprise us now will likely be popular in America in a year or two.

I believe fashion originates in Western Europe, then infiltrates New York and California. Couture-deprived Midwesterners will not see these trends until they are *pasado de moda* (out of style), when Europe and the coasts of America have moved on to still another fashion craze.

Uncle Chuck buys less-than-conservative sportswear and I, a smart outerwear jacket in a color surely to rise with the impending fashion tide of California.

With rigors of the day behind us, we dine early. At half-past eight, we are the only patrons at Trattoria Roma.

We eat Italian in the capital of Spain, sorting through plans for tomorrow: the world's foremost works of art in Madrid's museums, topped off with an evening fraught with passionate flamenco.

[1] *Almohades* (From *al-Muwahhidûn*, or "those who affirm the unity of God"): Ancient tribes from the High Atlas—Algeria, Morocco and Tunisia.

CAUGHT UP IN *LA PASIÓN ARTÍSTICA DE ESPAÑA*

I experienced a dozen-or-so flamenco shows in the United States, primarily in California, New Mexico and Florida. Had I sensed duende *in those performances? Once I did, I believed, at the opera in Santa Fe, New Mexico. There I saw a dancer named María Benítez with facial gestures believably tragic. Her body moved like liquid gold. I felt a connection with her. I hoped the show we booked in Madrid would live up to that benchmark....*

On this cool, bright morning, we ramble in direction of Parque del Buen Retiro to plot our day, admiring sidewalks animated with smartly attired businesspeople overtly on missions of importance. Splashing fountains take the edge off the hubbub. Freshly sandblasted buildings sparkle in sunshine. Madrid is a jewel.

"I am falling in love with this city," Uncle Chuck remarks as we converge upon the grand park. He steers me toward formal gardens just beyond Paseo del Prado. "Madrid they consider one of the cultural centers of Europe. This city is vital, aristocratic, well-planned, pristine," he sighs.

I, too, am charmed. The largest metropolis in Spain, with population of more than three million, Madrid amazes but does not overwhelm. We feel safe in her midst. Gothic, baroque and modern touches camouflage any indication of its roots as *Majerit*, a Muslim stronghold. Alfonso VI later renamed this city *Madrit* when it became capital of Spain in 1561. The only quandary here is the boundless number of monuments and museums. Where to begin?

We pause for a string of joggers to pass, then claim a stone bench in the park's Plaza de Independencia. Settled onto the cool slab, we turn our attention from granite and bronze monuments to methodically clipped shrubbery and autumn-kissed foliage to a pond reflecting birds flying upside-down. With a city plan unfolded between us, I run my finger down the column of cultural highlights.

"Look, the Prado, directly across the street. Let's start there, then move on to a *tapería* for lunch, cab to Centro de Arte Reina Sofía and...."

Uncle Chuck clears his throat and taps at a spot on the map. "There's the royal palace—a must...."

"Can't we do it all?"

"Let's spend the day leisurely, young man. No marathons, please. We're here for only two days. Save a site or two for next time."

We cross the busy *paseo* to Museo del Prado, a grand aggregation of art. On the steps, I'm overcome with anticipation, eager to take it all in. Though, considering the Prado's bragging rights to a reputed eighty-six hundred paintings, we will concentrate on favored artists.

Keen El Greco, his mastery of *sol y sombra*, I head directly to galleries featuring his work. In a matter of minutes, El Greco's Mannerist style envelops me; the unearthly cool light in his pigment, riveting emotionalism in melting, elongated figures and faces in moribund greenish-blue. Color plates in my university textbooks, mere photographic reproductions, were moot when compared to savoring these potent canvases firsthand.

On two floors are found works of art by the deaf artist Francisco José de Goya, a retrospective of drawings, cartoons and paintings. Goya's Black Paintings are macabre, gripping. *Had their otherworldly subjects influenced the musings of Stephen King?*

Goya's *Executions of The Third of May* yanks me back to 1808, to a sobering moment following the uprising of Madrid against French troops on the second of May. The subject of this painting immortalizes brutal annihilation by French gunfire in blackness of pre-dawn, the onset of Spain's War of Independence (The Peninsular War). A lineup of *Madrileño* patriots, eyes spiked with horror, quivers just inches from French soldiers' bayonet-tipped rifles. Slumped forward, a Franciscan friar prays in desperation, his tonsure highlighted in the flare of gunfire. Amidst bleeding corpses, another victim kneels with outstretched arms, poised in the gesture of the crucified Christ, a gut-wrenching distortion crossing his face.

Celebrated as the pinnacle of protest, this ruthlessly straightforward painting evokes anathema for atrocities of war. Goya, having sketched the massacre by moonlight, accentuated the brutish moment in history by picking out details of torment in brighter colors: sheer drama in livid facial expressions, white-hot gunfire illuminating the night, and crimson rivulets flowing in the street.

I step slowly backwards, until my calves meet the edge of a bench. With my eyes still fixed on the horrified eyes of the man in the crucifixion pose, I ease down, onto the seat. *Interesting, how Goya captured this powerful scene after dark, as he had painted so many illustrious canvases in his candlelit studio* As I wonder, Uncle Chuck's voice recalls me from my trance.

"Did you see the Diego Velázquez gallery? It's on the main floor, in the back—in a fetching, domed room."

As a zombie, I follow him down the steps. I drink in splendorous paintings as Uncle Chuck reflects from a padded bench. From dark backgrounds spring serene court scenes of children and dogs interpreted with restrained palette, to shocking tableaux of death and suffering. Baroque influence of strong, burning light in refined technique strikes a riveting chord.

My compadre enjoys the comfort of his front row seat while I absorb canvases by Rubens and Brueghel. He catches up with me in one of the Italian galleries.

We check out paintings by Ignacio Zuloaga, the artist who owned the castle we saw at Pedraza. When I tear myself away, we cab back in direction of Plaza Mayor. Uncle Chuck asks the driver to recommend a spot for lunch. The answer: "El Museo del Jamón" (The Ham Museum).[1]

We queue in a heady, quasi-delicatessen. Meaty mobiles of copious hams, sausages, joints and hocks dangle from the ceiling. Throngs of coeds and businesspeople adeptly order in Spanish. Tourists are flummoxed.

Elbowed up at a narrow counter in this bustling gallery of meat, we enjoy *jamón serrano* sandwiches with ice-cold beer.

"Now, the Reina Sofía?" I ask.

"With a late evening planned, I'm in need of a nap. Maybe I'll poke around antique shops. Why don't you take a taxi to the museum? Besides, I don't care for abstract art."

As the cab pulls curbside, I feel betrayed. The boxy, austere Centro de Arte Reina Sofía bluntly counterposes the Neo-Classical façade of Museo del Prado. I pay up, then board one of the glass elevators.

Uncle Chuck is better off with his shopping or siesta. Having seen the classics at the Prado, he would disparage these neoteric, innovative works as irrelevant and tasteless. Yet, as a former student of art history, I enjoy the originals. From minimalist, flat space of Joan Miró to Salvador Dalí's surrealistic nightmares to whimsies of Juan Gris, I let my imagination run wild.

Wonder if Uncle Chuck would have jostled at the works of Pablo Picasso, particularly his masterwork *Guernica*; Homeric in physical dimensions and impact, the black, white and gray pigments passionately depict the master's loathe of war. The subject: a Basque village under the attack of Nazis, wholesale carnage resulted from Nazi coalition with Spain's own Franco. Writhing animals. Expiring victims. Clutching her lifeless infant, a mother wails into the mouth of a bull. In throes of a maniacal military experiment, fellow subjects scream and retch. Conical tongues lash from gaping mouths. A dead man sprawls on the ground, in his right hand, a broken sword and a flower; a pentagram brands his left hand. Another man personifies the pose of crucifixion. Though abstract, *Guernica* embodies a comparable brand of chilling realities of war, as does Goya's *Executions of The Third of May*.

> Spain is the only country where death is a national spectacle, the only one where death sounds long trumpet blasts at the coming of spring, and Spanish art is always ruled by a shrewd *duende* that makes it different and inventive.
>
> —Federico García Lorca

"Enjoy your modern-art tour?" Uncle Chuck asks as I return to the room.

"I'm on sensory overload," I answer. "Care to join me for a drink?"

We head downstairs to Bar Taurino, the hotel's emporium of spirits. From crimson walls, regal black bulls' heads leer through glassy eyes at executives swinging deals, at tourists reminiscing of the day behind them. The glass-eyed *toros* maintain their glower as my *sangría* quenches. Loathing animal trophies, the more time I spend in this room the more troubled I become.

Back in the lobby, we leaf through international newspapers, catching up on world events. Uncle Chuck suggests shopping on La Gran Vía. We head out in a cab. The district becomes mayhem, teeming with after-work traffic and flocks of humanity.

Ostensibly, Spain's melting pot simmered longer than America's. The only Asians we see, however, are tourists, and we note only the occasional black. The makeup of people in outlying areas of Madrid we find chiefly dark-haired and swarthy. Here in Madrid, faces fluctuate from alabaster-white to olive to brown. Denizens of the north are lighter, some of them sandy-haired, even blond. Were those northern folk pollinated by Celts, Gauls and Visigoths?

When we return to the Reina Victoria, the concierge who booked a flamenco show for us stands at her podium. She winks and says as we pass, "You will like the troupe this evening. From Andalucía, real *gitanos.*"

I pivot and head back to her station.

"Do they have *duende?*" I ask.

"Oh *sí*," she answers, "but many of the flamenco clubs here in Madrid have the style more opera than authentic *cante jondo.*"

But not where she booked us, she promises....

"Please, describe *duende*," I say.

"*El duende, el duende,*" the concierge murmurs, furrowing her brow, casting eyes heavenward. Now, she relaxes her forehead and speaks. "You know if you have it. You know when you sense it in someone else. Difficult to explain...."

Here we go again.

She continues, "*La fuerza,* ah...vitality, the energy, the inspiration! *Espíritu*, a spirit that takes over the body. When you have the *duende*, you must release it. The Gypsies do this with song and dance. Painters express the *duende* on canvas."

I am satisfied with her answer, for now.

When we arrive by taxicab at a quarter till ten, the neighborhood around Corral de la Moreria courses with traffic, sidewalks with *Madrileños* and a smattering of tourists. We pay and tip our driver, then merge with the throngs, following a group inside the nightclub.

The smoky-blue room buzzes with conversation. We are ushered to a table not far from the stage. Glasses of Rioja *blanca* in hand, we peruse the limited menu, agreeing on salads and paella for two. Soon, the room overflows with patrons.

We order a pitcher of *sangría* as musicians climb a flight of three steps. Each takes his place on squat wooden stools along the back of the stage. Some in the audience applaud listlessly. Others resume chattering.

Onstage: three musicians, two holding *guitarras*, another clinching a wooden board between his knees. Now, two women in long sheaths form-fitting to the knees settle into seats alongside the men.

House lights pale. One of the *tocaores* cues with a hollow *tok*—igniting a refrain, a distinctive six-measure *compás*, sweet, deliberate. The *cuadro* shouts words of encouragement over bouncy music and *palmas*: *one-two, one, two, three, one-two, one, two, three....*

The man with the board pounds out a cadence compelling his troupe into locomotive action: guitars, *castañuelas*, fancy heel-work, arrhythmic *palmas*, gradual, then hitting on all cylinders.

Over fervent applause we hear, *"¡Ole!"* and *"¡Por Dios!"*

Now the *cantaor* wails hoarsely in melismatic style, a tragic song resembling a dirge.

> *El que canta, su mal espanta.*
> He who sings scares away all his sorrows.
>
> —Spanish proverb

The troupe performs a filigreed arrangement of attitude, *palmas*, stomping, rueful canting. *"¡Ayy!"* they shout. Midway into the number, as though through contagion, the two women take center stage with fancy heel-work, a tempest of red to purple swirling through spotlit bluish haze. *"¡Ayy!"* Moving sleekly to the tempo, at times hiking hems above knees, *"¡Ayy!"* they shout, *"¡Ayyay!"*

Uncle Chuck leans across the table, gesturing with a tilt of his head, "Over there, in the shadows...."

Raven-maned figures, elegant of carriage, of head and shoulders, a man and woman, stand near the stage, she in ruffles to the floor in a form-fitting, white frock peppered in black polka dots, he in bolero vest over a bloused white shirt and red cummerbund and painted-on pants. A strum spurs this couple to the stage with fanfare from the *cuadro*, from aficionados. The melody, six beats to the measure, accent on the third, pulses harder, louder, harder. Center stage, the intensely postured dancers concentrate not on themselves but on each other, their black eyes blazing.

The couple moves fluidly, climactically to clacking *castañuelas*, beating the planks with their feet. *Tocaores* pluck and thrum, the singer's guttural requiem cracks, hurtling us back to Spain's Golden Age of the Muslims to antecedent Judaic culture and campfire Gypsies.

Our dancers part then close their lips, though saying nothing. The male dancer, a stilt-legged bird, struts luridly, seducing his mate. Glistening rivulets follow contours of his throat, into his shirt. She beckons artfully with slender fingers. His hands remain clenched.

With a husky thrum of *rasgueado,* the number ends. The dancers are spent. So are we....

As the stars sit alongside the others, they breathe heavily, swabbing their faces and décolletés. While the dancers build up steam, guitarists perform an *intermedio.*

The rousing performance perseveres, now with all three women whirling across the stage accompanied by skillful guitar work, thunderous footwork. Yet, the audience hungers for more of the courting birds of paradise. The sexy dancers oblige solo, then duo, exhausting us, right up to the *fin de fiesta.*

¹ Museo del Jamón: Madrid hosts three such delicatessens, all under the same ownership. We sampled the one at Carrera de San Jerónimo 6.

AN ITALIAN-FRENCH WONDER IN THE CAPITAL OF SPAIN

When traveling, I covet each moment. Then, with a blink, it's time to leave. I want to live in Spain. Please, dear God, for at least a few years?

Breeeee–breeeee. Breeeee–breeee....
Within blackness, I reach for the phone.

"Buenos días, señor," booms a clear male voice on the other end. Oh, the wake-up call I made, yet forgot....

My head feels foggy. In sleep, I journeyed to Andalucía, drawn there to distant chattering of *castañuelas,* to a crackling campfire of *los Gitanos.* Women in flounced dresses clicked their heels while men with faces red as flames palmed seductive staccato. Mood took over when one of the men leapt to his feet and wailed. I was really getting into it when the distinctive falsetto of a European telephone pulled me back to the real world.

"What time is it?" Uncle Chuck asks.

"Eight o'clock, on the button."

Resolved in our course of action for this last day of vacation, we make our way under pallid firmament to a café called Oskar's. Standing alongside black-haired executives at the counter, I capture the barman's attention,

"¿Dos cafés con leche y dos jugos de naranjas, por favor?"

From a glass case, we select buttery croissants and sticky buns to accompany our potent coffee.

"The Royal Palace?" Uncle Chuck asks.

I nod. "And a tour of Toledo or El Escorial? There's Valle de los Caídos, too. We can take a train or a bus tour."

"All of that? We know Spaniards keep late hours, yet I believe their monuments close before dusk. As I've said, look to the future."

Back at the hotel, we snatch up our cameras and ask the porter to hail a cab. In a matter of minutes, our driver drops us alongside a square at Calle de Bailén near a colossal granite palace known to *Madrileños* as Palacio Oriente.

The palace is not yet open, so we traverse the concourse, admiring sugar-white statues of Spanish sovereigns in Plaza de Oriente. We wander back to the palace, discussing its Neo-Classical façade. Are the noble pilasters Ionic, Dorian or some of each? We gaze up to limestone balustrades, to finely hewn details, mind-boggling feats of architectural embellishment by Italian mason-maestros Juvaro and Sacchetti who based this façade on Gianlorenzo Bernini's rejected architectural scheme for Paris's Louvre.

The palace hunkers on burned ruins of a ninth-century Berber *alcázar*. From our outlook, we catch glimpses of the snow-capped Guadarrama range and teal-gray Río Manzanares cutting through a yawning *vega* (plain) below. Crowds gather. By half-past nine the palace doors swing open. We buy our tickets, then pass through the entry to a brain-rattling memorial to centuries of oppression.

"Imagine," Uncle Chuck marvels, "people living in this manner...."

This is grander than Palacio Real de la Granja near Segovia, but the two share in resplendence their interiors. Room after room—two thousand in all—highlight the apogee of French opulence. All but mere spaces are plastered with painted masterworks, and needlework in jewel tones. Cool, marbled spaces gleam with gilt, ivory, ebony and lapis lazuli. Ornate plaster ceilings drip bronze and crystal chandeliers. We are told that one of them weighs in at two tons.

A particularly sumptuous chamber, Sala de Porcelana, sparkles in tiles of white, gold and green. Carlos III had an affinity for porcelain and had this room designed to accommodate his minor compulsion. Another hall, Sala de Gasparini, sports a Chinese ceiling, a masterwork of polychrome in bird-and-flower relief.

The crowning glory of this Spanish palace, we decide, is Salón del Trono (Throne Room). As we stand in the red silk damask-lined, gilded and mirrored salon, I visually block out tourists, thoughts drifting back to an era when this temple of abundance endowed more than museum. I imagine coronations here and state affairs, royal weddings. We look in wonder at the royal perches of Rey Juan Carlos and Reina Sofía guarded by four golden lions by sculptor Benicelli, at finely wrought Venetian lamps and intricately inlaid consoles.

La Biblioteca Real cerebrally impresses. This royal library houses more than four hundred thousand volumes, including an original edition (1605) of Miguel de Cervantes's *Hidalgo Don Quixote de La Mancha*.

"Tired, Uncle Chuck?" I ask.

My motivation is lunch. Nevertheless, Uncle Chuck is on a mission, poring through his brochure and responds, "I wouldn't mind getting off my feet, though not before we see the music room, the armory...."

We admire more rococo lavishness under watchful eyes of guards as our guide herds us through chambers.

We're not going to see all two thousand rooms, are we? This Spanish palace is, after all, larger than London's Buckingham Palace. I am grateful to learn that our junket takes in only a dozen or so.

The palace arrayal neglects not a detail. Noteworthy Museo de Música harbors precision instruments by Stradivarius, together with fragile keyboards and other antique instruments. The armory gleams silvery-gray with medieval armor, including mounted models.

Next agenda: a gory display of torture mechanisms. This awakens memories of Boris Karloff movies. I take morbid fascination in a grisly rack, shivering as we inspect a cobwebbed iron lady. I imagine Inquisitors flailing heretics with the maces. When I mention to Uncle Chuck the dark stains on a club, he steers me away; I expect toward the gardens. To my relief, he's ready to leave.

At the close of the tour, we flag a taxi for Restaurante Botín at Plaza Mayor, the restaurant immortalized by Ernest Hemingway and, consequently, a tourist magnet. All four levels of the illustrious dining emporium are booked to their ancient rafters. As we are partial to uncrowded *comedores* and hate to wait for seating, we move on toward Puerta del Sol. On Carrera de San Jerónimo, we drop in on Restaurante Madrid 1 for *tapas* and *cervezas*. Munching seafood *croquetas* and anchovies, we plan the rest of our day.

Uncle Chuck decides to skip his customary nap, lest he spend a restless night. We leisurely stroll through Parque del Buen Retiro, watching dog-walkers and beggars. Mothers and nannies coo into perambulators. Joggers exhale vaporous puffs. The cool breeze caresses; the sky lowers with rusty cloud-cover.

With spirits and feet refreshed, we walk to El Rincón Esteban at Santa Catalina 3. A proud maître d' escorts us to a cozy alcove. We surmise immediately the patrons are compatriots.

Uncle Chuck launches his meal with voluptuous crab bisque; my first course, a slice from the house terrine of pâté, an ambrosial delicacy pink and velvety, flecked liberally with truffles, set off by a basketful of crispy toast cut on the bias and a bottle of agreeable Rioja *blanca*.

Four Americans at a table to my right bandy one-upmanship banter among themselves. Obstreperously, they relate tales of second and third homes and stock hunches paid off, successful offspring, five-star cruises. I prefer flamenco for dinner entertainment....

Turning deaf ears, we savor entrées of delectably broiled *rape* served with buttered asparagus alongside golden-brown medallions of potato.

"I wish we had more time in Spain, Uncle Chuck. Andalucía calls me. Alcalá de Henares would be an easy day trip from Madrid, and wouldn't it be great fun to stay over in Pedraza?"

HEAVY

"Spain is heavy," Uncle Chuck remarks as we settle into our seats on the plane.

"Heavy?"

"Yes, heavy with religion, with arrogance. Even the food is heavy."

To appease my Anglocentric uncle, our next trip must be to "lighter" England. Meantime, I dream of my return to an earthier Spain.

ADIÓS ESPAÑA MÍA

I stared through dual panes of a tiny window, scouring the ground for landmarks as our 767 made its ascent above majestic Madrid. Parque del Buen Retiro quickly diminished to the size of a postage stamp. I then saw the spine of the imposing Guadarrama from God's perspective.

As the jet penetrates a dense layer of clouds, beads of moisture race across my window. Two weeks of pure pleasure, drama, artistic masterworks and time-honored villages disappear behind us, yet stir foremost in my mind.

Before I discovered Spain, Italy was my favorite foreign country. As do Spaniards, Italians impress me as passionate people. But, oh my, the Spanish. To my experience, Spaniards transcend the virtue, with passion to spare. At each turn, with each pore, I sense passion and mystery in Spain. Italy has not the equivalent impact.

Sipping from a glass of crimson Rioja, I thumb through my journal. I close my eyes, listening to the acerbic call of a Gypsy:

Si mi corazón tuviera
vidrieras de cristal
te asomaras y lo vieras
gotas de sangre llorar.

If my heart
Had little glass windows
You could look in and see
It weeping drops of blood.

—Anonymous Andalusian son as quoted by Federico García Lorca

MÁS ESPAÑA

Eleven months escaped before I answered the call of Spain. During the interlude, I devoted considerable energy to researching the life and times of a candidate for sainthood—Junipero Serra, the Franciscan missionary who headed Spain's colonization of California in the late-eighteenth century. I believed that Serra's virtues included duende.

Fray *Junipero Serra was born in 1713 on Mallorca (Majorca), the largest of Spain's Balearic Islands. A logical point for accessing Serra's Majorca was Madrid's Barajas airport, with a layover of three days in that grand city before continuing on to the island. I succeeded in coaxing my favorite traveling companion to join me, so on a fine spring morning we were off again for an Iberian infusion.*

Mark Twain would have alluded to my quest as "variegated vagabonding." I called it rapture....

Uncle Chuck read a rave review about Villa Real, a smart hotel in the heart of Madrid. We hedged our bets and booked lodging there.

Our room at Villa Real is not prepared when we check in at the desk. Likely, our jet-lagged faces, or burdensome luggage and camera gear compels the lady to extend her generous proposal: for the price of a moderate room, she gives us a two-story suite. And I didn't even have to make Uncle Chuck cry in public.

"Admirable," Uncle Chuck intimates with a big smile as we ease into our fashionable accommodations: a commodious sitting room, two bedchambers with tastefully papered walls, real Roman mosaics and two baths—one fitted with a jetted, marble, soaking tub. A spiral, marble staircase joins the dual levels and each floor sports a balcony fronting on Plaza de las Cortes.

Unpacked, freshened up, we traipse to Plaza Mayor to decompress. The square greets us like an old friend with comforting ambiance and mid-afternoon sunshine. Richly hued flags wave on the breeze. The plaza exudes a warm, familiar feeling. After a riffle through artisans' stalls, we purchase gravures and drawings, then relax with luxurious espressos.

"Lunch at Botín?" I suggest.

"Last time it was packed. But, let's give it a whirl."

The Guinness Book of World Records rates Botín, established in 1725 as a roadhouse: "Earliest Restaurant in the World." We arrive at a popular restaurant not as jammed as we had seen it before, yet the old roadhouse echoes resonantly with lively *mentidero* (gossipy din) and music.

Settled in, we gaze to seasoned brick and glazed tiles, to darkened rafters sagging under tilted ceilings.

"It says they have a *Libro de Reclamaciones*,"[1] I read from the menu.

"What's that?"

"A complaint book."

"That keeps them on their toes," Uncle Chuck laughs. "For their sake, I hope you find your meal satisfactory."

Before long, complimentary *croquetas* stuffed with shrimp arrive with a bottle of Rioja *blanca*. We relish rustic bread and lightly dressed salads, following with *cordero asado* (roast lamb) sweet and tender with the redolence of wood smoke, a whisper of thyme.

"That's all for me," announces Uncle Chuck as he shifts in his seat.

I select sweet *leche frita* (fried custard), preferring not to share as Uncle Chuck looks on covetously.

On our way out, we peer into the kitchen, into the faces of dozens of roasted, caramel-colored piglets kneeling in casseroles stacked to the ceiling.

Laden with added pounds, we affront the crowds in Puerta del Sol, Madrid's fan-shaped sector considered Spain's "Times Square," and which accommodated a literary quarter in times of old. Here, Miguel de Cervantes Saavedra perished on 23 April 1616, the same day Shakespeare died. We poke into shops along Calles de Cervantes and Lope de Vega, snooping through antiquarian books, prints, period furniture, paintings and *santos*. Tormented by sticker-shock, we make our way back to our hotel's crimson and chrome-trimmed bar.

At the bar, seats of ultra-modern, tall stools vanish under soft derrières of the customers. We slide into smartly upholstered chairs at a well-dressed table. As we graze on almonds and olives and imbibe from perspiring glasses of icy gin, we can see a bar-side salon, a virtual museum-gallery of Roman and Greek artifacts, and framed mosaics in mellowed tones, plus black and cinnabar amphorae.

While Uncle Chuck rests, I muse upon the day. My attempt to watch Euro-television proves futile as I flip through channels. I understand Spanish if spoken slowly, but the talking heads are adrenaline-charged.

Lolling in my Roman tub, I inscribe postcards. After a filling lunch, dinner seems unreasonable, so I'll suggest a *tapería* for a light supper.

We squeeze through Calle del Prado's wall of pedestrians, landing at a lively *tapas* bar called Alemana. Understanding only the random word on the menu, we elbow our way up to the counter and point. The barman jots down our choices. Back at our table, we discover that we have ordered cheese croquettes and a kind of seafood, battered. And what are these? Chicken livers, we decide. We enjoy our nibbles with a pitcher of *sangria*.

Jet lag and *sangria*....We shall sleep well tonight.

[1] A law in Spain requires all hotels and restaurants to provide *Libros de Reclamaciones* (complaint books). Government inspectors periodically review these snitch-books.

castilla-la mancha

N

Bay of Biscay

France

Pyrenees

Portugal

Spain

MADRID

Balearic Islands

Atlantic Ocean

Mediterranean Sea

Africa

1. Toledo
2. El Escorial
3. Valle de los Caídos

CASTILLA-LA MANCHA

The fading day: Toledo's dynamic cathedral and works of El Greco, a relaxing dinner....

Before drawing the draperies, I stepped onto the balcony, my aperture on spectacular Madrid. The sky deepened to indigo; the air was seasoned with rain and Castilian cooking. Slick avenues shone obsidian black. In the mist, I indulged in a cigar and a glass of "welcome" vino tinto from the concierge. The wine was good.

To my left posed the pale gray façade of Congreso de los Diputados, Madrid's classical courthouse. A guard paced amid floodlit columns, maintaining his lonely vigil. The Congreso looked majestic, even more so from my height than when we walked by. In the distant horizon, spires of Iglesia de San Jerónimo loomed behind an eerie sheath of pale green glow. When we visited that church earlier in the day, a beggar thought we were priests.

Down below, Madrileños moved resolutely along sidewalks: el paseo under a glistening mantle of umbrellas. Vehicles hissed through the streets, casting luminous reflections of red and white trails.

On that balcony, I redefined my own conventions, believing I had verged on heaven. I recalled a local expression, "When I die, give me a window from heaven so I can look upon my city."

IMPERIAL TOLEDO AND OPEN PALMS

In A.D. 1087, Felipe II made Toledo capital of Castile. Throughout its golden era (fourteenth to sixteenth centuries), Toledo blossomed as an intellectual-spiritual center and became headquarters of Catholic Spain for five hundred years. Besides hosting a grand cathedral, Toledo imparted spoors of Islamic and Judaic provenance, yet the rich history predated even the arrival of Muslims and Hebrews.

Toledo was seminally the capital of an Iberian tribe called by the Romans

Carpetani. *Romans took over in* B.C. *192 and named the real estate* Toldtum. *From 534 to 712, Toledo served as Visigothic headquarters under King Recarred who called it* Tolaitola.

Heading out to explore Toledo, we first need to learn the ropes of Madrid's train station. Our concierge sketches a map and inscribes the word *cercanías* (commuter trains). Having experienced frustration at European train stations, we solicited the gracious young woman's assistance to help us find the train to Toledo.

"What you will look for at the station," she says, aiming a slender finger at a word she scrawled.

She hatches an *X* through the word *AVE.*[1]

"Do not go to that area," she says with a smile. "Enjoy your day in Toledo. *Hasta luego.*"

From the hotel, we hike, appreciating spring scenery. Clouds of chestnut blossoms scent the air; white petals carpet the sidewalks to Estación de Atocha. We pause for a transient tour of sixteenth-century San Jerónimo El Real, a noble, twin-towered church we see from our balconies at the hotel. This church is all that remains of a former Hieronymite[2] monastery commissioned by Isabel I de Castilla. As we exit, a beggar with a scraggly beard holds one of the big doors for us, and extends a bony hand for *almas.* *"Padres,"* he calls us. Must be our haircuts.

Ahead, we see Atocha, modern and widespread. Inside, throngs of commuters and signs overwhelm, yet we manage to locate our section, and purchase tickets. Arrived early, we make prudent use of time, visiting a snack bar for lunch, then ride the escalator to a platform below to sit in the midst of chain-smokers.

A horn blares. *El tren* thunders into the tunnel, and grinds to a halt. Aboard a non-smoking car that reeks of smoke, we roll into feeble daylight through back scenery of suburban Madrid.

With trumpeting of horn and abrasion of steel, our train pauses at each whistle-stop between Madrid and Toledo. As we jiggle along, views underwhelm until, in forty-five minutes, we verge upon the mysterious profile of Toledo. From the train, we ogle a cache of history recorded in stone, an imposing city clinging to an escarpment of granite. Toledo purveyed an amalgam of cultures from Romans and Barbarians to Visigoths, Jews and Muslims, and harbors one of Spain's foremost cathedrals.

Meandering through Estación de Ferrocarril on Toledo's outskirts, we debate how to access the old town. Shall we hail a cab? Walk? While I am keen on walking, Uncle Chuck is not. A brown, wrinkled man with a stogie between his cracked, stained teeth comes to Uncle Chuck's rescue.

"*¿Señores?* English? I speak some English. You want the tour?"

"*¿Cuánto es?*" Uncle Chuck asks.

"Two thousand pesetas," the leathery man replies.

Uncle Chuck figures "whatever," not to have to walk, and forks over the bills.

We fold ourselves into the back seat of a tiny car, looking forward to a private excursion.

Our driver circles Calle de Circunvalación above a ravine cradling the snaking Río Tajo. He points out an anesthetizing view of the cathedral. We see the bluff-side, four-turreted *alcázar*. About this fortress, our driver says, "Seminally a Moorish fortress, rebuilt in the sixteenth century, renovated in the twentieth, ravaged by fire three times in between."

Toledo piles upon itself within a ring of Gothic and Moslem walls. The firmament roils with violet-tinged clouds. I squint to blur a clutch of television antennae and construction cranes. Startling, this dramatic spectacle, and proof that El Greco's powerful *View of Toledo* was more than a stylized scene.

To our surprise and discouragement, we rocket past Puente de Alcántara, a massive Roman bridge with one and one-half arches. So goes our view of Puente de San Martín, a footbridge from 1203, Puente Nuevo (New Bridge), and vestiges of a pontoon-style span dating to Arabic rule, the Baño de la Cava.

"Best look quickly," Uncle Chuck laughs, "or you'll miss the sites!"

Along the way, we manage fleeting glimpses of original fortified walls largely in ruins.

The old man exhales a puff of blue-gray smoke and glances from the corner of his right eye. With eyebrow raised, he inquires, "Do you like the arts and crafts?"

"Well, yes," I respond, wondering at his question.

"Then, I take you some place unique, very amazing."

We veer off the ring road, delving into the guts of a brick-and-stone city, clacking up a steep, constricted alleyway. Our driver stops with a jerk, then wrenches up his emergency brake.

"There, you go inside," he gestures with his cigar, in the direction of a rustic façade. "You will find the famous swords, see how they are made. I wait for you."

With cameras in tow, we tour ground-level ateliers, watching as sweaty men in leather aprons at anvils and grinding stones hammer blazing red steel into silvery-shafted wonders. The burly blacksmiths plunge blades into water for tempering, then burnish them to gleaming perfection. A voluminous gift shop on the second story houses gaudy-handled daggers, swords, colorful embroidery and Damascene-ware.[3] Added to this, shelves of pottery, Mallorcan pearls and inlaid boxes, all tagged with breathtaking prices.

"I believe I can live without a sword or any of this," Uncle Chuck says.

We exit the building. Our driver sputters in Spanish when he notices our empty hands.

"The tour ends," he grunts.

Evidently, he missed out on a kickback.

"Can you please deliver us to the cathedral?" Uncle Chuck asks.

The petulant fellow releases the brake, plunges the car into first gear, and we lurch and zigzag through the labyrinth. After silent moments, he drops us in a compressed avenue flanked by massive Santa Iglesia Catedral Primada and gift shops. The car doors barely close when our tour guide zooms off to shanghai other unsuspecting souls back at the train station.

The position of this cathedral, as the one in Burgos, hems in, next-to-impossible to regard at intimate range. The redoubtable temple supplants a Visigothic church and former mosque.

We buy tickets in the gift shop, then cross the street behind a crowd, and step into cool, voluminous Santa Iglesia.

We've seen plenty of cathedrals, yet never before have we experienced such resplendence. Bundles of marble columns stretch from multi-foil arches to intricate vaulting. Side chapels gleam with gilded touches enlivened by light shed through 750 stained windows. The enormity of this structure staggers: 390 by 199 feet and more than 107 feet high in the nave. We tour the five aisles and apsidal chapels, principally on our own, but occasionally pausing to eavesdrop on an English-speaking guide.

In awe, we study the high altar's lacy *retablo*, a profusion of finely hewn statuary and flourishes in polychrome overlaid with gold or silver. Behind and above the altar, we discover *El Transparente,* a perforated dome, yielding light, bringing to life layers of gold-leafed saints and angels, gleaming marble, trompe l'œil glimpses of heaven. Narciso Tomé crafted this phenomenon considered the finest example of *churrigueresque.*

Shuffling on in astonishment across a smooth marble floor, we appraise the choir of deeply engraved, wooden stalls, golden panels, and a jewel-tone rosette oculus.

We absorb paintings and statues representing centuries of ecclesial art, scenes depicting the Holy Family's life and Goya's *Expolio* (Christ stripped of His robes) scintillating in vibrant strokes of red, ochre, green, blue.

We queue up to enter a confined space where six are allowed to enter as others file out. This is the Treasury, a storehouse of sacred vessels in gold and silver, scores of them encrusted with precious stones and pearls. Glass cases glow with Ciboria, censors, chalices, missal stands, crucifixes, and a royal crown of Isabel La Católica. Among these treasures counts a phenomenal, ten-foot-tall monstrance purportedly fashioned of gold begot from the Americas by Columbus.

We drift outside, squinting in burning light, our heads steeped with divine imagery, with centuries of loves' labors.

Blocks distant, we gaze back at the asymmetrical mass of cathedral, at a soaring spire on the left, and a *Mozárabic*[4] chapel dome on the right. Deeply arched portals and layered tympana are *plateresque* in style and the façade, *Manueline.*[5]

The cathedral swarmed. The streets are quiet. Uncle Chuck reminds of siesta-time; it's off-season besides. We plunk down at a *taberna* patio under a leafy canopy. Relieved, off our feet in the splendid spring air, we toss back ice-cold beer with *tapas*, fancy puffs enfolded with fish mousse and caviar.

On a second wind, we hike through town, discovering *Mudéjar*-style gates including rotund Puerta de Bisagra with an escutcheon of Emperor Charles V (Charles I of Spain). Farther along looms the exotic, fifteenth-century Puerta del Sol with golden crenellations, and further along, the brick-and-stone Puerta de Cambrón. The latter gives way to El Judería (Jewish Quarter), the twelfth-century community of more than sixteen thousand Jews.[6] Beyond the gate, we tour one of Toledo's synagogues, Santa María la Blanca, a Catholic Church-cum-synagogue dating to 1203 and constructed in the *Almohad* style. Under an umbrella of caliphal, horseshoe-shaped arches and filigreed details, we take our time absorbing the mystique of this White Church.

We follow our map to La Casa Museo de El Greco, twisting, turning through a maze of roads, past brick facades, randomly well kept, others tattered.

El Greco, "The Greek" (Dominikos Theotokopoulos, 1541-1614, born in Crete), studied art at Venice, then made Toledo his home from 1577. The *casa*-museum, purportedly the great artist's home, is not. This home belonged to Samuel Levi, treasurer of Pedro I El Cruel. Yet, El Greco did reside in the general vicinity of this *casa*.

We step in to tour the medieval-style *casa*, browsing galleries of the maestro's eloquent portraits and reverent scenes. One grabs my attention. I study it at length. The subject is San Bernardo, namesake of the San Diego suburb where I live. El Greco exaggerated Bernardo's figure in height, and garbed him in charcoal-gray cassock with three-knotted cincture. St. Bernardo's face wears a grave expression, the huge eyes soulful, the flesh, livid green.

Beyond are rooms of artworks and a replication of El Greco's studio. On an easel rests the stirring portrait *Saint Peter's Tears*. The setup looks as though the artist just stepped out for fresh air.

Less than an hour before the first evening train leaves for Madrid, we step up our pace and again find the center of town. In keeping with peacefulness we encountered in Toledo this spring day, we see scant vehicular traffic and not a taxicab in sight. I would walk back to the station, but Uncle Chuck has walked his feet off. He approaches a *Toledano* on the square.

"Taxi?"

The grinning man extends a hand, palm up. Uncle Chuck tenders a coin.

"*¿Más?*" asks the grinning man.

Uncle Chuck sputters under his breath as he deposits more coins into the man's hand.

"*¡Ahí!*" exclaims the man, pointing directly across the road to a yellow plastic box attached to the side of a brick building. On the box, overtly painted in big black lettering: TAXI; inside, a telephone.

"Oh, that's how it's done," Uncle Chuck grumbles as we cross the street.

"How had we overlooked it?" I laugh.

A young woman approaches the yellow box. She's an American student named Jennifer, on sabbatical leave from MIT. She asks to share our cab. During our brief ride to the station, the three of us barter viewpoints on Spain. Jennifer's field of study is engineering and she's researching Toledo's bridges.

Back in Madrid, Uncle Chuck refuses to trudge the stretch between Atocha and the hotel. Rolling along in a tiny BMW taxi, we fondly recall Restaurante El Rincón Esteban.

The snug *comedor* beguiles. Following a warm reception, we nibble *tortilla a la española* with sips of Rioja Gran Reserva 1991. We proceed with smooth, zesty gazpacho dotted with diced cucumbers and crunchy croutons.

"A flavorful albeit unidentifiable cut of beef," as Uncle Chuck describes it, gets his nod. I indulge in subtly smoky, exquisitely juicy *pollo a la parrilla* (broiled chicken). Served with our entrées: *verduras* (vegetables) prepared in the manner of ratatouille.

This restaurant turns out chocolates, with or without dessert. Awaiting the confections, we sample from a frosty bottle of *anís* (licorice-flavored liqueur).

While we dined, the sky opened. Weather has not put a damper on the nocturnal penchant of *Madrileños* for *el paseo*.

El Paseo—
¡Vamos a andar! ("Let's go for a walk!")

Southern Californians incline to cocoon themselves behind air-conditioned walls in gated communities. Spaniards, particularly city dwellers, aim their gaits beyond their living quarters, feeling restricted in apartments or town houses with considerably fewer square feet than the median Southern California tract home. The average Spaniard appears to me more gregarious, inquisitive than the average American. I believe Spaniards long to experience life beyond their abodes.

Whatever the motivation, in Spain, an energy pulses on the streets as dusk mottles the sky. I sense this, though to a smaller degree, in Italy where they call the nightly stroll *passeggiata*. In Europe, quitting time from work comes later than in America because of extended lunch breaks, or siestas. When set free from their toil, Spaniards celebrate life, visiting with each other at outdoor cafés, in plazas, on street corners. This delightful practice they call *el paseo* (the stroll).

After work, Spanish city dwellers dress to the nines, then strut proudly to a favorite *tapas* bar, tavern or square—a virtual pub crawl, called *tapeo*. Hundreds of Spaniards rove along, a nocturnal human landscape discussing everything under the moon. These revelers laugh or commiserate, inhaling life. They call themselves *Los Gatos* (The Cats), and focus on camaraderie, on family, on making the best of the moment. Then, from nine to ten P.M., The Cats return to their homes, or to a restaurant for *la cena* (dinner).

I envy these celebrants of dusk. Why has this enchanting Spanish custom not been adapted in Southern California, as have architecture, religion, cuisine and our second language? As so much more in Spanish culture, *el paseo* will always intrigue me.

No duerme nadie por el mundo. Nadie, nadie.
No duerme nadie.

Out in the world, no one sleeps. No one, no one.
No one sleeps.

—Federico García Lorca, from *"Ciudad sin sueño"* ("Sleepless City")

[1] AVE ("BIRD"): Spain's high-speed train.

[2] Hieronymite: After the hermetic philosopher Hieronymus Girolomo Cardanus (1501-1576).

[3] Damascene-ware, also known as Toledo-work: Damascus-inspired craftwork of black enamel inlaid with gold, silver and copper wire.

[4] *Mozárabic/Mozárabes*: From the Arabic *must'aribûn*, "Arabized," or converted Spanish Catholic servants (*dhimma*) of the Muslims.

[5] *Manueline*: Late-Gothic style inspired by sea ornamentation and using the florid, complex form of late-Gothic decoration. This style was developed in Portugal and prominent during the late-fifteenth and early-sixteenth centuries.

[6] All Jews were expelled from Spain in 1492.

EL ESCORIAL Y VALLE DE LOS CAÍDOS

We registered for a tour of El Escorial, "The Slag Heap"—so named because the site once served as a smelting dump—a sixteenth-century monastery-basilica-pantheon about thirty miles from Madrid. Our excursion would include La Valle de los Caídos (Valley of the Fallen). Each site ranks among Spain's noteworthy memorials.

When abroad, we always preferred the company of natives. At times, tours—even dining rooms—submitted none.

In our hotel's huge breakfast room, Uncle Chuck says, "Good case for dining out."

"A convention," I remark, gauging a utilitarian space occupied by a hundred or more of our compatriots.

The day brightens with air cleansed by last night's rain, just right for a stroll. We saunter in the direction of Plaza Cánovas del Castillo, dodging traffic through the intersection—red lights mean "god willing" in Spain—within earshot of splashing Fuente de Neptuno, to leafy Paseo del Prado. Amidst racks of postcards, vendors busily arrange displays of lace, plastic-ribbed fans and vividly hued, fake Hermès scarves. Others hang shawls or brightly-colored lithographs of toreros and flamenco artists.

On surrounding lawns, youth—tattooed or pierced or both—sit cross-legged, smoking. An older couple plays with their dogs. From his bench, a Bohemian fellow feeds popcorn to ravenous pigeons. On each corner, hawkers pass out leaflets of yellow or pink. Before depositing a handful of these into a trash receptacle, I notice the handbills promote concerts, rallies, restaurants and political puffery.

Across the plaza, near Hotel Palace, scenery alters notably to executives smartly dressed and coifed.

Uncle Chuck read in an American travel magazine that the Palace, commissioned by Alfonso XIII in 1912, had undergone an entire makeover in the late 1990s. We step in for a look.

As we pad across custom-dyed carpeting under dazzling chandeliers, we see a menswear shop. Uncle Chuck eyes a pair of dressy shoes. He applies his finest negotiating skills, to no avail.

"This isn't Tijuana," I remind him.

"Where do you think Mexicans got their knack for negotiation?" Uncle Chuck counters.

In a conservatory set beneath a splendid stained-glass dome, we settle in at a table. Ambiance clashes vividly with a pithier elegance of our Villa Real's Roman accents and clean, modern lines. Ladies in extravagant hats, some with veils, resemble props for the *belle époque*-style décor of this regal hotel. We take it all in as we nurse frozen vodkas.

After a lunch of *tapas*, we return to Villa Real for our tour appointment.

A woman in a smart navy suit calls for us, and we follow her sprightly gait down the sidewalk to a bus. After stops at three more hotels, we shuttle from Madrid in a northwestern direction.

Dense urban landscape stretches to farmland and mountainous views as Madrid melds with the distance. In forty-five minutes, we approach the foot of Monte Abantos on a southern slope of the Guadarrama, the range that separates the provinces of Castilla-La Mancha and Castilla y León. We pass slowly through San Lorenzo El Real, a snug village teeming with college students and tourists. Just beyond, the severe gray hulk of El Escorial looms on the horizon. Soon, our bus eases up a long driveway, parks behind a queue of others. Our guide advises us to return in one-and-one-half hours.

In the sixteenth century, Felipe II (1527-1598) commissioned the design of this monastery-basilica known as El Escorial—as a memorial to his father, Carlos I—to architects Juan Bautista de Toledo and Juan de Herrera. Introverted King Philip saw his new compound as a means of celestial insurance; thus, his mortal remains rest under spiritual functions of a grand church and monastery. From above, this architectural marvel resembles a grille, in memory of San Lorenzo, the martyr roasted on a grille.

> …El Escorial…where geometry borders on dream and the *duende* wears the mask of the Muse to the eternal punishment of that great king [Felipe II].
>
> —Federico García Lorca

Crunching along a floe of crushed rock, we catch glimpses of stunning gardens. Extensive architecture comprises the drab granite palace of nine towers, sixteen patios, fifteen cloisters, eighty-six staircases, one hundred miles of passageways, three hundred monks cells, fourteen hundred doors and 2,673 windows.

We queue with our group. In three languages, we hear of faded tapestries, jewel-toned frescoes, Pompeian-inspired ceilings and elaborate furnishings. During German and Spanish commentaries, Uncle Chuck and I stray for careful perspectives of artworks, to peer through wavy-glass windows to precisely clipped gardens below us.

Behind our guide, we step upon intricate metal grating near the foot of each of the second floor's multi-paned windows. About these grates our guide explains:

"Below are the old rotting rooms. Royal corpses were conducted there for funerary procedures, including the natural rotting of bodily remains. Grates afforded a method of escape for baneful odors through palace windows. A multi-step process effected not mummification, but clean, bleached skeletons then surrendered to marble and bronze sarcophagi. The sovereigns' urns, identified with nameplates, are on display in a rotunda-style crypt."

We pass through more art-filled galleries and hallways, down a marble-and-jasper staircase and into a dim antechamber. Within octagonal Panteón de Reyes (Pantheon of Kings), twenty-six ornate caskets coffer in niches honeycombing walls all the way up to a lofty domed ceiling. A blazing chandelier and golden cherub sconces illuminate this mauve-and-gold sepulcher. On the coffins' sides: ALFONSVS, PHILIPPVS and CAROLVS, among others. Says our guide, Habsburg and Bourbon monarchs, with few exceptions, are entombed here.

Our expedition proceeds to the adjoining basilica. Contrary to El Escorial's austere exterior, depths of this church shine brightly in gilding and marble, with richly hued oil paintings. Captivated by artisanal details beneath the barrel-vaulted transept, my eyes scour masterfully conserved artwork. The subjects are saints, celestial scenes intricately painted and incised. One of the frescoes, *The Martyrdom of St. Lawrence* applied by Titian, vividly depicts the saint's fiery death on a grate.

Our guide sets us free to prowl through luxuriant gardens. The sun soothes as we amble between neat hedges alongside pluvial fountains and weather-eaten statues. Suddenly, our guide reminds that our time at El Escorial has drawn to a close.

"One reason I'm keen to tour on our own," I complain, as we slide into our seats on the bus.

Our guide takes a head count. Two in our lot are missing—a delay guaranteeing abridgment of our tour of Valle de los Caídos.

With the laggards aboard, our bus slowly ascends the granite Guadarrama, then rolls through pine forests along mountainside pastures peppered with grazing *toros*. At the top, an effulgent, four-hundred-fifty-foot stone *Santa Cruz* greets us. The falling sun models behind the cross a mystical corona. At the base of this sacred symbol, chiseled into a live granite mountain, we recognize sculpted Evangelists and the Cardinal Virtues. We stand in the midst of a monument to tragedy, a memorial commemorating thousands who fell during the 1936-39 Spanish Civil War.

As we trail our ensemble up the steps of a basilica carved into a mountainside, an infinity of geography overwhelms from our aerial outlook. On the horizon spreads hazy, 302-square-mile Madrid.

Inside the basilica, enormous, sculpted guardian angels stand at each side of the narthex. Between them, a garrison of stone-faced military guards paces. One of these officials swiftly informs that use of photographic tripods is strictly *prohibido*. I must leave mine in the lock-up.

I catch up with the tour, which has moved on, one-third the length of the chilly nave. Our guide's voice reverberates between the walls.

"If not for these grilles that intersect the nave," he explains, "this church would exceed the length of St. Peter's Basilica at Vatican City."

St. Peter's, proclaims a papal decree, will forever maintain its status as having the longest nave in the Christian world. Since the church of Los Caídos exceeded the length of St. Peter's, the Vatican ordered a wrought-iron, statue-studded screen with gates installed, thus abridging the official span of Los Caídos.

We penetrate an inimitable nave burrowed from sheer rock. In contrast to opulent catacombs of El Escorial, the repository of Los Caídos impresses for different reasons. For one, this moody basilica memorializes Spain's Civil War. Besides Franco (*Generalísimo* Francisco Paulino Hermenegildo Teódulo Franco Bahamonde, 1892-1975), forty thousand soldiers and civilians lie buried here—a mean number compared to the war's more than three hundred and fifty thousand casualties, reason to give one pause. My body responds with *escalofríos* (goose flesh).

> Treacherous generals: Look at my dead house, look at broken Spain.
>
> —Pablo Neruda

Along the attenuated nave, we pause at chapels and ossuaries. On cold walls between, Belgian tapestries render the *Apocalypse* in fields of burgundy and gold. As we marvel at the human achievement of blasting a cathedral from solid granite, clinging moisture reminds us we are deep inside a mountain.

Above the sanctuary soars a mosaic-lined dome, an artistic marvel incorporating a million dazzling squares. The tilework depicts Spanish military heroes, martyrs and saints abreast of Christ and the Holy Mother. Under the sanctuary floor lie Nationalists José Antonio Primo de Rivera and General Franco. Spaniards' disdain for fascism considered, these heartless men entombed within such noble surroundings bewilders me. More surprising: batches of fresh floral tributes upon stone slabs inscribed with the names *Rivera* and *Franco*.

The forty-five-minute allotment for our tour scarcely satisfies. Herded into the bus, we then briskly plunge down the precipitous track to the motor-way. We will fly tomorrow to Mallorca, so a return trip to El Escorial or to Los Caídos on our own is impractical on this holiday. We vow to never again join a group tour.

1. Palma
2. Binissalem
3. Petra
4. Bon-Any
5. Pollença
6. Alcúdia
7. Can Picafort
8. Capdepera

9. Artà
10. Manacor
11. Sineu
12. Santa Margalida
13. Santa Eulalia
14. Muro
15. Monestir de Lluch
16. Ses Païsses

BALEARES

Mallorca: An Enchanted Isle

A mile below, surf ebbed silently, flowing in soft bands of turquoise blue and bottle green intermingled with hues of lapis lazuli and violet, all dotted with downy tufts of white. We gazed upon the glistening Mediterranean lapping the shores of Mallorca.

I distinguished through our jet's shadow a cluster of architecture known as Palma, the island's capital. Skiffs and launches swayed from their moorings in the lazy bahía (bay). Sun-worshipers basked like lizards upon the sandy periphery. From our perspective, it was paradise, and we would presently set down in its midst.

As landing gear whines and ratchets down, I peer from my window to Palma's harbor, likely the ultimate view *Fray* Junípero Serra beheld of his homeland. With heavy heart, in an English vessel, Serra departed his island home for the Americas on 13 April 1749. From Palma, he sailed to ports of mainland Spain: Málaga and Cádiz, then on to Vera Cruz, *Nueva España* (New Spain, later Mexico), never again to return to family or comforts of home.

I am closing in on Mallorca, where Serra was born. The purpose of my journey: to study the noble friar's pre-New-World life. Serra spent fifteen years in my home state of California. Now I would visit his homeland.

Junípero Serra—The Man Who Saved California From Russia

Imagine the Golden State a part of Russia, British Columbia or even France—possible, had *Fray* Junípero Serra agreed to turn back from Spain's Sacred Expedition to colonize California.

Eighteenth-century British and French traders ranked supreme on the seas. With Russian fur-trappers, colonies sprang up along the western shores of North America. Spain had already snared California, but considering the encroaching Russians, Carlos III grew serious about colonization. At the head of spiritual matters for Spain's Sacred Expedition to California was a zealous Franciscan missionary named Junípero Serra.

Serra, born Miquel Joseph Serre on 24 November 1713 in Petra de Mallorca, was the progeny of peasant farmers. As a youth, Miquel's parents encouraged him to frequent the nearby convent of Sant Bernardi (Saint Bernardine), where Franciscans conducted an elementary school. At a tender age, Miquel excelled in Latin, and particularly enjoyed reading the lives of saints. Miquel's parents and teachers, recognizing his intelligence, enrolled him, in 1729, as a philosophy student in Palma's convent of San Francisco. One year later, Miquel received the habit as novitiate at Convento del Santa María de Los Angeles de Jesús, just outside Palma.

In 1731, Miquel took vows as a Franciscan friar, trading his secular name for Junípero. He was ordained a deacon in 1736, and to priesthood in 1737. From 1739 to 1742, *Profesor* Serra taught philosophy at Palma's Convent of San Francisco. Among his students were two friars, Francisco Palóu and Juan Crespí, who later joined in Serra's missionary work in Mexico and California. Palóu also became Serra's biographer.

In 1742, Serra earned an S.T.D. (Doctorate of Sacred Theology) from Llullian University at Palma where he worked as a professor. There, he determined to become a missionary to Mexico, but given his preoccupation with studies and teaching, Serra's longings for missionary work in the New World were distracted. On feeling a reawakened call, he accepted his lot and enlisted as missionary.

On 13 April 1749, Serra, then thirty-six years of age, and Palóu sailed from Palma to Málaga, then to Cádiz, the first legs of a five-thousand-mile journey by sea to Mexico City. The Mallorcan friars arrived in Mexico, landing at Vera Cruz, after a layover at San Juan, Puerto Rico on 7 December 1749. Serra chose to walk the 275-mile tropical stretch of *El Camino Real* (The Royal Road) from Vera Cruz to Mexico City. On that peregrination, an insect bit Serra. The injury exacerbated, leaving him thereafter lame in one leg.

Serra's missionary career began in the rugged Sierra Gorda region of Mexico. There, he worked eight years among Pame Indians before his transfer to Loreto, capital of Baja California. At Loreto, Serra served as administrator of the peninsula's fifteen previously established Jesuit missions. Within a year, he learned of the Spanish Crown's forthcoming temporal and spiritual colonization of Alta California, and enthusiastically volunteered for the expedition. Later, he was appointed administrator of the future California missions. From April 1768 to January 1769, Serra coordinated with Joseph de Gálvez (Inspector General of the Viceroyalty of New Spain) the Sacred Expedition to Alta California.

Accompanied by two guards and an attendant, Junípero Serra, with Governor Gaspar de Portolá, began on 28 March 1769 a 95-day, 750-mile journey north from Loreto to the shores of San Diego Bay. On 1 July, when Junípero and his land party arrived at San Diego, they found two supply ships lilting at anchor. Serra sang a Mass on 16 July, founding California's first mission. Serra and the infirm troops remained at San Diego while Portolá, Crespí and a band of soldiers marched northward to Monterey Bay. Disheartened, the troops returned to San Diego, not realizing they had found Monterey.

Back at San Diego, most crewmen had fallen ill or had died from scurvy. Supplies waned. Portolá threatened to abandon the expedition if a supply ship did not soon arrive. With zeal to the tenth power, Junípero Serra rejected this cynical notion and prayed a fervent novena. Nine days later the ship arrived, and all was saved.

Had it not been for Serra's determination, California's destiny was vulnerable to fall under dominion of another power not as easily defeated as faraway Spain when Mexico declared her independence, as Mexico fell under fire by American troops; hence, California was easy game for America.

Junípero Serra went on to found eight more missions, and resided at Mission San Carlos Borromeo del Río Carmelo at what we now call Carmel, California, for the remainder of his life. Early in his administration of the California missions—which, after his death, numbered twenty-one—Serra journeyed to Mexico to petition the viceroy for Indian rights. The outcome of this petition became known as a bill of rights for California Indians, the first piece of legislation aimed specifically for the province of Alta California.

Fray Junípero Serra went home to God on Saturday, 28 August 1784. Pope John Paul II beatified Serra for sainthood on 25 September 1988. In stone or bronze, Junípero Serra's likeness stands in public places of distinction, including Sacramento's State Mall, and Statuary Hall in the United States Capitol. Californians proudly call Junípero Serra—a determined and stalwart man—their founding father.

Although it's early spring, as we deplane onto the shimmering tarmac of Aeropuerto de Palma, a sultry haze envelops us. Enduring the blast-furnace atmosphere, we lug our bags to the taxi stand.

The route to town is pockmarked with metropolitan fringe: homely row housing, a proliferation of highway over- and under-passes, scores of diesel-spewing vehicles. Suddenly, show-stopping scenery: old sentry towers and ramparts fronting on the Mediterranean, bobbing masts hatch scenery on one side, palm trees and ancient architecture lending sophistication to the other. Majestically poised on a bluff, overlooking the bay, a beautiful mass of cathedral stretches the imagination. Artist-writer Santiago Rusiñol once said of this spectacle, "The cathedral is an island in the heart of an island."

As we reach Palma's old town, our driver skillfully weaves through constricted streets through bustling Plaça Rei Juan Carlos. We stop at Calle Jaume III, a one-way, stone-flagged lane to our lodging in the core of Palma.

Weighty plate-glass doors clunk at their hinges, opening to the lustrous marble lobby of Hotel Born. Through an expansive arcade, we see a benchmark Mallorcan courtyard shaded by stately palm trees. This hotel, built in the 1500s, restored and converted in the eighteenth century, initially served as a town-mansion for the Marquis de Ferrandell.

Vaulted chambers overwhelm with curvaceous staircase, sienna-colored marble columns, walls and floors overlaid with gleaming travertine in taupe, together with leather-upholstered chairs and sofas accenting the grand space. As I take it all in, I imagine sumptuous sleeping quarters beyond.

As we register, Uncle Chuck pales when told there is no lift, nor porters to transfer our hundreds of pounds of luggage up three rigorous flights.

"Not to worry," I say. "I'll carry your bags to the room."

As I make a fourth endeavor with the balance of our gear, my clothing grows moist, and I gasp for breath.

Beyond the lobby's beauty, we find Hotel Born more hostel than hotel. No air conditioning. Hard, paltry beds. The ascetic Junípero Serra would have felt right at home. Our sparkling-clean bathroom is en suite, though outdated. So goes the cramped bedchamber.

"Take a breather," Uncle Chuck prescribes. "Why don't you freshen up, and meet me in the lobby?"

I catch my wind, change clothes, then tackle steep flights to the lobby. With Uncle Chuck, I head in direction of the sea on Passeig des Born.

We disregard shills at each alfresco café who solicit as we read posted menus, then land at Restaurante La Plaça.

Cradled in cushioned wicker chairs on the boulevard's shaded side, we're entertained by live comic drama and aggressive restaurateurs. Each storefront occupies a grinning man, bent at the waist, striving to wave passersby into his establishment. One of these salesmen points at sandwich signs as he rubs his paunch and rolls his big eyes with ecstasy. Other cons use a more direct approach, blocking a walker's path, then gently escorting the credulous soul, by an elbow, to a sidewalk table or into a restaurant.

Spanish menus and dubious exchange rates flummox us gullible tourists. The air drifts with dainty white petals and dusty pollen, eliciting sneezes and tears. Waddling between tables, an elderly woman in tattered black frock takes advantage of the allergy season, peddling packets of tissue. Given this wily old beggar, coupled with high-pressure restaurateurs and an exorbitant tariff for a pair of omelets plus a bottle of wine, we wonder if we have landed in a tourist trap.

With not a thing in particular scheduled for the rest of the day, we gather up cameras and city plan, then make for the cathedral and its neighboring palace at Plaça de la Almoina.

Because of our off-season journeys in Europe, attractions are frequently closed when we seek them. Added to this, the banker's holiday—we believe they have one of these each week in Europe—when all but frolic puts on hold. At times, we discover restoration under way. And today we find Palma shut down except for its restaurants. The cathedral is closed. So goes the palace. Yet, we appreciate exterior details of these colossal structures together with exemplary views from our lofty position facing the harbor.

Though the highly touted Arab baths lie just up the way, notions of siesta beckon Uncle Chuck. To coax him to the baths presents me with a challenge.

"I'm sorry, young man. I need a respite. Aren't you tired?"

We return to the Born and scale its seventy-two steps and four landings, through two lengthy corridors to our confined quarters.

Rested, adjusted somewhat to the island's humidity, we rise after two hours. We'll explore prospects for dinner. A man behind the lobby's front desk suggests La Lubina, a fish house at the yacht harbor.

Into a balmy evening we stroll, past the cathedral and across frenzied streets to a quay-side promenade. Ambling along the docks' planking, we admire moored sailboats, flags of sundry nations snapping above the decks of larger vessels.

We scan faces of one-story, wood-paneled buildings for signs of our *comedor*. When we spot La Lubina and though the evening is young, the hungry file in en masse. Fortunately, we procure one of the last available tables.

Akin to fish houses in America, Lubina imparts a relaxed presentation: acoustically impaired, fragrant of brine, decorated with blue oilcloth table coverings and white napkins. But here on Palma's wharf, wide expanses of glass highlight a pretty harbor tinged with vivid sunset silhouetting the launches.

Over the din, Uncle Chuck orders salad with *gambas* and I, savory *caldereta de peix* (fish soup). We split an order of *navajas* (razor clams, described on the English side of the menu as "sea jackknives") and baby clams tweaked with an unctuous sauce of tomato, olive oil and refreshing fennel. Having fancied the Castillo de San Diego we tasted in Madrid, we enlist a bottle of this cool, crisp white wine to accompany our luscious seafood feast.

"Shall we skip dessert?" Uncle Chuck suggests.

"No way. Look, they have *crema catalana* (rich custard under a shell of burnt sugar) served with *helado* (ice cream)."

The confluence of textures is superb. I relish each smooth, flavorful bite. No need to look up, to know someone across the table fancies a spoonful.

The sky buffets black as velvet as we aim toward the Born. Spotlights bathe a noble spectacle of feathery palms fringing the avenues. From an island greensward, a statue of Ramón Llull[1] watches over his city from a lofty pedestal; and trussed within a warren of buttresses, the cathedral blazes in golden luminescence against ebony firmament. Glorious, the site, this night, on an enchanted isle.

---

[1] Ramón Llull (1232-1316): Mallorcan/Catalan scholar and mystic revered as Doctor *Illuminatus* and whose writings were pivotal to Franciscan thought in *Fray* Junípero Serra's day.

FOR WHOM THE BELL TOLLS

Generally, and given my experience, church bells on the continent go silent after midnight. Not at Palma de Mallorca....

Tossing, turning on my monkish bed, I heard the tolling of midnight. Again I heard bells announce the first hour, then the second, before nodding off.

When I arose at eight, Uncle Chuck mentioned his rousing to the clarion calls at three and four o'clock.

Caffeine.... I crave caffeine. My impotent shower scarcely restores, so with fuzzy gray matter, through bloodshot eyes, I scramble down hallways and all the stairs.

A coquettish woman wipes clean the stems of an espresso machine behind her counter. *Fray* Junípero Serra would have averted his eyes. Gazing over her shoulder, she smiles sweetly and asks if I care for coffee. Her eyes....

"*Sí, sí. Grande y con leche, por favor,*" I manage.

As the long-haired beauty's machine hisses and sputters, I contemplate delicacies teasing from the buffet: fresh fruit, hard rolls, an intriguing pastiche of tarts—stuffed or robed with prunes and figs, others with withered tomatoes, anchovies, olives, eggplant, courgettes and onions. I load a plate, then turn to the coffee lady. She gestures toward the patio with a tilt of her head, then follows me with a copious cup of steaming *café con leche*. There is no one else here. I choose a table out of range of trajectory from birds roosting in the palm trees.

In cool morning mist, I savor richly brewed coffee. Mmm...delectable, medicinal. Dreaming of another coffee, I sample pastries, and leaf through a travel primer, reading of Mallorca's checkered history. Romans vanquished this island's indigenous people (*Talayotic* tribes) in the second century before Christ. Phoenicians and Greek adventurers made brief advents here, as did Vandals and Byzantines. "Palma" stems from the Roman appellation *Palmaria*, or Victory Palm. Since that epoch, possession of the island passed between Berbers, Catalans and Imperial Spain. From 1979, the Balearic archipelago has been autonomous. Mallorca apes the other islands at roughly 60 miles wide by 40 deep, with 344 miles of coastline. And nearly half of Mallorca's 615,000 residents live in Palma.

I look up to see Uncle Chuck walking hesitantly from the coffee counter to my private terrace.

"Overcast," he mentions, looking to the milky-white sky. Now, he casts his eyes toward my plate of crumbs. "You've already eaten."

"Sorry. I needed coffee, and it went so well with the tarts. Care for some?"

The coffee lady brings Uncle Chuck's order. I delay, with my third cup of the compelling elixir.

When we return to the lobby, a deskman hands me a note from Dr. Bartomeu Font Obrador,[1] a native of Palma, the world's foremost authority on the life of *Fray* Junípero Serra. Dr. Font's colleague, our mutual friend and eminent American author-historian, Reverend Monsignor Francis J. Weber, put us in touch before we left California. Dr. Font will, says his message, meet us at the hotel at ten o'clock tomorrow morning, then lead us on a Serra tour.

Into a mild, white day, we head up tree-lined Passeig Mallorca between a warren of fashionable shops—*cerrado*, each of them.

"It's Sunday," I remind Uncle Chuck, "in a Catholic land."

"Shall we find a church?"

"That won't be any trouble."

We walk one block toward the sea, drawn toward a litany issuing sweetly from rugged stone Iglesia Santa Creu (Church of the Holy Cross). Mass just commenced. We slide silently into a pew, then follow along as best we can. Unlike churchgoers in America, there are no shorts, no T-shirts and, auspiciously, no pagers or cellular phones. Here, respectful congregants dress in their Sunday best, men wearing sport coats or suits with ties, the ladies in dresses or skirts, and hair covered with veils or kerchiefs. When I was a youngster, people in America dressed this way for Mass.

Shuffling from church into a brighter day, toward the harbor, we pause to train our cameras on an eclectic scene. Moorings hatch the shoreline; misty mountains fill the distant prospect. In the mid-ground stands an extremity of old city walls, Mirador de la Seu, a sentry tower flouting the Mediterranean. In the foreground pose abstract sculptures fashioned from rusty scrap metal: a primitive warrior brandishing a spear, alongside a twelve-foot-tall stork standing guard over a wire nest cradling a metallic egg.

We pick our way through a tangle of byways, and cross over Avinguda d'Antoni Maura to an attractive building. We imagine this is a church or convent, but discover it to be the fifteenth-century Llotja, a Gothic mercantile exchange designed by Mallorcan architect Guillem Sagrera. We admire a façade of battlements with arched apertures and dual slender turrets all fashioned from yellow stone. A tympanum frames an ethereal bas-relief angel (Ángel de la Mercadería). We discover, inside this old exchange, an exhibition hall beneath ribbed vaulting borne on spiral shafts—stony palm trees?—and superb examples of Gothic devotional art. My favorite is a Virgin in solemn repose, an enormous corona of gold radiating from her lovely head.

"Let's visit the cathedral," I urge.

"I'm certain Dr. Font will conduct a more thorough tour than we'd have on our own. Save the cathedral for tomorrow," counters Uncle Chuck.

Sun shifts into overdrive, and we again bog down within sub-tropical milieu.

We hike back over the *avinguda* to Parc de la Mar, and up Conquistador at Jaume II to Plaça Major, the main square. Palma's *plaça* presents a paradox, lackluster, unlike the principal squares of Madrid or Salamanca. We walk on with no temptations, straight through the plaza, down a flight of worn stone steps. Just outside the plaza, we discover an inviting watering hole on Riera, and claim a pair of shady seats on the sidewalk.

"Ah, this hits the spot," Uncle Chuck sighs behind a moustache of *cerveza* suds.

Two voyeurs in Palma, we people-watch from our table, cheek-by-jowl with coursing traffic.

Uncle Chuck blots a wisp of foam from his lips and announces, "Lunch."

In a roundabout way, we venture, making our way back toward Plaça de la Reina to the vicinity of our hotel, strolling through sweet-scented plazas. Vendors hawk freshly cut flowers: stargazer lilies, snapdragons, daisies, iris and daffodils. We continue our trek under a shady canopy of elm trees thoughtfully planted along these pretty boulevards.

Must have made a wrong turn, as we have landed at Plaça de Sant Francesch. Across the square, we spot the church and convent germane to the life of Junípero Serra.

After lunch, I escort my exhausted travel mate back to our stringent quarters. With cameras, I return to the balmy old town's core.

Choosing the cathedral as landmark, I then reference my map, noting a legend detailing access to Palma's vestige of Islamic culture, the Banys Arabs (*hammâms*, or Islamic hot baths)—likely, a part of a caliphate palace from tenth-century *Medina Mayurqa,* an independent *taifa*, or petty dynasty. I've heard this site touted as one of the best-preserved Moorish bathhouses in Iberia. When I reach it, there is no one else here, just the ticket vendor, who gladly accepts my pesetas.

Adjacent to the exotic bathhouse, I look in wonder at a limpid well, at peaceful terraced gardens of aged citrus trees granting shade from a relentless sun. I bow my head, passing through a cramped, keyhole-shaped door and step into another time. Dank, hollow chambers cool me. Redolent of mortar and stone, this bathhouse interior glows mysteriously. I move toward the source of the light: thin rays seeping through eight-pointed, star-shaped apertures in the brick domes. The sun renders the interior an exquisite palette of earthy shades on limestone and rosy brick, ancient pilasters in tones of cinnabar and yellow ochre. I make photographic studies, then examine a conception of this bathhouse, as an artist believed it to have looked in its days of Moorish glory. Back then, this spa furnished a *frigidarium* (cold bath) and sudatorium (sweat room) for Moorish bathers. I grasp the chambers' significance, given the sauna-like atmosphere of this city.

Damp, fatigued, I head toward the Born, but trudging finds me lost. My clothes grow soggier as I roam through streets, up pedestrian ways, down blind alleys. Spotting no familiar landmarks, I meander on. Many people in the streets speak German. Seems there are more Germans than Mallorcans in Palma. Eventually, I spot the cathedral, and trek back to the hotel.

> I speak Spanish to God,
> Italian to women,
> French to men,
> and German to my horse.
>
> —Attributed to Carlos V

When I awake from siesta, I suggest cocktails.

"Splendid idea," Uncle Chuck beams, and we liberate ourselves from our scanty quarters.

A prevailing sea breeze caresses us as we approach the marina. At a dockside table, we order scotch and soda, breathing in salty air, admiring a flotilla of boats warped off the crystalline cove.

Uncle Chuck wonders where we will eat.

"We had seafood last evening. I'm in the mood for lamb or goat, rustic food," I tell him.

"The area behind the Llotja brims with shops and cafés. Let's wander over for a browse."

Dodging a snarl of traffic on Avinguda Gabriel Roca, we pass by the aristocratic Llotja, rambling along a narrow lane called Carrer Llotja de Mar, through air adrift with redolence of grilled meat and onions. Restaurateurs drag framed menu stands outside the doors of their *comedores*. We appraise the lists. Each of them tempts, given mouth-watering aromas suffusing this alley of restaurants.

Forn de Sant Joan just opened for dinner, at seven o'clock! On the menu: lamb, kid and beefsteaks. We nod in kind. On the ground level, we see a rustic bar and kitchen, and above, a beamed-ceiling loggia. We trail our host upstairs, to a table exquisitely set alongside a bay window open to a pleasant breeze.

We are the only English-speaking customers. Few Spaniards count among us, though Germans are in constant supply. We wonder at the Germans' fascination with Mallorca.

Uncle Chuck peers above his tall menu.

"So, will it be lamb or goat?"

"I can't decide. What tickles your fancy?"

From the enticing menu's abundant choices, Uncle Chuck selects a seafood salad judiciously tossed in vinaigrette, and I, salad of tomatoes and anchovies with creamy garlic dressing.

"I don't understand your taste for anchovies," Uncle Chuck mentions with a grimace.

"Here, try one. Anchovies taste better on this side of the world. I believe Europeans keep the premium catch for themselves, their olives and olive oil, as well. The exported products are rarely as good."

"Thank you, just the same. That jolting flavor will taint my palate for these remarkably fresh baby mussels and clams."

What ensues surpasses our first courses. Uncle Chuck attests that he tastes the finest filet mignon ever, chargrilled, delectably smoky, flavorful, tender as a mother's love. I make an analogous comment of my *cabrito* (kid) roasted with big garlic buds. We complement our tasty entrées with a bottle of Puerta Vieja Rioja 1996, a heady red with legs.

"Postres?" our charming *mozo* inquires.

Uncle Chuck begins, "No, I believe…."

I interrupt. "Yes, please. May we see the cart?"

No cart, though our *mozo* presents a tray of tantalizing wonders. We select strawberries plotted on swaths of whipped cream, overlaid with burnt sugar. Oddly, the waiter describes this creation as "crêpes."

Following our superb meal, we wander through mild dusky air and return to our cubicle at the Born, trusting we will survive the force of clangorous bells.

[1] Dissecting a Spanish name: Doctor (Ph.D.), Bartomeu (given name, *Català* for Bartolomé, or Bartholomew), Font (father's surname) and Obrador (mother's surname).

The Sun Also Rises

We rose at half-past seven, neither of us well rested.

Besides bells, a German-speaking woman droned in alto pitch from an abutting terrace in the wee hours of morning. Feasibly, she and her male companion had been out on the town. Three floors beneath our windows, confines of the courtyard amplified their post-revelry dialogue, a timbre as though the night owls sat in our room. I stumbled to the window and hissed, "ssshhh!" but they piped down for only a moment.

At eight o'clock, Uncle Chuck grumbles, "I wish we knew which room was theirs. I'm tempted to make a racket just outside and give them a taste of their own medicine."

We pass an idle hour with coffee refills, grumbling about the culprits who kept us awake. As other guests take tables nearby, we size them up. Which of them were the early-morning chatterboxes? The late-middle-aged *Herr* and younger *Herren* decked out peculiarly for this early hour? He sports a dyed comb-over, a suit of synthetic fibers, too many rings. She has long hair still damp from the shower, an immodest dress and acrophobic stilettos. How does she manage the cobbles on those rangy heels? *Were they the noisy night owls, or do the guilty ones sleep it off still?*

At ten o'clock sharp, the desk clerk summons us to the lobby where we meet a handsome, older gentleman, light of complexion with finely chiseled features and salt-and-pepper hair. A stranger to hard labor, judging from his meticulously manicured hands, this dapper man wears an olive-green cardigan sweater with matching trousers, green-and-rust-plaid sport shirt and expensive though well-used leather shoes.

"I am Bartomeu Font Obrador," the jaunty man says.

We shake hands in turn. All formalities aside, Dr. Font announces, "Today we visit Iglesia y Convento de Sant Francesch; maybe more. But first, I have surprise for you."

From the start, the good doctor's charming demeanor puts us at ease.

We accompany Dr. Font through the alley to Passeig des Born, fully expecting he will show us to his car. Instead, he escorts us on foot through the city to the baroque *ajuntament* (town hall).

Quivering with pride, he beckons, "Come, I show you the archives."

Dr. Font knows already that I will appreciate an opportunity to view documents, maps and artwork associated with Junípero Serra. Our indulgent host leads us to rooms punctuated with paintings of Serra's colleagues and of Serra himself. He arranges for me to photograph the portraits, plus the town hall's collection of records relevant to the conquest of California.

Back in the streets, I believe our guide to be a public figure, or at least a well-respected man about town. At each turn, men embrace him, and women peck his cheeks. He introduces us as *"mis amigos norteamericanos."*

Dr. Font could be seventy years of age, or a bit older, yet he treks with a sprightly gait, swinging his arms. I am impressed with not only his erudition, but with his fine manners. Turning to Uncle Chuck, he inquires, "You okay, *senyor?*" Uncle Chuck's okay and getting a charge out of the proud hidalgo, who so graciously shares with us his time, perspective and knowledge.

Weaving through Palma's streets, we reach the Gothic basilica of Sant Francesch, and reflect outside on a fine bronze effigy of Serra with an Indian disciple. With a sweeping gesture, Dr. Font enlightens us that this church is second only in size to the island's great cathedral.

The yellow Santagñí stone rigs flat, its blandness relieved with a *plateresque* rose window and baroque portal filigreed with vegetal motifs and statuary amidst a decorative pediment and two stout towers. Among personages depicted on the exterior: St. George on horseback, St. Francis of Assisi, Duns Scotus and Ramón Llull. The church and adjacent convent were commissioned by Jaume II and raised by Franciscans on foundations of a mosque in the thirteenth century.

Within the single-aisle basilica, we stroll and stop, staring up in awe to a shimmery baroque altarpiece, and from arched stained windows to age-encrusted, ribbed vaulting.

Twenty-three side chapels scintillate with sacred treasures, but pale when compared with the reredos. Against a backdrop of blinding gold stand Saints Francis of Assisi, Anthony of Padua, Clare, Bonaventure, Louis IX of France, Roch, Catherine of Bologna, Dominic, the Immaculate Conception and Blessed Ramón Llull. St. George on horseback crowns this captivating scene. Junípero Serra delivered the dedication sermon here on 29 October 1739, after this altarpiece was installed.

As we trail behind, Dr. Font reminds me that Serra preached a final sermon (10 April 1749) on his native isle in this church, his home church for eighteen years. He points reverently at a *trona* (pulpit) from where the ardent friar spoke on occasion. Junípero's contemporaries deemed his oratories "worthy of being printed in letters of gold."

In a chancel chapel rests the marble sarcophagus of Blessed Ramón Llull, one of Junípero's luminaries. Dr. Font asks a caretaker to turn up the lights. I make photographs, silently say prayers, then move along to the sacristy. This chamber, generally off-limits to lay-people, brims with colorful vestments including Serra's, in skeins of rich coloration. An enormous choir book is the same used by Serra when he officiated as priest from 1738-49. On a ledge are reliquaries: one with a relic of the *Vera Crucis* (True Cross), another embracing the mandible of Ramón Llull.

A flaming sun climbs in the sky. Again, the atmosphere warms; too warm, in our estimation, for springtime. Dr. Font sheds his sweater and we, our blazers. We accompany him to the Royal Friary of Sant Francesch abutting the fine church. This vintage structure quartered the Franciscan Province of Mallorca in Serra's day. Dr. Font applies the knocker. The knock is answered with the equivalent sense of familiarity and respect we encounter in the streets, this time from a friar. Stepping inside, we behold a communion of Moorish and Gothic architecture in a comely patio and ambulatory centerpieced with a well inscribed "1658." The tranquil, methodically landscaped environment proposes postcard views. Our eyes widen at a majestic tower, formerly a minaret, piercing a sky of clear, cobalt blue. Lobed arches and pilasters of Islamic design hem a cloistered patio where Serra studied and meditated during his early adulthood, after arriving in 1729 from his hometown of inland Petra. A reflective setting.... In a flight of fancy, I sense *Fray* Junípero Serra's sandaled footfall against rough flagstones.

We walk to Iglesia de Santa Clara (from 1246) where a nun prays in stage whispers near the sanctuary. Dr. Font mumbles to her. She floats to the sanctuary, turns up the lighting, bringing to life an eye-popping altar screen.

As we hike to the next site, Uncle Chuck, with stomach on alert, invites our congenial guide to join us for lunch.

"Most kind of you, *senyor,*" Dr. Font obliges. "But my wife and I have an appointment this afternoon. Maybe another time." Smiling, he continues, "*Hihan més dies que llonganisses.* (There are more days than sausages.)"

Dr. Font says we will visit one more site and resume our tour tomorrow. We will then see the cathedral.

Hiking along, I inquire, "Dr. Font, please tell me about *duende.*"

"Where have you heard this word, *hijo?*"

"In America."

"What do they know of such things?" He smiles wryly. "*Duende* is a ghost, but not just a ghost. *Duende* may be a trance...."

Well, it didn't hurt to ask, although I'm not satisfied with his answer. For the time being, we will stick to Serra trivia.

> A mysterious power which everyone senses and no philosopher explains.
>
> —Manuel de Falla (on *duende*), "*Nocturno del Generalife*"

Next venue: a library known as Archivo del Estado. Ah...that aroma of mildew we bibliophiles admire....

From impressive collections, Dr. Font calls to our attention a cache of handwritten manuscripts by Junípero Serra. At my choosing, our host removes cracked vellum-bound works from sagging wooden cases for perusal and photography. Marveling at pages written in fastidious, italic hand, I am astonished that we are not required to slip into cotton gloves before handling the precious material. Gingerly, I turn crumbling, curled letters and papers as I record them on film.

Replete with Serra nostalgia, I follow Dr. Font and Uncle Chuck back to the Born where we say goodbye, agreeing on a time to convene again in the hotel lobby tomorrow morning.

Uncle Chuck spots an attractive *comedor* named Chopin. We know that composer Frédéric Chopin spent a winter on this island with his common-law wife and author Baroness Dudevant (aka George Sand) more than one hundred and fifty years ago.

Not belying its courtly façade, the interior of this dignified restaurant is tastefully appointed in ivory napery, blond wood-tones and pastel, trompe l'œil scenes dancing upon walls.

Uncle Chuck opts for the *menú del día,* and his order brings creamy asparagus soup and morsels of beef served with fingerling potatoes. I order à la carte, with prelude of delicate consommé bobbing with tiny ravioli, continuing with supremely al dente noodles married with morels, napped in cream. Over our pleasant lunch, we discuss the Mallorcan tongue.

"You understood Dr. Font," Uncle Chuck remarks. "But then, you've always done well with language and accents."

"Actually, we spoke mostly English. I must say he's better versed in our language than I am with his. The *Mallorquín* tongue speaks Catalan, with Arabic and French expressions thrown in just for fun."

"I noticed *sant* and *san* for saint. *Calle* for *carrer. Paseo* becomes *passeig.*"

"Don't forget *avinguda* for *avenida* and *plaça* for plaza."

"That word he used for town hall? Not the Castilian *ayuntamiento,* but close."

"We are so near mainland Spain, yet the cultures, even the weather vary so. In Spain, it's cool and dry. Madrid is modern, with its share of concrete and glass skyscrapers, yet this capital city of Mallorca has smaller buildings chiefly constructed of stone—ancient stone. Palma gives more of an Old World feeling. Agree?"

"Yes. Now, shall we shop or siesta?" I ask.

"Can we siesta, then shop?"

After a good rest at the Born, we traverse three long blocks to Palma's fashionable shopping district on Carrer Verí.

I wait patiently as Uncle Chuck wanders aisles and ducks into dressing rooms to try on shirts and trousers. One of the shops, called Charlie Hombre, signals Uncle Chuck. He fancies the name, but finds nothing that suits him. Uncle Chuck formerly purveyed men's clothing and enjoys the sartorial as much as I do the ecclesial.

We walk to the main *passeig* and plunk down in chairs at a sidewalk café. Uncle Chuck orders beer and I, Coca-Cola®. Hardly a day goes by without this, my favorite beverage. Uncle Chuck calls it my Coke habit. As we sip icy beverages, a fountain on Plaça Rei Joan Carles I grabs our attention. From its basin soars a limestone obelisk balanced on backs of four bronze turtles and aloft, a bronze bat poised for flight. When we inquire, our *mozo* explains its intent—commemorating the royal visit of Spain's Queen Victoria, though the fellow hasn't a clue as to the bronze animals' implication.

"I dream of that fish baked in salt—you know, at the restaurant down by the water the other night," Uncle Chuck tells me.

I'm game, and we're off for the docks.

We pause on the brink of the harbor to reflect on La Capella de Sant Telm, a tiny chapel steeped in glow and shadows of burning sunset. We imagine fishermen and explorers-of-old pausing here for prayer before embarking on journeys at sea.

This evening, Restaurante La Lubina is not as crowded as the other night. A young woman sits opposite us, dining alone. I nod to her. She smiles, introducing herself as Sonia, from Connecticut. She wonders, as do we, about the numberless German speakers on this Mediterranean island.

"And Asians!" she exclaims. "I've come here to see natives, not tourists."

Yet, she appears to enjoy our company and commiseration as we chat throughout mealtime.

Sonia enjoys the fish baked in rock salt. Asked if it's worthy, she beams.

"What brings you to Mallorca," I ask, "besides the natives?"

She launches into a itinerary of "doing the islands." After Mallorca, she will visit Menorca and Ibiza. Though a youngster, Sonia has taken in the epic sites on mainland Spain, and now moves beyond. We're envious; Connecticut is so much closer than California to Europe.

This evening, the sea salt-encrusted wonder is *rodaballo* (turbot). Rolled out with regalia on a trolley, the dish resembles a mound of diamonds garnished with parsley and curls of lemon peel. With two large spoons, our waiter cracks the glistening crust, adeptly removes steaming, snow-white fish and de-bones it with the skill of a surgeon. The scrumptious outcome: moist, flaky fish, not at all salty.

After bidding our compatriot good night and bon voyage, we amble into the cool foggy evening. Gazing toward Old Town from the water's edge, we marvel at orderly rows of palm trees. What a poetic statement they make against soft, creeping fog. The grand old city glows subtly within her misty shroud, the majestic, floodlit cathedral with its pinnacled buttresses commanding the scene.

Stimulated about the continuation of our Serra tour, I pray for sleep.

The Germans are Coming

If church bells tumbled through their motions in the early hours, we did not hear them. Nor did we awake to Deutsch *whoopla from the courtyard.*

"I frankly don't recall nodding off," admits Uncle Chuck. "Yet I believe I slept for a good eight hours."

Not bothering with blazers, we instead throw on cotton shirts and chinos, for the weather and to be more in keeping with the mode of Dr. Font, though Dr. Font is smartly attired in sport coat and dress trousers.

Smiling, he asks, *"¿Sa Seu?"*

We hike with him down the Passeig to Plaça de la Reina, passing under a spread of enormous plane trees. At the end of the square, Dr. Font points out a pair of stone sphinxes in knight's beavers, leonine aberrations designating Palma's Roman past.

The clime ratchets ardent as we reach *Sa Seu* (The Cathedral). Spires, flying buttresses, outcroppings of statuary bathed in golden radiance offset a sky painted in broad strokes of vivid blue. Dr. Font explains that the cathedral's eastern façade is partly the work of Guillermo Sagrera, the talented artisan responsible for Palma's Llotja.

Dr. Font speaks briefly in *Mallorquín* to the ticket taker. They embrace. We are all allowed to enter at no charge.

"This *catedral* they began in 1229, to celebrate Los Católicos's defeat of Mallorca's Moslem rulers," our informed guide tells us, "and completed in 1604. Jaume I (1213-76) of Cataluña and Aragón dedicated this cathedral to the Blessed Virgin."

I shall remember always my first impressions of this wondrous temple. Unlike gloomy cathedrals we have toured on the continent, this one glows. Sunlight streams through stained windows, modeling spectrums of gold, heliotrope, green, red and blue along fourteen octagonal pillars. Richly amplified within this drenching of prismatic radiance, munificent gilding, Gothic arches and ribbed brick vaults are more the accouterments of palace than place of worship.

Dr. Font does not have to point out the significance of a colossal, alabaster *púlpito*. Must be fourteen feet high, at least, this pulpit resembling a gigantic baptismal font intricately incised with biblical scenes and niches relieved with saints and the Holy Spirit. The steps are the same Father-lector *Fray* Junípero Serra scaled on the Feast of Corpus Christi in January of 1742, 1743 and again in 1744. Above, a lectern dwarfed by enormity of this richly engraved rostrum. Way up there, Serra also spoke on the topic of the Holy Eucharist in 1743, according to Dr. Font.

On a distant wall flares an illustrious rose oculus, considered one of Europe's finest. Forty-two feet in diameter and constructed of more than twelve hundred sections of stained glass in the design of a six-pointed star, this window blazes violently, adding more rays of color to stony environs.

Mesmerized, we shuffle through the echoey stone chamber, one of Europe's widest naves, up to the sanctuary. Dr. Font points to a golden canopy suspended above the main altar.

"Is by Antoni Gaudí. You know Gaudí? Come. We see his work better from above."

We trail Dr. Font, crouching through a small door, up two flights of stone steps to the choir. From here, we appreciate the vastness of space from an angel's perspective. We are captivated by Gaudí's delicate mobile crafted in finely gilded wrought iron, symbolizing the intrinsic elements of the Eucharist. A masterful baldachin, suspended from high above by chains linked with huge, multifaceted glass beads, is legitimately Gaudí's interpretation of an abstract rosary. As I set up my tripod, two German tourists step into the choir.

"Private tour," Dr. Font cautions, wagging a finger at them. "Please go."

"Dr. Font," I ask, "why so many Germans in Mallocra?"

"Please," he says gruffly, "we discuss outside."

We scale another flight of steps to Capella de la Trinitat. In alabaster sarcophagi rest the remains of Jaume II and III. Jaume I de Aragón the Conqueror is entombed back in mainland Spain.

Lids of these coffins by Frederic Marès realistically detail effigies of two Aragonés kings—pronounced *kinks* by our host—resembling living, sleeping men powdered white. The monarchs' feet rest upon pillows shaped as lions. Sweet cherubim hold open books of scriptures near the kings' peaceful faces.

We return to the sanctuary, then walk the side aisles, reviewing opulent chapels with baldachins twisting between images of saints. We see more Virgins in repose, such as the one that we'd noted in the Llotja exhibit, and others wreathed in golden rays as other depictions we've seen of the Virgin of Guadalupe.

As we pass through the nave, Dr. Font cites a stained window framing a portrait of Junípero Serra holding a California mission; flanking his figure, an American Indian.

The baptistery imparts solemnity, untouched by dusty rays that penetrate other quadrants of this cathedral, though pretty with a fine painting of Christ's Baptism set amid faux marble pilasters with Ionic capitals in rosy tones.

We shuffle outside to the old chapter house, peering through a thick glass floor exposing underpinnings of Palma's Roman *castrum* (fortified town). The only remains: a geometrical pattern, footings of ruinous columns. Vertigo grips as I take baby steps across this transparent floor. Just beyond, glass transitions to marble in a museum where we view ecclesiastical treasures at ease: a scrap of Christ's tunic, a reliquary of the True Cross and a leathery piece of Saint Sebastian's brain.

On the streets again, I quiz Dr. Font on Mallorca's German invasion.

"¡Ah! ¡Esos alemanes!" he cries out. "They spoil our beautiful island, disfigure the coastlines, put up high-rise apartments and hotels. They make second homes here, building so many expensive *casas* and villas that average Mallorcan citizens cannot *affor'* their own.

"But this is *nothink* new," he says. "Centuries ago, Visigoths invaded Roman Spain."

He goes on to explain that Germans arrive in droves on a weekly basis. Mallorca's pleasant climate makes package tours from Germany attractive.

"I understand they fly round-trip from Frankfurt for little more than twenty-five-thousand pesetas." (US$150)

He points as we encounter a pushy band of Germans on the sidewalk.

"See! How assertive and rude, *forgettink* they are guests. Are we in Germany, not in our native land?"

Uncle resolves to keep his German heritage a secret from our host....

We proceed to Llullian University, an eminent school known in its glory days as the Pontifical, Imperial, Royal and Literary University of Mallorca—where *Fray* Junípero studied philosophy and theology. Little remains of original buildings from 1483, though one wing stands preserved. Elegies to Llull and Serra adorn the walls. Junípero Serra earned his S.T.D. from this university in 1742 and went on to teach here, before leaving for missionary work in the Americas.

After pausing for Coca-Cola®, the doctor takes us to Archivo del Convento de San Felipe Neri de Palma with its cache of fine manuscripts, including those written by Serra as a student. Again, he allows me to remove fragile documents from storage and display cases. I find enchanting, Serra's illustrated Ptolemaic chart with moveable paper wheels allegorizing the pre-Copernican view of planets and sun orbiting the earth.

Dr. Font says he will lead us to one more site before he departs for another appointment.

"When are you *leavink* for Petra?" he asks.

I answer, "Tomorrow morning. As there were no rooms available at Petra, we booked at Binissalem—an easy drive, we expect."

"I will meet you at the Serra Museum in Petra at fifteen hours then?"

The three of us ride in a cab to Convento de Santa María de Los Angeles de Jesús, a convent where Junípero Serra received the Franciscan habit as novitiate in 1730. Only a row of ruined Gothic arches that once delineated a cloister remain of the original convent.

On our return to the Born, we pass through Plaça Major, described by Dr. Font as *"Plaça de Almas."* Extended palms and sad eyes taunt us each step of the way. Befitting, Dr. Font's nickname for Palma's main square.

"I find the beggars charming," I tell our host. "I've seen them in Madrid, in Santiago, all over Spain."

Dr. Font smiles, reminding me I am on vacation. He alludes to the beggars as *depredadores* (predators).

In the alleyway fronting the Born, we exchange hugs with our host.

"¡Bon dia tinguin! (Have a good day!)," he says heartily.

We wish him *"buenas tardes,"* then repair to our room to freshen up.

"Whew," Uncle Chuck breathes. "I'm bent on a nap."

His stomach wins out. We make flight to a restaurant for a late lunch. Wandering in a direction opposite the tourist trap, we pause at Restaurante Cuba.

After a meal of *tapas* and salads, we hike back toward the cathedral, to pay homage to Palau Real de la Almudaina. Gracing this stone fortress, a slim reflecting pond splits a garden in two, an aspect hinting of Palma's Muslim dominion. Amazingly, the royal palace is open and we file inside to tour imposing military headquarters. This site's derivation officially stems from Roman occupation, when it thrived as a *castrum* dubbed *Gymnesia Mayor* in B.C. 121. Consecutively, Vandals, Byzantine and Muslim conquerors overtook the *castrum*. From A.D. 903, this palace served as seat of Arab viziers and, in the Middle Ages, of Aragonés kings. I wonder if it was then that Palma chose St. Sebastian as patron, since Sebastian immunized the faithful in facing arrows, a suitable safeguard for soldiers.

We see precious little clue of the Moors' sway as we wander through Flemish painting-and-tapestry-festooned corridors, royal chambers, Fireplace Hall and a graceful courtyard. We pause between cascading shocks of fuchsia bougainvillea, near a gurgling fountain fed from the mouth of a stone lion. Overall, the palace exterior divulges a gray and golden pile of stone, though inside, a Gothic palace.

Spanish ascendancy smacks unmistakably in opulent throne room and royal crests, suits of armor guarding halls and cannon defending portals. After a lengthy tour of corridors and chambers, Uncle Chuck lets go a sigh of relief when we discover the highly acclaimed Chapel of Santa Ana closed for restoration. On the way out, we see youthful Mallorcan military guard maintaining a steady vigil.

Uncle Chuck's stamina wilts, so I accompany him back to the Born. As he hunkers down, I strike out to visit Iglesia de Santa Magdalena, a church recommended by Dr. Font.

Dr. Font said I would find the 1679 *iglesia* just up the alley from the Born, on a passageway skirted with wall-to-wall seigniorial mansions from the sixteenth through seventeenth centuries. The occasional mansion's massive wooden door stands ajar, shielded with intricate *rejas*. Peering between bars, wondering at splendid courtyards, I sneak photographs. A block distant, I spot the massive stone *iglesia*.

Inside the cold, eerie church, I hear the murmur of prayers and clacking of beads. I pass silently by worshipers, in direction of the main altar, and gaze up into a Roman-style dome. Alongside one of the side aisles, I glimpse a shrine. Within a glass coffin lies the incorrupt corpse of the island's patroness, Santa Catalina Tomás. Tiny face, hands and feet protrude from her habit. Her taut, withered flesh glows waxen yellow, her eye sockets vacant. Though she died young, Catalina's knuckles look arthritic.

> Humble little saint, flower of the mountain,
> flower of the hawthorn so pricking,
> who now perfumes our land
> from the balconies of Paradise!
>
> —Miquel Ferrá

In Spain, faith hangs heavy on the air. Spanish culture intertwines intensely with Roman Catholicism, though a mere one-fifth of the population attends church services regularly. Seminary admissions and ordinations have fallen throughout the majority of Spain's provinces—attributable largely to growing indifference amongst those under the age of fifty. Still, more than ninety percent of Spaniards are deeply ingrained with Catholic faith. *Does Spanish passion spring from deep religious belief, or religion from passion?*

> Nothing in life is more wonderful than faith—the one great moving force which we can neither weigh in the balance nor test in the crucible.
>
> —Sir William Osler

Back at the Born, I rifle through brochures in the lobby. When I share my ideas with Uncle Chuck, he reminds me of the concept of tourist trap.

"I wonder where the locals dine," he says.

Uncle Chuck has been cooped up too long. I follow him to the lobby. The deskman suggests Asador Tierna de Aranda, just up the street.

We set out into a cool evening, to a candlelit *comedor* where we unravel the puzzle of our menus. Passing on wine, we opt for scotch and soda. We each order what we conclude to be sweetbreads, from their description on the menu, but turn up grilled mushrooms and baby green beans. We segue with ethereal lamb chops served with sliced, fried potatoes. Dessert proposes a righteous finale: sensual crêpes stuffed with melting vanilla ice cream, topped with gooey, caramelized walnuts.

We retire early, anticipating our journey to Binissalem and Petra tomorrow. With marathon tours and a heavy meal behind us, we drift off moments after falling into our stiff beds.

Bona nit.

The Son of Peace, a *Deutsche* Samaritan,
an Expat Rocket Scientist and a Swiss Gastronome

Conceivably, my longing to live in Europe, particularly in Spain, endears me to expatriates. Expats have mastered the concept of seizing the moment, of living spontaneously. Exemplars were Hemingway, Greta Garbo, Josephine Baker and Peter Mayle.

We would soon meet a pair of expatriates not as eccentric as the celebrities mentioned above, but nonetheless enviable. And were they truly eccentric, or did they embody the virtue of duende?

Each time I plod down to the lobby for coffee, then breakfast, I lug baggage to a lock-up on the main floor. I'm eager to shove on to the next leg of our itinerary, but my travel mate insists on shopping Carrer Verí again. So, after breakfast, with one last gaze at the coffee lady, we head to a haberdashery where Uncle Chuck buys a sport shirt. Now, happy with his *recuerdo* of Palma, we return to the Born and call for a shuttle.

We paid in advance for a mid-sized car, yet the leasing agent has no record of our order. As we stand with luggage in a tiny car-rental office, phone calls are made, emails sent. At last, the agent sets our situation straight and dispatches a man to collect our vehicle. When a half hour later he arrives— he had to wash the car—we stuff our gear into the trunk of a small Chrysler sedan. Shortly, we're bound eastward toward Binissalem.

"Guess they consider this mid-sized in Europe," Uncle Chuck grumbles, shifting his bottom in the driver's seat. "But it's new, clean and, I'd expect, fuel efficient."

As on mainland Spain, motor-ways of Mallorca are supremely engineered and well-regulated. Once we abandon the merging flurry of Palma's interchanges, we course effortlessly along. With the capital city behind us, splendid views come forth: a less-settled interior of clustered, village-crowned hills, set amidst endless acres of almond orchards and olive groves.

An American journalist noted Binissalem's guile, deeming it Mallorca's wine center. The reviewer lauded also a superlative bed-and-breakfast hotel called Scott's, a restored eighteenth-century *palacete* (seigniorial estate). According to the article, guests of Scott's bask in stellar ambiance and hospitality. We booked a room at Scott's for three days as a staging point for exploration of Serra's hometown, Petra de Mallorca. Binissalem ("Son of Peace" in Arabic) broaches twenty-five minutes east of Palma, forty minutes northwest of Petra.

No inkling of vineyards once we reach the village, yet we suspect they flourish in the general vicinity. As Binissalem's population is only five thousand, locating Scott's should be a cinch. I unfold the rave review.

"Let's see....says the hotel is near the church square. Look, there's a steeple."

We roll through a slumberous town of stony façades with great wooden doors, and old town houses, seigniorial mansions, all abutted against one another. As we approach what appears to be the town commons, I keep my eyes peeled until I see a stone *casa* with a shiny brass plaque engraved in refined script: *Scott's*. The façade faces a plaza with a fetching church and campanile of mellowed gray stone.

We pull over, park and lock the car.

"See the sign," I warn. "No parking allowed."

We climb back in and Uncle Chuck turns the key. *Nada*. He tries again, with still no results. "Fine. We're stranded, smack in the middle of an island halfway across the world, parked illegally," he grumbles.

Repeated attempts to fire up the Chrysler prove futile. We step out and open the hood. As we stare in wonderment at hoses and wires, a car pulls up. The driver mutters in German.

We implore, "English? *¿Español?"*

In English, the fellow asks, "Problems with your car?"

We nod.

Legally parked, he approaches Uncle Chuck.

"The key bob, please?"

Surrendering the keys, we watch the fellow inspect the bob. He chuckles.

"*Ja!* You have engaged the auto-theft mode," he suggests.

Given this Samaritan's engineering counsel, our rental car ignites with a turn of the key. Uncle Chuck unwittingly pressed its button after parking. Embarrassed, though grateful, we thank the fellow.

"Maybe Germans aren't all bad," I say with relief.

I ply the bell at Scott's. A voice calls from above, "Yes? May I help you?" A man in bathrobe leans from a window on the second story. He is middle-aged, his accent either American or affected British.

"We've booked a room," I call up, announcing our names.

"Oh, yes, we expect you. I'll be down straightaway."

In five minutes, a thick door swings in from the austere façade, disclosing an elegant interior. Scott's, a town house of an eighteenth-century nobleman, looks smart in its careful stonework and flagstones. Interior appointments include Oriental rugs, padded benches, subtle yet effective lighting and tasteful floral arrangements. From the lobby, we glimpse a typical Mallorcan courtyard awash in sunlight, the liquid yellow rays flooding interior corridors.

The fellow who let us in is Dr. George Scott, strapping, handsome, mustachioed, and now dressed. He welcomes us warmly and inquires about luggage.

"I'll send my son to collect it for you. Please, won't you sign the guest book?"

His wife Judy is away now, George tells us. She will return later today.

"She outclasses me with check-ins and such," he admits. "So then, I'll show you to your room."

Behind him, we cut through a pleasant courtyard. Pots of flowers and wrought-iron furniture propose an inviting retreat beneath a venerable lemon tree growing from an old well converted to planter. Veering right, our journey continues up two flights of steps to bright, cheerful chambers done in tones of soft blue, white and beige—our quarters, looking out upon the courtyard.

"Ben will be here with your luggage momentarily," George says with his perplexing accent. "Settle in, relax. Help yourself from the bar off the patio, if you wish. An honor system. You'll find a pad on the bar. Jot down what you take. We'll tally things up later."

How many guests are honorable?

Looking ahead to our appointment at Petra, we wait for Ben to arrive with the luggage. Ben is a shy teenager, lanky, brunette, with a mesh of braces camouflaging his teeth; he looks nothing like his father. Depositing our bags, he declines a tip.

Referencing our map, we pursue Petra via the route of Inca and Sineu. Rolling along, we enjoy sylvan views of *Es Pla*—the fertile plains of Mallorca's interior—ancient loam dotted with grapevines and fig trees. Almond orchards rain pink petals on the air. George Scott mentioned that, only weeks ago, those almond trees resembled fluffy pink snowballs.

In forty minutes, the hill town of Petra (Rocky) comes into view. With time to spare before our appointment at the Serra Museum, we drive through crooked tracks in pursuit of a restaurant, inching along, marveling at the milieu of this settlement: peaceful, ancient, a virtual time capsule of stone dwellings on cramped lanes. With exception of power lines, this sleepy village appears stopped-in-its-tracks since Serra's youth.

And here Petra is the firm rock of the apostle, cradle, land, inheritance, beginning, and source.

—José Garcia Nieto, "Song of *Fray* Junípero"

"This isn't exactly a booming metropolis," I mention as we slowly roll through town. "So we can't be finicky. Look! There's a bar."

"Where?"

"Stop."

"Please, don't do that!"

"No, I didn't want a photograph. The bar is called 'Stop.'"

We pull into a tiny car lot, then cross a dusty path to a rustic roadhouse. Delectable aromas greet our nostrils. Tellingly, the customers are local, likely *Petrenses* (Petra villagers), an excellent sign.

I explain to our waiter that we are pressed for time and ask him, *"¿Menú del día para dos, por favor?"*

The pleasant man lays the table with hearty bread, bowls of glossy green olives together with an earthenware jug of white wine and bottle of water. Next come *greixeras* (casseroles prepared with lard) of delicious *frit mallorquí* (Mallorcan stew): an ensemble of sliced *sepia* (cuttlefish), broad beans, peas, potatoes, artichokes and bacon enveloped in flavorful sauce. When Uncle Chuck mistakes cuttlefish for boiled egg, I let him believe so. Assuming lunch is over, we are astonished when our *mozo* brings breaded pork cutlets and nests of shoestring potatoes. When we finish, he proffers plates of cold, juicy orange sections.

La cuenta comes to sixteen hundred pesetas (under US $10), for two of us.

"Without a doubt, the best value imaginable," Uncle Chuck says. "That luscious stew with boiled eggs, a meat course, and wine included."

"Let's pay up," I insist, glancing at my watch. "Dr. Font expects us in fifteen minutes."

We dash to the opposite end of the village and park near Carrer Junípero Serra with our right-side tires on the sidewalk, as the street impedes narrowly.

Uncle Chuck says, "Imagine attempting to maneuver a Cadillac around these parts."

Dr. Font awaits us in the museum's front patio. We are dressed in ties and blazers; this time, Dr. Font is attired casually.

Though small, El Museu Serra harbors a comprehensive repository of mementos concerning that favorite son of Mallorca, *Fray* Junípero Serra. Besides a plenitude of manuscripts and paintings, points of interest include models of missions Serra administered in the Americas, plus Native American artifacts: arrowheads, baskets and clay pots. Dr. Font leads our tour of meticulously displayed material. In the museum library, he proudly shows us his two-volume doctoral thesis on Serra's life. These leather-bound books, with spines at least three inches thick, are generally protected behind locked glass doors.

Just up the street, Number 6 Carrer Barracar Alta discloses *Casa Solariega*, Serra's birth-home, a commonplace façade of durable stone with arched portal. Mounted alongside the door, a plaque inscribed in *Mallorquín*:

Ancestral home of the Venerable Father
***Fray* Junípero Serra, OFM, Apostle of California**
1713-1784
The Town Council and People of Petra

On the heavy, worm-eaten wooden door hangs a branch of bay laurel. A pilgrim or Serra devotee, no doubt, placed it there. I know the significance, having learned of circumstances relative to the birth of Junípero Serra. In olden Mallorca, says tradition, when a boy was born, parents affixed a sprig of laurel to their front door.

Dr. Font presents the humble *casa* to us as though it were his own. The sparsely furnished, flagstone-floored parlor presses in on us with thick, lime-swabbed walls. Only two others compose the ground level. Dr. Font tells us the larger chamber quartered the family's mule. As the Serras labored as paisanos, he tells us, a mule was their most valuable possession. A worn stone track transects the *casa* to this interior stable. Opposite the mule's quarters, we see the *cocina* (kitchen) with primitive wood stove and hearth.

We climb to the loft, to two additional rooms: the larger, used by the Serra family for dying fabric and for storage. Young Miquel Joseph (Junípero's christened name) and his sister Juana shared this utilitarian space for sleeping. A mere alcove off the hallway furnished sleeping quarters for their parents.

Amazing, walking in the footsteps of the illustrious Junípero Serra. I have done so in his California missions, yet at this moment I feel more endeared to him on his native soil.

Dr. Font escorts us out back, to two rustic *hornos* (ovens) under a lean-to shed. Lovely, coral-hued roses bloom against a postage-stamp-sized speck of land once used as a corral.

Next, we walk a short measure through quiet streets to Iglesia de San Pere (Church of Saint Peter), where Serra and his family worshiped. An austere church, boxy in conformation, a thin turret on either side of the stony façade relieving banal design, as does a huge rose oculus and seven Romanesque windows along one of its broad sides. At the opposing end soars a hexagonal bell tower with pyramidal peak. Considered late Gothic in style, this church constructed of stone from the Santagñí quarries was begun in 1582, completed in 1766.

With exception of the Neo-Classical *retablo* installed in the nineteenth century, interior appointments were familiar to Serra.

A niche on one of the church's dark side aisles harbors a reliquary encapsulating a bone fragment of Serra, who was buried at Carmel, California. The Gothic font in which infant Miquel Serre was christened in 1713 occupies the sanctuary. The font later served as birdbath in the church garden, but in the mid-twentieth century, a priest moved it back inside, to the surety of the church.

As I make photographs, Dr. Font speaks with the *párroco* (parish priest) who presents to us a musty, bulky registry of baptisms. Under the date of 24 November 1713, the priest points out hand-written words *Miquel Joseph Serre*,[1] an entry made by The Reverend Bartomeu Lladó, who officiated at baby Miquel's christening.

When we step again into daylight, a statue across the street captures my attention: a stone depiction of a woman with demure countenance, Santa Catalina Tomás standing alongside the fifteenth-century Franciscan church and former convent of San Bernardino (Sant Bernardi, dating from 1607). Miquel Joseph studied there. Down the street, in a Renaissance church, Dr. Font introduces us to Sant Bernardi's guardian, Father Juan Martí Gandía, OFM, a stout "Friar Tuck" sort of fellow who speaks no English.

As we approach the sanctuary and its gleaming baroque reredos, Dr. Font points to stones in the floor marking the tombs of Serra's parents, his sister Juana and brother-in-law Miquel Ribot.

The sanctuary's gilded columns and flourishes frame polychrome statues of the Immaculate Conception, angels, and saints including John Capistran, James of Marches, Bernardine. Flanking Capistran stand other saints for whom the California missions are named. Exquisite friezes, murals and tiles underscore the allure of this holy scene.

Dr. Font escorts us back down the nave to a grotto with *rejas*. Behind these metal grates stands an exquisite *Belén* (Nativity scene). Adoring pilgrims, each Christmastime, solemnize this shrine with hundreds of candles. Clergy suspends Eucharistic bread from the ceiling, a galaxy of wafers, a custom pre-dating Serra's time and has to do with the significance of *Belén* (or Bethlehem, *beth le hem*—land of bread).

"Soon I must leave you," our gentle host says. "But you stay in Binissalem not far away, so come back to Petra; visit again. Now you know what to look for."

As we escort Dr. Font to his car, he cites more Serra memorabilia along the way: plaques, tiles and a grand statue of the saintly friar in the town's tiny square. When we reach his car, he opens the trunk, removes books and presents them to me. There are five, all authored by him. We embrace, bidding farewell.

"Come back to Mallorca," Dr. Font says. "And I may see you one day in beautiful California, or in Rome for the canonization of *Beato* Junípero Serra. *¡Amar a Dios, mis amigos! ¡Amar a Dios!*"[2]

As he drives away, I turn to Uncle Chuck. "I'll miss that gentleman. How terrific, having our own personal guide."

"This old gentleman requires a nap. What do you say we head north?"

Up in the room, Uncle Chuck snores. I lounge in Scott's delightful courtyard, drinking in warm, unsullied air. As I sit under a lemon tree, scrawling in my journal, a tabby checks me out and decides to keep me company. Sensing someone near, I look up. A charismatic, ample, brunette woman sashays onto the patio.

"Good afternoon. I'm Judy Brabner Scott," the woman intones with a distinctive British accent.

I introduce myself and rise, to shake her hand.

"Oh, you mustn't be so formal," she scolds. "We run an informal country inn. Please, relax."

Judy reviews the litany of the honor bar. I await Uncle Chuck, I tell her, and ask, "Can you recommend a good restaurant for dinner?"

The bright-eyed woman looks to the sky and shrugs. "Let's see.... Try La Suiza! The owner is a gentleman and a wonder in the kitchen."

This dark-haired, brown-eyed woman has Latin qualities. When she mentions Spanish place names, her accent rings credible, her eyes sparkle with charisma. I sense *duende*.

"Mrs. Scott?" Uncle Chuck asks, stepping onto the terrace, looking well rested. He greets our hostess and the gray tabby.

"Judy, please, and we call my little kitty-puss Alonso. I was just explaining to Terry that we are casual here."

"A drink, Judy? You, Uncle Chuck?"

"Yes, indeed," Judy acquiesces with a chuckle, and snuggles into a padded seat between us at a wrought-iron table.

The sun drops as we sip smoky scotch. George joins us and sits back, stretching his long arms heavenward, near-silhouettes against a russet sky. With fingers locked behind his head, elbows in the air, he declares with a wide grin, "Isn't this the life? You must try it; do the expatriate thing, you know."

George Scott is a writer, retired from his career as aerospace engineer in Chicago. Judy, from England, bases her career around the restoration and interior design of historic buildings, including this beautiful inn. She includes Elizabeth II among her design clients.

After chatting with the Scotts, we excuse ourselves, then make our way through the slim streets of Binissalem to a tiny Swiss restaurant.

As usual, we dine early by Spanish standards, so there are scant tourists in this *comedor*. A pair of them across the room swap not a word, nor even a taste, during their entire meal. We order a bottle of Parellada *blanca*, a local wine. During our meal of crisp salads and grilled langoustines, the Swiss owner-chef pays us a visit. As we finish our entrées, he recommends his *crêpes à l'orange*, a masterful melange of orange segments commingled with soft vanilla ice cream wrapped in tender, freckled pancakes.

We venture through twilight back to Scott's.

"You'll love your bed," Uncle Chuck testifies. "So far this inn lives up to the accolades. I'm impressed with the quality of sheets and pillows, the cleanliness, Old World ambiance. I will, however, make one complaint in the morning. The beds are on casters. While I napped, the bed had a mind of its own; a moving nap, you could have called it."

[1] Serre: Original *Mallorquín* spelling of the surname Serra.

[2] *Amar a Dios:* "Good day;" literally, "Love God"—one of the first Spanish expressions *Fray* Junípero Serra taught his native Californian converts.

SEIGNIORIAL SPLENDORS WITH BUMPER CARS

Over the centuries, Mallorca was invaded relentlessly, yet each intruder imparted its own engaging attributes. Modern man added little or nothing of cultural interest, ruining the coastlines with a barricade of multistory flats and hotels, fast-food restaurants, trinket shops. Nevertheless, inland milieu of magical Mallorca remained pure, even into the twenty-first century.

Before the days of mass tourism and German sunbathers, pearl factories and estate agents, this island's economy was strictly agrarian. Unspoiled inner floes, for the most part, endured as they did in days of old. Before long, Uncle Chuck and I discovered our preference of the fetching interior over Mallorca's coastal glitz.

Rich toned church bells toll the hour of six A.M., invading the sub-consciousness. I stir, yet choose to stay in my well-appointed bed. What a pleasant disparity from the bare-bones accommodations at Hotel Born. According to the Scotts, our beds are handmade, multi-spring models with mattresses firm yet not the least bit rigid. Deluxe sheets spun from rich cotton percale smell of the great outdoors. Goose down fills fluffy pillows and duvets. All so comfortable, making it tempting to sleep in.

When bells resound again at seven, I squint from my downy nest. Conspicuously, Uncle Chuck and I engaged in an unintentional game of bumper cars during the night. Our beds are askew, at right angles to each other—his headboard two feet from the wall.

My radar detects the fragrance of coffee wafting through our windows. Stretching, yawning, I shuffle to the shower.

Faceted pump bottles brimming with lotions, shampoos and conditioners accouter the oversized tub. I lather up and wash my hair with a medicinal potion and haplessly this seeps into my eyes. But the water feels soft and warm, so I linger in vaporous luxury.

Drying then wrapping myself with a fluffy Turkish towel the size of a sheet, I step up to the sink for a shave. A ruby-eyed demon stares from the mirror, eyeballs blazing red, pupils constricted to mere pinholes, lids thick and swollen. Is it *duende*, my inner demon coming forth? I panic, then remember the shampoo.

Now really in need of a caffeine fix, I urge Uncle Chuck to make haste, warn him about the brown shampoo, then gallop down the stairs in sunglasses.

Scott's dining room occupies an adjacent wing one level up. I cross the courtyard to reach its stairway. When I arrive for breakfast, only three are here: Mallorcan women in starched uniforms of gray and white. I imagine they've seen it all, including now, a man in shades at breakfast time.

After three cups of heavenly coffee, still awaiting Uncle Chuck, I step out onto the sunny terrace bridging two wings of this *palacete*. Enjoying the view with a cigar, I indulge in another jolt of caffeine. From the bridge, I look across the street to a turreted steeple and octagonal apse of the church rising above plane trees. Birds serenade, maintaining a conservative distance from Alonso, who skulks along the balustrade.

"He fancies ham," calls Judy from the stairs. "Happy to see he's made a friend. Beautiful morning, isn't it?"

When finally Uncle Chuck arrives, he joins me for breakfast on the terrace, asking, "So, what are the plans for the day?"

I have no ham on my plate, so, tossing a scrap of salmon to my feline buddy, I ruminate aloud, "Well, our tour of Petra was abridged. One option, head back for a better look. With Mallorca so small, I guess a drive anywhere takes under an hour. What did you have in mind?"

I expect Uncle Chuck to accede with my notion of revisiting Petra. Almost always an agreeable travel companion, he willingly—or with my prodding—probes beyond the beaten path, sharing corollary interests in cuisine, antiquity and history. I guess this is why we travel together so well.

"I liked Petra," Uncle Chuck says. "Maybe there's another terrific restaurant, or we could pay another visit to bar Stop...."

Judy interrupts, "I apologize for eavesdropping, gents. There are actually two fine dining rooms in Petra. Another of our favorites you will find nearby, in Sineu—El Molí, in an old mill. You'd love it!"

We thank Judy for the suggestions and mention our roller-derby beds. She will have the casters removed or put rubber cups under them before day's end.

"I apologize," she begs, "but we've only just completed the restoration. Still working out the kinks."

We head for Petra, soaking up along the way bucolic panoramas. Our windshield frames a cornflower-blue sky, red poppy-dappled fields, carob groves, silvery olive trees, shiny-green citrus. On approach to charming Petra, we perceive its characteristic campaniles, one rising at San Pere, the other, distinctly Islamic, from Sant Bernardi.

We tour again the Serra Museum, biding our time, making photo studies. I want another survey of Serra's birthplace, but the door won't budge. We borrow a key from the museum's caretaker, an elderly woman, who greets us warmly. We let ourselves into the Serra homestead for a private tour.

According to our hostess in Binissalem, one of Petra's stellar restaurants occupies an old bodega called Es Celler. In this small village, we easily find it and descend a flight of stone steps to its cool depths. The vaulted space with wine-barrel décor clatters with the buzz of *Mallorquín,* and wafts fragrant of wood-fired wonders. Settled at a rustic table of wine-stained, brown planks, we order a bottle of *vino de mesa Fray* Junípero (*tinto*) as we peruse the menu.

"All looks tempting," Uncle Chuck remarks, "but I favor the *lechón* (suckling pig). You?"

I choose grilled quails. Each of our delicious entrées comes with fried potatoes and salad. We purchase bottles of *Fray* Junípero wine to carry back to America, deciding to uncork them for the occasion of Serra's canonization.

Following our fine lunch, we will drive to the nearby shrine of Bon-Any, favored by Serra. He preached a sermon there on Easter Tuesday, 1749, then bade his fellow *Petrenses vaya con Dios* for the last time. Shortly thereafter, he sailed for the Americas. He was thirty-five years old.

Non recedat memoria ejus.
The memory of him shall not depart.

—Solomon

From Petra, we see the church of Nostra Senyora de Bon-Any cresting a hill. Though a stone's throw away, to reach the summit requires treacherous hairpin turns, up steep lanes, wending 506 feet above Serra's hometown. We pass a *Vía Crucis* (fourteen positions, each with a station of the Way of the Cross).

In *Mallorquín, bon any* means good year. In 1607, after two years of drought, when processions of rogation failed, townspeople invoked the divine will of the Holy Mother—their Protectress of Fields and Harvest—for rain. Rain it did. When crops prospered, peasant-farmer *Petrenses* put up a barrel-vaulted shrine above Petra in 1609 to honor their Lady.

Donau-nos bon any, O Lady, for key to the good year art thou.
—"Prayer to Our Lady of Bon-Any"

The prototypical, twin-towered church was replaced in the early-twentieth century, yet many of its details are original, including sections of a rose window and a spellbinding, sixteenth-century polychrome Lady and Child in a shrine behind the main altar.

From the top of the hill, we gaze to the distant village of Petra and beyond. They say that, on a clear day, three-quarters of Mallorca are visible from this point. Lingering here, just the two of us in this peaceful hermitage, we pray for loved ones living, as well as others at home with God, lighting candles in their memory.

As we head north toward Binissalem, we decide to explore, so purposely overshoot the exit to our home base. We wind up in Santa Margalida for a rest and *horchatas* (cold, almond-flavored soft beverages) at a bar. There isn't much to see in this tiny burgh called *Hero* by Romans and *Abenmaaxbar* by Berbers, save a fine church styled in fashion akin to one that looms above the plaza near our inn.

Heading toward Scott's, I insist on stopping to record a promising scene. Even Uncle Chuck deems this one worthy: a field ablaze with crimson poppies, a stark white goatherd grazing upon them. We rest here, listening to jangling bells at the throats of goats, as we inhale bracing ocean air that drifts to this inland sample of heaven on Earth.

"Now what?" asks Uncle Chuck as I clamor again to pull over.

"Look," I say, pointing out a farmer who leads a mule-drawn cart of green hay.

We stop again for vistas of antique grain towers, plus windmills driven by lacy, wooden fans in the shapes of enormous spiders' webs. Afield spread pastures of downy sheep, vine-clad slopes and measureless panoramas of the Mediterranean on the distant horizon—a photographer's paradise.

Back at Scott's, we relax on the patio with *cervezas*. Judy emerges from a corridor, asking about our agenda this evening, and makes a recommendation.

"Restaurante Robines, just across the street. Nothing fancy, mind you. The waitress is rude, so don't say I didn't warn you. But the food is rustic and consistently good."

Only the waitress lives up to our hostess's description. The food tastes good, yet far from superlative. Finally gaining the brat's attention, Uncle Chuck orders lamb chops. I exult in the prospect of *sepia*, until the coarse waitress blurts, "No!"

Are they out of it? Or does she not want me to have any?

I order *sopa mallorquína*. Not available, either. Taking a deep breath, I point at my menu, to an item unfamiliar, but it is available: a respectable version of dry soup of sausage, black olives, prawns and rice. Arranged upon the rice, mussel shells heaped with seafood au gratin. Our capper: *vino* Macabeo.

"What a pair of night owls," Uncle Chuck jokes as we arrive back at our soothing quarters by half-past nine.

Our soiled clothing has been laundered and folded. Moreover, rubber cups moor our beds, so no carnival rides this evening.

COASTAL KITSCH

Again, we were induced by the German incursion of Mallorca—our noble lair in the obscure village of Binissalem having been invaded in the still of the night. Near midnight, a resounding Teutonic humdrum issued from beneath our windows. Two women and two men engaged in a late-night soirée on the patio, the monotone jabber broken only by occasional outbursts of shrill laughter from one of the Frauen.

Given the interruption in sleep, we lingered in our comfy beds until eight o'clock, when a vociferous cat fight roused us. I considered the shrieks were more of the strident guffaws we'd heard in the night. We also sensed the rumble of trucks.

Scott's bestows a splendid country house. We ramble throughout, puttering in the courtyard after breakfast, admiring flowers unraveling petals of yellow and purple in the sunbeams. Old stone walls pulsate in golden hues. Pretty, butter-yellow shutters lend monochromatic distinction to this natural palette.

Limestone touches bestow high and low. Here, a fine balustrade hems a bridge-terrace off the breakfast room; there, cleft walls rise from the patio's periphery. Ancient urns and finials grace the surrounds. Beyond a sweeping, semi-circular arch deploying the bridge, we locate the inn's Roman-style bathhouse with pool and spa.

Upstairs, we walk through sumptuous parlors where guests are welcome to read or socialize—genteel chambers stretching beneath coffered ceilings, tastefully outfitted with antiques, overstuffed sofas and chairs, potted palms. Black-and-white, checkerboard marble floors border fine Oriental rugs. Paintings and mirrors in gilded frames bedeck pastel walls.

I sense Uncle Chuck's inclination to linger, to recharge in this captivating environment, yet I encourage him to press on.

Just outside, we find the source of raucous trucks we heard from our beds. The square fills with vendors arranging produce and wares for the weekly market.

Crossing the street, we hear a racket at the back of an open van. A stodgy fellow unloads wooden cages of chickens, rankled cargo complaining as though aware of their imminent demise. We cross through the leafy square in shadows of the pocked stone Church of the Assumption. We peruse picture-perfect arrangements of teal-blue Swiss chard, burgundy beets, green-and-white leeks, ivory garlic and mushrooms, and tan almonds. Farmers arrange sun-dappled brown eggs and pink sausages, squashes, turnips, barrels of oily olives in red, green and purple. Other vendors unload buckets of multicolored flowers, an array of gaudy trinkets and leather crafts. Locals haggle with vendors as children tear through the plaza, screaming-falling-tripping-scraping their knees.

In front of the fine old church stand life-sized sandstone statues of a peasant couple, she wearing a Mallorcan headdress and holding a basket of grapes and he, pummeling must in a carved stone *lagar* (wine press).

Before noon, we head out in our car for the northeast coast.

"Let's see what the *bahías* propose," I suggest, running my finger across the map in my lap. "We'll stay on this highway all the way to Alcúdia."

Ahead, we glimpse a sapphire-blue sea and signposts for the town named *al-Kudia* ("Town on a Hill") by Muslim settlers. Stone fortifications and arched gates glow tawny in the sunlight, presenting an inviting arena for exploration.

"This book mentions a Roman theater, a museum," I inform Uncle Chuck, but he is bent on seeing the coast. We steam on.

We arrive at the brink of a cove, Bahía de Alcúdia, a breakwater of massive concrete blocks enfolding an elliptical bay. Brightly painted fishing boats sway along the coastline, sunlight capers upon the water. A continuum of periwinkle-tinged mountains spreads beyond. At the *puerto*, we linger for photographs, then climb to a higher point where we spot a commanding shoal known as Isla de Aucanada, a postage-stamp isle verdant and uninhabited except, perhaps, by a keeper of a lonely lighthouse. Behind us, lavish pieds-a-terre, villas and an imposing country club cascade along gentle slopes.

We ply back to gain our bearings, continuing south through a marshy preserve called Albufera. Rolling through coastal Can Picafort jars us back to the present. We grouse about the modern mishmash of high-rises, fast-food restaurants, tawdry amusement parks and legions of plump, sunburned Germans lumbering along the beaches. No *duende* here....

"Let's get out of here," I insist. "This cove reminds me of Dr. Font's peeve."

Tooling south toward the geographical center of Mallorca, Sineu (called

Sinium by Romans), we pursue another dining emporium recommended by Judy Scott. From Sineu's outskirts, we spot its signature mill sporting enormous wooden blades, Restaurante Molí d'en Pau.

When we reach the lobby, heavenly aromas seduce us. The popular *comedor* hums with conversation as we're ushered through the packed room to a corner to decipher menus.

We choose a regional, sleek white wine, Palacio de Arganza 1994. Uncle Chuck orders pork tenderloins with French-fried potatoes and green salad. Feeling more adventurous, I select lettuce hearts laden with tomatoes and anchovies, together with delicious *bacalao* baked with *pimientos*.

"Later we'll have ice cream," I suggest to Uncle Chuck, when the waitress mentions dessert.

With an imposing temple dominating a main square, Sineu characterizes Mallorcan towns. The Church of Mare de Déu dels Ángels from 1248 undergoes major restoration. Clouds of plaster-white dust permeate the cavernous space as construction workers blast away at the stonework.

Parking spots are scarce in this diminutive village. We retain our coveted space near the church and hike Sineu's lanes in pursuit of dessert. With our cones, we pace through the labyrinth of narrow pedestrian ways. Suddenly, three neatly dressed schoolboys scoot up to us, one of them urging, *"¡Senyores! ¿Fotos, por favor?"*

The *muchachos* noticed my camera bags and imagined their faces will land on the page of a magazine. I pose them in a postern, finding their ethnic makeup intriguing. One of them looks as Spanish as it gets; another exotically Moorish, while the third—a freckled redhead—appears distinctly Frankish. After I bracket a series of frames, the bright-faced *niños* scoop up books and backpacks, then scramble up an alley, high-fiving and yelling, *"¡Celebridades!"*

"I do favor these interior villages," Uncle Chuck remarks as we return to our car. "The coasts are ruined with all the glitz."

Rolling toward Binissalem, we pass a length of runners, the first one bearing a flaming torch. Sun favors the landscape, mellowing flocks of grazing sheep, groves of nut trees and more of the rustic windmills. Between the kilometers, coloration of stone varies from ocherous to rosy-beige.

When we arrive back at Scott's, Judy invites us to join her family for a light supper.

After restorative naps, we make for the pool. I swim laps while Uncle

Chuck soaks in the spa. Feeling on top of the world, we dress for dinner. George introduces us to Rachel and Jon, a couple from Germany. *Oh, terrific....* But it happens Rachel is Croatian and Jon, Swedish. The six of us enjoy the balmy evening terrace-side.

The Scotts lead us to the dining room where we enjoy cool, smooth gazpacho, nova lox with all the trimmings and a bottle of *vino* Moll *blanco*. The Scotts' children join us: Ben and his attractive sister Chessie, a year older than Ben. Over dessert of vanilla flan, our discussions of international affairs and travel agendas persevere for an hour. George uncorks more wine.

With plans to leave early tomorrow for Santa Eulalia, Uncle Chuck and I excuse to our room for packing.

A NOBLEMAN'S SUMPTUOUS GRANGE

In modern times, only the wealthy could maintain centuries-old seigniorial mansions, palatial farmhouses, even the smaller villas of Mallorca—a scattering of which were transformed into museums or hotels, as was Scott's, a large family home with rooms to let for the bed-and-breakfast trade.

Scott's, emblematic of Mallorcan town houses, snuggles between others of similar size and conformation, constructed of golden stone with at least two stories, each sporting a central courtyard.

In the countryside, old farmhouses once the quarters of wealthy land barons wended toward commercially run inns—edifices, too, constructed of stone, engulfed by acres of fragrant citrus groves and vineyards, almond and olive orchards. Soulful dwellings, steeped in shadows of history and earthy patina, comfortable, accoutered with a juxtaposition of all things old and new.

We enjoyed our brief stay at the Scotts' town house. Next, we would sample pleasures of an ancient farmhouse.

Alonso, exceptionally dapper in gray tiger stripes, lurks intrepidly. From the terrace, I scramble up to the room to grab my camera, hoping to make a portrait of my feline *amigo*.

"Here you go," says Ben, smiling behind wired teeth, a piece of ham dangling between his fingertips.

I place the bait on the balustrade and no sooner step away than Alonso vaults up alongside the ham. I manage only two shots as he devours. When the last bit disappears down his gullet, he leaps to a rooftop to intimidate birds.

"Shall we make tracks, then?" Uncle Chuck urges.

He doesn't care for cats, preferring dogs. I love them all.

George and Ben, lugging bags, escort us to our car. George apologizes on behalf of Judy, who left for Palma to "fuss with a porcelain basin that had not met with her approval," George explains. "Do come back and stay with us again," he invites, as we bid adieu.

We drive via Santa Margalida to an area known as Santa Eulalia, not a town at all, by appearances, anyway. For miles, land stretches flat through agricultural fields dotted with rustic farms and creaky windmills. To pass by the discreet signage of our hotel would be easy, as buildings sit back from the road at the end of a lengthy track.

As Scott's, Hotel Casal Rural Santa Eulalia is also a seigniorial mansion, but larger, and on a *finca*. According to descriptions in a brochure, this estate's initial document dates back to 1242, with additions made through the sixteenth century, and of late, refurbished as a fine hotel. A line of marquises owned the mansion's agricultural holdings in earlier times.

The butterscotch-toned palace dazzles in well-proportioned lines growing from a sandstone promontory. Ubiquitously, fiery bougainvillea clings to rough yellow walls, and Spanish lavender scents the warm air.

"Stunning ranch house," Uncle Chuck remarks as we step from the car.

Electric-blue sky deliciously sets off yellow stone and dusky-green olive trees. From this rise where the mansion perches, we survey sweeping, cultivated land. The Mediterranean shimmers on the remote horizon of the eastern shore.

We pass under a carriage arch into a courtyard graced with potted flowers, a lone olive tree and vintage sundial. Checked in at the stony lobby, a beautiful *fashionista* says our luggage will arrive presently in room fifteen.

Tucked away in this pristinely restored *casal*, number fifteen boasts large spaces: foyer, bedchamber, lavish sitting room, enormous bath with hydrotherapy spa and separate shower. Reproduction-antique furnishings, fine rugs and wall hangings enhance our quarters. A private walled terrace, accessible from the sitting room through French doors, extends our commodious space outdoors, admitting pastoral scenery eclipsed by immeasurable mountain views.

After unpacking toiletries and placing sport coats and trousers on hangers, I gather up cameras and tripod.

"But we've just arrived," Uncle Chuck complains. "Can we please put our feet up and enjoy this gorgeous inn?"

"There's time for that later," I say. "I just read of Pollença this morning, a village, not far away."

"One of these years you should make a holiday in the Caribbean, on one of the smaller islands where you unwind on the beach, with little else to tempt you."

"I'm unwound," I tell him, "and ready to explore."

We head toward the northern coast via Sa Pobla to Pollença, a settlement named *Pollentia* by the Romans. We course through town in pursuit of an intact Roman bridge, Pont Román. At last glimpsing the squat span beyond the hubbub of the village, we pull over. I photograph from all possible angles this aged stone, double-arched and buttressed viaduct stretched across a parched riverbed. Mopeds and miniature European cars scarcely squeeze through its breadth intended for equestrian traffic.

Uncle Chuck is famished. We hike to the middle of town. With myriad dining gambits, we drift in quandary.

"¿Senyor, por favor?" I inquire of a pint-sized, middle-aged man on the street. *"¿Donde hay un buen restaurante?"*

The well-proportioned wee fellow needs a shave. He smiles, introduces himself as Miquel and gestures for us to follow. Behind him, we trudge up streets, down alleys to a smart-looking establishment called La Fonda, a bustling, alluringly fragrant *comedor*. Miquel approaches the host, who frowns at his book, then glances around the room, and shrugs. The restaurant is fully booked, with no one ready to leave.

"Come," says Miquel with a genial smile and gesture of hand. "I take you to another good restaurant."

Again, we wind up and down streets, landing this time at swank Restaurante Clivia. Now we are ravenous, and relieved when the host obliges. Ushered to a stylish, skylit room, we're surprised Miquel has not joined us. I return to the front of the restaurant and see Miquel sitting at the bar. He thanks me for the offer of lunch, but explains that he has had his. He will settle for a whiskey, *gracias*.

The Mallorcan demeanor reminds me of the Portuguese. Unlike bolder, mainland Spaniards, these people are generally more reserved, even shy. *What must they think of brash Americans and German intruders?*

As we peruse menus in a stately room accented with potted palms and orchids, Miquel shows himself in the doorway.

"Beber a la salud; gracias, amigos," he toasts, lifting his snifter in our direction, then turns back to the bar.

Settled in, we order martinis. With our drinks come *bocadillos*: one sausage slice apiece.

Skeptical of proportions to follow, Uncle Chuck mentions under his breath, "This must be one of those overly fussy French places."

But we delight with bowls of hot, creamy soup. The chef used a generous hand of potatoes, leeks and asparagus. Salads arrive artistically plotted with avocado and prawns. To round out our luncheon, we sip freshly brewed coffee. Uncle Chuck enjoys a baked apple, and I, a lemon-pistachio sundae.

We walk to Museo Municipal (a former monastery), closed today, but we enjoy its pretty cloister. We head toward the *ajuntament* where our city map denotes the proximate 365 steps to sixteenth-century El Calvari (Calvary chapel). We ascend the steep, cypress-framed flight, stopping on landings to catch our breath, admiring a tumble of rustic *casas* along the way. Reaching the top, we ponder the inconsequential, gray-and-beige façade of a chapel and miniature *campanario*. We step into a cool, barrel-vaulted interior for prayers and relaxation. Outside again, we marvel at boundless views before making a dizzying descent back to the village.

"To the *casal* for siestas?" Uncle Chuck asks enthusiastically, now that we at last locate our car. We trekked our feet off in search of it.

I have one more tour in mind, a seventeenth-century monastery in the northern mountains. True to his simpatico demeanor, my travel mate complies and we head off through the foothills to Serra de Tramuntana.

Uncle Chuck agrees the detour was time well spent. Richly textured with snaggle-toothed peaks of ashen gray and unspoiled valleys, this scenery ranks among the best we have viewed. Mounting arduous switchbacks, we discover dry-stone walls, corrals for herds of black-and-white sheep. Above, teal pine forests inspire against flawlessly blue sky.

Refurbished as overnight accommodations, the one hundred cells of Monestir de Nostra Senyora de Lluch attend chiefly Mallorcans who flock to this site in droves, making pilgrimages, paying homage to a precious icon of Our Lady. In the thirteenth century, an Arabic shepherd boy named Lluch, whose family converted to Christianity, found a statue of the Virgin. The boy gave it to a church, but pirates stole it. Amazingly, bad weather deterred the scoundrels, and the statue found its permanent home at this monastery named for the boy who rescued it.

At this lofty, remote hermitage, thin air stifles, though pilgrims approach in force and European youths camp upon surrounding fields.

We saunter leisurely through gardens, under leafy canopies, noting an eye-level *Paso de la Cruz* (Way of the Cross) upon slender steles. Pausing for snapshots, we relax to the music of sparkling fountains. Trails of humankind file toward the compound's center. We queue up, trailing pilgrims, to a baroque church. In it, we discover what the fuss is all about—the statuette rescued by the shepherd boy—a precious image called *La Moreneta* ("The Dark One"). This haunting icon, a standing Virgin, holds the Christ child in her left arm, rather than seated with Him in her lap, as other examples we have seen.

> But from each hollow of Spain
> Spain comes forth.
>
> —Pablo Neruda

Hiking back in direction of the car park, we regard a weather-beaten stone convent and a stable with intact mangers. A museum tempts, but Uncle Chuck is pooped. We head back toward Santa Eulalia.

After siestas, we dress for dinner down below in the original wine cellar, now the hotel's exceptionally fine restaurant.

Gentle glow from frosted sconces caresses limestone and brick vaulting with golden luminescence. Fresh flowers and soft candlelight grace tables, and an army of black-and-white-clad waitstaff stands at attention.

We embark upon a paramount dining experience with complimentary *frits,* tiny ramekins of vegetables blended with onion and kidney. We proceed with creamy vegetable soup floated with chopped, al-dente haricots. With a bottle of local Chardonnay, Uncle Chuck relishes *pato a naranja* (duck *à l'orange*). I enjoy delectable rack of lamb. We relish on the side, deftly plotted dabs of spinach, cauliflower florets and a mushroom the size of a skullcap.

The uneasy staff proposes much of their attention on an aristocratic-looking couple and their entourage. When we mention the celebrities to our *mozo,* he quietly informs that the two holding court own this *casal.* They're in from Palma for the weekend.

"*¿Postres?*" our waiter queries as his busboy clears and de-crumbs our table.

Desserts seduce us. We choose two for sharing: "cheese pudding," as described on the English side of the menu, "dry flan with texture of cheesecake," and a heavenly tart of sliced pears crusted with almonds, served warm under vanilla ice cream.

Following our superb repast, we pad outside. Alcúdia twinkles on the distant horizon. Meadow-side, we listen to bleating sheep, the lowing of cattle, as a whisper of salty air blissfully cools.

While we were away from our room, staff turned down beds, leaving behind chocolates and a basket of fruit. I set the French doors ajar before slipping between linen sheets of my cushy bed, in an elegant farmhouse-hideaway on a magical isle.

Mallorcan Culture, from *Talayotic* Iberians to Neoteric Hoteliers

Spain grew impossibly rich not only from cultural influences of France to North Africa and India to Persia, but from cultures long vanished. Modern inquisitors were grateful for durable building materials used by prehistoric tribes—tangible records of history, legacies in stone. Nigh this flotsam, we sensed ancient ethos.

Gentle breezes seep through gauzy draperies and a rooster's loquacious yodeling fills my ears as I awake fully refreshed at seven o'clock. I don robe and slippers, step onto the veranda, squinting in the growing light and espy beyond the promontory, a hay-stuffed stone shell of a barn girdled with yellow wildflowers. On tiptoes, a copper-and-black cockerel cranes his neck, crowing vociferously. His harem clucks and bobbles through weeds, pecking the ground. Sheep's bells tinkle stridently from afar, and upon the moist air drifts the fragrance of nutty-sweet almond blossoms.

"Better get a move-on if we're going to do the measure of touring you've suggested for the day," Uncle Chuck calls out.

At eight o'clock, we arrive in the hotel's cellar for a proper breakfast.

Ah, another day of exploration. We pass southward, through wild Albufera and dreadful Can Picafort, then continue to the old Islamic settlement of Artà, a village dating back to the Bronze Age. As were its neighboring towns, Artà was invaded by cultures including Phoenicians, Romans, Berbers and Aragonéses. We make out thirteenth-century fortress battlements cresting this town's highest elevation and approach the fortified site, plying up narrow lanes between ochre-and-cinnabar-washed abodes graced with stately palms and splattering fountains.

Up top, we pick our way through a semi-restored fort. Pyramidal finials cap each of multiple crenellations, an ominous spectacle. On foot, we inch higher, mounting a confined flight of steps to a precarious banquette. Uncle Chuck views the village from our dizzying course. I am on tenterhooks, my forehead beading with perspiration, mouth dry and trembling hands cold and clammy. Uncle Chuck pokes fun at my vertigo condition as I slowly inch sideways, clinging precariously to a wall.

Uncle Chuck waits patiently as I slowly descend steps from the ramparts on my butt. We move on to the town's two historically significant churches. One of them, Santuari de Sant Salvador d'Artà, looks unduly restored, a church clinging to a slope, overlooking parts of the city we had not viewed from the ramparts above. Splendorous panoramas stretch from mountains in the west to the sea in the north and east.

Inside the church, behind the high altar, we assess a primitive rendition of a long-faced Virgin and Child. As it is *Día de las Madres* (Mother's Day), we light candles to honor the Holy Mother, as well as our own.

We exit cool comfort to torrid outdoors, then descend a lengthy flight toward thirteenth-century Iglesia de Transfiguracío del Senyor that breaches the site of an Arabic fortress. This golden-brown Gothic church boasts a rose window engagingly framed with swaying pine branches. Through pointed arches in the church's upper story, pigeons flutter through darkness.

Around the next corner, we settle in at a bakery-café for iced coffee and melodramatically delicious *ensaimadas* (sugar-dusted buns). On a wall hangs a plaque in relief of Sant Marçal (Saint Martial), patron of bakers. We've noted his image in other bakeries on Mallorca and as well in mainland Spain. These plaques are many times sculpted in bread. Though, I believe Elizabeth of Hungary, Michael the Archangel, even Peter the Apostle, looked after bakers.

Why did bakers chose Saint Martial as their protector? The account of the obscure saint is, after all, sketchy. I have heard the tale that Martial hailed from Palestine and the Church celebrates his feast on 30 June. Two Epistles in the Bibliotheca Patrorum are attributed to him; and, as Martial preached Christian tenets in the Province of Limoges, does the French connection associate him with culinary matters? Could it be the assertion Marital raised a man from the dead is a metaphor for rising bread? Hagiography cites another Saint Martial, from Zaragoza. Even less is known of him, apart from his persecution-martyrdom in A.D. 304. I mention to Uncle Chuck the other Martial's correlation to bakers.

"These things stem from conjecture," he guesses, changing the subject in his typically Anglican mien. "And so, what's next in the program?"

"Ruins of a megalithic settlement," I say, reaching for my map, "just south of here." I pray this will not bore Uncle Chuck rigid, as do my comments on hagiography.

> ...thou hast delivered a thousand sentences condensed in the compass of a few words....
> —Miguel de Cervantes, *Hidalgo Don Quixote de La Mancha*

Driving to the edge of Artà, to rusty tracks of a former railway mentioned in my book, bustle gives way to farmland. We discern, at the edge of a field, a massive wall of a Stone Age village, Ses Païsses. An old man in a booth sells us tickets for one hundred pesetas (US$1.20) each, and we walk across pine-needle-and-rock-strewn lanes to one of Mallorca's versions of Stonehenge.

A STONY LEGACY OF MALLORCA'S ANCIENT SETTLEMENTS

An Iberian *Talayotic* band, members of a race noted for dexterity with the slingshot, settled Ses Païsses in Mallorca around B.C. 1300. The prehistoric tribe erected great stone piers and beehive-shaped huts (*talaiots*) fashioned from local gray stone. In a roundabout way, *Talayots* were responsible for the name Baleares (Balearic Islands). Early Greek settlers on Mallorca called slingshots *ballos*. Subsequently, Roman invaders named the island *Balear Maior;* hence, "the archipelago's largest island, occupied by a tribe that used slingshots." After Greeks and Romans, Muslim corsairs named this region *Artà.*

We pass under a primal dolmen (stone entablature), gazing from our elevated path, to crude underpinnings of a Neolithic village. Warm winds whistle hauntingly through the pines, along massive boulders that once shaped an archaic community of dwellings, cisterns, towers and shrines.

Throughout the ages following the extinction of Artà's precursory culture, local farmers pilfered pieces from the prehistoric quarry. As we tromp around the ruins, we look beyond, to rugged gray stones in corrals and barns lying outside this preserve.

> Who made you? What is your name? What strong hand lifted your rocks? Was it the ancient giants of the dead race that left you as an eternal memorial?
> —Miquel Costa i Llobera, *"A un claper"*

We head eastward to a hill town not far from the coast, founded in A.D. 1300 by Jaume II: Capdepera, home of Mallorca's largest fortress. The challenge is not in locating Capdepera's medieval stronghold, but in securing a parking space in this tourist-packed village. We wind through streets for fifteen minutes until, at last, a small truck pulls out of its tight space at a hillside curb. Uncle Chuck wangles into the spot, turns the wheels hard and ratchets up the emergency brake. Uncle Chuck is a terrific driver, precisely why I put up with him....

The grounds of fourteenth-century Castell de Capdepera swelter as we hike the steep grade. At midpoint, views steal our breath. We look down to a jumble of buildings, out to the horizon, to an edge of glinting sea. From here, Capdepera's highest point, we see churches of Sant Bartomeu and Nostra Senyora de la Esperança.

Stepping through an archway, we behold the guts of a gargantuan fort with square and round towers guarding this hillside. Slung across a stone corbel lies a handsome tiger tabby, a dead-ringer for my *amigo* Alonso in Binissalem. Bathing under sunshine, this cat pays no mind to countless visitors passing by. Above loom battlements festooned with crenellations unlike the spear-shaped motifs at Artà; Capdepera's are purely rectangular, strictly utilitarian.

From the steamy grounds, snapdragons and geraniums swoon in sunburned pinks and fuchsia. We gawk up, into a cylindrical *talaia* (watchtower) known as Torre de Miquel Nunis. A cochlear staircase, designed after a nautilus shell, snakes against interior walls.

We relax in depressant refuge inside the fort's pint-sized *capella*. This chapel embraces a fine painting of *Our Lady of Hope* (patron saint of Capdepera) and a convoluted Gothic cross of orangewood. Resting on pews in serene coolness, we read of this site's occupation over the centuries by Roman, Islamic and Christian conquerors.

When we return to our car, it's still blocked. Uncle Chuck folds back our driver's-side mirror and the closest culprit's passenger mirror. With skillful finesse, he manages to inch out unscathed.

"Your driver deserves a siesta," Uncle Chuck exhales, "but this doesn't come cheap!"

Back in our room at Santa Eulalia, I grab a *cerveza* from the mini-bar and head for a shady end of the terrace. Cool afternoon breezes fan me as I catch peek-a-boo glimpses of the hazy Mediterranean. I have just nodded off in my easeful canvas chair when Uncle Chuck wakes me. We order more beer. He wants to navigate the grounds.

We follow a path through newly mowed lawns, to a stout rise of stone steps terminating at a dazzling turquoise lap pool. Encompassing fields evidently run rich with sandstone, for sandstone monoliths upsurge from shimmering water. Beyond the flagged deck, another flight of steps extends to a palm-fringed, Olympic-sized pool and a spa.

"Can I make a case to spend more time here?" pleads Uncle Chuck. "Besides these inviting pools, there's a gym and sauna opposite the restaurant. Have you noticed?"

It's late afternoon, hours until the dining room opens. We take advantage of the interval, cycling and treadmilling in the gym.

"I'm hungry," I tell Uncle Chuck at six o'clock.

"Shall we head into Santa Margalida?" he suggests.

Shortly, we land at a square in the tranquil town of Santa Margalida. Just steps from the plaza, a bar beckons. We pass through a beaded doorway. The proprietors, a lovable working-class couple in their late fifties, greet us as regulars. Scribbling on the chalkboard behind the bar indicates only *tapas* available this evening. We order a ration of *tumbet*: traditional Mallorcan stew of potatoes, tomatoes and peppers. The *senyora* graciously offers heartier fare, but we will have to settle for potluck.

Between bites of *tumbet*, we nurse a bottle of Reserva Cosecha 1991. We're elated when, after twenty leisurely minutes, our charming hostess surrenders sizzling plates of *berenjenas rellenas*: eggplant halves brimming with pork and tomatoes, a vivid regional dish, and the best potluck imaginable. We dig into this homespun fare with abandon, understanding little that blares from a television behind the bar. Nevertheless, money speaks an international vernacular. Coffers of the local lottery are at an all-time high and since we hit the jackpot with dinner, Uncle Chuck takes a gamble, purchasing ONCE (lottery) tickets.

The Spanish Lottery

The lottery is an even bigger deal in Spain than in the rest of Europe or in America. In Spain, lottery kiosks stand at street corners of metropolitan areas. Vendors sell tickets on the streets, at times walking into restaurants and public squares to hawk chances. And bettors can buy tickets in bars, cafés or other places of business.

Spanish lottery tickets, resembling small bank notes, include the daily ONCE—pronounced *ohnsay*: Organización Nacional de Ciegos de España—and twice weekly Lotería Primitiva. Four times weekly, officials draw Bonoloto. Lotería Nacional runs prize-draws almost every Saturday. Special lotteries called Extraordinarios, largest of which is El Gordo (the Fat One), are drawn annually near Christmastime (usually on 22 December). Spanish lotteries reach the equivalent of five million dollars, even more. Bettors also take chances on *décimo* (one-tenth of a number).

Back at the hotel, I watch twilight cycle to violet. In a blink, it blushes to fiery russet and ebbs with a flash beneath the horizon.

From our quarters, I phone America to wish my mother *feliz día de las Madres* before retiring at midnight. In trunks and bathrobe, Uncle Chuck heads through star-studded darkness to the spa.

¡BEN DINAT!
(I HAVE DINED WELL!)

The aspect of fine dining always proposed one of the highlights of my travels; serious food served by professionals, in a pampering environment. In America, the art of cuisine and the experience of dining are not as revered as they are in Europe, so the best of regional food must figure into my sojourns abroad. How delightful that we took one of our transcendent culinary experiences in Mallorca at the humble hometown of Fray Junípero Serra.

Our cockerel neighbor crows mightily.

"What time do those chickens get up?" I groan from under my pillow.

"He's been at it for hours," Uncle Chuck answers.

No wonder, at a quarter past nine. Showered, in trunks, we cut through dewy lawns to the smaller of two pools, a heated one.

In the breakfast cellar, Uncle Chuck takes a swig of coffee, then thinks aloud, "Not much more around here to see."

"Manacor," I hint, "Mallorca's second-largest city, though its population counts under twenty-five thousand. Manacor traces its origins to B.C. 123, at that time a Roman holding. Maybe we'll find ruins."

"You and your ruins."

Late morning, we travel southeast to discover the unimpressive city of Manacor. From the looks, little remains of a Roman possession once known as *Cunici*. For the most part, we see boxy tenements, infinite trucks, delivery vans and smokestacks spewing virulent fumes. We locate Majorica, Manacor's renowned pearl factory.

The interior looks smart with counters fitted and filled with Mallorcan cultured pearls in shades modulating between shimmering white to pink and luminescent gray to ebony. These authentic-looking pearls, manufactured from a mixture of powdered seashells compressed with fish scales, are radiant and weighty, though priced at a fraction of the genuine articles. We look through trays of single, double and triple strands, plus earrings, pendants, tie tacks, rings, brooches and bracelets, as we determine gifts for friends back home.

Back in the car, I reach for a guidebook to read about Manacor.

"None of this looks too inviting," Uncle Chuck grouses. "Let's head out."

"Visit Petra again?"

"Try that other restaurant recommended by Judy Scott? Dr. Font said it was excellent, as well."

Driving northwest, we enjoy views of Petra from a fresh approach. Trundling up the hill, we see only one sign of life gracing the otherwise deserted scenery: an *anciana* (elderly woman) clad in black, hobbling on a cane through a shadowy alley.

"The others are in the fields, no doubt," I tell Uncle Chuck.

"Or on siesta," he adds.

Near the Serra Museum, we browse a pedestrian way, walls gleaming with majolica-style tiles: portrayals of Indian converts with *Fray* Junípero at each of his nine California missions. We discover also a tile display of the five missions under his administration in Mexico's Sierra Gorda.

In the center of town, a statue of Junípero Serra dominates the main square. Dr. Font had only pointed this out to us, from a distance; now, we have a more intimate look. Guillermo Galmés Socías sculpted this gray stone into a compelling apostle. Dedicated in 1913, the memorial commemorates the bicentennial of Serra's birth. From his elevated position on a pedestal, Junípero stands vigilant, viewing the church of his baptism and the convent he attended as a youth.

Nearby, we see Sa Plaça, a restaurant-hotel on a square by the same name, a crusty old *casa*, home to the Dams, a husband-and-wife team. On the upper story, the Dams let out three rooms as accommodations. The main level supplies a quaintly civilized *comedor*.

Senyora Dam, a petite woman in her mid-forties, greets us demurely.

Smart in silk blouse, tailored skirt and needle-nose pumps, she escorts us through a maze of finely dressed tables. We step outside to a palm-shaded courtyard bursting with yellow and red cabbage roses, cooled by a gently splashing fountain. Asked if we may drink here while perusing menus, the *senyora* nods politely, then quickly retreats. She returns with her husband.

"Gentlemen, welcome to Petra," *Senyor* Dam says. "What is your pleasure?"

The handsome, raven-haired man in white apron and red scarf speaks English with a brusque rasp. We speculate that he has undergone surgery for throat cancer. His manners and broad smile make us feel at home. He pours *cervezas* as his wife proffers menus. I drool.

"These selections," I say. "Judy Scott knows her restaurants."

The beer refreshes. So does the fountain dribbling melodically into a basin of orange fish. It's tempting to linger in this placid setting but our stomachs win the debate.

Senyora Dam leads us to a pleasant dining room of pale plaster walls, floors of terra cotta, and dark-beamed ceiling. Magenta swags divide chambers of neatly dressed tables, and antique fiddle-back chairs upholstered in brocade. A tall pendulum clock in a slim case graces a corner, suites of modern paintings and mirrors in gilded frames on the walls. A forest of stemware gleams upon tables and crystal chandeliers sparkle overhead.

The *senyora* brings with our wine complimentary duck pâté, olives, bread and rolls. *Senyor* Dam delivers superb courses that follow, the ritual unfolding at leisurely pace. We are his only customers.

Uncle Chuck begins with *ensalada mixta*, followed by a plate of succulent lamb chops punctuated with tiny potatoes and medallions of green and yellow squash.

I take the adventurous path with a demi-portion of Mallorcan stew brimming with cuttlefish, herbed meatballs, potatoes and peas—the ordinary made extraordinary, a luscious communion of flavorous textures enrobed in a cloak of spicy tomato sauce, served en casserole.

We refresh with intermezzo sorbet. For crescendo, I savor wood-oven-baked breast of guinea fowl served with char-grilled Mediterranean crayfish, a symphony of flavors. When the *senyor* arrives to pour more local Muscat wine, I toast, applaud and call him "maestro."

Though plied with *alta cocina*, we predict our French-trained chef likewise excels in finales. We agree to audit the *postres*. *¡Por Dios!* Enticing bonbons, picturesque pastries, chocolate Charlotte, golden-brown macaroons, moist and dry flan, fig mousse, fresh and glacé fruits.

We stammer and stare until our host-chef puts finger to temple, smiles with his eyes, then hustles to the kitchen. Back at our table, he presents a generous plate. We behold a chef d'œuvre of sweets with a dab of each of his superb pastries plus homemade coffee-almond ice cream. Upon and around tantalizing morsels, *Senyor* Dam tastefully piped *coulis* of kiwi and strawberry. Rock sugar crystals border the platter, a Disneyland arrangement of whimsical confections.

"Are we in heaven yet?" I ask.

"Speak for yourself, boy. I intend to enjoy many more meals as superb."

Oh, the travails of travelling with a senior....

By four o'clock, we have eaten all of the evidence. We arrived at one. Taking copies of their brochure for hopeful future reference, we thank our kind hosts for a grand luncheon.

"Can you imagine dining that way every day?" Uncle Chuck gasps as he climbs into the car.

Yes. Santa Eulalia for siestas.

Meanwhile, back at the rancho, the temperature drops. We pull on sweaters and drive to nearby Muro. The capering sun adds a peachy glow to the horizon, an enhancing backdrop for near-silhouettes of multiple windmills springing from rolling plains.

"Do you realize," I ask, "Mallorca has no rivers? All of the island's fresh water courses underground."

Uncle Chuck is unimpressed....

We pursue signposts through unpaved lanes to Muro, a Berber stronghold called *Algebelâ* in A.D. 840. Penetrating this tiny village through rugged stone gates, we note the imposing, amber-hued church of Sant Joan Baptista from the sixteenth century.

A swank restaurant stands on the square. Closed.... We meander up the street to a *tapas* bar. Those inside this brightly-lit emporium give us the once-over, then resume their hunched-over posture. Invasion has fructified Muro-Mallorcans. There is no mistaking Moorish roots. We order gin on the rocks and request the roster of *tapas*. "No *tapas* today," we are told.

"Bottoms up, boy," Uncle Chuck mutters. "Let's head back to Santa Eulalia. We don't need any more to eat."

Proceeding cautiously south along an unpaved track, we drive between dusky fields drained of color. We pass a shepherd, minding his flock of bleating sheep with a crookneck stick.

By half-past nine, we return to our enclave, our tummies still full—and the gin didn't hurt at all. Before retiring, we opt for a leisurely swim by starlight, wistfully imagining a prolonged sojourn on this enchanted isle.

TREASURED MEMORIES

The Mediterranean spread swarthy-gray, and dwindling Palma roused as we surveyed from above. Our antiquated jet shuddered as it broke a barrier of clouds. Then suddenly we gazed upon a counterpane of orange-neon glow. Within moments, sunlight blazed through my window.

The hour soon approaches for set-down at Madrid. Late afternoon, we'll board another flight, back to reality. I bear heady memories and an insatiable longing for Spain.

madrid otra vez

 1. Alcalá de Henares
2. Consuegra
3. Córdoba

Madrid *Otra Vez*

I craved another immersion into Spanish culture. Eleven months after our tour of Mallorca, Spain called me like the unquenchable reprise of a distant bell, torturing my soul with memories of her.

Time: late autumn, in the aftermath of 11 September 2001. Uncle Chuck succumbed to fear, but my Spanish attack transcended rumors of terrorism. I somehow managed to persuade Uncle Chuck to join me in another excursion to glorious España. While Americans quaked in their boots back home, we concentrated on a realm of Spain called by the Muslims al-Andalus (Andalucía).[1] Airlines had cut back the usual number of flights, so to land in Seville would have involved layovers.

Enamored of Madrid, we chose its tarmac, planning to spend two days recovering there, then driving south. Plotting the journey, I dreamed of Iberian scenery and architecture, moody skies and cante jondo. *In Andalucía, the essence of Muslim Spain, I knew we would delight in plenty of its deep song.*

"Good thing," says Uncle Chuck, sardonically, "we chose a direct route to Spain."

More than twenty-five hours elapsed between San Diego and Madrid. Our rigorous junket included a layover at JFK and a lengthy delay at London's Heathrow. Another ten minutes and Uncle Chuck would have bolted for the Cotswolds.

Our spirits lift as a taxi whisks us toward Spain's capital. But shortly, after passing through Puerta de Alcalá, Madrid's triumphal arch, traffic grinds to a stop. Our cabdriver lifts her hands from the steering wheel, shrugs and growls, "*¿Que pasa?*"—and a number of expletives, as well. Uncle Chuck finds disconcerting a woman cussing, particularly of this one's reverential age. Generally, Spanish women are more normally reserved than their

American counterparts, especially in the company of strangers. I suddenly regret not having learned Spanish profanities in addition to menu mastery.

For five minutes, we sit at a clogged intersection. Our driver breathes deeply, sputtering more words we really do not understand. Car horns resonate. All around us, collective diastolic pressure soars, dark eyes roll back, hands gesticulate. Meantime, we have plenty of time to savor the eighteenth-century Neo-Classical gate of Alcalá, a tribute to Carlos III in granite and limestone ashlars by Francisco Sabatini.

Honking subsides, our driver exhales and we glide along as though nothing happened, reverting to a more characteristic demeanor. Moments later we stop curbside at Hotel Palace where our husky driver lugs bags from the trunk, rebuffing my assistance.

A fellow in gray tails and stovepipe hat opens the cab's doors, greets us and assists our driver with luggage. Porters snatch up bags and trail behind, up a flight of marble steps. Doormen nod politely as they hold open heavy plate-glass portals.

We agreed to spoil ourselves on this trip, having dreamed of one day indulging in Hotel Palace's extravagance. The moment has arrived.

The aristocratic lobby of the 1912 Palace sparkles with glittering chandeliers. Brass gleams brightly and gargantuan floral bouquets impart a pleasant milieu. Faux classical door frames hem trompe l'œil scenes. And precision is a notion well mastered by uniformed staff.

No sooner do we enter our quarters than porters arrive with luggage. As they arrange it on racks, one of them explains the minutiae of our room's safe and mini-bar, then wishes us a pleasant stay.

Our accommodations are rich in pale to deep shades of green, burgundy and ivory, furnished with overstuffed chairs and sofa, and cherry-wood writing desk. Padded, damask wall coverings repeat in tufted headboards. An enormous bathroom sports butter-yellow, filled-travertine marble, heated towel racks and a bouquet of fresh roses.

Our room with a view renders apertures onto the traffic we escaped, replete with cacophony of car horns.

I need a shave and crave a shower, but cannot wait for a cigar and a drink. Stubbly and smelly, I leave Uncle Chuck to the luxuries of a bath.

In the lobby's mezzanine level, I pause to consider the splendors. La Rotonda unfolds as an opulent expanse beneath an enormous Art Nouveau stained-glass dome supported on classical columns. On our last visit, we enjoyed cocktails in this pleasant environment.

An army of businesspeople blabbers into cell phones, pacing about the area girdling the dining room, seeking their assigned conference halls. Other guests, ostensibly as jet-lagged as I, relax in overstuffed seating, savoring cocktails. Within eyeshot is a smartly appointed, dimly lit bar.

I collapse into a seat in the richly paneled room. Ah, back in Europe where *camparisoda* is one word and attentive service comports as an art. Sitting back, I puff my cheroot and sip my bittersweet aperitif, winding down, getting back into the rhythm of being an artist, feeling content with the milieu, in a country I adore.

A refreshed, dapper Uncle Chuck joins me. I desert him with his cocktail and make haste to shower off jet lag and to dress for the city. I prefer to linger, but quickly dry myself with a thick, beach-sized towel and don dress shirt and tie, trousers and blazer.

With utmost precision, doormen spring forth, obliging from corners unknown as we step into briskness of late afternoon. Traffic creeps through overburdened routes, sirens blare, indelible car horns complain. We jaunt toward Plaza Mayor, dodging determined strides of smartly dressed *Madrileños*. Admiring spinning tiers of confections through *pastelería* (bakery) windows, I catch our reflection. We are on the beat in Spain again and loving it. We carry on, sniffing out a place for dinner, stopping for menus posted outside restaurants.

Well aware of this culture's proclivity for dining late, we agree to drop into Restaurante El Rincón Esteban. They serve early.

El Rincón's door is ajar; a solitary light shines from the kitchen. When we pull back the foyer's olive-green velvet drapery, a cook spots us. Shortly, the jolly proprietor engages lights and greets us, flashing us his familiar smile.

"*Señores,* good to see you again."

We wonder if his treatment is a tad ingratiating.

A *mozo* steps up to our table. He is the same.

"*Señores,* welcome. You forget *el paraguas* (an umbrella). I chase you down the street with it. How have you been?"

They do remember; amazing!

"Isn't it refreshing," muses Uncle Chuck, "some things remain the same? Back home, we find so many restaurants plagued with clueless staff and exasperating lapses in service. American waitstaff hop from job to job. For them, service remains a lost notion."

As lost as my umbrella would have been....

Waitstaff are all eyes, no ears. Regaled as though we were visiting aristocracy, we lament on the sad state of affairs in Californian restaurants. Typically young American waiters tend to deem their jobs little more than gigs as they put themselves through college, or earn a stipend between careers. Here in Europe, waiting on tables exemplifies a profession adeptly mastered.

Following a well-tended dinner, we toast our arrival in a beloved city.

At half-past nine, locals arrive. We have seen only two other foreigners. No doubt, terrorist attacks on America impacted tourism.

We trudge through the frigid night to immerse ourselves in comforts of the Palace. We have been up for thirty-six hours.

[1] Andalucía: From the Arabic *al-Andalus*.

FROM ALCALÁ DE HENARES TO PARADISE
AND SISTERS WITH VOICES, NO FACES

Sleep came slowly, given effects of time zones crossed and clamorous streets below. Swapping fresh air for tranquillity, I put down the dual-paned windows before I retired, but opened them when acrid cigarette smoke seeped into our lair. I believed smoking was an aerobic exercise in Spain.

Into a clear cool day, we walked two blocks to Cafetería Oskar. Again, the same man squeezing oranges behind the bar, the mozo *with the friendly smile, locals mobbing the space, incessantly chattering between sips of coffee.*

Uncle Chuck and I looked forward to exploring beyond Madrid. Our curiosity would lead us to Alcalá de Henares, thirty minutes distant. With map in hand, we strolled down Calle Atocha toward Madrid's train station under a wintry sky of deep azure marbled in white.

At the bustling station, we locate the *taquilla* (ticket window) for the *cercanías* (metro train). We aim toward the platform, through a colorful bazaar. Musicians and magicians perform on the sidelines. Vendors' stalls brim with books, brightly hued textiles, electronic gadgets and toys. Trains depart every twenty minutes for Alcalá. There I hope to honor the saint associated with my hometown, San Diego.

San Didacus (Diego) de Alcalá de Henares, the Saint Who Slept with a Prince

Diego was born circa 1400 at San Nicolás del Puerto near Seville in the province of Andalucía. He lived as a hermit before joining the Order of Friars Minor at Arizafa near Córdoba. Diego served as a missionary in the Canary Islands, and was guardian of the Franciscan community on Fuerteventura from 1445-49. He journeyed to Rome in 1450, working there among the poor. In the Eternal City, Diego gained a reputation for miraculous cures.[1]

Diego spent his later years at Alcalá and died there on 12 November 1463. At Alcalá, he served in the university's infirmary, attending the sick, abetting the poor. Miracles of healing are attributed with Diego's intercession. We see his image often depicted with a crucifix and loaf of bread or bouquet of roses.

The most popular miracle associated with Diego transpired a century after his death, involving Don Carlos, son of Felipe II, King of Spain. Don Carlos tumbled down a stairway, rendering him unconscious. King Felipe rallied physicians who determined the diagnosis bleak. Fearing this son's imminent demise, Felipe charged local Franciscans to place the incorrupt cadaver of Diego in bed with the prince. Don Carlos awoke next morning, completely recovered, claiming that in sleep, he'd envisioned a friar in a Franciscan habit lying beside him. He and his father, the king, petitioned Rome to canonize Diego. Besides a second miracle, Vatican officials proved that Diego exemplified theological and moral virtues, plus his vows of Obedience, Poverty and Chastity. Pope Sixtus V entered Diego's name in the Catalog of Saints in 1588. In the twenty-first century, more than five hundred years after Diego's death, devotees contend his incorrupt corpse emits a pleasant aroma. Believers seek his intercession still.

In addition to his patronage of San Diego, California, San Diego de Alcalá endows the namesake of California's proto-mission. Though born in the district of Córdoba, earthly remains of this fifteenth-century Franciscan rest in the city of Alcalá de Henares.

We climb aboard the train at twenty past ten in the morning. We have bountiful seats from which to choose, with only the random student aboard. A careworn man faces us. Slight of frame, hollow-faced, missing teeth, he stares at his lap with the plaintive, red-lidded eyes of a basset hound. His clothing is drab and tattered. Across the aisle, another aged passenger passes a rosary between her spotted, knobby fingers as she mouths silent prayers.

Then she dozes, as our train rocks and sways between depots en route to Estación de Alcalá.

After a brief journey, we disembark and duck into a cozy bar for espressos.

Alcalá, a cache of history, was bestowed with the high honor of World Heritage City for recognizing its celebrated citizens, for preserving its monuments. "Alcalá" is a corruption of an Arabic word for fortress and Henares, a river idling through this illustrious town.

"We're here for only the day," reminds Uncle Chuck. "Let's focus on a couple of sites, have lunch, then return to Madrid by sundown."

I question whether we will unravel all of Alcalá's mysteries in a day. After all, at Alcalá, Columbus first met with Queen Isabel the Catholic and here Isabel gave birth to Catherine of Aragón, one of the wives of Henry VIII. This city harbors medieval walls, an open-air sculpture museum, an archbishop's palace and the *Complutum*—remains of a Roman road and villa with a bathhouse complex. Given Uncle Chuck's edict, it's clear we need to distill our itinerary. Heaven forbid he miss his distilled spirits in the Hotel Palace bar.

Eminent among Alcalá's monuments are Colegio de San Ildefonso (alumni includes St. Ignacio Loyola) and home of Miguel de Cervantes Saavedra, author of one of the world's first novels,[2] *Hidalgo Don Quixote de La Mancha*, 1605 and 1615. Nonetheless, our focus remains to locate the tomb of San Diego.

Bristling from effects of caffeine, we roam through town. We detect a distinct clacking overhead. The exotic vibration, resembling the percussion of castanets, turns out to be storks. These robust birds migrate annually from Africa to Spain, nesting here during wintertime. The clacking made with the beak reputedly signals excitement or love. *Had Isabel, Cervantes and Diego heard the same clatter?* Overhead, the grand birds form a black-and-white phalanx against an azure-painted sky. Other storks visit their crude nests of twigs atop bell towers, on ledges.

The oldest college in Alcalá, San Ildefonso, founded by Cardinal Gonzalo Jiménez de Cisneros in 1498, survives as one of dozens long vanished from one of Spain's notorious centers of learning. In 1537, Juan Gil de Hontañón designed this college's ornate façade overlaid with *plateresque* escutcheons, keystones amid arches, spandrels and finials.

El Patio Trilingüe del Colegio Mayor de San Ildefonso, the residential college, rises three stories above colonnaded archways encompassing precisely clipped shrubbery, a graceful stone fountain, plaques hewn with

Alcalá's coat of arms, images of professors and saints. In the cloisters, we discover all doors bolted. On our way out, we meet with a stone statue of Cardinal Cisneros in the courtyard. In one of this town's printing shops, Renaissance journeymen published, under Cisneros's commission, the *Biblia Políglota Complutense* (in Greek, Latin, Aramaic and Chaldean—the polyglot Bible).

Just across the courtyard, Uncle Chuck spots a restaurant smart in white plaster coat with eyebrows of bright blue awnings.

Our waitress is friendly and fluent in English. I quiz her on Diego's resting place. She hasn't a clue. Wonder if she knows who he was....

A middle-aged customer overhears my query; she suggests an inquiry at the convent next door. Someone there will surely know how to find Diego's tomb.

Fronting old Convento de Clarisas stands another statue of Cardinal Cisneros, this one fashioned of bronze, crowned with a miter. Moving beyond the statue's staring eyes, we step cautiously over a timeworn, wooden threshold into the Claritians' reception hall. Here we encounter an elderly man buying egg-yolk sweets known as *yemas*. The vendor, a nun, we cannot see, as she stands concealed behind a *torno* (revolving counter). Managing Spanish, I solicit the man's help. Though he speaks no English, he endures my broken Spanish. As he questions the faceless woman, I hear monotone words *"iglesia magistral"* issuing from the screen. The gentleman winks and escorts us outside. He points, makes two left turns with additional gestures, smiles and wishes us well.

With the kind man's directions, we move fleetly to Calle Mayor, the main route through old Alcalá de Henares. Each side of this tight passageway defines with medieval arcades, a lineal forest of columns carrying second-story apartments. Our footfalls echo through a corridor of shops, pharmacy, grocer and restaurants.

Just emerged from the arcade, we practically trip over Museo Casa Natal de Cervantes, a 1950s reproduction of what purportedly resembles Cervantes's birth-home, reared on foundations of the original where the author was born in 1547. We pay a brief visit to this tiny, two-storied *casa*.

The ground level encompasses a portico centerpieced by a fountain, a typical Spanish courtyard, upstairs, replications of bedchambers, a primitive bathroom, a prim salon, an exhibit of puppets in medieval garb. Engaging rooms harbor rare copies of Cervantes's *Hidalgo Don Quixote de La Mancha* in Spanish, Japanese, German and other tongues. Illustrations in these books tantalize. Each artist interpreted the "Distinguished Gentleman of La

Mancha" in distinctive style and color.

We move on, down the street, admiring a rash of convents and churches. When at last an enormous, cathedral-like church comes into view, we cut across a park and make our way toward it, only to find bolted doors. This is becoming a trend.

There's a sign: *Museo Iglesia.* We step inside a museum. I tell the ticket seller, *"Por favor, uno normal y uno viejo."* She corrects me, smiling at Uncle Chuck, saying, *"Jubilado; no viejo."* He pays the senior fare.

We wander, admiring treasures: the bell tower from the ambulatory, a stone sarcophagus of Cardinal Cisneros, centuries-old sacred vessels, a fine painting of San Diego.

On the way out, I ask the ticket seller if San Diego's body is in the church.

"Oh yes," the young lady replies. "Will you be here on 13 November?"

"Regrettably, no," I answer.

"The twelfth," she explains, "is the anniversary of his death. But we open his urn on the thirteenth. You may visit Diego's shrine after six o'clock this evening when the church opens."

We see a *taberna* directly across the street. As we while away our time with *cafés con leche,* moody sunset dapples lazily moving clouds with rosy glow. We watch from the bar as dusky hues evolve to rich persimmon, deepening to burgundy, to violet. As the sky blackens, floodlights bathe the *magistral* church and its rusticated tower in radiant yellow, the roosting storks as silhouettes. We have now glimpsed this inveterate temple and campanile throughout the day, under all phases of light, natural and electric.

I want to come back, to see Diego's remains.

"Why would you forfeit time in Andalucía to look at another desiccated corpse?" Uncle Chuck asks incredulously.

THE *MAGISTRAL* CHURCH OF ALCALÁ DE HENARES

Santa e Insigne Iglesia Magistral, dating to 1136, rebuilt in 1497, ranks as one of only two in the world with the title Magisterial, meaning that all of its clergymen required university masters of Doctrine. The church, considered by some a cathedral, was built over the graves of Justo and Pastor, Roman children who died as martyrs. Cardinal Gonzalo Jiménez de Cisneros commissioned architects Antón and Enrique Egas to build this church in Gothic style. The belfry was created in the mode known as Herreriano and completed in the seventeenth century.

Clamorous bells resonate six times. We roam across the street where two women stand outside locked gates, and take our places behind them. A man arrives with a jangle of keys. He plies a five-inch skeleton key to the lock and swings open huge, creaking gates.

The interior of this massive, scantly lit church manifests solemnity. Chapels span each side of the nave of forty-three pillars. *Where is Diego?* Now, as though drawn here, we discover the tomb. Peering through *rejas*, we admire in candlelight Diego's chased silver casket. His portrait hangs above. Just outside the shrine blazes a sconce of "candles." We feed an excess of pesetas into a metal box for sixty seconds of light. At once the entire affair glows brightly, each candle ignited with an electric bulb. We pray to San Diego, then turn to the gentleman who let us in, to explain the purpose of our pilgrimage. He opens the *rejas*, then kindly proffers holy cards and booklets on our hometown's patron saint.

Our pilgrimage consummated, we now retrace our steps through town. The ebony sky glistens with a sea of stars. We approach the train station, dodging a mob of youths just arrived and geared to celebrate the evening. Night falls cool. We shiver on the platform for fifteen minutes.

Youthful passengers head off to Madrid for parties. Unlike mid-morning's coaches, this evening's cars bulge to standing room only.

As our train eases along the rails, I survey fresh, young faces—some Moorish, others with red or blond hair—a veritable nexus of cross-pollination. As our train chugs forward, teens jabber on cell phones and among themselves. Like their peers in San Diego, California, these young people sport tattoos, pierced lips, eyebrows and noses.

Back in Madrid, Uncle Chuck insists on a cab ride back to the Palace. "I believe we've walked enough for one day," he tells me.

Once dressed for dinner, we set out for a restaurant called La Finca de Susana. Night air chills as we course inner streets of Madrid, admiring illuminated architecture and memorials, tempted by aromas drifting from *cervecerías* (bars).

"Walking distance?" complains Uncle Chuck.

"Maybe it's just around the next corner," I keep encouraging.

We walk until exasperated Uncle Chuck announces he can go no farther. He flags a cab, just as I catch my second wind, beginning to enjoy our *paseo*.

"Back to the hotel," he says, "and we'll ask the concierge to recommend a restaurant in the immediate vicinity."

The endorsement this time: Restaurante Paradis at Marquis de Cuba 14, right across the street. We step happily into warmth, into a dining room smartly decorated in ultra modern and sporting an apple motif. On each table rests an immaculately burnished crimson orb. The forbidden fruit is the subject of paintings here: still-life bowls loaded with red and golden apples, cubist trees bogged down with abundant autumn fruit and Eve presenting the forbidden morsel to Adam.

Uncle Chuck looks at his watch. "We dine in the manner of Spaniards this evening, at ten o'clock."

And we had been on *el paseo grande* as we pursued another restaurant for an hour. We deserve martinis and a good dinner.

At the end of our martinis, we sip creamy soup of wild *cep* mushrooms afloat with roe of sea urchins. Uncle Chuck carries through with lacquered duck over couscous and I, with the restaurant's signature *fideuà*. Lacquer on the duck, we surmise after a taste, the chef made with brown sugar, cloves, cinnamon. My entrée, a version of *fideos* (paella prepared with vermicelli rather than rice) is flecked with mushrooms, topped with a fat slice of seared *foie gras*.

Our *mozo* tenders nougat-style cookies with *la cuenta*. Smiling, we return to our suite at half-past midnight.

"We've become real night owls," boasts Uncle Chuck as he loosens his necktie. Now, limply, he asks, "Can we please take it easier tomorrow?"

[1] Weber, Msgr. Francis J. *San Diego. The City and the Saint.* Monterey, CA: Hilleary & Petko, 1992.

[2] The world's first novel was *Tale of Genji* by Lady Murasaki Shikibu (1011); the second, *La Celestina* by Fernando de Rojas (1499).

FIESTA TIME

Spain's deeply religious populace understood the notion of "party," for characteristics of the spiritual and the spirited come forth in their fiestas (festivals) and ferias *(street fairs).*

The most popular of Spain's festivals, Semana Santa *(Holy Week), manifests an eternal state of fanfare throughout the country—though exaggerated in Seville—from Palm Sunday through Easter. From villages to big metropolises, streets swell with merrymakers during fiesta. Images of Christ and the Virgin parade through towns on the shoulders of* costaleros, *followed by decorated floats and revelers. Flowers are ubiquitous, the breeze aloft with fragrance, singing, dancing, color and pomp. And after Easter come ferias.*

We had no idea our day in Madrid conceded fiesta. Nevertheless, in short order, we found ourselves caught up in the fanfare.

Wind blows frightfully raw and Madrid is a veritable ghost town. Asked about the peacefulness, our *mozo* at Oskar's explains. Today launches the first of three fiesta days to honor Our Lady of Almudena, Madrid's patroness and namesake of Madrid's cathedral.

"It will not be so peaceful later on," he says with a smile.

Uncle Chuck and I program our itinerary. He would rather spend the day couched in the luxury of Hotel Palace, but sites in Madrid remain unexplored by the two of us. First stop, Templo de Debod, an Egyptian temple; next, the cathedral.

Uncle Chuck objects to hiking two miles or so to the western side of town. I call for a taxi. Our porter summons the first from a long line of cabs always parked near our hotel.

"Parque del Oeste, por favor," I tell the driver and we are off through deserted streets.

Park of the West looks paltry compared with Parque del Buen Retiro, though pretty and green under piercing blue sky. We scale steep concrete steps to reach the temple.

Daylight bathes the Egyptian shrine, two of its principal gateways casting reflections of ancient forms on a lengthy reflecting pool. Spanish engineers rescued these reconstructed piles—originally built in Nubia, along the Nile, for Pharaoh Zakheramon—from the Aswan Dam project. The Egyptian government donated the dismantled temple to Spain in recognition of the heroic rescue.

We pluck against a chilly bluster as we reflect on the temple's age, its admirable survival. To thwart the cold, we pick up our pace toward the cathedral and pause at Plaza de España, site of a Civil War barracks, built over as a public square. From a pond at its center rises El Edificio España, a memorial to Cervantes depicting Don Quixote with other characters from the celebrated novel. Dedicated in 1957, this massive stone obelisk was once the tallest concrete structure in the world.

Near noon, avenues around Plaza de España course with foot traffic. We have landed in one of Madrid's busiest intersections and insanely popular squares. Car horns echo, pageantry abounds, sidewalks are runways for tender- to middle-aged ladies in flowing gowns, lacy mantillas on *peinetas* (combs). Gentlemen deck out with great plumed hats and capes. Merrymakers parade down boulevards and children yell, running hand in hand. The elderly shuffle along in dark clothing.

We drop into a claustrophobic bar called Cañas y Tapas (Draft Beer and Snacks). Warmed and sated, we again endure the climate.

After three long blocks, we sense something amiss and consult our city map, struggling with it against the wind. We are on La Gran Vía, not Bailén, as intended. We turn back to find Bailén.

We reach Plaza de Oriente between the royal palace and cathedral, a square abandoned to a riot of colorful ruckus. Here we see more ladies in black mantillas, brightly patterned *mantones* (fringed shawls) and gentlemen in capes. A crew of cameramen captures the resplendent scene, filming from rooftops of local broadcast vans. Vendors hawk *churros* and flowers. Devotees in throngs approach the cathedral to honor their Lady. Before joining in the procession, we step aside to inspect the cathedral of white stone under blue-gray, slate-topped turrets and spires.

As we follow the flock up the cathedral's steep steps, beggars plead mournfully, *"¿Almas, por favor?"* One of them, an old woman swaddled in black, save her soulful eyes and hands, conjures her own tears, soliciting with open palm. Gaily attired revelers ignore the beggars. We follow suit.

Though enormous, this cathedral does not impress us, as have other Spanish cathedrals. Madrid's cathedral, a youngster mostly completed in the late-nineteenth century, was finished in the late-twentieth century. Yet detailing astonishes, from noble vaulting to stained glass windows to chapels embracing finely wrought statuary. By European standards, the sanctuary endows scant superfluity, though the vault is remarkable in interleaved panels of brilliant red, gold and blue. An enormous crucifix floats above the altar.

Shuffling among devotees on a carpet of rose petals, our senses fill with color and aroma. Continuing behind a solemn crowd, our path wends to a staircase against a wall of the transept, at its apex, an altar bearing a life-sized statue of Nuestra Señora de la Almudena. All file past her image, some leaving *ofrendas* (offerings) of flowers.

To exit the cathedral, we press against a tsunami of worshipers filing in, squeezing dodging between elbows until we at last manage our way to the front steps. We halt briefly, catching our breath and to admire across Plaza de la Armería the intricate façade of El Palacio Real.

"I'm past the point where I enjoy that sort of fanfare," Uncle Chuck breathes. "Either that, or I'm claustrophobic in my old age."

Had the clime been a tad warmer, I would have loved to linger at the fiesta. I understood that, after all of the spiritual adulation, the parties were wild.

Not surprisingly, we are the only customers at Café Ricordi; everyone else attends fiesta. Seating choices include casual bar or intimate room of six napped tables and yawning fireplace. We choose the room. Seated, we crane our necks to study trompe l'œil scenes in the domed ceiling: a fresco of picnickers, musicians and a Franciscan friar.

Buñuelitos de huevos (deep-fried, breaded, boiled eggs) begin our meal. We split a large *ensalada mixta*. With a bottle of Marqués de Riscal *blanco*, we savor *dorada*—luscious whole fish baked in olive oil, tingling with garlic, topped with green and red peppers.

Thick-lipped cups of tea and coffee will fortify us against bitter weather.

As we pay up, a cackling party of revelers takes a table nearby.

"I'm glad they didn't arrive earlier," whispers Uncle Chuck as we leave.

Wind whips through our jackets and Uncle Chuck has had it. We hail a cab back to our suite.

Tomorrow, we will make a road trip to Seville, the capital of Andalucía.

1. El Carpio
2. Córdoba
3. Seville
4. Cádiz
5. Algodonales
6. Ronda
7. Gibraltar
8. Málaga
9. Granada/Alhambra
10. Jaén

Andalucía

"Mistral" was not a phenomenon unique to France, Spain having her own version of those frozen, forceful winds that chilled to the bone, numbing face and fingers. Reports promised temperate weather to the south. We looked forward to reveling in its thawing warmth.

We collect our reserved Peugeot at the airport, then ease into traffic on M-40. In short order, we pick up southbound N-IV through outskirts of Madrid. The expanding metropolis yields its aristocratic milieu to suburban density and industrial parks for miles beyond. Eyesores eventually give way to landscape free of urbanization.

The efficient, litter-free thoroughfare cuts through a sweeping *meseta*. Scenery bristles with craggy grapevine stubble on one side, gray-green olive trees on the other. Randomly, we spot *huertos de almendros* (almond orchards) and ghostly, squat windmills, a couple of them bedecked with lacy wooden fans, others crumbling cylinders with no blades—scenery calling to mind the backdrop of Don Quixote. Rolling along, we tilt at clusters of wizened windmills dotting the hillsides of Consuegra. I want to stop for pictures, but Uncle Chuck remains hellbent on making time.

Road-weary after two hours, we draw up to a *venta* (roadside inn) for a pick-me-up and a stretch. I leave cameras in the trunk. The vicinity rambles monotonously, volunteering no glimpses of windmills or castles. The short walk from car to bar is treacherous in a blustery gust following us from Madrid.

Delaying table-side, we watch as truck drivers feed coins into slots, then curse and kick the machines. Fueled with *cafés con leche*, we hit the road.

Landscape unfolds in shades of green, punctuated occasionally with ruinous stone barns, then views even more splendid, as we weave round hairpin turns of the Sierra Morena. Glimpses at this elevation remind us of craggy granite pinnacles we savored in Picos de Europa years ago.

Winding down a southern slope of the sierra, the province of Andalucía spreads before us. The sky yields rich shades of blue, and far-flung olive groves brighten undulating terrain with monochromatic shimmer.

I share with Uncle Chuck that Rome vanquished the Carthaginians, taking Andalucía in B.C. 206. Romans called the region *Betis* and according to legend, Hercules founded what would become the provincial capital: Seville. Spain's largest region, Andalucía, became autonomous in 1982. Exotic with overlays of cultures, likely Arabic or North African—Andalucía is, after all, only eight miles from Africa.

At noon, we discuss lunch. Uncle Chuck suggests dropping in for a sandwich at one of the N-IV convenience restaurants. My heart longs for a more engaging circumstance. I scan scenery northeast of Córdoba, sighting a Moorish tower-crowned hill in the distant prospect. We pull off the freeway, piloting toward the site, maneuvering cautiously up a narrow road toward the *torre*. This is El Carpio, a prim town dappled in early-afternoon light.

DISCOVERING EL CARPIO

The obscure village of El Carpio (The Hill), established as a pueblo in 1325, graduated to status of Berber stronghold during the eleventh century, territory that became a ward of the emirate of Córdoba. By 1240, Fernando III conquered the powerful position with its small yet salient Islamic *alcázar*. The Muslim holdings were distributed among the Spanish royal court's beneficiaries, including the clan of Méndez de Sotomayor.

Only the Tower of Honor, also regarded as Torre de Garci Méndez, remains of this village's castle-fortress built under orders of Garci Méndez de Sotomayor. The *Mudéjar*-style construction of brick and mortar by master-mason Mahomat was completed in the fourteenth century, according to an alabaster tablet removed from the rubble and put on exhibit in the Palace of the Dueñas at Seville.

Also founded by Garci Méndez was El Carpio's parish church, Nuestra Señora de la Asunción dating from 1360. Little remains of the original known in medieval times as Iglesia de Santísima Trinidad (Church of the Holy Trinity). The church crumbled to ruins by the sixteenth century. Improvements made from the seventeenth to eighteenth centuries included three naves, barrel vaulting, a *bóveda* (dome) and a crypt under the main altar containing relics of Sotomayor marquises.

We step into a restaurant off the deserted main square.

"Have we just dropped in from outer space?" questions Uncle Chuck, as dark brown eyes follow us somewhat askance.

Given El Carpio's remote position and no mentions in travel sourcebooks, little wonder this restaurant's employees and customers—with nuances of Muslim ancestry in their features—regard us as novelties. El Carpio would not be considered a tourist magnet. On the other hand, we felt invisible in Madrid, having been swept up in the capital city's bombast, nearly mowed down by pedestrians, as though we were ghosts. But here in El Carpio, blue-color folk—olive pickers or processors—surely consider their community strictly residential, likely not having traveled far beyond the foot of their hill.

Excusing myself, I step outside to photograph the *torre* of taupe-colored stone with terra cotta accents. I make studies of the church, an enticing medley of sandstone and brick accented with carmine and arched portals, *campanario* and filigreed clock tower. The rustic structures' earthy palettes rest gloriously against a backdrop of clouds whipping through deep-blue sky.

When I return to the café, no one gives me a second look. The locals have recovered from the initial shock of a rare tourist invasion. Our table is set with *tapas*, including *migas*: deep-fried and breaded minced fish, garlic and herbs. As we lunch, farmers chatter at the bar; other customers watch a ceiling-mounted television or play pinball games.

La cuenta, including beer, totals 850 pesetas, half the cost of a simple café breakfast in Madrid. Refreshed, we proceed toward Seville.

Rolling along the first stretch of Ruta del Califato,[1] we savor the widespread range of Córdoba. I have dreamed of including this city in our itinerary, but this will have to wait for another trip. Passing by, we make out the random, historic edifice amidst Córdoba's smudge of modern apartment buildings, hotels and office towers.

Although I know the roads I'll never reach Córdoba.

—Federico García Lorca

We catch glimpses of the snaking Río Guadalquivir and, on approach, behold the architectural splendor of distant *Sevilla*. At four P.M., we pull into the city. I examine a map for crossroads near Hotel Alfonso XIII. We canvas corners of buildings for street names. Passing by old city walls, we soon encounter an eclectic melding of old and new, glimpsing *Mudéjar* architecture and spotting the mighty Torre del Oro, a landmark proximate to the Alfonso.

Twice we circle one-way routes. When at last we arrive at our hotel, an army of livery-clad staff opens and holds our doors, removes luggage from our trunk and escorts us to the reception.

"Welcome to *Sevilla*, gentlemen."

A young fellow greets us as though we are familiars, checking us in graciously. With passports and card-keys exchanged, we ride a lift to the second floor.

Elevator doors open and we step into Moorish heaven. Our grand hotel, commissioned by King Alfonso XIII as an *Hispano-Mudéjar* palace, speaks of Moorish revival at every turn. Completed in 1929, Hotel Alfonso XIII extends a comparable level of comfort to the Hotel Palace in Madrid, yet disparate in décor and not as fussy as the Palace. Public rooms and corridors are fitted with inlaid marble floors, pierced oriental sconces, horseshoe arches, ceramic tile in arabesque patterns brilliantly colored. The main level hems an open-air patio with fountain and potted palms. Faïence mosaic scenes in blue, green, mustard and white inset the stairwells.

We find guest rooms accoutered in the manner of a kasbah with dark marquetry ceilings, Moorish-style headboards, thick draperies and richly hued Moroccan fabrics. Our unique, sparkling-clean bathroom is overlaid with slim, vertical strips of tile in tones of cobalt, white, iridescent copper. Our windows overlook a verdant park and the waterfront beyond. And to our delight, no car horns....

Downstairs, making our way to the courtside lounge, we admire, through an arcade, a soothing fountain. Nursing martinis, we comb over our plans for *Sevilla*.

Mostly Spanish guests cloud the lounge with pale-blue smoke. One lady puffs one cigarette after another, lighting next with last. In a noxious fog, Uncle Chuck chokes and suggests we quit the lounge for fresher air.

We ask the concierge to recommend a flamenco club. The convivial fellow with meticulous goatee makes our booking for tomorrow and suggests Plaza Santa Cruz for its restaurants this evening. We head out in that direction.

Milieu is pristine, all scrubbed and tweaked as though city officials expect a documentary film crew. Babbling fountains and lacy palms refine the scenery. Sidewalks are plotted with decorative concrete pots; from each grows a specimen orange tree impeccably clipped to spherical preciseness.

Horse-drawn surreys reconvene at taxi queues.

Two blocks from our hotel, we step into lengthening shadows of the cathedral, a mass of carved stone crowned with dome and spires, held aloft by flying buttresses—the color of old ivory in late afternoon's glow.

CATEDRAL DE SEVILLA

Five-aisle Catedral de Sevilla (Church of the Holy Savior), the most sizable in Spain, ranks third grandest in the world after St. Paul's in London and St. Peter's Basilica in Rome and was at one time the largest religious monument in all of Christendom. Seville's cathedral is the largest Gothic church in the world and, according to *The Guinness Book of World Records*, boasts an area greater than any other church. The present structure, designed by Alonso Martínez, Simón de Colonia and Juan Gil de Hontañón, rose on Roman stones, the foundations of a twelfth-century *Umayyad* chief mosque. Architectural survivors from 1184 include a skyscraping *alminar* (minaret) converted to campanile, and an old ablution courtyard known as Patio de los Naranjos (Court of the Orange Trees). The Christian church (1248-1401) progressively supplanted a Friday mosque. Gothic fabrication was carried out from 1434 to 1517 and Renaissance additions made from 1528 to 1601, with baroque chapels appended between 1618 and 1758. Three portals and the southwestern wing were added in 1825 and 1928. The city's patroness, Virgen de los Reyes, presides over the high altar.

The cathedral's bell tower, a former minaret stretching 228 feet—and forty-eight-feet square—evolved gradually over the years, yet retains germinal Arabic characteristics from its footing to more than two-hundred feet above ground. Within the tower, thirty-five sloped ramps in thirty-four sections stretch upward through seven vaulted rooms. Legend has it, after Fernando III conquered Seville in 1248, he rode on horseback to the top of this tower, admiring from there a view of his tenancy. Thereafter, the bell tower was fabricated to be the most beautiful on earth. Crowning the top of this eye-catching campanile, a cupola aloft with a weather vane fondly named La Giralda, from *giraldillo*, "a thing that turns." This bronze vane turns with a female warrior brandishing a plume and shield symbolizing faith.

Let Posterity say that those who created it must have been lunatics.
—Anonymous statement regarding construction of the Cathedral of Seville

Farther afield, we penetrate a bustling neighborhood, El Barrio de Santa Cruz (Holy Cross), formerly the old Jewish quarter. Constricting the lanes, a warren of patriarchal buildings presses in on us—bulging structures swathed in chalk-white plaster trimmed in ochre and blue, some of them homes, others shops or restaurants. As dusk softens the sky, we promenade amongst legions of *Los Gatos* on *el paseo*. Lively din of Spanish folk music heralds the advent of evening. Each step and glance down an alleyway unfurls a scene abundant with color and the still air is redolent of grilling meat.

Near the plaza, we drop into a lively restaurant, but quickly change our minds. Thick with cigarette smoke, the clamorous room looks dingy. We ply on, landing at Restaurante Las Escobas. Besides *tapas*, we may select from the dinner menu. Seville is credited with the invention of *tapas* and boasts more than one thousand bars where we may enjoy them. This evening, we opt for à la carte.

Gazpacho spikes pungent with garlic, more than other versions we've tried. I like it. Uncle Chuck suggests sharing a pan of paella. No surprises, only morsels of chicken, chorizo and a smattering of shellfish and peppers dot the bed of saffron-and-tomato-sauced rice. Flawlessly snappy, dry Marqués de Sierra 1990 raises our spirits.

Striking back to our hotel, we pause at luminous Santa Cruz Square. Black velvet sky adds to the splendor of La Giralda Tower.

This evening we will fall asleep in a city beyond compare, in a grand hotel commissioned by a king.

[1] Ruta del Califato (Route of the Caliphate): the old route between Córdoba and Granada.

[2] Fernando III: 1198-1252, canonized by Pope Clemente X, 1671.

DISCOVERED: COLUMBUS AND *NOCTURNO DE ANDALUCÍA*

I gained deeper understanding of this concept of duende, *recognizing the virtue in aspects of Spanish culture, in the eyes of her people. I would soon be stung by* duende—*in exhaustive, unadulterated measure.*

At half-past eight, Seville still sleeps under crisp blue sky. We strike out for the cathedral, but find it closed. Back, toward the river, we discover a lively café called Coliseo. *"¿Limpia?"* inquires a shoeshine man lurking outside. I wear suede loafers, so avoid his solicitation, but the man confronts

Uncle Chuck in smart leather shoes.

Caught up with me, Uncle Chuck mumbles, "They didn't need a shine."

We eye breakfast behind a glass case on the bar: husky rolls, *jamón serrano* and *cafés con leche* to savor but quickly, stuffed between Spanish businessmen reading newspapers and leisurely sipping coffee. I'm antsy to explore.

We hike over to Puente San Telmo, one of Seville's six bridges spanning the medieval trade route Río Guadalquivir. From this *puente*, we see the dodecahedral Torre del Oro, an imposing, thirteenth-century defensive tower, a landmark edifice, lone survivor of a pair built by *Almohades* in 1220 near the finale of Spain's Moslem period. Time was, the bridgehead fortification towers formed corners of old city walls. Enormous chains, linking the towers at the harbor's entrance, were a means of keeping enemy ships at bay. The handle Torre del Oro stems from days when the bastion's turret gleamed with gold brought from the Americas. Though naked of gold today, this golden-brown tower shimmers with the mounting sun. In the foreground, moored tour boats bob along riverbanks; in the background, La Giralda looms above the beautiful city.

From the other side of the bridge, a pink-and-yellow palace mirrors in the teal, glass-smooth Guadalquivir. The subject: Palacio de San Telmo, a drop-dead palace with sandstone portal chiseled in florid *churrigueresque* style. In 1682, this was a school for sea pilots and sailors, named—conspicuously, as was this bridge—for the patron saint of navigators.

Farther along, we walk up San Fernando, discovering Jardines de Murillo, an engaging park just outside the walls of the royal palace. Under rows of sycamores, we tread on a carpet of yellow leaves, pausing at an obelisk commemorating the Genoan-Italian expat, Cristóbal Colón (Christopher Columbus, 1451-1506).

Sunny rays gently caress the scenery. The mistral is truly behind us. As we wind deeply through Barrio de Santa Cruz, street musicians entertain us. Between whitewashed, centuries-old dwellings, we glimpse sequestered patios along alley walls, and occasional tilework memorials to saints, to Columbus. Without realizing it, we are lost.

Our predicament resolves when we turn a corner and follow our noses to an aromatic square. We case out restaurants' posted menus for future reference.

It's noon when we reach Plaza de Triunfo near the cathedral. La Giralda's twenty-five bells toll uproariously, expressing hundreds of pigeons from lofty perches. We watch a neck-breaking repertory of swinging bells, a cloud of orbiting birds, until all hushes again.

Three long blocks away, Leafy Parque de María Luisa beckons. Arrived there, we step through an arched stone gate, then amble along a path through a sun-splashed forest of specimens imported from Latin America. Again we startle, then wax quixotic. Through lacy trees, we catch eye-popping views of a pavilion, a monument with water features fashioned in 1929 for the Iberoamericana Exposition. This is majestic Plaza de España, constructed in the form of an amphitheater.

The enchanted plaza teems with bused-in tourists and horse-drawn carriages. White doves and gray pigeons wing through minaret-style towers above extremities of a three-story masterpiece. Jets of white water dance twenty-or-more feet above fountains. Footbridges gleam with multicolored *azulejos* (glazed tiles); balustrades of blue and white ceramic span a semicircular moat. Ducks wriggle their cute bottoms between dives through an ultramarine surface and tiny boats convey merrymakers under bantam arched bridges.

We move slowly alongside, inspecting brilliant tile scenes of Spain's fifty provinces. The sun's radiance undulates playfully upon water, reflecting a blaze of polychrome tiles. Merchants clack castanets above a pageant of fans and miniature bulls. Others sell ice cream and *churros*. Enthralled with the fanfare, we hail a surrey for a jog around the plaza.

Twenty minutes into the ride, I tell our cabby, "La Plaza de Santa Cruz, *por favor.*"

Bouncing behind a clip-clopping equine-engine, we drink in a banner day. We ask to be dropped at El Tres de Oro, a restaurant we agreed upon earlier.

The cozy bar-*restaurante* is neat as a pin. By appearances and by what we hear, the customers are Spanish, assuring, we believe, parochial cuisine.

"I feel like a martini," Uncle Chuck exhales.

We order gin on the rocks, swirl it round carefully and pour it into wine goblets, leaving the ice in our lowball glasses.

"Now this is a good, homemade martini," I tell Uncle Chuck. We've at last learned our lesson in ordering a favorite cocktail in Europe.

Uncle Chuck starts with *ensalada mixta* and I, with salad that looks like an overgrown flower: endive leaves arranged as petals spread with Roquefort. We proceed with selections from the open grill: smoky *pinchos a la brasa* (shish kebobs) of cubed pork and vegetables, plus grilled *rape* served on a puddle of saffron sauce dotted with shrimp.

Though *postres* tempt, we decline and linger, nursing *cafés con leche*.

On the way to the cathedral, we browse *tiendas* (shops), each abundant with enticements from fine-looking, hand-tooled leather to colorful pottery to exotic tiles.

At the cathedral, we step under a bower known as Puerta de San Cristóbal o de los Príncipes. Leaning against a wall sits a gaunt, bearded man whose looks and demeanor conjure notions of the *Ecce Homo*. With thin, grimy hand extended, he groans for *almas*. We proffer coins, then inch our way behind a queue to the *taquilla*.

Cristo moreno	Brown Christ
pasa	passes
de lirio de Judea	from the lily of Judea
a clavel de España	to the carnation of Spain.
¡Miradlo por dónde viene!	Look where he comes!

—Federico García Lorca, "*Saeta*" ("Arrow")

Inside, we see a wing of galleries bedecked with oil paintings of Christ, the Holy Mother, saints, former monarchs. Along traffic-worn corridors, we peer into a vestry, to a marble-paved patio, as we aspire towards capacious depths of the temple.

Dwarfed by more than seventy-six thousand square feet, we stand agape. Fluted pillars stretch from their pedestals to infinitesimal vaulting. Boundless, drab space distinguishes vivid jewel tones of stained-glass windows high above a choir with spectacular *Mudéjar* stalls and baroque organ boxes.

"It would take a day to tour this cathedral," Uncle Chuck prescribes.

Tallying the chapels listed in his brochure, he comes up with thirty. Each chapel awes, with La Capilla Mayor (The Main Chapel) the crowning jewel. We're blinded by golden *retablos* behind three gilded sets of *rejas*: altar screens traced with friezes of angels, prophets and evangelists, scenes from the lives of St. Paul and Christ—forty-four figures in relief and sculpture. A fourteenth-century Gothic crucifix crowned with octagonal caissons provides the centerpiece.

Behind Capilla Mayor, we find domed Capilla Real (Royal Chapel). Here, in a silver coffin, lie the remains of Fernando III, patron saint of Seville. Through glass panels, we view this mummified saint-king, gawking at his long, pointed shoes and withered hands. Fernando, an ascetic, fasted himself to death. Uncle Chuck does not understand my fascination with this.

The *duende* does not come at all unless he sees that death is possible. The *duende* must know beforehand that he can serenade death's house and rock those branches we all wear, branches that do not have, will never have, any consolation.
—Federico García Lorca

Still spellbound, we discover the tomb of Christopher Columbus, a draped coffin held aloft on the shoulders of four sculpted heralds symbolizing the four kingdoms of Spain. Tourists take photographs of each other near the legendary hero's imposing memorial. Around the corner, the tomb of Christopher's son Hernán is paradoxically unimposing.

Sacristía Mayor reveals heavenly paintings by Goya, Murillo and Cano, and a relief hewn by Juan Bautista Vázquez. The vaulting fascinates in its stylistic confluence of *Mozárabic*, Gothic and Renaissance.

We stagger out, through an original, bronze *Almohad* door onto Patio de los Naranjos. Neat rows of orange trees in full fruit spring from cutouts in the stone-and-brick courtyard. The trees take their nourishment from irrigation channels intersecting this ancient patio. In Muhammadan times, the faithful washed in the central fountain before prayer (ablution). *What a phantasmic place.* Standing amidst orange trees, in shadows of the tower—a frozen-in-time minaret—I imagine Muslims called to prayer, purifying their bodies ritualistically in this courtyard, then removing their shoes before entering the mosque.

ABLUTIONS

Wudû (the lesser ablution)

The believer must first say, "In the name of God!" He then washes his hands three times; three times, he rinses out his mouth and snuffs water back into his nostrils, pouring water into his hand for both of these acts.

Next, he washes his face, from hairline to neck, the chin and openings of the nostrils. He combs out his beard with wet fingers, if it is thick, and washes it, if it is sparse. He then washes his hands up to and including the wrists, three times.

He proceeds to the rubbing of his head, including the ears; this rubbing he does with both hands, going from forehead to nape of the neck, and back.

He washes three times his feet, including ankles, taking care to pass his fingers between the toes. Finally, he raises his face toward heaven and recites: "I witness that there is no god but Allâh, the Unique, who has no partner. I witness that Muhammad is His servant and His messenger."

Ghusl (The greater ablution)

The greater ablution involves, as a strict duty, the intention and washing of the entire body; this washing should include rinsing of the mouth and nostrils.

It is *sunna* (praiseworthy, but not necessary) to say: "In the name of God!" and to rub the body with the hands....

It is not obligatory in the greater ablution to cut off the body hair, if one washes the parts with plenty of water.

One may accomplish the lesser and the greater ablution, providing one formulates the intention of doing so....

—*Great Religions of Modern Man. Islam.*
John Alden Williams, ed. New York: George Braziller, 1962.

Awe mingled with fatigue augments the mesmerizing effects of a bubbling fountain. From jowls of stone lions, crystalline water flows from shell-shaped ewers, percolating over fluted lips to an ample basin. We relax, puffing cigars at Plaza Virgen de los Reyes, a square just outside the cathedral. Pigeons preen and sip and visitors make snapshots. We exhale, deeply.

"Siesta-time," says Uncle Chuck.

En route to the Alfonso XIII, I tell Uncle Chuck that Seville gained her riches through trade and mining in the Americas between the sixteenth and eighteenth centuries. Jangling her profits, she bartered much of her wealth for art and architecture.

"A good portion of it they evidently poured into that sumptuous cathedral," he adds.

We slumber for more than two hours. At a bit past seven, we step into a cool evening. My excitement builds as I look ahead to the flamenco show we booked for ten o'clock. Uncle Chuck suggests a walk around Barrio de Santa Cruz before dinner.

In twilight, we meander through a labyrinth of alleyways, enraptured with a spirited Latin beat pulsating from street-corner musicians' trumpets and electronic keyboards. *El paseo* in *Sevilla.* Vendors peddle roasted *castañas* (chestnuts) and sardines from smoky grills. Up and down streets, *tiendas* open for business. We see, behind brightly lit windows, merchandise ranging from chocolates to weight-loss products, negligees to woolen scarves. We have evidently wandered beyond the tourist zone.

The deeper we penetrate the barrio, the more this neighborhood bustles with the brio of Sunday evening celebrants. Music issues from bars and the essence of spices and roasted meat perfume the air—the embodiment of *ambiente* (crowded, noisy), just the way Spaniards like it.

"Shall we head for that restaurant now? Modesto, I believe it's called."

Uncle Chuck has dinner on the brain.

Our course reversed, we see nothing familiar. Lost again.... Uncle Chuck flags a taxi. Piled in, we ask for Restaurante Modesto. (Options when lost: 1. Admit and ask for directions. 2. Hail a cab.)

At lively Modesto, we order *sangría* and sip while casting decisions. We start with *crema de patata ahumada con crujiente de beicon*: smoked, creamed potatoes with crisped bacon. For entrée, Uncle Chuck selects *ternera con alcachofas*: stew of veal and artichoke hearts in wine, and I, *choto en salsa de ajos:* grilled kid enlivened with garlic sauce. I cannot speak for Uncle Chuck's, as he has abandoned not a scrap, but mine invokes culinary sublimity, salsa spiked with just enough garlic, and the meat melts in my mouth. To wrap up our meal, we split a plate of *tocino de cielo* (heavenly bacon), dense, ivory custard frosted with sweet caramel. The color of this dessert, so say the Spanish, resembles the pig's snout. Furthermore, Spaniards consider *tocino de cielo* the pork we eat in heaven.

Proceeding cautiously now, we heed directions given by our concierge to Los Gallos. Without getting lost, we find our flamenco club deep within the Santa Cruz Barrio.

We are surprised at the confined space of the club, but not at the cloud of smoke. The room accommodates forty people, all smoking. We should travel with oxygen....

Ushered between child-sized chairs at the foot of the *tablao* (stage), we squeeze between other patrons' knees and the brink of the stage. Each table the size of a medium pizza, intended for sharing by two, includes the ever-present ashtray and scarcely enough room for drinks.

A cramped stage, fifteen feet in breadth, ten in depth, frames a backdrop of roosters (*los gallos*) painted in bright, impressionistic brush strokes.

Two *tocaores* in flared sleeves stride up from the back of the room, one of them middle-aged and balding, the other youthful with flowing wavy hair. Each grips his *guitarra*. Once settled, the men tune their instruments, then nod in kind. Red spotlights engage. *Cante chico* commences. Strumming, the musicians smile and guffaw, the younger man tossing his tresses. The older man scowls, then bursts into lively *bulería*.

House lights come down. Red spots infiltrate and mood takes over. Subtle foot-taps, gentle strums lure a statuesque figure out, her glossy black hair pulled tautly into a bun. Framed with precisely arched brows, kohl-fringed eyes flash like jewels. Through haze of pinkish cigarette smoke, the enchanting apparition floats marginally controlled. Posture is everything. I know I'm breaking out in a rash.

Our enchantress alights at center stage. Frowning, she arches her back, raises graceful arms like a ballerina, throws back her head and stomps once. *Ay!* To raking staccato, she cuts loose, blinding us with a vortex of white petticoats. Melody simmers. Arms waver flame-like above her head in sensuous, serpentine pantomime. Adrenaline seizes. Again, again she jockeys between restraint and erratic vent. Pouting mouth, pumping legs, stormy petticoats. Restraint…. Savage temperament! Restraint…to the final throb of riveting catharsis when, all too soon, she exits behind a windy whorl of red and black. I exhale.

Two more men join those on stage. Guitarists break into a lively ditty, a blur of fingers strafing guitar strings. Accompanists counter with voice and percussion. Now, a coquettish Gypsy regales us, a petite firecracker with deep-fringed neckline of scarlet a-frenzy. Her *zapateado* and sensuous gesturing of hands escalates impromptu strumming, plucking, clapping, stomping. A singer springs from his stool and goes berserk. Exalted as though by grief, he cants in fierce *voz afilá*. Tension grips the room, the energy, contagious. I lose my head, crying, "*¡Olé! ¡Eso es!*"

As four musicians pursue their improvisation, I notice for percussion only cadent hands and heels, hypnotic music sounding more Arabic than Spanish. Flamenco, raw and pure….

Just as I settle down, out walks a *cantaora* garbed in mourning black. Her supple complexion glistens olive-brown, her eyes, lethal. She claps twice, breathes in deeply. I drift into a trance as she belts out a poignant ballad: unrequited love shared in visceral *siguiriya* style.

> *El día paso con pena y la noche con dolor,*
> *suspirando me anochece, llorando me sale el sol....*

> The day is full of troubles, and the night full of pain,
> twilight falls on my sighs and the sun rises on my tears....
> —Anonymous Gypsy lyrics, as quoted by Federico García Lorca

"¡Así se canta!" cries a man behind us.

The nightingale smiles sweetly. Now, passion takes flight. Her face writhes as she pursues her stormy tale. She clutches her bosom; tears sparkle in her fiery eyes.

For one breathless moment, she pierces me to the quick, warming me with my own fire. She gazes at me tenderly, then leers and points as though I stand accused! With quavering resolve, I refrain from crying out *forgive me!*

The wronged woman disappears. All goes black.

> If you are touched by music, you are touched by love in a very pure way.
>
> —Pepe Romero

Another silhouette emerges. Swelling spotlights reveal a *bailaor*, haughty, at center stage. Hair drifts to his shoulders disheveled, greasy. Not the physique of a dancer, but tall, beefy, double chinned. In high-waist pants, he struts like a horse—or, is he a satyr on high heels?

A refrain ignites his spirit. Clumsily, this hulking man assaults a *farruca*, stomping across the boards, a number more burlesque than serious dance. I slide down in my seat.

"Tiny Tim," Uncle Chuck remarks.

I laugh out loud, wondering if the fellow will cut loose on a ukulele.

Following *Señor* Tim's number, all of the beauties alight again on stage, pulverizing the floor, swirling in *fin de fiesta* splendor.

Amidst thunderous applause, *"¡olés!"* and *"¡baila!"* we squeeze through the smoky room to crisp outdoors. As we head toward our haven, I walk on air, reveling in afterglow.

"That was *duende*," I tell Uncle Chuck. "Remember the show in Madrid? It looked rehearsed, choreographed. What we just saw was spontaneous and *raw*. Did you see that singer point at me? The one with hunger in her voice?"

"She pushed your buttons, didn't she?"

"Wow. I used to think Edith Piaf was intense, that Billie Holiday had bluesy technique, but that woman in black really suffered. I felt hypnotized when she looked through me with those laser eyes. I believed what she told me, although I understood few of the words. I wanted more."

"Well, I understand *buenas noches*, young man. It's been a long day for this old *americano*."

A TALE OF TWO CITIES

Sevilla *(population 700,000), once a thriving* colonia *of the Roman Empire—and birthplace of Hadrian and Trajan—Julius Caesar named* Hispalis *when he captured the region from native* Tartessians *in* B.C. *45. Nearby, the Romans built* Itálica. *Berber conquerors later called the territory* Ish-biliya *and ruled there for hundreds of years. After the Reconquest, New World discoveries filled* Sevilla's *coffers with gold from the Indies, from trade through her port on the Guadalquivir, still one of the Iberian peninsula's most active river ports.*

Besides her wealth of architectural and artistic masterpieces, flirtatious Sevilla *beguiles with cultural treasures: a museum of fine art (Museo de Bellas Artes) eclipsed only by Madrid's Museo del Prado, an art school and a university formerly a tobacco factory that inspired Georges Bizet's opera and character Carmen. The mythical Don Juan[1] was born in Seville, securing for the city an important role in the world of literature. Added to this, Seville boasts a real treasure, Archivo General de Indias. Carlos III commissioned the archive in 1785—in La Casa Lonja, a commodities market—as a grand storehouse for records and maps relative to Spain's colonies in the Americas. This archive of an empire houses an eighty-million-page paper trail dating from 1492 to the de-colonization of Spain's holdings in the Americas in the early 1800s. I dreamed of delving into the collections, knowing the inventory included letters in* Fray Junípero Serra's *hand.*

My concierge kindly rings up the archive. He frowns when a recording tells him, "Shut down for renovation for two months." To bury myself in the archives ranked high on my list. I am gravely downhearted, having traveled so far, only to discover the archive closed. The sensitive concierge notices my desolation and ventures to gain special dispensation. He phones his friend at Seville's city hall, but his valiant endeavor is denied.

Over breakfast at Coliseo, Uncle Chuck and I discuss possibilities for today's exploration. The sky lowers, so the *archivo* would have been an appropriate venue. And a tour of Córdoba requires more than a day trip.

"Check this out," I say, passing Uncle Chuck a travel book opened to a spread on Cádiz.

"Claims to be the oldest inhabited European city, settled by Phoenicians as their trading post in eleven hundred B.C.," he reads aloud. "Later controlled by Carthaginians and then Romans. Set on an isolated limestone promontory...once home to Hannibal...where Julius Caesar first held public office...sacked by Sir Francis Drake...Spain's capital for a brief period...port from which Columbus made his second voyage...."

"And *Fray* Junípero Serra set sail from there, as well," I contribute.

"I should have guessed," grunts Uncle Chuck.

Back at the hotel, a valet delivers our car from the garage and we set out for Cádiz.

Sailing southwest on the *autopista* (toll highway), we encounter geography less remarkable than we saw north of Andalucía. For miles, landscape stretches from black-and-white cotton fields to tilled-under farmland to random thickets of blue-green pines. On our left loom smoky-blue mountains, on the right churns the white-capped Guadalquivir. For gasoline, we stop north of Jerez de la Frontera, the sherry capital. Uncle Chuck forfeits a king's ransom to fill our tank.

On approach to the hazy port of Europe's oldest city, we make out shapes of docks and davits, huge freighters, a forest of sky-raking structures. Ships under construction, freighters, stevedores, oil refineries crosshatch the scenery. We travel along a momentous peninsula thrust into the Atlantic at least a mile. We pass fishermen and canneries to reach the old part of town, knowing we've found Cádiz when a peculiar cathedral comes into view.

We have ventured from a gem of a city to discover the *Taza de Plata* (Silver Bowl), a bleak, homely port. As it has taken two hours to get here, we will try Cádiz. Near the cathedral, we pull into a public garage and descend into its depths.

The tempestuous Atlantic defines Cádiz on three sides. From the water's edge, beyond a seawall of massive concrete blocks, extraordinary views propose in spite of overcast sky. We spot the fortress. Nearby, the cathedral rises above pastel boxes—apartments swathed in pastel pink, blue and yellow. The off-white Catedral Nueva presents a synthesis of baroque and Neo-Classical flair, sporting an enormous cupola of glossy ochre tiles and two domed spires. We've heard rave reviews of the cathedral's ecclesial cache. And the tomb of composer Manuel de Falla can be found within the nave. We cross over.

We recoil to the discord of metal against stone, earsplitting bursts, sputtering jackhammers. Workmen at one side of the palatial cathedral rend a section of concrete plaza. Other grunts labor diligently inside. Through one of the portals, we peer from scaffoldings to dust-masked men in overalls laboring in near-darkness. We walk along the periphery, striving to find a way in.

"They've shut the whole place for repairs," Uncle Chuck tells me. I can tell he is crushed.... We move through the plaza, Uncle Chuck dreaming of a *marisquería* (seafood restaurant). I dream of visiting Falla's tomb. He was, after all, the master of *duende*.

Bar La Caleta proposes a likely spot with outdoor tables on a palm-fringed plaza proximate to the sea. The heavens have cleared, affording essence of salty air, views of cruise ships and gulls aloft. Uncle Chuck stares at a mound of cold broiled shrimp in jackets, with legs, heads and tails intact. Between sips of flinty-dry *vino de la casa*, a white Rioja, he struggles with his order of *gambas a la plancha*.

"These taste of the sea," Uncle Chuck mentions, "though I'd fancy them not as briny. Moreover, I'd prefer not to shuck and clean them."

My salad measures large enough for two. I share. Uncle Chuck forsakes his *plancha* after dissecting a fourth shrimp. He samples my tasty *gambas al pil pil*—a regional casserole of peeled shrimp in bubbling garlic oil, punctuated with chiles, but it's too spicy for him.

Between bites on the sunny *terraza*, I read to Uncle Chuck about the evolution of the name Cádiz. Phoenicians named it *Gadir* (Fortress), Greeks renamed it *Gadeira*, and Romans, *Gades*. Berbers called it *Jeziret Kadis*. Under Spanish monarchs, the port finally was known as Cádiz, an anchorage for Spain's Silver Fleet. Sir Francis Drake sacked this city in 1587. In 1812, Cádiz became Spain's capital, when the nation's first constitution was declared here.

"We'd have been better off to relax back at Seville," Uncle Chuck huffs, "and read of all this in your travel books."

We order *tortilla a la española*, splitting the luscious wedge between us. Instead of dessert, we sip more Rioja.

Cádiz sports outstanding museums, including Museo de Cádiz with fragments dating from Phoenician occupation. We saunter through steep, cobbled mazes, on a spoor to find those relics. Unlike tidy Barrio de Santa Cruz back in Seville, neighborhoods of Cádiz come to light poor and unkempt. Gleeful urchins play *pelota* in the streets. Alleyways teem with cats and dogs, notwithstanding signs warning:

PROHIBIDO
JUEGO DE PELOTAS
Y DEFECACIONES
CANINAS

We stumble upon Oratorio de San Felipe Neri, one of the museums we wished to visit. Damn! It closed for the day thirty minutes ago.

"Let's head back to Seville," Uncle Chuck suggests. "Cádiz won't head my list of recommended destinations," he suspires. At least he didn't snicker....

I acquiesce. In spite of Cádiz's storied past, it holds none of the allure of enchanting Seville.

With relief we exit the peninsula, speeding northeast, arriving at Seville in time for Uncle Chuck's siesta. I soak in my jetted tub with journal and a glass of Barbadillo sherry.

"What's for dinner?" Uncle Chuck asks from his bed.

I carried from America pages on Seville torn from a magazine. An article mentions Egaña Oriza, an outstanding restaurant just two blocks from our hotel. I tell Uncle Chuck where he'll find the pages in my luggage. Propping himself up on one elbow, he reads.

"Let's give it a whirl."

It's not yet dinnertime in Spain. So at the wee hour of seven o'clock, we dress in warm togs, then set out for sightseeing.

We walk to the banks of Río Guadalquivir, enjoying a captivating panorama of Torre del Oro. As we stand in the black chill night, we indulge in kaleidoscopic views: golden reflections of the *torre* mingled with shimmering ribbons of gold, green and orange rippling in lights from the shore.

KA-BOOM!

"Basque protesters," Uncle Chuck implies as salvos echo, chattering between the banks.

We've seen *insurrectos* (rebels) in the north of Spain, even in Madrid. But way down here, in Andalucía?

KA-BOOM - M - M!

A wreath of smoke issues near the *torre*. Yells and chants follow more blasts, more echoes. Some things are best left unexplored. We flee, hiking to southern extremities of Jardines de Murillo, to swanky Restaurante Egaña Oriza.

It's still early as we plop down in the bar. As we consider a list of *tapas*, a waitress fills our prescription for gin on the rocks. The first round of *tapas* is petite, crispy pastry cups heaped with chopped prawn, sprinkled with dark gray caviar.

The restaurant opens in thirty minutes. We peek inside. A menu of regional dishes and a refined room tempt us, but we're wilting.

"Shall we carry on now, with more *tapas*, then consider it a day?" asks Uncle Chuck.

We order slices of roasted pork loin, served cold on toast wedges, plus *buñuelos de bacalao* (cod fritters), pungent anchovies in garlic-spiked olive oil, and *croquetas caseras de jamón* (ham croquettes).

A Gypsy limps into our exquisite bar. Grasping a cup in his grubby hand, he begs for pesetas. As the forsaken man approaches our table, the manager snaps, *"¡Adiós! ¡Buenas noches!"* The beggar returns to the streets. Uncle Chuck believes a sorbet would have been a preferable intermission.

We savor two desserts, a light-as-air pastry shell enfolded with vanilla ice cream under a landslide of wild strawberries, and an apple tart prepared in the manner of *tarte Tatin*, topped with heavy cream.

Laden with an overabundance of *tapas* and sweets, we hope another walk will foster sleep. We cross the *paseo* and step through open gates of the university. Above a portal, a floodlit white statue of Gabriel the Archangel blows his horn. Beneath him, Spanish youth swarm, yammering into cell phones. We discover a pleasant courtyard and linger for photographs.

I accompany Uncle Chuck back to our room, then return downstairs to the lounge. Seeking a table, I navigate through the smoke-filled quadrant and snag a seat near a bronze bust of Alfonso XIII. Between sips of *anís seco*, I complete my day's journal.

Tomorrow we depart this miracle known as *Sevilla*. My heart longs to stay. Seville, without question, impresses me as the paradise of cities; lovelier than Rome, more graceful than London or Paris, even prettier than Florence or Venice. Though I have marveled at the glories of those other European cities, I had not felt the overwhelming sense of belonging, the twinge of *terra cognita* that I do here in Seville. Moreover, I discover myself—a Catholic—considering the concept of reincarnation. Such thoughts indict me as "designer Catholic," according to my friend Monsignor Weber.

Nevertheless, I have experienced déjà-vu moments in Seville. *Sevilla* speaks—no, sings—to me. I feel that, if only I spent more time here, I would unravel the meaning of *duende*.

[1] Playwright Tirso de Molina (Gabriel Téllez) introduced the Don Juan character in 1632.

ADIÓS SEVILLA HERMOSA, HOLA RONDA

Quien no ha visto Sevilla, no ha visto maravilla.
He, who has not seen Seville, has not known marvel.

—Anonymous

Luggage sat packed, zipped and set for deployment to the town of Ronda, one of Andalucía's pueblos blancos. An early breakfast under our belts allowed time to explore one more of Seville's attractions before we lit out.

Near ten o'clock, we wend our way to a section of old city walls built of rammed clay by *Almohades*. Not far away, we step up to Los Reales Alcázares that rise on foundations of Roman acropolis and Muslim *alcázar*, a structure hailing from the reign of caliph 'Abd ar-Rahmân III (A.D. 913), when Seville furnished the *Almohades'* Andalusian capital. Before Berber reign, a paleochristian basilica and Visigothic buildings also occupied this site. Berber residents included Al-Mu'tamaid and Abû Ya'qûb Yûsef. Today we will see splendid palaces from the fourteenth century, constructed for Pedro I El Cruel. Of these sumptuous accommodations—the modern royal family's official headquarters in Seville—select chambers are open to the public, the royal apartments off-limits.

From Plaza de Triunfo, we move toward the fortress's carmine-colored

Puerta del León. Between crenellated bastions and portal, a tile crest depicts a lion wearing a crown and clenching a crucifix in a front paw.

Inside the old palace, a ticket seller hands us audio devices with our site maps. We advance to an open-air courtyard known as Patio del León (Courtyard of the Lion), passing under leafy arbors of green tinged with red, through splendidly honeycombed arches. Before us lies splendid Patio de la Montería (Courtyard of the Hunt), an intricately carved plasterwork arcade. Beyond this enclave we enter El Patio de las Doncellas (The Courtyard of the Maidens) replete with convoluted carvings, strap-work, *Nasrid*[1] arches and columns. In this court, eunuchs purportedly sacrificed hundreds of virgins to Moorish emirs.

We negotiate *salas*, discovering *Almohad* horseshoe arches, faïence panels, wainscoting of sinuous Kufic inscription laced with lozenge designs. Post-Reconquest touches in *Nasrid* motif—sanctioned by Peter the Cruel, circa 1350 and by his successors—come forth throughout the palace. Notwithstanding, historians consider this entire complex Spain's purest example of *Mudéjar* architecture. Sala de Justicia (Court of Justice), a fourteenth-century chamber and twelfth-century *Almohad* patio just off the courtyard are the oldest parts of these *alcázares*.

Salón de Embajadores (Hall of Ambassadors) blooms in *Nasrid* architectural flourishes. We glimpse neck-wrenching aspects of surviving *Almohad* details and an incredible cupola swathed in crimson, green and gilt. In 1526, Carlos V and Isabel of Portugal (parents of Isabel La Católica) staged their wedding beneath this dome.

Uncle Chuck's love affair with European antiquities piques as we enter resonant quarters of Charles V known as Sala de Tapices (Hall of Tapestries) and Sala de Fiestas (Hall of Festivals). A trove of Flemish tapestries, ornamental clocks and inestimable paintings abound. We drink in splendors of sumptuous artworks, then step onto the sun-drenched patio of El Jardín Estanque de Mercurio (The Garden Pool of Mercury). This setting stuns in its beauty. In the midst of formal, terraced gardens, flowers and palm fronds sway in rhythm with the arpeggio of running water. Between walls plastered in cantaloupe hues lies a *terraza* centerpieced by a leaden fountain with Mercury aloft. An outburst of water gushes between a cordon of peristyles, then into a reflecting pond beneath the winged messenger of the gods.

From Mercury's garden, we turn our attention below. Terraces of painstakingly clipped hedges neatly follow serene ponds, raked gravel pathways, palms, cedars, more fountains. The scene takes the breath away....

Moors, then their conquerors, welcomed cool retreats from Seville's summers in these comely environs, their *hortus conclusus* (enclosed, inviolate garden).

Concluding our tour, we glimpse an ancient Arab bathhouse, then exit through colorful Patio de las Banderas (Court of the Flags). On the way out, we gaze through a carriage-way to flapping banners, through orange trees, to a commanding view of the mighty Giralda Tower.

At half-past eleven, we depart Seville, disengaging regretfully under dazzling cerulean sky. As we drift south on A-4, the highway we traveled to Cádiz, I locate on our map the town of Las Cabezas de San Juan, what turns out to be a dismal town with a crossroad leading us east to our destination at Ronda. Playing with the radio en route, I find stations serving up Gypsy music, and drift back to the captivating flamenco show at Los Gallos.

Rolling along, we survey rich, freshly plowed soil, hillsides terraced with almonds and olives. Meadows yield luxurious green, and deep-blue mountains stretch across the horizon. We spot random *pueblos blancos*, isolated, whitewashed towns cascading along intermittent hillsides. We plan to lunch in one of those villages settled for protection from invasion, just ahead, in the foothills of the Lijar.

Algodonales is a prim *pueblo blanco* two-thirds the way to Ronda from Seville. In second gear, we drive a precipitous track to the town center. We park near pleasant Santa Ana church and admire its campanile of sandstone trimmed in burgundy. At the opposing extremity of Algodonales's square, a golden fountain spouts twelve glistening arcs, symbols of mountain springs that have nourished local populace since the Neolithic era.

We cannot decide from among the town's cafés, so I ask the clerk at a compact *supermercado,*

"*¿Donde hay un buen restaurante?*"

She shrugs and smiles at a stocky, middle-aged man who has just picked up his sack. The man takes me by the crook of my arm, from the store, down a footpath to Calle Mayor. Uncle Chuck follows.

"*Ahí,*" the cordial fellow advises. He points a stubby finger toward a restaurant near the church. "*Muy bueno,*" he assures and wishes us, "*Buenos día y buen apetito.*"

Nothing fancy, this oblong restaurant has a bar along one side, six wooden tables on the other. On walls hang framed, faded sepia panoramas of *pueblos blancos*. The bar hums with earnest conversations among young men; local farmers, we decide, affirmed by rough hands and soiled overalls.

A friendly woman delivers menus, slips of pink paper listing but four *tapas*. I want *ensalada*. With none available, we order beer and sandwiches, Uncle Chuck's, *caña de lomo* (pork loin) and mine, *serrano* ham. The woman breaks lunchtime ritual and graciously makes a salad for us. I love Spain.

With hunger quelled, we again loop through the tapering grade, then merge onto the highway below. Just when we believe scenery cannot be better, it is with each passing kilometer. A-wheel on sinuous mountainside roads, we spot more isolated villages glistening in white from strategic positions. As we pass through Grazalema Natural Reserve, we sigh at vistas of an emerald-green lake cradled within a mountain cleft. We spot an occasional ruinous hilltop *atalaya* (watchtower) and sensing the best lies ahead, yonder the specter of Ronda strikes.

The village of Ronda, cleaving to a rocky shelf of Serranía de Ronda, is a spectacular, vertical village established in days of prehistory, acquiring wealth as a fundamental trade zone during Roman occupation. Moslem Ronda gained importance as a Berber *taifa*, one of the last Muhammadan bastions. Conquered in 1485 by the Catholic Monarchs, Ronda's Islamic aspect thereafter blossomed with churches, convents and Renaissance mansions.

Since the eighteenth century, Ronda is known for its Puente Nuevo, a bridge constructed mid- to late-1700s, stretched across a gnarled limestone chasm more than three hundred feet wide. The gorge named El Tajo plunges four hundred feet to the floor of the Guadalevín River valley. Protected behind *murallas*, the old Muslim stronghold perches atop one side of the ravine. Post-conquest Ronda was spawned on the other side of the new bridge.

Had we planned more auspiciously, we would have entered Ronda through her old city gates, driven through the old town and across Puente Nuevo to the *parador*. Instead, we enter the new town and pass the old bullring. We stop short of the bridge where stands Parador Nacional de Ronda, a cliffhanger at Ronda's northern fringe. Next time, we will know better.

Our *parador's* 1761 exterior contrasts a modern interior. Originally a town hall, this historic aerie with Renaissance façade ranks as one of Spain's most conveniently located *paradores*.

We had requested a room with a view. Our suite sports two balconies; each affords a panorama stretching to distant western mountains from where we came, to a valley floor quilted with farmsteads and dotted with ruins. From our outlook, we see groves neatly planted plus Moorish walls and rusticated city gates. Boundless mountains fold deeply in indigo-blue shadows. Our position will not exactly blow the gauge on an altimeter, but stepping onto the larger of our balconies, I halt short of the railing and go numb.

The dizzying dimensions have not the anxious effect on Uncle Chuck. Ensconced at the balcony's edge, he admires the vista, making photographs. I enjoy the panorama from a safer range, behind him, in the sitting room.

"You're not embracing the experience from in there," Uncle Chuck teases.

Familiar with the classic scene of Puente Nuevo in travel essays and guidebooks, I feel cheated that we had not experienced, on our way in, the view of the illustrious bridge from the other side.

Heading out, we seek vantage points for picture taking, where I will not flinch from the height.

We hike to the new bridge, tarrying to study its eastern contours. From here, we see seventeenth-century Puente Viejo (Old Bridge) spanning two weathered precipices above an arid riverbed. Ronda's medieval folk fashioned this bridge, also known as Puente San Miguel, on foundations of a Roman span.

We traverse the New Bridge to Calle Tenorio, heading toward a cobbled square. Determined to pinpoint an access for my photo mission, I trudge ahead, leaving Uncle Chuck to his sightseeing. He catches up with me as I contemplate a steep flight of stone stairs.

"You go ahead," he prods, after gauging the series of steps. "I'm not going to risk a heart attack."

With camera bag and tripod in tow, I slowly descend switchback steps to a succession of hairpin paths leading to the canyon floor. I pause at turnouts to evaluate the spectacle of Ronda's lofty setting. Views infect more as I trek sweaty palmed toward a likely outlook, to record bracketed exposures of wondrous stone span stretched between greenery-dotted vertical cliffs, a golden and verdant spectacle plunging to a riverbed. Remote terrain strikes a landscape in triptych within three handsome arches. Our *parador* looms above, just to the left.

When I have at last memorialized each scenic angle, I pack up my camera gear and turn to head back. Above stands the minute figure of Uncle Chuck. He looks over a stone balustrade, plausibly miles removed. The return excursion takes my breath away. Though I paused at each turn of the steep track, I am winded upon my return to the top. I did not look down once....

Breathing heavily, I plod in sync with Uncle Chuck's leisurely pace. Walking astride, delving deeper into Ronda's old town, we are drawn to an intriguing campanile. We traverse a compact plaza to discover the minaret-turned bell tower of Santa María La Mayor, a splendid brick church.

Incorporated between the fifteenth and sixteenth centuries into a former mosque, this collegiate church hints of Islamic glory. Inside, we find a thirteenth-century horseshoe arch, a *minbar* (staircase-like pulpit) and a *mihrâb* (prayer niche facing Mecca). The rich stucco, filigreed touches date from the Islamic *Marînid* Period.

Quietly, we walk between massive pillars, across marble floors. In this dim church hang fourteen bronze plaques depicting the tribulations of Mary, an extravagant high altar of silver and hauntingly beautiful shrines embracing statues of saints, of the Virgin. This church, dedicated after the Reconquest to the Virgin of the Incarnation, poses a curious fusion of Gothic and *plateresque*.

Following our tour of nave and vestry, we scale the minaret's worn-stone steps to a balcony. From here, we appreciate a late-afternoon perspective of Ronda's *ayuntamiento* across the plaza.

"Martini?" I ask Uncle Chuck.

"Pregnant thought," he replies.

On a back street across from our *parador*, we discover Café-Bar El Torero Restaurante. Inside are only four others: the proprietor-manager, a cook and her husband with a spunky Yorkshire terrier. We park at the bar and study the wall. Autographed portraits of toreros hang above and between fifths of liquor. In each photo, posed alongside a bullfighter, stands the restaurant's owner—a tall striking man with moustache and generous, wavy hair. Celebrities in the photographs range from newcomers Enrique Ponce and Javier Conde to the illustrious Antonio Ordoñez.

As we relax with gin martinis, the courteous owner introduces himself as Jaime Alles. When he mentions my camera equipment, we engage in genial conversation. *Señor* Alles proffers coffee-table books chock-full of idyllic views of Ronda, then proudly discloses the lore of his hometown plus tales of *bandoleros* (bandits) that dwelled in caves of outlying mountains as recently as the 1950s. Alles comes to life as he launches into anecdotes concerning famed toreros and aficionados.

"You know of Orson Welles and Ernest Hemingway. They came to Ronda frequently." *Señor* Alles continues with a chuckle, "*Señor* Welles *eez weeth* us in Ronda *estill*. When he die, *heez* ashes they *esprinkle* on the *estancia* of the greatest torero, Antonio Ordoñez."

Uncle Chuck asks, "Where did they bury Hemingway, or sprinkle him?"

"Idaho," *Señor* Alles and I answer in sync. "Buried, not cremated," I add.

Señor Alles details Hemingway's love of Spain and *afición* for the *corrida.* I am impressed with Alles's *Hispanidad* (Spanishness), with his knowledge of a great American author.

"Antonio Ordoñez, he call Hemingway Papa Ernesto," Alles says reverentially. "*Eso deed* aficionados."

This flesh-and-blood Spanish exemplar glows as he reminisces. I glaze over. But when he mentions *duende,* I sit up, interrupting his litany.

"*Señor* Alles?"

"I am Jaime," he warrants with a broad mustachioed smile.

I correct myself, "Jaime, please tell me about *duende.*"

"Ah, *eez* not easy to *esplain. Los* toreros have *eet,* deep *een-eside.*"

I slump. How does something as inhumane as bullfighting embody the *duende?*

"Please, tell me more," I say.

Jaime's nostrils flare as he rejoinders, "*Duende eez contagioso,* ah, the contagious passion. *Eez* how a person look at you, when you *esee heez esoul,* feel *heez* longing...."

Jaime turns his attention to the walls. Now, he grips the edge of the bar, gazing back at me.

"Do you under-*estand la corrida?*" he growls.

Jaime is impassioned with the ritual of bullfighting. He named his restaurant for the fighters. The wall in front of me screams allegiance to toreros. How do I tell this man how I really feel?

"I do not understand it," I manage.

Jaime inhales deeply, leans across the bar, locks his eyes with mine. I smell his pomade.

"*Eez* simbólico, ah, symbol—symbolic! When the matador *keel* the bull, he *keel* oppression. *Eez* living art. When you know *Espanish* history, then you understand *theez simbolismo.*"

By now, I believe all Spaniards have *duende.* But how could I have it, when I will not step foot into a bullring?

¡Que no quiero verla!	I will not see it!
Dile a la luna que venga,	for I do not want to see
de Ignacio sobre la arena.	the blood of Ignacio on the sand.

—Federico García Lorca, "*La sangre derramada*" ("The Spilled Blood")

Jaime turns, grabs a bottle and pours a whiskey. *What comes next?* The cook and her husband come to my rescue. The dog belongs to them. We exchange tales of canine idiosyncrasies and unconditional love.

Uncle Chuck and I drink up, bid them all *hasta luego* and return to the *parador*. We savor the day, waving goodbye to a sunset from one of our balconies. A fiery orb slips behind a breadth of mountains, a suitable interval as we aspire towards dinner. Jaime told us that El Torero serves before eight P.M. We're pleased.

"I'm so happy that you broke custom back there, at the bar," Uncle Chuck says.

"Meaning what?"

"Well, generally you speak your mind. Yet you didn't tell Jaime how you feel about bullfighting."

"I didn't want him to throw me out or poison my drink, did I?"

As we quit our suite at half-past seven, the New Bridge glows in floodlight. Peace blankets the town. The air chills and penetrates.

El Torero's warmth and subtle lighting welcome us, as do mouth-watering fragrances drifting from the mezzanine-level kitchen.

We order a bottle of Rioja *tinta*, indulging as our waitress presents great steaming bowls of soup, *de vegetal*, comparable to minestrone, and *de ajo*, garlic-based, thickened with bread, floated with a poached egg. Uncle Chuck cannot resist farm-raised chicken served roasted with French fries. I venture *rabo de toro* (tail of the bull), rich, fork-tender, prepared in the manner of oxtail, served in its own casserole. *Wonder if my order pleases Jaime?*

Jaime sits at the bar. Between slurps of soup, he chats with customers, discussing *la corrida*, no doubt.

With *anís dulce:* sweet, anise-flavored liqueur, we relish *arroz con leche*, rice pudding transcribed as "rice milk" on the *tarjeta de postres* (dessert menu).

Back at our *parador* by nine-thirty, we enjoy a twinkling black firmament. We perceive far below us a snaking trail of miniature headlights and occasional flickers from camera strobes—flashes that will not reach their subject, El Puente Nuevo in floodlit radiance.

Venganza Dulce del Toro

An American, nostrils twitching like an eager hound's, followed his nose into a Spanish restaurant. *What was that seductive aroma?* Seated, he caught wind of an enticing dish on the next table. *That's it; what I smelled.*

The American questioned the *mozo*, "What is that man having?"

"*Criadillas,*" the waiter replied.

"In English, please," said the American.

"Bull's testicles."

The American paused a moment, then said, "I'll have some."

"I'm sorry, *señor*. We have no more *criadillas*. Come back tomorrow, after the *corrida*."

The American, dreaming of a tasty meal, returned next day and ordered *criadillas*. But when the *mozo* placed the order under the American's appreciative nose, the American stared in disappointment at a plate of testicles smaller than those he'd coveted the day before.

"Waiter," he cried. "These are so small!"

With a shrug, the *mozo* replied, "*Pero, señor.* You see, sometimes the bull, he wins."

---

[1] *Nasrid:* A dynasty founded by Muhammad ibn Yûsuf ibn Nasr, a member of the Arab Banû l-Ahmar family. *Nasrids* built the Alhambra palaces at Granada.

CALIPHAL OBSOLESCENCE, SPANISH FRIES ON THE SIDE

At seven A.M. the timbre of water awakened me. Uncle Chuck was in the shower. Perched on the edge of my bed, I gathered my bearings, stretched and shuffled across the room to peek at Nature's stereoscopic presentation....

Mustering gritty resolve, I creep cautiously through sliding doors, over threshold, onto the balcony. A breeze carries pungent whiffs of leafy smoke from N-gauge bonfires far below. Silence deafens, as though someone has pressed a mute button.

I inch forward, swallowing hard. Now, with firm grip on the rail, I peer for the first time over the brink. Distant valley floor fills my view-plane with shadowy-gray flat scenery shielded yet from the rising sun. I clutch the railing tighter and spot, way below, the tiny ribbon of road where we saw headlights and camera flashes last night. I recall tales of Spain's Civil War, when prisoners were hurled into this gorge. I feel dizzy....

Uncle Chuck sunders my trance.

"Get yourself ready, boy," he tells me as he pulls a sweater over his head. I rush through the drills and join him downstairs.

Through a breadth of arched windows, the dining room frames postcard vistas of Ronda's old bullring and diminutive Plaza de España. I single out Uncle Chuck, coffee in hand at a table with a view, and wave to him from the buffet.

From generous offerings, I choose a wedge of *queso* Manchego *fresco* (young, mild sheep's cheese) a crusty bun, granola. Uncle Chuck runs the gamut of the buffet.

"This will tide me over for one of your marathons," he says. "Shall we have one more cup of coffee and hit the streets?"

Across the new bridge, along dewy cobbles we tread to *La Ciudad*, the old part of town. We pause for snapshots of redbrick Minarete de San Sebastián, a slender tower standing a lone sentry of pre-Reconquest mosque. I wait patiently for a delivery van to vacate before framing the fourteenth-century monument with my camera.

Carefully picking our way down a steep slippery byway, we ponder Palacio de Marqués de Salvatierra. Through a finely wrought stone gate called Arco de Felipe V, we examine the palace's Renaissance-style limestone walls set with pre-Columbian figures. The *arco* was the original passageway to Puente Viejo. Around the next bend, we study the seventeenth-century bridge not as filigreed as its eighteenth-century counterpart traversing the gorge near our *parador*; the Old Bridge linking the breach of El Tajo not as precipitous as the height of our balcony. This smaller bridge rests upon a single semi-circular arch. Beneath, a ribbon of the Guadalevín thinly flows. We follow a bank of this trickle along old city walls to the Baños Árabes, savoring Ronda's ancient structures through blurring mist.

Guidebooks and local brochures tout Ronda's Arab bathhouse as the *best preserved Arabic baths of the Iberian Peninsula*. Fashioned from brick, with domed ceilings carried on sturdy piers, this venerable structure hails from the turn of the fourteenth century. Moorish bathers used the same water mill, aqueduct and heating systems as did their Roman predecessors.

We pad across an uneven brick terrace, moseying through a series of horseshoe arches and into cool depths. Domes are perforated with *lumbreras* (apertures) shaped as Muhammadan stars, cobwebbed apertures admitting weak light, casting obscure, eight-pointed stars onto tile floors. I remark on this structure's correlation to the Arab baths in Palma de Mallorca.

Now we backtrack, seeking out Puente Árabe, a holdover from the era of the baths. Trivial in design, this bridge rises from one forthright arch maintaining a narrow passageway.

Farther along, we locate eighteenth-century Fuente de los Ocho Caños (Fountain of the Eight Spouts) alongside a primitive stone church called Nuestro Padre Jesús, Ronda's oldest, dating to the late-fifteenth century, Gothic in style, its *campanario* constructed later in the Renaissance period. The fountain that supplied drinking water to ancient residents runs cool and clear today. We ponder seeping spouts, imagining medieval townspeople gathering here with *jarras* (water jugs).

What was it like then? Did those earlier denizens appreciate the beauty of Ronda, the natural beauty garlanding this city's lofty position? Did medieval folk take this majesty for granted, or were they too engaged, eking out a living, rebuking errant Inquisitors, fighting off bandits? As they collected water from the fountain, what were the subjects of their gossip—or did they gossip at all?

Chilled and craving caffeine, we hike back to the new town, settling at a café snuggled within the bustling arcade of Plaza de Socorro. Warmed with espressos, we step across the plaza to Iglesia de Nuestra Señora del Socorro, a smart church of whitewashed sandstone carrying a pair of fine towers. Traversing the plaza, then through a passageway, we face Plaza de Toros, Spain's oldest bullring (opened 1785), whose architectural engineer José Martín de Aldehuela also designed this town's Puente Nuevo. Martín plunged to the afterlife while inspecting his bridge. Just the thought of it makes me dizzy.

Out front of the bullring, we photograph bronze statues, depictions of Spain's most illustrious *matadores*: Antonio Ordoñez (1932-1998) and Pedro Romero (1754-1839). Jaime Alles told us this was a favorite haunt of Welles and Papa Ernesto.

I am smitten with Hemingway's work, though at odds with his *afición* for the bullfight. Though fascinated with Spanish *afición*, my position on animal cruelty precludes any interest in the spectacle. Having given considerable thought to Jaime Alles's mordant words, I now consider *la corrida* more diversion than entertainment.

Uncle Chuck suggests a visit to the historic bullring.

"It's vacant," he consoles. "This isn't the season for bullfighting."

"No, thank you," I counter.

I went to the bullfights in Málaga, in Lorca, in Barcelona. What perversity in the Spanish character demanded this sickening spectacle? You couldn't blame Franco for this, although it must have been a tremendous safety valve for all the frustration of fascism. The *corridas* depressed me, and I was glad to abandon the effort. But the events were inescapable, always on television, constantly in the newspaper.

—Paul Theroux, *The Pillars of Hercules*

Northward, we track down austere Iglesia de la Merced, to capture it on film. Inside this 1585 church, we discover one of the incorrupt hands of Saint Teresa of Ávila.

Uninterested, Uncle Chuck complains, "I'm cold."

We peek through windows of a cozy spot called Restaurante Polo. "Looks pretty good," Uncle Chuck remarks. He sees the familiar words *chuletas de cordero* (lamb chops) on the posted menu.

We stand at attention until a Spaniard, who does not look Spanish at all, ushers us to a table, then opens poster-sized menus and offers them to us. Uncle Chuck will not brave the more exotic fare. I prime my palate for stuffed *boquerones*.

"Now, what are these *boquerones?*" he asks.

I interpret, with assistance of my pocket phrase-finder, "Whitebait, described as stuffed with spinach, *pimientos*, deep-fried."

"I'll pass," he says, sticking with his decision for lamb chops.

The well-kept room is accented with dark wooden beams athwart tilted ceiling, and wallpaper and table dressings of blue and white.

With a perspiring bottle of crisp Rioja *blanca*, we split an enormous salad. Uncle Chuck requests his French fries *seca* (dry), having been assigned too many versions of Spanish fries sodden with olive oil. Tiny, pink lamb chops receive a rave review and his potatoes, "prepared exactly as I'd hoped." My tiny, plump fish propose a party for the palate, uniquely dressed, not stuffed as described; instead, vegetables robe the fish.

After a satisfying lunch, Uncle Chuck becomes better acquainted with his mattress.

We hadn't looked at city walls or gates up close this morning, so I'm off with camera in hand. While the antique village lolls peacefully, the only souls roaming Ronda's streets this chill afternoon are a couple off-season tourists and an *anciana* pulling a wire cart of groceries.

From the foot of Arco de Felipe V, hazy blue hillsides climb to the southwestern horizon. Emerging from a bank of white mist in the mid-ground broods a fortress-like edifice of sienna-colored brick, buttressed, cut with angular lines in its pediment garnished with carved finials. This was a Renaissance church, Iglesia del Espíritu Santo (Church of the Holy Spirit), dating from the fifteenth century, when it was a fortified tower. Beneath the church, sun-drenched hillocks stretch dappled in hues of chartreuse tumbling gracefully to the feet of stone walls.

In the direction of Holy Spirit church, well-trodden, craggy, flagged pathways wind to the *murallas*. Two impressive gates pierce massive fortifications, one from Muslim occupation, the other dating from the Reconquest. The Muslim gate is Puerta de Almocabar (thirteenth century), the other, Puerta de Carlos V (sixteenth century). Along the thick wall, under mighty parapets, additional gates fill in with stones. Under half a mile of these walls remains intact from a link that hundreds of years ago encompassed the southern extremities of Ronda.

Up an alley, a cat enjoys lunch, only his hindquarters discernable from a trash dumpster, his rear feet gripping the rim, tail swaying in ecstasy. I frame this humorous scene through my viewfinder, but the whir of advancing film alarms him and eight or nine other felines that launch from the can and scatter throughout the alley. Annoyed, they regard me from a distance, surely not as annoyed as I, having missed a zinger of a photograph.

As I return to the room, Uncle Chuck is ripe to leave. I muster energy.

On the way to El Mercadillo, the new part of town, we duck into a confectionery to enjoy waffle-cones of praline ice cream dense as taffy.

We have not yet explored the northeast end of Ronda, so we have a prowl through its neighborhoods. Beyond plazas and shops, we chance upon Iglesia de Santa Cecilia. In this chilly, candle-scented church, we move quietly, admiring a gaily-painted retable under a dome of white, and an image of St. Cecelia glowing within a halo of gilded stars.

Though I grew up in a Catholic home and have seen my share of shrines and statues, such are far bigger deals in Spain. Halos are larger, plated with silver or gilded with gold. At the feet of these religious icons, lie *ofrendas*: flowers, rosaries and devotional medals known as *milagros* (miracles). And candles flicker ubiquitously, real candles and even electric versions. Isabel La Católica's vision for Spain stands strong as ever in the twenty-first century. It dawns on me that the notion of *duende* induces such devotion.

SYMBOLS OF FAITH

We encounter assertions to pietistic conviction in Spain's general population at her shrines and churches. One sees these symbols of faith at side altars. Besides candles and flowers, we find amulets of silver or gold—bearing likenesses of saints—known as *milagros*, some configured as legs or arms, others representing heads or hearts. By way of illustration, if one's leg were diseased or lame, he would pray to a saint associated with leg injuries or diseases. If cured, the formerly afflicted deposits an appropriate icon shaped as a tiny leg at the foot of a saint's statue, as a gesture of gratitude and respect.

Milagros are depicted in portraits, as well, in symbols and other representations of specific intercessional acts of the subject saint.

Most moving of these testimonies, plus assertions of manifestation of miracles, are pairs of full-sized, well-used crutches or other walking aids occasionally discovered at or beneath the shrines.

> Righteousness comes from faith, hoping against hope that God's promises will be fulfilled.
> —*Romans 4:13, 16-18, 22*

With noses and fingers numbed from cold, we return to our room for international news on television. Uncle Chuck thumbs through a magazine, stumbling upon a review on a *comedor* called Don Miguel. Descriptions glow. We decide, at six o'clock, to relax there with a cocktail.

"I'll bet they make good martinis at Don Miguel," Uncle Chuck says.

Don Miguel's bar occupies a softly lit, smoky cellar. We order drinks, then carry them up to the lobby and sip while leafing through travel magazines. This lounge is peaceful, with no cigarette smoke, for a change.

When the restaurant opens, we are first in.

We order a bottle of Barbadillo Rioja *blanca*. Uncle Chuck begins with salad sporting a mile-long list of ingredients: sweet and bitter field greens, hearts of palm, shredded beets, cured sheep's cheese, kernels of corn.... Corn? This must be a new trend in Spain. I have read of Spaniards' disdain for what they call "food for pigs, food of Mexicans."

I order *sopa rondeña*, unlike the version we enjoyed at Torero, the broth entirely absorbed in great chunks of bread, with an undertone of chiles.

Uncle Chuck proceeds with roasted duck, moist, tender under a layer of crackling skin. My entrée, a trout, leers back at me. This handsome fish is grilled, dappled with bright salsa of fresh pineapple and almonds, duly superb. Finally, we find it tough to resist luxurious crêpes filled with warm loganberries and topped with a mountain of fluffy whipped cream.

"A shame we leave tomorrow," I lament to Uncle Chuck. "I'd love to sample more of this regional cuisine."

As peace falls on the village, I puff a cheroot on the balcony—a conservative three feet from the rail—scanning winking stars for my favorite constellations, and bidding Ronda good night.

CUISINE OF ANDALUCÍA

No mystery why the Andalusian diet appeals to me, as I find comparable fare within an easy drive from my home in Southern California. I have sampled gazpacho—Andalucía's signature soup, in effect, puréed salad of tomatoes and other vegetables blended with garlic, vinegar, oil, bread, served cold—all over the southwestern United States. Rarely do I sense these versions as superlative as Spain's. Paella—found all over Spain, but the cradle of this dish was Valencia—I have eaten in America and in Spain. In both countries, renditions range from lamentable to sublime. Spicy food I love, the more *picante*, the better.

Cuisine of southern Spain includes cured meats, spiced sausages, wild game, fish, and a liberal dose of olive oil—none of this deviant from food styles of regions north of Andalucía.

Though ragouts are knocked out throughout Spain, *cocidos* (one-pot stews) and *potajes* (bean stews) generally taste spicier in the south. Offal is more popular in Andalucía, where the occasional restaurant lists *riñones* (kidneys), *sesos* (brains), *hígado* (liver) or *criadillas* (testicles) on menus.

Tomatoes, peppers sweet and hot, and honey, cooks use liberally throughout Andalucía. Fried fish, including *sepia* abound. Vegetarians find agreeable dishes of legumes and vegetables known as *pisto* (stir-fried).

Recipes intrinsic to Andalucía include *flamenquines*: deep-fried, breaded veal or ham, and *al pil pil* preparations: Basque adaptations of seafood baked in oil, with garlic, chiles. Unlike the cuisine of Castile and Galicia, Andalusian food spikes with flavors of Middle Eastern and oriental sway, with cumin, saffron, cinnamon, paprika and lemon commonly detected. Other characteristic ingredients include olives, oranges, artichokes, chickpeas, even tripe (*callos*).

Though *tapas* abound throughout Spain, these delectable snacks originated in Andalucía. A signature entrée, *rabo de toro* resembles a spicy rendition of oxtail stew. Favorite Andalusian dishes, such as soup known as *ajo blanco,* incorporate crushed almonds. In the south, cooks add a splash of sherry to main dishes and likewise to *postres*.

Across Spain, desserts include flan or its variations. In the southwestern United States Mexican restaurants serve sensuous flan. For the most part, luscious Mexican caramel custard mimics its rudimental Spanish equivalent.

FROM RONDA'S BRIDGES, BULLRING AND ARAB BATHS TO A CLOISTERED RETREAT IN GRANADA

In the midst of skylarking, one sometimes forgets to check the itinerary, as Uncle Chuck and I did at Ronda....

With car trunk packed and backs to El Tajo, we trundle over Puente Nuevo, squeezing through cramped streets of old Ronda past sights now familiar. Wind buffs the sky luminous and the temperature is agreeable, in the mid-sixties.

At the foot of the hill, throngs erupt from ship-sized tour coaches. We will long remember splendors that still lie ahead for these visitors newly arrived.

We roll through Ronda's massive gates, scanning signposts for Antequera, a recommended route to Granada.

Eastbound, soon the road climbs through mountains honeycombed with hideouts of yesteryears' wily *bandoleros*.

"Funny," I mention, "as we checked out of the *parador*."

"How so?" asks Uncle Chuck, his eyes focused on the road.

"The lady at the desk asked if there was a problem with our room."

"And she wanted to know why we weren't staying another night," Uncle Chuck adds.

"It's not as though they need the business, with all the tourists just arrived."

"Those buses make only a day trip," Uncle Chuck points out. "Did you have enough breakfast?"

Given his penchant to make tracks, I knocked back more than my customary ration, having helped myself to an Uncle-Chuck-style breakfast.

"Where are we now?" Uncle Chuck quizzes, after traveling twenty miles.

With a partially unfolded, poster-sized map on my lap, I scout for signposts to gain my bearings. We have ventured beyond Serranía de Ronda, on approach to a southern range designated on my map as Santa Bermeja.

"Well, it appears we're headed south. We want east," I answer.

"So, relax. Enjoy the views," Uncle Chuck says. "We're not going to turn around now."

My map shows no major connectors before Málaga. I suggest we persevere Costa del Sol, then trail that southern coastline, then proceed north from Málaga, proving a banner choice, for the route cuts with mile upon mile of serpentine mountain roads and bird's-eye views of heart-stopping scenery dotted occasionally with lime-white *pueblos blancos*.

As we creep along momentous switchbacks of the unspoiled Santa Bermeja range, we trail a laggard convoy of trucks. At a pullout, the huge trucks turn in, allowing a string of cars, including ours, to speed ahead.

Dropping down, we approach the seaside village of San Pedro de Alcántara. The Mediterranean ripples before us. Through haze, we glimpse the Rock of Gibraltar on the distant horizon.

"Stop the car!" I yell.

"What's wrong?" my nonstop driver asks. "And please, don't do that again unless there's a problem."

"Please, pull over," I insist.

Amazingly, he grants my request. We turn back.

Clutching camera bag, I sprint across two lanes of highway to a bluff with sweeping panoramas of exquisite villas. Trucks wheel by, the same convoy we passed miles back. After they pass, Uncle Chuck catches up with me as I reflect from a bluff.

"Homes of movie stars, athletes or such," he suggests, as we soak up an enviable tableau.

Agape, we drink in celestial scenes of dream homes against a panoramic backdrop of blue granite mountains, a mid-ground of lush pine forests and beyond, a vista saturated with the breadth of the sea.

"Must be nice," Uncle Chuck remarks. "Now, let's carry on. It's a long way to Granada."

I would settle for a humble abode, just to live in Spain....

We wind down the mountainside, enraptured with blissful San Pedro, a slope sown randomly with noble villas and modern pieds-a-terre, an enclave exuding a self-confident air. Lissome palms hem ribbon-like, hillside roads, adding grace to terraces of countless swimming pools.

We visualize an equivalent scenario beyond, at coastal Marbella, but this haunt of the rich and famous parallels Miami Beach in its brash forest of high-rises.

Before us, the shimmery Mediterranean scrolls in hues from sapphire blue to violet. The expansive sea holds our attention as we traverse miles of Costa del Sol by the towns of Fuengirola and Torremolinos, each as overrun as Marbella. We proceed along the *autopista*, above and around the achromatic sprawl of Málaga, an old Phoenician stronghold.

"Challenging," Uncle Chuck remarks as we scan the vastness of this maritime city. "Good thing we don't have to go in."

A gentle spray of rain brightens our windshield as we advance northward from Málaga. With the sea behind us and an aluminum-colored sky overhead, pastel scenery presents less than spectacular. For miles, we see but rolling hillsides neatly tufted with olive trees and tobacco fields, with only the random outcropping of rustic farm breaking the pattern.

Tierra seca,	Dry land,
tierra quieta	quiet land
de noches	of immense
inmensas.	nights.
(Viento en el olivar,	(Wind in the olive grove,
viento en la sierra.)	wind in the sierra.)
Tierra	Old
vieja	land
del candil	of oil lamps
y la pena.	and sorrow.
Tierra	Land
de las hondas cisternas.	of deep cisterns.
Tierra	Land
de la muerte sin ojos	of death without eyes
y las flechas.	and of arrows.
(Viento por los caminos.	(Wind along the roadways.
Brisa en las alamedas.)	Breeze in the poplars.)

—Federico García Lorca, "*De Poema de la Soleá*" ("Poem of the *Soleá*")

With no inkling of civilization for miles and Granada far afield, we pull into the first *venta* we happen upon, at Villanueva del Trabuco. On the tarmac, we hearten ourselves against a bitter blast of wind.

We step into a spacious cafeteria cold as the weather outside. Behind a marble-topped bar, haunches of cured pork dangle from the ceiling. Three stout men in quilted jackets lean on the bar, tossing back beer, belching appreciatively. Another man plays hunches on a one-armed bandit.

We've acquired a taste for *serrano* ham. Sliced wafer thin, this delectable treat tantalizes in translucent shades of burgundy marbled with creamy white. We order some on crusty bread plus two short glasses of draft.

I wipe crumbs from my mouth, eager to push on to the grandeur of La Alhambra at Granada. Uncle Chuck convinces me to linger for coffee.

In an hour, we reach the outskirts of Granada and slow to a crawl as we weave into the ancient city's plexus of streets and blind alleys. Behind a tangle of commuters, we finally extricate ourselves, adjusting our course after a lengthy delay. The easternmost approach to Granada proves practical, dispatching us directly up a hill toward La Alhambra.

Along this outcrop of Sierra Nevada, hemmed between a brigade of tour buses, we scour scenery for signs of Parador Nacional de Granada. At last, we set eyes on a signpost. Then, running out of signage, we stop to ask for directions.

At a snail's pace, we move alongside a growing parade of pedestrians, then enter a hillside forest cut with hairpin lanes. When asphalt gives way to cobbles, we bump along, arriving at the pinnacle, in the shadows of La Alhambra.[1] My heart sinks as I stare at austere piles of brick fortress with cubic towers.

"The wonders lie beyond these walls," Uncle Chuck speculates. "Think of them as theater curtains; the best is behind them."

> We leave the question to Allâh,
> who knoweth the secret of hidden things.
> Insight in matters of religion is better
> than insight in matters of knowledge and law.
> —Abû Hanifa, the *Fiqh* (Law)

As a tourist army marches abreast in our direction, negotiating the site tests our patience. Sightseers gawk, snapping pictures, oblivious to dangers of a moving vehicle and cranky driver. Uncle Chuck taps the horn, expressing the daydreamers to sidewalks.

From photos in travel brochures, we recognize the golden-pink, brick veneer and towering belfry of an old *convento-parador* at the end of the track.

Though built in 1495 on the foundations of a thirteenth-century Arab nobleman's palace with mosque, modern conveniences come into play the moment plate-glass doors slide open on an electric eye. Only a small number of Spain's *paradores* are modern constructions. The majority of these inns embrace renovated accommodations and high-tech features within ancient walls. An exemplar of *paradores* is this old Franciscan friary, Convento de San Francisco, El Parador de Granada—about as Spanish as Spanish gets.

Milieu strikes eclectic, the wall behind reception trimmed with an antique painting of St. Francis cradling his crucifix; a shelf beneath his image outfitted with computers, printers and credit card machines.

A goddess receives us. Her face—with supple, olive complexion, seductive purse of lips, noble *Roma* nose and bewitching eyes—could have inspired a classic painting. Reviewing our vouchers, this raven-tressed woman tells us apologetically, "I do not have you listed for today, *señores*." Pecking at her keyboard, she adds, "Your reservations are for tomorrow and the two days following."

Uncle Chuck and I look at each other in dismay. The goddess resumes her pecking.

"That's why they acted peculiar when we checked out of Ronda this morning," I tell Uncle Chuck.

"We have a cancellation," the woman says, "so we can take you."

We sigh....

She phones the *parador* at Ronda to credit our missed day, checks us in, then summons a porter. A short, thin, elderly gent in green uniform appears and gathers up our luggage. He leads the way, whistling a cheery ditty as we stroll behind through dim corridors hung with old paintings of saints. He puts down a bag, points to a canvas of St. Anthony, now, to himself.

"I am Antonio," he boasts, then resumes his whistling.

I glance up, as we pass a landing, to a radiant stained-glass window etched with the Franciscan coat of arms: crossed arms of Christ and Francis of Assisi, each hand skewered with stigmata. Our quarters are just beyond, through a private sitting room with chamfered corners and Oriental rug bordered in tile patterns of sienna, bone and green.

"The friars didn't live in such comfort," I mention to Uncle Chuck as we check into our smart accommodations. I'm engaged with the size of this room, with its Moresque-style furnishings, posh fabrics and pristine bathroom.

"Señores, por favor, " Anthony proposes as he pulls back heavy draperies, "your view."

What a view. Through grand, arched windows, our eyes feast upon a rose garden and reflecting pond; farther afield, postcard panoramas of orchards, a blissful vega rising from a narrow gulch.

The elderly gent arranges our luggage on racks, then grins, lingering attentively for a tip. We hear his whistle trail off as he heads back toward reception.

Unpacked for four days at Alhambra, we set out to explore our digs—a stopover, since its days as an inn, for Arthur Rubenstein, Rita Hayworth, the British Queen Mother, General Franco, President Lyndon Johnson and Victor Mature. Grace Kelly and Prince Rainier honeymooned here. Uncle Chuck wonders: which quarters were theirs? I still would have preferred another day at Ronda.

Arrived one day early in Spain's most popular *parador*, we feel fortunate to reside in the oldest section, a two-and-one-half-storied convent encompassing an open-air courtyard. Wings appended in the early 1900s, though architecturally harmonious with the antiquity, do not hold the enchantment of the original convent.

A dozen-or-so paces from our room, we enter a cloistered patio. Here I imagine Franciscans at prayer, reminding me, though on a smaller scale, of Patio de los Naranjos at Seville's cathedral. Similarities include orange trees and a nuclear fountain, flagstones cut with irrigation channels, a lofty cypress soaring beyond the dormer story to the height of an adjacent belfry. Stone columns delineate an arched cloister bearing the weight of a loggia. Perimeters of the ambulatory are set with long, wooden benches. Modern touches include café tables and wicker chairs set around the fountain and, yes indeed, rocking chairs.

We pursue through a gloomy corridor that leads us back to a shrine we noticed on our way in. Mindful of a marble tomb, we pass under a scalloped arch to investigate, and find ourselves inside a *mihrâb*, the only section preserved from the property's Islamic pedigree. Arabic inscriptions embroider interior walls, one side pierced with three *Nasrid* arches framing a *vega* beyond. Countless *muqarnas* (cells and carved stalactites) festoon the dome. At our feet, a marble slab identifies the tomb of Isabel the Catholic

(1451-1504). Isabel requested burial here in a humble grave, but her remains were conveyed to the cathedral's Capilla Real below us in the city, some years after the death of her husband Fernando (1516). The marriage of these Catholic monarchs sealed the fate of Spain's sultanate.

With our backs to the *mihrâb*, we see a diminutive chapel dating to Franciscan occupation. We peer into a scantly lit space, making out an ornate, gilded altar screen. Pews seat, at most, eighteen. On either side of the altar hangs a portrait, one of Isabel, the other of her husband Fernando. Outer walls are cut with niches of relics, marked with marble tablets.

As we poke about, we discover an elongated room, with hoary fireplace, converted to conference hall, formerly the friars' refectory. We admire statues and portraits, plus a crucifix ensconced within a nook along shadowy corridors leading us back to the lobby.

I stand nonplused. How ironic, how distressing, this Muslim shrine defiled with tombs and shrines of their conquerors. One of the Catholic Monarchs rested for a time under the floor of the mosque's prayer niche. Just down the hall, they stock and tipple liquor, and a game table sits in proximity to this formerly hallowed Islamic plot—all such forbidden in *al-Qur'ân* (the Koran).

We pass through an informal lounge filled with overstuffed furniture and reading material, to a bar looking onto an expansive cliff-side patio.

"The terrace?" I ask Uncle Chuck.

Shivering involuntarily, he says, "Not in this season, dear boy."

Carob, aromatic cypress, pomegranates and quince shade the lovely *terraza*. Shimmery fountains and views to Sierra Nevada (Snowy Mountains) invite. We park at a table in the cozy bar for scotch and soda. Bowls of plump, salty almonds and tangy olives accompany.

"When I see those miles upon miles of olive and almond orchards from the highway, I wondered what they do with all of them. Now I know," Uncle Chuck remarks. "Every drink in Spain comes with almonds or olives or both."

It feels good to be out of our car, footloose within the privileged environment of La Alhambra, the Muslims' replication of heaven on Earth. We discuss our schedule for tomorrow. We'll book a tour of the palaces and gardens.

I cringe at the thought of a tour as I recall our truncated visit of El Escorial and Los Caídos. But this is the only way they do it at La Alhambra.

"I feel like a nap," Uncle Chuck sighs, placing his empty glass on the table.

To dream of dinner, we retire to our cell for siestas.

Rejuvenated, we pad through corridors softly lit with Moorish sconces of pierced brass, through lounges abuzz with conversation.

This evening's repast in a graceful, yet comfortable dining room commences with a bottle of robust Rioja Banda Oro Paternina 1997. The wine favors our *bocadillos complementarios*. For first course, Uncle Chuck orders sautéed fresh pasta tossed with vegetables and soy sauce. I decide to try *ajo blanco*: a cool lake of almond paste, cream, olive oil and grape juice with mere parentheses of garlic. Garnish of chopped apples adds crisp texture to the cold soup. In a word: masterpiece.

Between courses, we study the room's appointments: antique stone details, marquetry ceiling in faux-Moorish design, breadths of glass proposing a twinkling black sky. The majority of our fellow diners dress casually—unduly so, for the most part, yet a few are respectfully attired.

Two waiters deliver silver-domed plates with much ado. As they synchronously lift the domes, delectable aromas drift from our plates and we behold Uncle Chuck's beef sirloin Pedro Ximénez with chestnut purée in sweet red wine sauce. And my country chicken *Alpujarra*-style. Each dish is superbly presented, the chicken with skin folded to the knuckles, giving the aspect of elegant gams with stockings unrolled. Arranged neatly about the meat selections: savory morsels of cubed, fried potatoes, pearl-sized cherry tomatoes and quintessential Brussels sprouts.

For dessert, we sample dabs of custards, petite pastries drizzled with bittersweet chocolate and tarts filled with custard and cream.

In a digestive fog, we return to our room at quarter past ten. Here, in comfortable beds, we dream of layers of history, of conquests pervading this hill where we slumber.

[1] *Alhambra: Al-qal'a al-hamrâ'*, Arabic for The Red Citadel; others define *al-Amra* as The Red.

TALES OF THE ALHAMBRA

When Moors first arrived in Spain in the eighth century, Christians were still barbarous. How, I wondered, did Spain's citizenry, under Islamic rule for eight hundred years, co-exist in peaceful harmony—when in the twenty-first century we still see religious wars? Spain's ancient Moslems tolerated other religions. As Moors reigned in Iberia (711-1492), faiths of Islam, Judaism and Christianity flourished in concord. Isabel and Fernando shattered that utopian spirit.[1]

The deeper I probed this extrinsic outpost, the phantom Alhambra, the more respect and compassion I felt for its ancient populace, the more I realized their terrestrial plat resembled the Paradise described in al-Qur'rân.

Greeting the new dawn, I revel in exquisite solemnity. In lusterless cool, this cloistered patio belongs to me. The air is sweet and still, the tinkling fountain flows gently into a *teja* strategically conducted from a spigot, directing a crystal current to a slender waterway. Vestigial geraniums yield faded petals to the bedrock. A statue of St. Dominic, with an air inquisitive, leers from his niche. I leer back. *Why are you here, in this Franciscan convent?*

"Ready for breakfast?" Uncle Chuck booms.

We are first in the *comedor*. A commodious buffet tenders succulent casaba melon slices with texture and flavor of vanilla ice cream, together with deep burgundy strips of *jamón serrano* and crusty rolls just-the-ticket. Stainless steel pots of robust coffee and hot foamy milk supply *cafés con leche*. Though second helpings tempt, we resist and hit the Alhambra's cobbles.

This brisk morning banks of mist linger within the deep Darro Valley. Fountains splash and warble. We drink in chaste air as we await our tour.

Before nine-thirty, others gather. Now, Concha greets us. This bright-eyed, redheaded Spanish woman in horn-rimmed glasses will lead our three-hour tour of the Alhambra palaces, fortress and Generalife (in Arabic, *jannat al-'arîf*: the artist's garden).

Like a gaggle of geese, we follow Concha to the esplanade. Here she splits us into three language groups: Spanish, English and German. Once divided, our cortège tallies smallest, with only Uncle Chuck and me, two Brits, a French couple and Concha. Germans and Spanish-speakers, Concha assigns to other guides.

We trudge on, passing trinket and bookshops and halt at the foot of a church with a prominent belfry, Iglesia de Santa María de la Encarnación, built from 1581 to 1617 on foundations of the *Nasrid* Friday mosque. The yellow-stone pile rises opposite the resplendent Renaissance palace of Carlos V. Somehow these post-Reconquest edifices look out of place in an Arabic compound.

"Carlos ordered a great portion of the Moorish palaces destroyed, making room for his own palace and this church," Concha explains in flawless English. "In its Moorish heyday, this Alhambra sported twenty-three towers, four gates, seven palaces and a plenitude of dwellings for commoners. Carlos lived here for only two months, on his honeymoon. The church provided services and sacraments for the Catholic Monarchs."

Though an intruder within a Muhammadan realm, the palace of golden stone surrenders a masterwork of the High Renaissance designed by Pedro Machuca, a pupil of Michelangelo, in 1526. The quadrangular exterior stands garnished with pediments, Corinthian capitals and escutcheons. Between the gingerbread, overlays of rusticated stone impart the illusion of enormous, golden-brown waffles, the first level studded with heavy bronze wreaths dangling from mouths of lions and eagles. Inside the quadrangular building, we discover a ring-shaped courtyard of marble; above, a loggia carried on thirty-two peristyles. Grand, the overall sensation and though bare-bones cold, one of the chambers, Museo de Bellas Artes, embraces rare art treasures.

> ...the Italian Style
> the Florentine Style,
> the roomy, gloomy, spacious, severe, symmetrical
> Renaissance Style.
>
> —Gladys Wynne

We trail Concha to the centerpiece of La Alhambra, the enchanted Palacio Nazaries (Arab Palace), pulled back in time as we enter the Mexuar (from the Arabic *mashwar*: Council Chambers). Alabaster walls of these mysterious quarters evoke magic. Just outside, patios and passageways undulate with ciphers above, clad with faïence tiles beneath. Marquetry-strapped ceilings impart rich patination. An enclosure facing the Darro Valley sports lacy *ajimeces* (Moorish paired windows). We learn that common folk, such as ourselves, were not allowed in these courtly chambers during the sultans' reigns.

Concha pauses occasionally, to herd us into a corner where she shares snippets of La Alhambra's story-laden history.

"Granada, formerly occupied by the indigenous *Túrdulos*, came under powers of Romans and Visigoths who named this region *Illiberis*. On this hill called *La Sabîka*, Visigoths succumbed to Arabs in A.D. 711. From 1031, *Almorávides*[2] and *Almohades* ruled *Gharnatha*[3] until Muhammad ibn-

Abî'mir, a North African Berber, founded the Alhambra in 1241, establishing here his *Nasrid* sultanate. As king, Ibn-Abî'mir changed his name to Muhammad I. A contemporary of Fernando III, Muhammad I hailed from a tribe called *Beni Nasar*. Under Muhammad's rule, Granada became the wealthiest stronghold in Iberia and known as the Eternal City. They say Muslims made Spain great, bringing light to the dark Middle Ages. New crops and agricultural techniques came with them as they swept through Spain, introducing their modern world, developing arts and sciences, building elaborate palaces, schools, gardens and bathhouses.

"You will step across terraces of marble," Concha continues, gesturing for us to follow. "Beneath stretches a labyrinth of water courses supplying ponds and fountains throughout this complex. Water comes from the Sierra Nevada we see in the distance. Snow caps that range throughout the year," she says, pointing to distant mountains.

Concha emphasizes that much of this architecture went up in the reign of Muhammad's successors, Yûsuf I and his son Muhammad V. The Alhambra measures seven hundred-twenty meters (2,340 feet) by two hundred-twenty (715 feet).

We cross murmuring parterres to a marble patio, the Cuarto Dorado (Gilded Quarter), its center marked with a flat fountain. The prospect of Comares Palace across the patio intoxicates in proportion and in capricious detail, a façade richly historiated with Kufic relief and geometric fretwork, breached with five arched windows. Glazed tile patterns in shades of green, blue, rust and white enrich door frames and wainscoting.

Concha cites symmetrical designs as geometrical, others epigraphic: inscriptions, phrases or poems from *al-Qur'ân*; the absence of human or animal forms in the interior décor, an Islamic precept.

Spellbound as we are with these tangible metaphors, the effect eclipses with exaggerated splendors around the next corner. *Serrallos* (chambers of concubines) give way to Patio de los Arrayanes (Courtyard of Myrtle), a regal enclave cut with a hedge-lined pool mirroring images of lacy arcade and tenuous pillars.

We pass through Sala de la Barca (Hall of the Boat in Spanish and in Arabic, *al-birka*: pool). Just beyond, we marvel at extravagant details in Salón de Embajadores (throne room and Lounge of Ambassadors), at a ceiling that depicts the seven heavens of the Muslim cosmos in rich intaglio subtly colored. Here, Isabel and Fernando watched Boabdil (Abû 'Abd Allâh Muhammad XII), the last of Granada's *Nasrid* caliphs, sign the articles of secession. Boabdil's abdication marked the swan song of Muslim rule in Spain. Thereafter, the Catholic sovereigns held court temporarily in these palaces of La Alhambra, and in this lounge of the ambassadors, Isabel received Cristóbal Colón.

I am familiar with photographs of Patio de los Leones (Courtyard of the Lions), but unprepared for reality. This courtyard is a visual feast in a class by itself. Though twelve massive lions carrying the central fountain's weight are alabaster copies of originals, the overall context numbs. Legend proposes the innocuous lions represent the twelve suns of the Islamic zodiac. Four channels radiate from this fountain in directions of the compass, the four rivers. Numbers play an important role in Islam.

> And when Moses sought water for his people, so he said, "Strike with thy staff the rock;" and there gushed forth from it twelve fountains; all the people knew now their drinking place.
>
> —al-Qur'ân

The metaphorical fountain rests at the core of a symmetrical courtyard of bountiful peristyles, delicate, slender, balancing filigreed arches hemming Patio del Harén (harem): delicately garnished pavilions garnished amid a forest of delicate columns. Effecting Elysian space underlying masses of second-story walls of stone, this is architectural triumph, art and geometry impeccably conceived. Concha tells us this cool, marble oasis proliferated with flowering shrubs in the era of the sultans.

Sala de los Abencerrajes, a vestibule giving onto Patio of the Lions, lies adjacent the Dome of the Mocárabes (*Muqarnas*), an eight-sided star cupola. We gaze up into its lacy interior to sixteen windows broadcasting gentle illumination within snowflake-like ornamentation. To my eye, this resembles a wedding cake turned outside in, though Uncle Chuck indicts this an "ivory kaleidoscope." According to Concha, "the stellate decorations conjure up visions of star-filled sky." Whichever, we feast on a symphony of composition. Rapt with dizzying beauty, I recoil as Concha rekindles a bloody tale of rival nobles. Residents of La Alhambra invited the Abencerraj family here to a banquet, then massacred them in this gorgeous room.

At an extremity of the complex, beyond La Daraxa gardens and El Palacio del Partal, lies the oldest part of La Alhambra, after the citadel. Only a portico and tower, plus their rippling reflections in a pond, remain of El Partal's vastness.

We step into another gallery abutting the Lion Courtyard, Sala de las Dos Hermanas (Hall of the Two Sisters): more neck-wrenching ceilings writhing in arabesque, arches and squinches, domes dripping with pensile carvings in ivory-hued stucco. In fragile state of preservation, these handcrafted, stalactite-vaulted chambers strike splendorous in themselves, yet we detect remnants of faded embellishment showing shades of green, blue and gold, bringing to mind opulence even more exalted in the reign of the caliphs.

Dale limosna mujer,	Give him alms woman,
que no hay en la	for there is nothing
vida nada	worse in life
como la pena de haber	than the misfortune of
nacido ciego	having been born blind
en Granada.	in Granada.

—*Fray* Luis de Granada

On a path back toward the Mexuar, we cross marble-floored corridors between walls inlaid with mosaic patterns, rooms trimmed with incense niches, window seats and grotto-like alcoves. From these dreamily atmospheric chambers, views of the Darro Valley and Generalife Gardens propose from *miradores* (bay windows) delicately arched, latticed like bird cages.

Under the spell of La Alhambra, my imagination stirs. I hear piercing tones of a *mu'azzin* (muezzin) as he calls the faithful to prayer. I visualize silver and crystal sconces, smell them, along shadowy corridors, burning fragrantly with scented oils. My ruminations wander to eunuchs standing guard over the harem. Sultans recline on soft cushions, Arabic vixens' silhouettes tease behind gossamer veils. I picture heads rolling under bloody sabers of rival tribes. If one were so inclined to scratch the surface, he would find it all here, in mementos of Divine handiwork cloaked in oriental intricacies suffusing these legendary quarters and porticoes with Moorish mystery.

We shuffle on through resonant quarters known as Washington Irving's apartments, rooms let for three months to that legendary writer and American ambassador to Spain. Here, Irving so eloquently penned his highly acclaimed *Tales of the Alhambra* in the early nineteenth century.

"Are we ready for a break?" Concha asks.

"I'd break my own leg to sit down," Uncle Chuck whispers.

Our heads muddled with Arabian refinement, we welcome the hiatus for refreshments. Our tour will recommence after fifteen minutes, to the Alcazaba, the eleventh-century *Zirid* citadel.

At an outdoor kiosk, we idle in the cool morning air, warming our hands with fumy cups of coffee. Two in our group are from Great Britain, a married couple in their early forties. Helen hails from England and Jim from Chicago. Jim has acquired a British accent, having lived in England for fifteen years. Uncle Chuck and I enjoy Helen and Jim's company, comparing travel adventures as we shiver and sip.

Helen has made four trips to Spain, but, like Jim and us, this is her first visit to Andalucía. We all classify Alhambra as the heartbeat of Spain, the essence of what we seek here.

Concha rounds us up. We trail her to the fortress, an enormous stone pile reared on foundations of Roman and Visigothic fortresses in the thirteenth century. Under Moorish occupation, this *alcazaba* housed up to forty thousand troops at a time. We scale time-honored stone steps to a site of Barrio Castrense—excavated soldiers' quarters and primitive toilets. We mosey over to ramparts for commanding views through embrasures of Granada's quaint Albaicín (old Islamic quarter).

The massive structure beneath us recalls a momentous history. Visigoths, Muslims, then Catholic Monarchs laid it nearly to waste. These lofty ramparts bear marks of chivalry and ravage. And here we are, part of an army of tourists, adding our own footfall to this remnant of a dynasty.

When we reach the watchtower known as Torre de la Vela—a survivor of the eleventh-century fortress erected by the *Zirids*—Concha invites us to hike to the top. From our lookout, we spot pink Hotel Alhambra Palace, its *Mudéjar* tower and dome peeking above the semicircular city of Granada far below.

Concha directs us up toward the *parador*, telling us of its history, then we march behind as she passes through gates to enchanted gardens of the Generalife—a breezy oasis from Granada's blistering summer heat, the *Nasrids' hortus conclusus*.

> It is He who sends down to you out of heaven water of which you
> have to drink, and of which trees, for you to pasture your herds, and
> thereby He brings forth for you crops, and olives, and palms, and
> vines, and all manner of fruit.
>
> —From "Alif Lam Mim Sad, " *al-Qur'ân*

Along a curvaceous path, we wind between chestnut and poplar trees, cedars, box hedges. As we peer through windows cut through cedar trees, we discern ruinous foundations of buildings that did not survive the journey through time.

"We do not mean a general life when we speak of this retreat," Concha remarks with a smirk. "The name Generalife comes from the Arabic *Yannat al Arif*, or Garden of the Architect. In the fourteenth century, *Nasrid* kings visualized this Generalife as their summer palace. The Muslims foresaw their vanquish and, before their forced exodus from this *Andaluz* stronghold, built a terrestrial paradise as close to heaven as human labor and the graces of Nature could provide. Their perfumed gardens succored refreshment for body and soul."

A case of gentle steps leads to terraced gardens on a brow of the hill above La Alhambra. Exuberant verdure retains dewiness from dawn. Here, in the midst of musical fountains, we breathe in moist coolness, lingering at a balustrade, basking in the context of a visual feast. Below us stretch cypress-flanked lanes, rose arbors, fine stone balustrades, impeccably clipped hedges and mazes.

Padding along brick-flagged borders of goldfish and lily ponds crisscrossed with arcs of glistening water, we glimpse beyond the garden pavilions of the Nazaries. Not unlike interior corridors of the Alhambra palaces behind us, the magical courtyard of Generalife writhes in delicate relief, colonnaded with a host of finely hewn pilasters. Though late in the season, these gardens bloom in petaled profusion amidst jets of water waltzing across slender Patio de la Acequia (Courtyard of the Canal, *al-sâqiya* in Arabic). We peer through bowers of pomegranate, across the *vega* to our *parador*, to La Alhambra and the Sacromonte beyond. The latter, a hill honeycombed with caves, was home to Gypsies until the mid-twentieth century; now it is a tourist mecca.

I wonder at the view of La Alhambra, amazed at blocky exteriors sequestering such intricate beauty, singular harmony of space and proportion in stone and water. I imagine this relates to Islam, having to do with notions of Divine insight, a oneness with Nature.

Though sunny, it's wintry. We earnestly pursue the *parador's* warmth, repairing to our oasis for lunch.

Uncle Chuck luxuriates in a siesta-time; I write in my journal. Looking up from my desk, I turn my attention to the dale, relishing from this privileged viewpoint Moorish structures and terraced gardens of Generalife, delusional profiles under a surly El Greco sky.

I lie down, only to rest my eyes, but nod off, dreaming of tales of the Alhambra.

Uncle Chuck wakes me at six P.M.

We set off, passing by the night-lit *mihrâb*, the Isabel shrine, wandering through corridors, down a short case of carpeted steps to the bar. Spotting the British couple, Helen and Jim, we join them to discuss our tour. I ask what they do. She is a writer and he, a film producer. Helen thrills that she sleeps near the tomb of Isabel the Catholic, a visionary, medieval feminist. We enlighten Helen. The crypt is vacant; the zealous queen now sleeps in the city below.

We invite our friends to join us for dinner, but they will dine later. First, they will make a night tour of the *Nasrid* palaces.

"Night tour?"

"Indeed," Jim answers. "They open certain rooms for the price of a ticket and that wondrous tracery is illuminated. Better still, we understand only a few people take the tour, particularly this time of year. I intend to have fun with my camera."

As we take our table in the *comedor*, I urge Uncle Chuck to join me in a tour tomorrow evening. He nods, though I'm not sure he's heard me, engrossed as he is with the *propuesta de menú* (menu proposal).

We kick off our dinner with grilled, boned partridges on nests of salad dressed with cabernet-sauvignon vinaigrette. Uncle Chuck progresses to *chuletas de ciervo con pan de zanahoria y compota otoñal*: venison chops with carrots and autumn compote. When he read these words on the menu, he said the name was longer than the dish. Yet the portion is generous and the meat falls easily under the knife. We taste, discussing his autumn compote.

"Why didn't they simply describe this as squash purée?" asks my Anglophile uncle.

I have *rape mozárabe con piñones*, Arab-style monkfish sheathed in a lemony cloak studded with toasted pine nuts.

"Tasty," I remark. "But I like my monkfish naked, unadorned, chargrilled, served with lemon-butter, period. Why do some chefs gussy it up so, blurring the flavor of the fish?"

We match our selections with a bottle of Castillo de San Diego. A bracing day.... We will slumber well upon this eventful hill.

¹ In the twenty-first century, more than 15,000 Muslims live in Spain. Until 2003, the only mosques were makeshift affairs in apartments, storefronts or garages. On 10 July 2003, a mosque was dedicated at Granada, the first of its kind in more than five hundred years.

² *Almorávides*: From *al-Murâbitûn*, or people of the Ribât—a fortified monastic foundation, a base from which to conduct the Holy War or to serve as a place of religious retreat; Berber nomad tribes from the Sahara, which invaded Spain in 1086.

³ *Gharnatha:* Granada

A Pricey Sprig of Rosemary and a Stunning Bride

…It is love for what is related and similar…. for like inclines to like….as experience, report, and history all testify. This too necessitates loving God, because of the inner similarity which does not go back to resemblances of feature or form, but to inner significance, some of whose meanings we may mention in books, and some of which it is not permissible to write, but which must rather be left under a covering of dust until the traveler stumbles upon them in his path.

—From "al-Ghazálí, " *Ihyá*

Adjusted to the convent's routine, I took my time grooming and dressing, to arrive in the dining room by eight A.M. Uncle Chuck lagged, as usual. I craved coffee, lots of good, muscular coffee. I emptied an entire pot before Uncle Chuck joined me.

"Care for a walk?" I ask.

"You go ahead. I'll relax," says Uncle Chuck. "Besides, we're going into the city later this morning. Enough walking for one day."

Spooning up the bottom of my pineapple yogurt, I bid him *adiós*.

Dressed snugly, I step into halfhearted light and hike across the steamy esplanade. Turning sharply to the steep descent along a hairpin path, I advance toward the *bosques* (woods). Bus-loads have not yet arrived. Ah, alone time….

I delay a moment, contemplating regal Puerta de la Justicia, the Gate of Justice emerging from a veil of white mist drifting eerily with Muslim legacy, with spirits of Iberian triumph and tragedy.

An open-palmed hand wrought into a 1348 keystone of crumbling barbican called *Xarea* dallies with me. So does another form configured as an immense key. These shapes hold mystical significance. *Is one the all-seeing eye of God? The other the key to Truth, to Salvation or to Paradise?* I wax melancholic in this Alhambra, the Muslims' terminal aegis in Spain. My reverie calls up the ghost of her last sultan, Boabdil, banished in embarrassment by Isabel and Fernando and forced to surrender the keys in 1492. Then, on his steed, Boabdil rode to a foothill of the nearby Alpujarras. Heavy-hearted, bleary-eyed, he took one look back at his ephemeral kingdom and wept. The hill, thereafter, was known as *La Cuesta de las Lágrimas* (The Hill of Tears).

> Your son looked to Granada
> And was consumed by pain.
> The mother replied:
> A woman cries with great agony
> For what a gentleman
> Has not been able to defend.
>
> —From the poem "Boabdil Loses Granada"

Roaming along, I inhale whispers of dewy fragrances from the wooded hillside, bracing atmosphere spiced with organic-spicy-loamy fragrance that comes only from purest Nature.

Beneath a mantle of noble elders, walnut saplings spring from a carpet of velvety green. Beams of sunshine penetrate fog, diffusing the dense thicket, exposing chunks of moldered, pink-brick structures. In all likelihood, these are vestiges of Berber walls and bastions. I stray occasionally from asphalt to leaf-strewn footpaths, examining fragments palpably overlooked when renovators worked their magic at La Alhambra. Yet, within misty shrouds and an entanglement of vines and brambles, these keyhole-arched monoliths recall an aristocratic epoch.

Where lanes converge, the melody of water draws me to an erotically suggestive fountain. A plaque identifies this as Monumento a Ganivet. I wonder at the significance of its bronze subject: an unrobed, mesomorphic male straddling an elk from the rear, holding it firmly by the horns. From the elk's mouth, a jet of frothy white water gushes into a green pool. Odd tribute, I muse, to the nineteenth-century philosopher Ganivet.

A Syphilitic, Nineteenth-Century Philosopher

Ángel Ganivet y García (1865-98) based his philosophical arguments on nineteenth-century debates concerning Catholicism, Positivism, Imperialism and Rationalism. Ganivet, who suffered from progressive syphilitic paralysis, implied Spain's past was a deviation of its true ethos. Two suicide attempts he made before he expired, drowned at age thirty-two in a river.

Imos silandeiros orela do vado
Pra ver ô adoescente afogado.

Let us go down, silent, to the bank of the ford
To look at the youth who drowned here, in the water.
    —Federico García Lorca, from *"Noiturnio do adoescente morto"*
                            ("Nocturne of the Drowned Youth")

I pick up my pace along footings of citadel ramparts. Sun strikes triumphantly, burning through haze, anointing old brick structures with a sheen of golden-pink luster. On either side of my moist, sandy path, slim ramps convey crystalline liquid from a mountain source, irrigating Alhambra's verdure. I squat down and plunge my hand into sparkling water. As droplets weep from my fingertips, I close my eyes, contemplating icy water from the melted sierra ice cap that nourished the Moors, purifying them during ablutions.

I open my eyes to grottos, waterfalls, ferns and honeylocust, to morning glories unraveling purple calyces toward emerging sunshine. Butterflies silently flit from purple to yellow flower. Black-eyed daisies dance like ballerinas on verdant banks. Larks call from bowers; other birds glide through, beyond the ancient arches.

As if placed here by God, outcroppings of creamy-flowered oleander and fuchsia bougainvillea abound alongside autumn-tinged brambles and firethorn in full red berry. Stalks of ivory belladonna droop under the weight of trumpet-shaped flowers. Above all, rise great ruddy-ochre towers of La Alhambra, the grandeur of Granada.

I long to lollygag, but Uncle Chuck is waiting. I retrace my steps under relentless sunshine. At the summit, I check my pace, catching my breath and gazing down alleyways into courtyards. There exists an entire world beyond the beaten path, abodes and private patios of a sparse populace on this enchanted hill.

Back in our quarters, I tell Uncle Chuck, "The Muslims truly understood the notion of heaven on Earth."

"Moreover," he adds, "they created heaven on Earth. Remember what Concha told us? Now, let's see how the other half lives."

One of Uncle Chuck's knees gives him a fit. He insists on a taxi. Previously, we noticed cabs on the plaza near Palacio de Carlos V. We walk over and pause briefly, until a taxi arrives.

"¿La catedral, por favor?" I ask, as we embark.

We zoom through wooded hillside along switchbacks akimbo until we reach the bottom, beyond La Puerta de las Granadas (The Gate of the Pomegranates). Our driver maneuvers left and quickly veers right through a throbbing city, then pulls over and points.

"La catedral," he croaks.

We jaunt up an alley, making our way to Capilla Real, fending off Gypsies who sell sprigs of rosemary. The royal chapel is closed, but, says a sign, open in forty-five minutes.

"Coffee?" Uncle Chuck proposes.

Sounds good to me. We drift past the Alcaicería[1] and its colorful *mercados*, shadowy alleys strung with multicolored banners, polka-dotted dresses and filmy scarves. Rows of baskets overflow with tacky trinkets, among them, chintzy piggy banks, squirt guns, costume jewelry, ubiquitous leather coin purses. Along the way, an African fellow engaged in a squabble with an Asian couple entertains us. Each parleys—shouting—in Spanish. With fiery drama, the African declares the corner as his; the Asians are intruders. Meanwhile, the Asians stoutly stand their ground. As amusing as they are, we maintain our pace.

Beyond the bazaar lay alleys less inviting, dirty byways lain with blankets, arranged with trinkets sold by nomads not unlike the people who fought over a coveted space.

At large, people in rags solicit. We make tracks and take refuge at a tiny hole-in-the-wall called Café Lido.

Served alongside our cups of cocoa are saucers of salty, greasy *churros*. Uncle Chuck tastes a *churro* and wrinkles his nose.

"Dunk it," I tell him.

We each dunk a greasy *churro* into pudding-thick hot chocolate. Heavenly fusion.

Uncle Chuck smacks his lips and remarks, "I'm glad our lodging's above.

Granada does not appear the safest place in the world."

Plucking courage, we hit the streets again, backtracking toward the cathedral, past the corner where merchants had their spat. The African usurped the coveted spot. The Asians sputter as they roll up their wares.

Sky blazes blue as we reach Plaza de las Pasiegas. At one end of the square stands the Gothic-Renaissance Catedral de Santa María de la Encarnación, a radiant façade fashioned of dust-colored stone in seamless symmetry. Between four pillared buttresses, three arches cradle five circular windows, at the center, a sixteen-point star. Beneath this conspicuous detail, a plaque bears the inscription *Ave María* and a medallion with a finely chiseled scene of the Annunciation.

We find the main entrance bolted, but gain access through a small side portal, stepping past guards into a gargantuan *catedral*.

This cathedral, commissioned by Carlos V in 1521, was completed in 1714. Architects included Enrique Egas, Diego de Siloé (son and pupil of Gil de Siloé), Juan de Mena and Granada-born Alonso Cano. King Carlos intended for the entombment here of his grandparents, Isabel de Castilla and Fernando de Aragón, near the site of his royal grandparents' ultimate conquest of 1492. Erstwhile, their bodies rested at the Franciscan convent where we lodge. The monarchs' corpses were later moved to their ultimate shrine under the cathedral's adjacent Capilla Real.

We walk through a brume of fine dust, a dreamy spectacle of light shafts streaming in through lofty stained windows. Workers on scaffolds sandblast fluted columns, their work nearing completion, as much of the interior smacks immaculate in matte white; uncleaned sections remain stained with centuries of grimy soot.

The sixteen-point star on the façade turns up a blazing stained oculus: a portrayal of a jewel-toned dove, *The Holy Spirit* encompassed by golden rays and seraphim. Nuns scoot through the chancel, polishing, sweeping, and arranging white gladiolus on the altar beneath an argentine baldachin. A golden arc within the silver canopy shields a sculpture of the *Lamb of God* between a pair of adoring angels in milky-white alabaster.

We marvel at *Twelve Apostles* in bronze, compelling busts of *Adam and Eve*, and the overall magnificence of this grand chamber of infinite side chapels and lacy vaulting. Now, we ferret our way out, heading for Capilla Real.

As we pass again through Gran Vía, two young women atop a soapbox entertain us, their faces, hands and clothing made up in gray. Motionless, these women pose as statues; against their platform rests a sack for *almas*. We move on, dodging a gauntlet of solicitous Gypsies all the way to the threshold of the royal chapel.

Against the wall of the *capilla* a man leans, exhaling plaintive strains through a four-foot-long wooden pipe inclined toward the pavement. He too presents a receptacle for alms. Beside the steps sits a dolorous fellow with an extended palm. One of his rolled-up trouser legs exposes a limb with great open sores; on his cardboard poster, one crudely scrawled word: *Leproso* (Leper).

Shaken, we step uneasily into shadows of the opulent shrine of the Catholic conquerors.

This royal chapel, commissioned by Isabel and Fernando, flaunts a style known as *Isabeline*-Gothic, designed by Enrique Egas and completed in 1521.

Where are the tombs? We shuffle into the chancel, a beautiful alcove overwhelming in details, in its gilded *plateresque retablo*. We identify, amidst carved saints, an apocryphal scene: Boabdil surrendering the keys of Granada. Beneath, his usurpers' cenotaphs: effigies of Isabel and Fernando in creamy alabaster, resting atop finely chiseled platforms. The Catholic Monarchs lie facing the altar in eternal attendance at Mass. Just below these intricate monuments, we discover access to a subterranean vault, the Catholic Monarchs' crypt, behind *rejas*.

Peering between bars, we see five humble, leaden coffins—four of medium size and one small. Larger caskets hold remains of the Catholic Monarchs, plus their daughter Juana La Loca (The Mad) and son-in-law Felipe El Hermoso (Philip the Handsome). The smallest coffin is that of the infant prince, Felipe de Asturias, son of Juana and Felipe.

Medieval Spaniards adjudged Juana mad after the demise of her handsome husband. For years she denied his death, kept his body unburied, expecting miraculous resurrection.

We move on, making room for a tour group, and inspect a gallery bedecked with royal banners. Here we study Isabel's amazingly small silver crown, her scepter and the filigreed sword and sheath of Fernando. Another room brandishes Isabel's collection of Flemish art.

On the way out, Uncle Chuck warns, "Brace for an onslaught of beggars."

"I've been thinking about those rosemary sprigs. I want one as a souvenir of Granada," I answer.

Given this, I slip into the clutches of the first Gypsy we encounter on La Gran Vía, a woman with deeply etched brown face, dyed-jet hair peeking from corners of her silk kerchief. Staring into my eyes, she rapidly murmurs in Spanish—and no doubt, *caló*, or gypsy—idioms escaping my comprehension. The old woman's eyes sparkle like polished obsidian as she looks up from my right palm, now from my left. She articulates the words *corazón, Jesús Cristo, Santa Cruz, carajo, por Dios.* Now, as the Gypsy palms a fragrant sprig into my hand, I pull pesetas from my pocket.

"*¡Más!*" she moans, glaring in horror. "*¡Más!*"

Embarrassed, I hand her a 1000-note. Not enough, still. The Gypsy's eyes well up with tears. I hand her another note.

"*¡Pero, señor, mis pobres niños!*" she laments with trembling voice.

Her poor children! Given her age, the children are in their forties, or older. Yet, still embarrassed, I ask her, "*¿El dinero Americano okay?*"

"*Oh, sí,*" she answers.

Pulling out American bills, I notice Uncle Chuck standing idly by in the alley, smirking.

"*¡Más!*" the Gypsy intones.

Suffice to say, our jockeying goes nowhere—for me, anyway. I hand back her sprig. She will not take it. I ask for my money. She will have no part of this, either, and grabs hold of my shirt-sleeve. Her moist eyes are irresistible, sparkling with *duende*. Nevertheless, breaking loose from her grip, I flee with my sprig in the direction of Uncle Chuck. The Gypsy yells after me as I join up with him.

"Why didn't you help me?" I implore.

"I wanted no part of that. *You* insisted on a *recuerdo*."

I repeat to him the Gypsy's words.

"She probably said," Uncle Chuck laughs, "that if you didn't give her more money, she'd nail your heart to the cross and send you to Hades. Now, how's that for *duende*?"

Not the least bit amused, I carry my expensive sprig, walking alongside my wiseacre companion. At Plaza Nueva, Uncle Chuck makes snapshots of a white marble statue: Alonso Cano defined in flowing lines. I'm miffed. Uncle Chuck knows this. We stroll through a bustling plaza graced with a Neptune fountain. While Uncle Chuck looks for a cab, I inspect a majestic bronze monument to Isabel and Cristóbal Colón. Her majesty sits upon a throne; kneeling at her feet, Columbus presents a vellum scroll.

Uncle Chuck, noticing a bus queue, suggests a ride back up the hill. We board a bus with an *Alhambra* marquee. We're fleetly shuttled away.

We've been intrigued with pale-cinnamon-tinged Hotel Alhambra Palace since our arrival on the hill. We disembark near this exotic hotel's car lot.

Inside, we time warp back to the era of Spain's sultans in a neo-*Mudéjar* edifice enrobing an interior not unlike a harem. The space, within a forest of horseshoe arches, employs friezes of sinuous caliphal inscriptions, rooms resplendent with comfortable sofas and chairs in arabesque patterns, and no shortage of Persian rugs or lustrous pillars of marble and malachite. What's more, brass chandeliers and sconces exaggerate this rich context with splendorous flair.

As I mumble my sense of amusement, Uncle Chuck interrupts.

"What you admonish as 'over-the-top,' young man, is a style of décor that surely filled the rooms of the Alhambra's *Nasrid* palaces. Flamboyant, yet it works."

We peer into the restaurant, to a landscape of rosy napery amidst a stained-glass emporium of mauve.

"*¿Señores?*" a kindly voice articulates behind us. "The dining room is closed. But you may order sandwiches in the bar or from the terrace, if you please."

The smartly dressed man escorts us to the bar, gesturing toward the terrace. We pinch through a tiny door to a mirador with heavenly views.

"This is it," Uncle Chuck exhorts, pulling out a chair.

Below us, an ocean of *teja* rooftops, a bird's-eye view of terra cotta barrel tiles tinged with mossy patination. To our right, the cathedral shoots skyward, to our left, a sweeping panorama of majestic, snow-capped Sierra Nevada. We order gin martinis, straight up. The bartender knows how Americans like them, icy cold with mere parentheses of vermouth. With sips of cool gin and more eye-popping vistas to snow-crowned sierras, we complacently munch sandwiches.

This afternoon affords opportunity for contemplation. Back at our *parador*, as I enjoy *café en vaso sombra* (strong coffee in a glass, with milk), I remove my expensive rosemary from my breast pocket. Spindling the aromatic sprig between fingers and thumb, I ponder the black-eyed Gypsy who begs for livelihood.

Gypsies embody the noble spirit of Spain. Their ethnic makeup and apparel substantiate physical and cultural attributes of centuries of invasion and cross-pollination—particularly Arabic and Indian. Gypsies I encounter are extraordinarily passionate, regarding matters of the heart, in their profound Catholicism. Gypsies personify mystery, with palmistry and such superstitions. Profundity shines from their souls, through their eyes.

Fancying Gypsies, I do not understand why they are considered pariahs, why such talented people find themselves at the bottom of Spain's well of poverty.

The Mysteries of Rosemary

Rosemary (*Rosmarinus officinalis*, botanically, or *romero* in Spanish), a fragrant herb with tiny, powder-blue flowers, imparts deeply religious significance in Spain. For Spaniards, rosemary symbolizes remembrance. Gypsies consider the herb a germane *recuerdo* for tourists. Furthermore, this mystical plant is said to have had flowers of white before the occurrence of a miracle associated with the Virgin Mary. Spanish Catholics maintain that the Virgin, while resting on the flight to Egypt, threw her cloak over a rosemary bush. Hence forward, the flowers bloomed blue. Among the superstitious are those maintaining the rosemary bush requires thirty-three years (the age of Christ) to reach full stature. Thereafter, the plant grows no taller.

I look forward to our after-dark tour of *Nasrid* palaces three hours hence. Meantime, I'll catch some winks.

After restful naps, we dress warmly. With our tickets inscribed *Visita General Nocturna—Palacios Nazaries*, we step into the cool night.

A brilliant crescent of platinum hangs in the inky sky. No tourists animate this scene as we cross the esplanade by Palacio de Carlos V, padding alongside the floodlit *alcazaba*. We hear chirping of crickets, the serenade of an owl, then wing-beats as the huge bird wheels overhead. The chirping hushes.

Met up with a retinue of twenty near the entrance of the *mexuar*, we are all allowed in at precisely eight o'clock.

A disquieting luminescence heightens exoticism, the *mexuar* unfolding further forsaken than during daylight, creepy and ponderous with spirits. We move into shadows of Arrayanes patio, where pillars and façades shimmer in the placid black pool, symmetrical embellishments mirroring the glowing aura.

We geese shuffle on through the *harén* onto Patio of the Lions. This courtyard and its lacy pavilions likewise engross, even more so than under natural light. We glimpse a scene straight from *Arabian Nights*, a ghostly apparition in diaphanous layers of ivory, her groom in impeccably tailored black tuxedo. The two look ravishing, archetypal dolls for a wedding cake. We watch as they glide across the majestic courtyard, followed by lens of videographer and eyes of family.

Wanting my own photograph of this magical scene, I twist a 300mm lens into my camera body and take aim. As the couple's faces come into focus, I am stupefied. From afar, the willowy bride conjured a remarkable sight. Up close, her face might compel a train to use a dirt path. I relax my finger from the shutter button, lower my camera and catch up with Uncle Chuck. From his questioning glance, I realize my face must register a shocking encounter.

Our tour includes Sala de Dos Hermanas under its enchanted Dome of the Muqarnas. As I drink in the splendors, a draft sweeps over me. *A raking saber.... Or an owl swooshing by?* In any event, it occurs to me we are here at the hour of the Abencerraj family's execution. Indeed, their spirits count among us.

Infused with Islamic refinement, allegory and a numinous encounter, we amble back to the *mexuar*, across Plaza de los Aljibes, along Calle Real to our convent for dinner.

Tomorrow is our last day in this charmed Alhambra. We resolve to make the most of it.

> ...the Gypsy is the most distinguished, profound, and aristocratic element in my country, the one that most represents its way of being and best preserves the fire, the blood, and the alphabet of Andalusian and universal truth.
>
> —Federico García Lorca, *Gypsy Ballads*

[1] *Alcaicería:* A *Sûq* (oriental bazaar) and former silk market during Andalucía's Muslim occupation.

POSTSCRIPT TOURS

I sensed duende *in unexpected places. One need not be a gifted poet like García Lorca or an accomplished flamenco performer to embody the virtue. Even beggars exuded* duende—*and they have engendered this within me.*

I fretted with these sentiments before falling asleep and awoke with notions yet unresolved....

"Why did I ever invest in the NASDAQ?"

I open my eyes. Uncle Chuck bewails the international market report as he stares at our muted television.

"You've eased into your holiday, at last," he says with a chuckle. "Realize what time it is?"

I squint at red digits on the clock between our beds. Half past eight…. So much for making the most of our final day in Granada.

We consider having breakfast delivered to our room, then lounging around the *parador* all day long.

"This is such an enticing place," I tell Uncle Chuck. "Let's kick the tires before we explore beyond."

We exit into a bright, gusty day. Antonio whistles blithely as he assists a guest with luggage. He nods to us, smiling.

A private, walled garden off the game room looks inviting. We walk through to an intimate courtyard of a half-dozen, Moorish-style fountains on the *parador* grounds. We deliberate a shallow, scalloped basin, thirty-six inches in diameter, resting directly upon the patio, a two-foot plume of water spouting from its center. Herringbone motif encompasses the space set with smooth black river stones, offset with chalky-white crushed rock. Morning glories and bougainvillea stretch along the campanile to mid-height. No bells accouter this tower's aperture. Two alabaster tanks in alabaster, emblazoned with regal crests, trickle within a leafy niche.

As we soak up casual elegance of our lair, a screen of tall cypress cloisters us from tourist central.

> Praised be my Lord for our sister water, who is serviceable to us,
> and humble, and precious, and chaste.
> —Saint Francis of Assisi, "Canticle to the Sun"

"Let's have a look over there," I suggest, pointing to a slim lane alongside the old convent.

Uncle Chuck perseveres behind as I traipse the muddy track, turning left to the pond we see from our rooms. We ease up to a moss-stained border, admiring reflections of residual roses that droop over its margins. Coppery fish dart beneath the placid surface.

Uncle Chuck aims a finger across the dry river valley.

"Pavilions of the Generalife," he commends.

Our view frames music in stone precariously poised on a terraced crest. "We stood right there the other day, looking in this direction," he says.

"What a picture," I sigh. "If only it were a bit warmer, we could have lunch right here."

Up Calle Real, we join the ranks of sightseers. We peer into a *bañuelo* (Arab bathhouse, or *hammâm*) closed for restoration, then push on.

271

Morning sun simmers, adding luster to formal Palacio de Carlos V and to the adjacent church. Fresh batches of mom-and-pop tourists arrive, staring in amazement.

A host of tabbies numbers among spectators who roam these *paseos*. The cats, sensing we are animal lovers, snuggle against our legs and cry for attention each time we traverse this quadrant.

Across the esplanade, three brawny cannons aim from the brink of the ramparts on yesteryears' foes. Just up the way stands a splendid survivor of Alhambra's Muslim occupation, La Puerta del Vino (The Wine Gate), a noble structure sparkling within a ballet of sunlight, the horseshoe arch of stone and mellowed brick tower steeped in amber-mauve hues.

As we near Hotel Alhambra Palace, we look forward to more views from its terrace.

Over lunch, we cast our eyes to snowy Sierra Nevada on the horizon, to a dilapidated, domed complex in the city below. Dust-colored walls sag under a roof wavy with rows of decrepit *tejas*, an intriguing old building capped with a handsome dome, overlaid with mosaic tiles in gleaming teal-blue and white. Our *mozo* identifies this for us as Iglesia de Nuestra Señora de las Angustias (Church of Our Lady of Angustias—Our Lady of Sorrows, patron saint of Granada), dating to the sixteenth century.

"Let's go below, to tour that old church after lunch," I suggest to Uncle Chuck.

"No, thank you, dear boy; it's risky business down there. Moreover, the only beggar we have up here on the hill is the occasional cat and look, these birds."

Three sparrows hop along the margin of the terrace, cocking their heads, staring desirously. We pluck from our toasted sandwiches, then place crumbs on the railing. In the spur of the moment, an air force of sparrows joins their three troops. The tiny tan birds instantly devour the crumbs, then nervously make their exodus.

"See," Uncle Chuck remarks. "The crumbs are gone and those feathery stalkers have flown away. Gypsies could take a lesson from the birds. Now, shall we see what's up the way?"

We hike up a grade, heading nowhere in particular. Beyond a towering cross of concrete, we spot an oasis, a walled villa known as Carmen de los Mártires.[1] Fundamentally part of Boabdil's kingdom, later a hermitage of Queen Isabel I, this property eventually passed through hands of Carmelite monks, then to General Carlos Calderón. Hubert Meersmans purchased the gardens and orchards in 1891 and had a palace built on the estate.

> So in a manner we united are, and one; yet otherwise disunion is our estate eternally.
>
> —Junayd of Baghdad, "The Ecstatics"

To reach the *carmen*, we crunch across gravel paths, delighting along the way in ferny grottos, watching water trickling about heads and shoulders of carved-stone wood nymphs. We continue to a courtyard of pedestals topped with Spanish sovereigns, among them, Carlos III.

Beyond, we spot a creamy-white *palacete* well proportioned with stately portico. Uncle Chuck would love to explore inside, but the mansion is closed. We peer through windows as we walk between them and a watery veranda, a Generalife in miniature. We pass under lacy *Mudéjar* arches, looking below to quiescent terraced gardens, to lacy tops of thirty-foot palms. In the midst sprouts a four-tiered fountain of stone.

"What a sanctuary this was for a fortunate Victorian; what peaceful beauty," Uncle Chuck remarks as we stroll.

From the court of palms, we pad down gently sloping ramps to a pond hemmed by Roman columns, teeming with waterfowl. Exotic ducks, snowy geese, black swans paddle through emerald water with their great orange feet. A waterfall splatters and froths at one end; at the other, lazy turtles sunbathe on rocky ledges. Bridges span the pond's narrows; at the core, a watchtower girds an island of stone. The centerpiece: formal gardens with classical stone urns, unruffled pool and spouting fountain surmounted with a sculpture of Neptune. Statues of saints pose in the shade, under a canopy of pine and cypress. All but a few of the statues lack heads, hands or both. A passerby mentions that tourists helped themselves to pieces of the statues.

I am grateful for four days in Granada; otherwise, we would have missed these details.

We roam back through the hinterland, up to our *parador*.

After restful naps, we don ties and coats. Under a crescent moon we walk, past imposing silhouettes of Moorish barbicans, into the woods, toward Hotel Alhambra Palace.

These *bosques* take on an eerie guise in darkness. Melodic splashing of fountains transpose with strident chirps of crickets. The only souls, besides us, are feral cats, though we sense others lurking. We pace cautiously in single-file along confined, dewy sidewalks of brusquely hewn blocks. Occasionally, a car rolls by on constricted switchback *paseos* just inches from harm's way.

"How did we find the hotel when we lunched there?" Uncle Chuck asks.

"For one, we could see the tower. I believe it's in that direction?" I recall, pointing toward a park. "Let's cut through."

A voice thunders from the *paseo*:

"*¡Señores! !Cuidado! ¡Gamberros!* (Sirs! Beware! Hoodlums!)*"* a middle-aged man shouts from his car, wagging a finger, warning us not to enter the park.

"Must have a reputation for desperados," Uncle Chuck breathes.

We thank the thoughtful gentleman, then ask for directions to the hotel. He points straight ahead, rolls up his window and peels off.

We persevere through blackness. Around the next bend, through a clearing, we espy the grand Moorish-style tower bathed in glowing spotlights. We inch down a steep asphalt track to the car park, wangling sideways through a jammed lot to reach the front steps of the hotel.

Sunk into an overstuffed suede sofa, we savor martinis. Surrounded with all manner of opulence, we notice still more details than on previous visits. Says the hotel's brochure: Alfonso XIII commissioned this grand folly, as he had the hotels where we lodged in *Sevilla* and Madrid.

At the magic hour, we make for the obscurely lit dining room, pulling up to a table on an enclosed terrace. We scarcely make out the sierra on the black horizon, but Granada twinkles with kaleidoscopic splendor, our aerial vista beyond an unparalleled dining adventure.

A world-class waiter, an elderly gentleman with *pundonor*,[2] together with his brigade of bus staff shower us with attention, each of them gracious, having mastered the concept of service. As if by magic, a waiter attends when needed and does not hover.

"This is, without a doubt, the best asparagus I have ever tasted," Uncle Chuck croons as he samples his appetizer.

His glossy, ivory spears are enormous, tender and flavorful. A mold of velvety salmon mousse sprinkled with lustrous gray caviar accompanies this first-rate overture (*espárrago frío con mahonesa*).

My first course is gazpacho. Onto its persimmon-colored surface, a busboy spoons chopped boiled egg, green bell pepper, onion and crispy croutons. Ah, luscious soup, cool, smooth, notches above others I have sampled.

"I want to eat like this every day," Uncle Chuck remarks, "notably if it included this level of service."

We share a bottle of Torres Viña Sol, carrying on with scrumptious bread and entrées. Uncle Chuck has *solomillo de ternera con salsa bernesa:* veal tenderloin on a puddle of béarnaise sauce and I, *pez emperador a la Granadina:* swordfish, Granada style. The fish is grilled, brushed sparingly with olive oil and piquant seasoning. Petite, creamy potatoes and shoestring-thin green haricots garnish our plates.

"*¿Señores, postres, cafés?*" suggests the headwaiter.

We surrender to the dessert presentation. Uncle Chuck relishes *tarta de queso* (cheesecake) and I luxuriate in a decadent wedge of *tarta de manzana* (apple cake) drizzled with cassis.

"Our *parador* is, what, a mile away?" wagers Uncle Chuck. "Let's cab back and avoid the prospect of hoodlums."

The headwaiter, evidently overhearing, scurries ahead to the front desk. When we reach the steps, our carriage awaits.

This was grand, our last day at La Alhambra. I know we will miss it.

My serene and happy reign in the Alhambra was suddenly brought to a close…while indulging in oriental luxury in the cool hall of the baths, summoning me away from my Moslem Elysium to mingle once more in the bustle and business of the dusty world. How was I to encounter its toils and turmoils, after such a life of repose and reverie? How was I to endure its commonplace, after the poetry of the Alhambra?

—Washington Irving, *Tales of the Alhambra*

[1] *Carmen de los Mártires:* Villa of the Martyrs. *Karm*, in Arabic, means vineyard. In Spanish, *Carmen* is Order of the Carmelites.

[2] *Pundonor:* refined sense of self-respect; honor

A Doleful Exodus and a Woeful Repast

Our Spanish holiday wound down. Moreover, we embarked from my favorite region in Spain. How long would it be before my return? I was not, after all, satisfied with my quest for duende. *My love of Spain began with that elusive word. Would I ever get my fill?*

"You have an appetite this morning," Uncle Chuck gibes.

I resist the urge to volley back cheeky. How well I know his propensity to drive at breakneck speed to reach a destination. What's more, I stall, regretting our departure after four mind-altering days on *La Sabîka*, the enchanted hill.

"Shall we pack and hit the road, then?" Uncle Chuck asks nonchalantly between sips of coffee. "It's already mid-morning and I believe we'll spend five or six hours on the road to Madrid."

Glumly, I fold my napkin, stack peseta coins on the table and saunter through corridors of saints behind my eager uncle. Somber best describes my mood as we fold clothes and gather tour books and souvenirs. I arrange my rosemary sprig between pages of a brochure, then tuck it carefully into a zippered compartment of my suitcase.

Smiling Antonio meets us at the reception. I sulk.

"Señores, hoy, no hay sol," Antonio laments with a commiserating look. A lackluster day, indeed....

After we settle our bill, Antonio carts our luggage, jauntily attending us to the car park. He assists in loading the trunk, then wishes us *buen viaje*. We tip him and shake hands. He waves, striding back to the *parador*, whistling a cheery tune no doubt. He lives in Granada, after all.

Pulling away slowly, lest we alarm a regiment of gawking tourists, we roll cautiously toward the main plaza.

As we round the last bend, I kneel on my seat, facing the rear window. Assuredly, Isabel and Fernando banished the Muslims, but not their fervent spirit. The hill called *La Sabîka* flourishes no longer with aristocratic caliphs and veiled courtesans, yet the vision lives on in poetic architecture, in décor, in luminance shed upon Spain's Dark Age. The glimmer has not waned, in that, their Eternal City, La Alhambra....

> Love every beautiful thing for its own beauty, and not
> for any satisfaction which can come from it....
> Beauty can be external beauty,
>   which is perceived with the eye of the head,
> or it may be interior beauty,
>   which is perceived with the eye of the heart.
> The first sort may be perceived by children or beasts;
> to perceive the second sort is the special property
> of men of the heart,

and none may share in it
who know only the life of the lower world.
All beauty is beloved by a perceiver of beauty,
and if he perceives it with his heart,
it becomes his heart's beloved....

—From "al-Ghazálí," *Ihyá*

Uncle Chuck takes a wrong turn onto the highway, sending us in direction of Motril-Costa del Sol rather than Jaén-Madrid. We take the first *cambio sentido* (turnaround) and head north. Fringes of Granada transfigure to tailored fields, orchards and now, to an endless range of olive groves from freshly planted saplings to their venerable, gnarled ancestors.

I pull a tour book from my car-door pocket.

"There's Jaén, just up the way. Can we pull in for a tour?"

Denied my request, I settle for fleeting glimpses of the illustrious hill town's profile under glimmers of struggling light. Jaén's engaging Castilla del Baños de la Encina, a noteworthy attraction, crowns the scene.

"Next you'll want a side trip to Córdoba," Uncle Chuck chides.

"I'm in no hurry to get to Madrid," I say, closing my book.

With old "James Dean" at the wheel, we career up the turnpike *a mata caballo* past blurred scenery, under fluctuating cloud conditions and levels of sunshine. When we reach the picturesque, granite outcroppings of Sierra Morena, I again petition to stop. Since we drove through this range only nine days earlier, its forests now blush with autumnal color. But one turnout proposed and our speed precluded stopping, once we spotted the breathtaking panorama.

Va-room!

"We *will* stop for lunch?" I ask.

"Absolutely. You name the spot."

I scan the map, intent on the notion of a beguiling encounter, such as one experienced at El Carpio en route from Madrid to Andalucía. My eyes focus on the map's finer print, those appellations designating smaller villages.

"Up the highway; let's see, Santa Cruz de Mudela."

"You watch for signs and give me notice."

We pull off the highway into Santa Cruz. No El Carpio, the bland town looks gloomy, spread narrowly across a level plain, its dreary storefronts and shops utilitarian.

"We'll find a snug café somewhere," I suggest.

We scour a lengthy south-north main route, but see nothing enticing.

"An entire waste of thirty minutes," Uncle Chuck grumbles.

How was I to know?

Again, we are off, racing with northbound traffic at 120 kilometers per hour.

"Aren't you hungry?" I venture again.

'James' admits, "I could do with a bite and a rest, plus it looks like the fuel tank's down to a quarter."

I'm not surprised when we swerve into the lot of a *venta*, La Pausa, a pristine, modern cafeteria near Valdepeñas. We belly up to the bar and order rings of fried *calamares*, a ham-and-cheese sandwich, a slice of *tortilla a la española* to split and glasses of red wine. Perched on tall stools, we eat with gusto from a Formica counter. The food is palatable, though I would prefer enhanced ambiance.

As we race through La Mancha, I dream the impossible dream rather than stopping for photographic studies of Consuegra's famous windmills.

más madrid

MÁS MADRID

With amazing facility, we arrived at Aeropuerto Barajas near sundown, returned our trusty Peugeot to the car-rental office, then rolled our luggage to the taxi queue.

Out front, the fellow in stovepipe and epaulets welcomes us again to Hotel Palace. A garrison of bellhops assists, one of them meeting us in our extravagant quarters with our luggage and an open palm.

I throw open draperies and look out over La Rotonda, the stained-glass cupola groining the lounge—an amenity not as commendable from above. The other three wings block imaginable views of the city. We had requested a quiet section, as the room we had two weeks earlier faced the ruckus of a street. What the previous room lacked in tranquility, it favored in prospects of illustrious Madrid.

"You can't have it all," Uncle Chuck says. "Furthermore, we won't spend our remaining days here in the room, will we?"

On a mission to find a photo lab, we hit the streets. As a measure of precaution, we will have our dozens of films processed locally. X-ray appliances at airports have cranked up since Osama bin Laden made his mark on America—and we know of X-ray's effect on exposed film.

It's a frigid evening, colder than any temperatures we experienced in Andalucía. But how gratifying it is to be out of the confines of a car and stretching our long legs in Madrid.

Three blocks from the hotel, we step into a camera store with lab. With aplomb, we leave our exposed films for processing.

"Now, how about a nip?" Uncle Chuck suggests.

Against a darkening sky glows the spire of Hotel Gran Reina Victoria. With a shudder of recognition, I see in my mind's eye this hotel's carmine-red bar with *toro* trophies.

"Let's find another place," I suggest.

"We're right here, and I'm freezing."

281

Reina Victoria's attractive lobby has not changed over the years, although Bar Taurino has seen better days. Bull-head trophies still leer, but need dusting. Carpeting, upholstery and wall coverings look a bit bedraggled. As we discuss this deterioration, the bartender winks.

We nestle into well-worn, overstuffed chairs in a corner of the cozy albeit tattered room. Nursing scotch and soda, we people-watch and debate our dinner prospects.

"Botín?" I suggest.

"We won't get in without a reservation, nor get out before midnight."

"Paradis?" I ask.

"Didn't care for it."

"Well, I don't care for this place."

"Let's look at the restaurant at Villa Real. I understand it's completely changed since we tried it years ago."

As we wander to Hotel Villa Real, Madrid's nocturnal milieu evolves, the capital city cloaked in surrealistic luminance, monuments and superstructures bathed in liquid green, red, blue and white. Streets lilt with vibrant nightlife, *el paseo* through perpetual din of car horns and wavering sirens. We see *Madrileños* dressed in the latest couture, perennially stylish Spaniards poised, impeccably tailored.

We step from the cold into the lobby of Villa Real, then stroll into retro-hip East 47 Restaurant.

"It's noisy and smoky," Uncle Chuck remarks. "But let's give the food a try."

Little contrast here from the cacophony outside. We turn tin ears to youthful patrons shouting above the pulsating blare of neo-disco cadence.

This restaurant transcends cutting edge; bleeding edge is more like it. At a zinc platter balanced upon wire-cable legs, a hip waiter slips us stylishly printed menus.

"How does the chef dream up these concoctions?" I say loudly over the painful music.

Uncle Chuck shouts back, "I wish we'd ventured Botín after all."

"Something to look forward to tomorrow," I yell back.

For our first course, we try warm potato soup swirled with truffle oil, floated with tiny purple flowers. We agree, over the clamor, it hits the spot on this chilly evening, though we eat up-tempo, in sync with throbbing music. And what are we supposed to do with these flowers? The course following looks downright quirky, though we are sure the chef considers it edgy—or *cocina fusión*, as they refer to this in Spain.

Uncle Chuck laughs at his plate. "How was this described in the menu?" he quizzes with a grimace.

"I don't recall the exact epithet," I answer, "but I expected warm pasta—and this is...so dark, so cold."

This presented before us on triangular plates, arranged under a sprinkle of toasted sesame seeds occurs room-temperature, purple-black pasta (presumably tinted with squid's ink) tossed with strands of seaweed and morel mushrooms.

We are not amused.

"I saw a film noir," I tell Uncle Chuck, "where the villainous lead character said to eat black food is to eat death."

Uncle Chuck pushes aside his plate of half-eaten pasta. He groans, "For my taste, ultra-trendy food—black or otherwise—is an utter waste of ingredients and money."

We have just experienced a complete absence of *duende*.

We refresh our palates with *cervezas* and then head out, our heads still thumping with techno-music. Back at Hotel Palace, we bask in warmth and comfort and, on this evening, in peacefulness, as our holiday draws to a close.

From the Palace to the Ritz,
then Back to Reality

We had not requested a wake-up call, nor did we set an alarm clock. I awoke to a rustle of paper and opened my eyes. Uncle Chuck sat in a wing chair by the window, reading the news. He glanced up, peering at me over his spectacles.

"Well, good afternoon."
Propping myself up on one arm, I peer at the clock. A quarter past nine....
"What time did you get up?"
"About an hour ago. I need a cup of coffee. Shall we have a pot sent up?"
"I'd rather get some at Oskar's."
"Well, get yourself ready, boy. The day's a-wasting."

"Ah, this I've missed," I sigh, with a first sip of luxurious *café con leche*.
"Let's see what's going on at Plaza Mayor and Puerta del Sol these days," Uncle Chuck suggests.
We return to frigid atmosphere. Though windy and cold, this city of

concrete glistens under bright daylight; bearable temperature, but it takes its toll each time we wait at attenuated traffic signals.

Inside of fifteen minutes, we have reached Plaza Mayor, Madrid's beating heart. All but three or four of its shops are shut tight for the season; no café tables with umbrellas, no artists painting. At the center of the plaza, a construction crew vibrates at the handles of jackhammers. We move beyond grit and racket, window-shopping in the arcades. When noise ceases, a siren call resonates, a seductive strumming....

"Listen," I say.

Pursuing the source, we spot a man with guitar. In the sunniest corner of the plaza he sits cross-legged, propped against a massive stone plinth. The middle-aged Spaniard strums sweet flamenco strains, floaty timbre illuminating the plaza. I remove my camera from its bag. The fellow acknowledges this and nods "Okay." We linger, savoring his dulcet solo, then toss pesetas into his box and move along.

Halfway across the plaza, a youthful, black-haired woman approaches and plunges a long-stemmed red carnation into my coat pocket. I smile, handing it back. She stuffs it again into my pocket, persisting in her ruse until I lose patience. Uncle Chuck watches. I don't care for any more of his diatribes.

"*¡No, por favor!*" I bark.

With this, the shocked woman seizes her straggly flower and scurries away. What? She didn't expect a barking gringo?

"You're learning," Uncle Chuck praises. "And you've experienced flavors of Andalucía right here in Madrid. A Gypsy propositioned you and we've heard live flamenco music. What more could you ask for?"

"Warmer weather?" I manage between chattering teeth.

Wedging through animated byways, we encounter a brawl. A woman complains to a pair of policemen in shiny, black plastic hats—officers of the Guardia Civil.[1] They have already apprehended the accused. One of the policemen lifts the culprit off the ground by his shirt collar.

> Those patent-leather men with their patent-leather souls.
>
> —Federico García Lorca

"Better behave yourself," Uncle Chuck warns.

I roll my eyes.

We march through the cobweb of streets to Puerta del Sol's plexus of shops, department stores, restaurants and confectioneries. The *puerta's* ten streets course with pedestrian traffic. No huskers, no musicians, nor contortionists out in force, as we have experienced on warmer holidays here. Uncle Chuck's on alert for men's shops. We duck into a smart one. Delaying for thirty-or-so minutes, we casually riffle, staying warm. After Uncle Chuck purchases a cardigan vest of cashmere, we return to windy alleyways.

The temperature will not much improve, we have decided. We pick up our negatives and contact sheets, then ply back toward Hotel Palace and happen upon an appealing restaurant, Tres Encinas. We scan a menu posted in the window and walk in, reviving our numbed hands.

This elegant *marisquería* is one of Madrid's seafood shrines. Though Madrid lies at the geographical center of Spain, hundreds of miles from its seacoasts, the capital city brims with fresh seafood. With the advent of refrigerated trucks, largess of the sea finds its way daily to tables of Madrid.

The host escorts us upstairs past trolleys heaped with ocean-fare to a formally decked table in a beautiful room.

Leaning forward, Uncle Chuck suggests under his breath, "We're into big tariffs."

"It's the last day of our holiday; let's splurge," I whisper back.

We order salads and a bottle of Vinícola de Castilla *blanco* and ask to see the trolley. A *mozo* wheels a chill bed of ice table-side. Upon it rests, between parsley-and-lemon garniture, an arrangement of black barnacles, orange crustaceans, tawny-colored bivalves. We gawk at spiny crabs, *percebes, cigalas, gambas, langostas,* all steamed—save freshly harvested raw oysters and clams on the half shell.

We select portions of each. After prying from shells with an array of tools, we savor sweet morsels with horseradish and pepper sauce.

Our *mozo* dresses salads of delicious white asparagus and chopped boiled eggs atop crisp beds of greens. Another server volunteers finger bowls, more napkins.

The menu proposes grilled or baked fish entrées, but we've had plenty, having polished off a bounty of cold shellfish.

"*¿Postres?*"

From the winking dessert cart, we choose ethereal pastry shells brimming with fluffy clouds of whipped cream, crowned with toasted almonds thinly sliced. Each bite, heavenly, between sips of rich espressos.

As I remove a cheroot from its canister, a *mozo* swoops to my side with a lighter. Another waiter brings shot glasses of *hierba.*

"*¿La cuenta, por favor?*"

"More than we usually pay for dinner," Uncle Chuck grumbles.

"Excellent meal," I counter. "Why can't we find meals like this in California?"

We again brave the outdoors, heading back to warmth of the Palace, to pass an idle hour reviewing our contact sheets.

Glancing at one of my sheets, Uncle Chuck asks, "Where did you take that one?"

"In Ronda, while you napped."

I'm busy at my journal, matching up pictures with places when Uncle Chuck rouses from siesta.

"Happy hour yet?" he asks groggily.

"Where shall we have them?"

"Let's see what the Ritz is all about."

Attired in suits and overcoats, we stroll to Madrid's other top hotel. Near the imposing façade, a doorman in navy uniform and cape walks a guest's two Cavalier St. Charles spaniels. Another attendant bows as he holds the door for us.

Smaller than the Palace's, this lobby is predictably chic, more than a tad off-putting. Soaring walls are veneered in marble and fruitwood. Above a short flight spreads a mezzanine lounge; the bar must be up there. We climb steps to a parlor dripping with French chandeliers, elegant in tones of buttery ivory and muted palette of coral and green, set with chic sofas and statuesque floral arrangements. We move past clientele attired in fur jackets and pearls, a veritable medley of face-lifts crowned with lacquered coifs tinted yellow or lavender. From behind tiers of finger sandwiches and bonbons, these tea drinkers follow us with their eyes, pretending not to look. Frankly, this scene is not our cup of tea. We pursue the bar.

"That must be it," I gesture.

Beyond the lounge where pretentious dowagers nurse tea, we discover the barroom. No one else occupies this brightly lit space, not even a barkeeper; but no sooner have we made ourselves comfortable, than a man steps up to take our orders for scotch and soda.

"I favor the clubby atmosphere of Hotel Palace's bar. That's a man's hotel. This is for the ladies," I mutter, stepping up to the bar to examine our tab.

"Enjoy your scotch?" I ask, glancing over my shoulder. "We're about to pay fourteen dollars each for our drinks."

No more overpriced scotch; we have reservations at Botín.

Our cabby drops us at the time-honored roadhouse, a shuttered brick façade glowing with carriage lamps. We step into ancient ambiance, to a table in the old bodega, a sixteenth-century wine cellar.

We follow the host down a steep staircase into a brick-lined, pointed-arch cellar. The premature hour of eight finds chiefly a basting of tourists.

On our table stands a slender vase with a single red carnation. Lost in reflection, I feel a pang for not having given money to the Gypsy girl at Plaza Mayor. I do not mention this to Uncle Chuck, but instead gaze about the room.

A gentle fireside glow dances on mellowed brick vaulting. Embers explode in a fireplace, hurtling sparks up the chimney. A couple talking to their plates interests me even more so. They must be Scandinavians.

In spite of the restaurant's celebrity status, I sense intrinsic warmth between these rugged walls. We feel welcome, unhurried, as do other guests—besides the silent pair—judging their gleeful mien.

"After that filling lunch, I plan to go easy," Uncle Chuck insists.

We order a bottle of Valdevegón 1996 and munch crusty bread. After deliberation, Uncle Chuck selects a joint of Aranda lamb. I opt for grilled sole. We share a ration of white asparagus with mayonnaise.

The silent couple dips into dessert. The only words exchanged during their meal were to the waiter. They must be fun at parties.

Our entrées are tender, moist, infused with smoky evergreen wood. We relish fat spears of asparagus, using only a trifle of sauce served on the side.

"Can't we extend our holiday? We haven't been to Extremadura, or even to Barcelona, Córdoba...."

Uncle Chuck interrupts, "All of that will keep for another trip. Now, let's get back to the hotel. Wake-up call's at four o'clock."

---

[1] Guardia Civil: The national police force of Spain, created in 1844 to replace the militia. These policemen typically patrol in pairs, on foot or on horseback.

Rude Awakenings

A knock at our door.... Groggy, disoriented, I squinted at the clock, discovered it was midnight. I asked, "Who's calling?" A female voice came muffled through the thick-paneled door. In sultry Spanish, she pleaded to be let in. Had she the wrong room—or was she one of Hotel Palace's amenities? We'd never know....

The four A.M. call rouses us again. Promptly we are off into blackness, to the airport to partake in our least-favored component of travel.

To reach Spain had taken twenty-five hours. Our return trip will endure for more than thirty. During lengthy flights and layover limbo, I make prudent use of time, scouring maps and books, planning our next excursion—to Barcelona, Montserrat, Cáceres, Trujillo, Mérida, Guadalupe, Córdoba.... Armed with determination, I still seek the essence of *duende*.

Yo vuelvo	I'm coming back
por mis alas.	for my wings.
¡Dejadme volver!	O let me come back!
¡Quiero morirme siendo	I want to die where
amanecer!	it's dawn!
¡Quiero morirme siendo	I want to die
ayer!	where it's yesterday!
Yo vuelvo	I'm coming back
por mis alas.	for my wings.
¡Dejadme retornar!	O let me get back!
Quiero morirme siendo	I want to die where
manantial.	it's origin.
Quiero morirme fuera	I want to die
de la mar.	out of sight of the sea.

—Federico García Lorca, *"El Regreso"* ("The Return")

1. Barcelona
2. Montserrat
3. Tarragona

CATALUNYA

LIFE IS A CABARET, OLD CHUM

Slowly I pivoted on my internal axis, absorbing, absorbing. Music permeated each pore, dew-laden air refreshed and a kaleidoscope of color dizzied the mind. Before me a golden-clad King Tut flashed the thumbs up; across the way, a demure Cleopatra nodded graciously in my direction. Over there, a middle-aged man balanced a soccer ball on his neck while pumping impressive pushups against flagstones. Iridescent roosters crowed, nearly drowning coos of doves and nervous chirps of quail.

Was I hallucinating? I wiped my bleary eyes, shook my head and paced farther, under a canopy of autumnal plane trees. I espied a cowboy, a living statue, and beside him, a copper-colored alien. Who were these characters? Where was the ringmaster? Turning my head, I came face to face with a wild man coifed in tangled dreadlocks. Barefoot, that war-painted aborigine in loincloth leapt away and shinnied up a tree! Next, I encountered a knight in scaly armor, brandishing a sword and perched atop a soapbox. The silvery cavalier winked, then bowed. Nearby, two hairy gorillas slow-danced to "Bésame Mucho" played sweetly on a saxophone by a bohemian fellow....

Roses and lilies flanked my path, their divine redolence floating upward. Perhaps this was heaven. An angel, after all, surveyed me empathetically.

Wait...the jet lag. This can't be real.

¡Viva yo! Real it is. I am coursing Las Ramblas in magical Barcelona. After a hellacious aero-marathon to get here from California—including a layover at London—I'm not sure whether this day-lit cabaret is fact or fancy. Uncle Chuck must believe it; he busily snaps pictures and tosses euro coins at the feet of jugglers and artist-mimes. Distracted by worldly matters, he glances to headlines in newsstands. For the most part, dailies focus on a messy oil spill off the coast of Galicia, the demise of the tanker *Prestige*. Uncle Chuck concerns himself with the stock market and threat of war with

291

Iraq, but he's energized. I barely keep up with his pace. We carry on between myriad mimes to musicians, postcards to comic books and mopeds to taxicabs. This one-mile stretch known as Las Ramblas fosters a vibrant, surreal celebration.

I again persuaded Uncle Chuck to join me for a sweet taste of Spain. Hitherto, we had not sampled Barcelona, Spain's second-most populous city, and largest metropolis on the Mediterranean. Catalunya's capital surpasses our wildest expectations.

On arrival, heavenly notions greeted us. El Prat de Llobregat (Barcelona's airport) is a dream, Customs a snap. Our brief journey by cab from airport to hotel was efficient, inexpensive. At Hotel Plaça Catalunya, a comely *senyorita* behind the desk greeted us as special guests with nurturing *bienvenidos*: warm smiles and tall flutes of cool sparkling *cava*.

Had we retained our original bookings, we would be more remotely situated, removed from the city's core. But fortune smiled and the location of our hotel overlooks the north end of Barcelona's famous Ramblas. Our American friend Annie put us in touch with Ignacio, her colleague in Barcelona. Ignacio insisted on securing for us accommodations close to the action. He'd succeeded.

We proceed along La Rambla. Onlookers huddle around an illegal scam called *trampa*, a slippery, three-card game the player never wins. Now, wait. A man in clown white, squatting on a toilet! I want to photograph this spectacle but Uncle Chuck grimaces, urging me on when the fellow grunts appropriately to the fixture. I settle for shots of other mimes outfitted as toadstools, a metallic-blue astronaut and the green caterpillar from *Alice's Adventures in Wonderland*.

As Federico García Lorca once exclaimed, I want this fantasy to endure. But after a mile's scenic hike, cabaret gives way to vehicular chaos. We have reached Plaça del Portal de la Pau and the Mirador de Colom, terminus of La Rambla, in the shadow of a two-hundred-foot monument[1] to Christopher Columbus—or Colom, as he is known in Catalunya. We understand that in nearby Montserrat, Columbus convinced Benedictine monks to arrange for him an audience with Queen Isabel, his benefactress for New World exploration. Here in Barcelona the Catholic Sovereigns welcomed Columbus upon his return from the Americas. His bronze effigy above us faces Africa, not America; nonetheless, a commendable tribute.

Sufficiently worn out, we head back in direction of our hotel, stopping a block short at Café Zurich. Plunked into chairs at an outdoor zinc table, we ratchet down, watching La Rambla from the sidelines, enjoying *ginebras con hielo*.

On this cool November afternoon, an accordionist plays "Lady of Spain," embellished by an accompanist's jangling tambourine. Tarot-card readers parked under plane tree bowers leisurely cast futures. Suddenly, shattering glass disturbs our euphoria. A truck driver, standing on his brakes to avoid a pedestrian, spilled a pane of plate glass from his rack. In a stroke of luck, no flying shards reached human targets and the errant pedestrian escaped injury. Two policemen arrive and idly watch as the driver cleans up his mess one shard at a time. An abyss in the concrete inhales, exhales currents of pedestrians delving into and coursing from the rumbling Metro.

"It took only twenty-four hours to get to Spain this time," I yawn.

"Some kind of record, I imagine," Uncle Chuck says with a smile and simpatico yawn.

Yes, Uncle Chuck is pleased to be here. Months ago, I believed I'd have to fly solo to Spain, but at last ditch, he agreed to come along. Nevertheless, he is ready to collapse. I know we'll retire early this evening in spite of the Ramblas' allure.

Glasses drained, we scan beckoning windows. Spotting an irresistible display, we step inside to peruse tempting comestibles along a glass-clad bar. I point at deep-fried *calamares*, snow crab claws (*¡estupendo!*), cold anchovies, olives, a crispy baguette smeared with olive oil and smashed tomato (*pa amb tomàquet*) and another topped with *serrano* ham—*tapas* to tide us over. And while nocturnal Barcelona simmers and scintillates, we will snooze by eight P.M.

[1] The finely carved base of Monument a Colom (installed 1888) took shape under the talented hands of Gaietà Buigas, the bronze statue by Rafael Arché.

CATALUNYA AND THE MEDITERRANEAN JEWEL KNOWN AS *"BARNA"*

Couched between the mountains of Collserola and the blue Mediterranean, with a year-round nearly perfect climate, Barcelona manifests an idyllic locale, accounting for its fiercely contested position checkered with subjugation and oppression. Until the first century before Christ, *Laietans* (Iberian tribal inhabitants of this seaside region of northeastern Spain) called their homeland *Laia*. Phoenicians, under their leader Amilcar Barca, conquered the indigenous tribe. The tale goes that the name Barcelona stems from the Phoenician conqueror's surname. Romans took over in B.C. 133, renaming the settlement *Colonia Favencia Julia Augusta Parterna Barcino*. Roman colonists at once erected decorative walls, which, by the third century, they reinforced with defensive bastions; but their colony fell in the fifth century A.D. to Visigoths, who made *Barcino* their Iberian Peninsula headquarters. And though Greeks did not capture Barcelona, they made settlements just north on the Costa Brava.

Islamic corsairs toppled the Visigothic crown in the eighth century, naming their prize *Barshiluna*—a transitory defeat, hence the absence of Moorish monuments in this region of Spain. Under Charlemagne, in 801, Franks laid claim to the coveted real estate. The Moors, returning in 985, were briskly defeated. Catalunya won her independence from Frankish rule by 988. In 1137, Catalunya joined with Aragón. United as such, Catalunya enjoyed years of prosperity, exporting wool and iron through her port, one of the wealthiest on the Mediterranean.

Aragón-Cataluña joined with the new nation of Spain when Fernando II de Aragón married Isabel I de Castilla in 1469, uniting Catholic Spain under one crown, effacing any sense of autonomy, ushering in Catalunya's era of *Decadència* (Oppression). When the greater part of Spain reveled in a Golden Age, Barcelona's port suffered in favor of trade through Seville, ensuing in economic recession for Catalunya.

Catalunya lost the twelve-year *Guerra dels Segadors* (Reapers' War, 1640-52) to France. A treaty returned her to Habsburg control in 1652.

Felipe V (Philip de Anjou, a French Bourbon) militarily seized Barcelona in 1714, suppressing Catalunya's identity. Under a dictum of Felipe, all local autonomous privileges were rescinded, including the Catalan language. In 1778, Carlos III lifted the ban on trade through Barcelona's port with the Americas, a victory short-lived, for the wrath of Napoleonic Wars in Spain did not spare Catalunya. In 1808, French troops left in their path considerable havoc. Spain began to lose control of her empire by 1850 and Catalunya felt the repercussions.

With Barcelona's industrial renaissance (*Renaixença*) in the nineteenth century, Catalan nationalism was on the rise. But on 23 December 1938, Franco's Nationalists bombed Barcelona and conquered the region on 26 January 1939 just before the end of the Spanish Civil War. Subsequently, Franco—whose goal it was to destroy Spanish regionalism—abolished Catalunya's language together with her proud yellow-and-red-striped standard.

In post-Franco years, Catalan independent nationalism flourished in a modern age, and the ancient Generalitat (Catalan autonomous government) was reinstated in 1980.

Barcelona, capital of Catalunya (until the ninth century, Tarragona served as capital), boasts a population of more than three million. Here, languages are two, *Català* and *Castellano*. Scintillating Barcelona, fondly called *Barna* by its citizenry, engenders a robust maritime, industrial/manufacturing, intellectual, financial center. Barcelona's port attests successful trade and tourism. The city supports a thriving cultural scene, one of the foremost globally. Though chiefly modern, much of Barcelona's turns of history stand recorded in stone.

The tapestry embodying Barcelona spreads wide and varied with colorful districts and neighborhoods. Considered the Modernist capital, *Barna* hosts more Art Nouveau architecture than any other city worldwide. Let us start where it all began, near the seminal Iberian settlement and Roman colony of *Barcino*, then move forward to *Barna's* ever-unfolding evolution.

CIUTAT VELLA (HISTORIC OLD TOWN) AND LAS RAMBLAS

• **Barri Gòtic** (Gothic Quarter): Spoors of Roman settlement are found here, beneath the streets, specifically foundations and reservoirs, viewable in the basement of **Museu d'Història de la Ciutat**. Crowned by **Església Catedral de la Santa Creu** (Cathedral of the Holy Cross), this historical center maintains the city's oldest Catalan-Gothic structures back-to-back with neoteric architecture facing the throbbing shopping artery of **Vía Laietana**. On weekends, in **Plaça de la Seu** (Cathedral Plaza) *Barcelonés* spontaneously join hands in the traditional Catalan ring-dance known as *sardana*. In this district, too, is the modern seat of government, **Palau de la Generalitat de Catalunya** and **Casa de la Ciutat** (the *ajuntament*, or town hall).

• **Las Ramblas:** *Rambla* (in Spanish: avenue), from the Arabic *ramla*, or dry bed of a seasonal river. Individual sections of the world famous strip, La Rambla, known as the "Backbone of Barcelona," stretches one mile from **Plaça de Catalunya** on the north to **Monument a Colom** in the south, with two narrow outer streets for vehicular traffic. Between, a spacious pedestrian mall abounds with artful effervescence. Las Ramblas' diverse sectors are five:

Rambla de Canaletes: Sip here from a famous fountain's four spouts to assure your return to Barcelona.

Rambla dels Estudis: Site of a former university, also known as "Rambla dels Ocells" because of the birds sold on this stretch.

Rambla de Sant Josep: Also known as "Rambla de las Flors" by virtue of florists who throng this sector. Just to the west, world-famous **Mercat Boqueria**, a farmer's market to top all farmers markets.

Rambla del Centre: Or "Rambla del Caputxins," home of **Teatre del Liceu** (opera house).

Rambla de Santa Mónica: Here we find **Museu de Cera** (Wax Museum) and, after dark, prostitutes.

LA RIBERA (SANT PERE AND PARC DE LA CIUTADELLA)

An area so named because of its ancient riparian position, this neighborhood of chic boutiques, restaurants, museums and ateliers occupies medieval buildings. In the Middle Ages, La Ribera furnished an important textile center. Metal crafts, ceramics and other fine arts were also produced here.

• **La Ribera:** This bohemian nucleus remains a haunt of artists and is home to **Museu Picasso** and a battery of medieval palaces, shadowy alleyways of charm and Catalan-Gothic **Església de Santa Marià del Mar**, the mariner's church.

• **Sant Pere:** A neighborhood bordering La Ribera, generally lumped into the same district. Here is found the church of **Sant Pere** and **Moderniste Palau de la Música Catalana** designed by Domènech i Montaner.

• **Parc Ciutadella:** Former site of a fortress designed to consolidate Madrid's military occupation in Barcelona under Felipe V, this greensward is now an urban park. Sights include **Parc Zoològic** (home to **Snowflake**, the world's only albino gorilla), **Museu de Geologia** and **Museu d'Art Modern**. Close by, **Estació de França**, Barcelona's bustling train station.

EL RAVAL

Tourist, beware! Apart from **Palau Güell** (on the margin of this district) and the Romanesque church of **Sant Pau del Camp**, much of the neighborhood west of La Rambla bears the earmarks of ghetto. Decades ago, El Raval's south end earned the inauspicious moniker of *Barri Xinès*, or Chinatown. Although no Chinese lived there, it presented to visitors a seedy district of drug dens and brothels. Today's populace includes Afghans and North Africans. El Raval is also home to a police station. (Having walked through this neighborhood, I am at odds with travel writers' avowal of cleaned-up status.)

Seafront

The maritime fringe of seven beaches, Olympic site and marina.

• **Poble Nou** and **Port Olímpic:** The old warehouse-factory district of Poble Nou was dismantled, making room for the 1992 Olympic Games. This is a dynamic neighborhood of apartment buildings, parks, shopping mall, sports center, beaches and restaurants. Port Olímpic sports a pair of twin office towers, sailboat moorings, restaurants, casino, nightclubs. La Vila Olímpica, blocks of apartments, housed Olympic athletes in 1992.

• **Barceloneta** ("Little Barcelona"): The city's old village of fishmongers, seafood restaurants, bars, cafés, beaches.

• **Port Vell:** Barcelona's busy port, hatched with masts of private sailing vessels, bustles with tourism, blares with fog horns of cruise ships. Pedestrian **Moll d'Espanya** accommodates merrymakers and tourists, providing easy access to the **Aquarium, Cine IMAX** and **Multicines.**

• **Montjuïc:** One of Barcelona's two hills and site of the 1929 International Fair and 1992 Olympic Summer Games is a source of civic pride. Surrounded by boundless acres of parkland, fountains and gardens, looms **Castell de Montjuïc** (fortress, now a military museum) built in 1640 by rebels against Felipe IV. Additional sites include **Palau Nacional** (housing **Museu Nacional d'Art de Catalunya**), **Fundació Joan Miró** and **El Poble Espanyol** (The Spanish Village), replicas of architecture from Spain's most notable cities.

Dreta de L'Eixample ("The Enlargement")

Developed in the nineteenth-century *Renaixença* (industrial-inspired renaissance), this was the first master-planned neighborhood (designed by engineer Ildefons Cerdà) to expand beyond the old city. Here, in **Quadrat** d'Or (Golden Quarter), stand testimonies to achievements of fabulist architects Lluis Domènech i Montaner, Josep Puig i Cadafalch and Antoni Gaudí i Cornet. The illustrious architects' Modernist architecture graces this district, but none so prominently as Gaudí's seminal work, **Temple Expiatori de la Sagrada Familia** (Expiatory Temple of the Sacred Family), the emblematic symbol of Barcelona.

ZONA ALTA (UPTOWN)

- **Collseroles and Tibidabo:** A foothill of the Collseroles mountains, Tibidabo looms across town from the hill of Montjuïc. **Tramvia Blau** (Blue Trolley) and a funicular railway are means of accessing its crest. Here, according to legend, Satan tempted Christ when he took Him up a mountain and offered Him the world spread at His feet. (*Tibi dabo*: "I shall give you.") Crowning this hill is Neo-Gothic **Temple Expiatori del Sagrat Cor** (Expiatory Temple of the Sacred Heart). Other sites include **Parc de Collserola** (an amusement park), a ruined casino, and **Torre de Collserola**, an award-winning, 945-foot-tall communications tower designed by London-based Norman Foster & Partners as a transmitter of television and radio signals during the Olympic Games.
- **Grácia:** Random Moderniste buildings, parks including **Parc Güell**, sophisticated shops and restaurants.
- **Horta** and **Vall d'Hebron**: Horta is a neighborhood of apartment buildings, plus the random old farmhouse and medieval fortress. At Vall d'Hebron were built Olympic venues for cycling, tennis and archery.
- **Pedralbes and Les Corts:** Residents of these exclusive neighborhoods include El Barça's *fútbol* stars.
- **Sants:** A former textile center, now a neighborhood of aging apartment buildings and sublime plazas.
- **Sarrià:** One thousand years old, this village-within-a-city is blessed with mansions, beguiling squares, deluxe boutiques and the district's own town hall. On the squares, one often finds groups performing the *sardana*.

PARKS

Barcelona charms with perennial verdant oases. Besides **Parc de la Ciutadella** and **Parc de Montjuïc**, there are Parc de les Aigües, de

Bederrida, de Carles I, del Carmel, Central de Nou Barris, Cervantes and del Clot. Parc de l'Espanya Industrial, de Estacío del Nord, Parc Güell, de Guinardó, les Heures, del Laberint d'Horta, de Joan Miró and de Monterols. Serra Martí, de la Trinitat, Parc Turó del Putxet and Turó Parc together with ubiquitous gardens and beguiling public squares.

MUSEUMS

Over and above the expected major metropolitan collections—fine art, historical, diocesan, zoological—myriad esoteric tastes are satisfied here in *Barna*. If you name it, you will discover it here, from shoes to holography, comic strips to erotica, textiles to football. There are—yes—museums dedicated to hearses, bulls and sewers. Caches of Egyptian, *Azteca*, Mayan and Incan art, plus museums decked with textiles, maritime and military themes, ethnology and archaeology round out the array.

In the opinion of an outsider, the arts are as important to a *Barcelonés* as the air he breathes. Top-notch artists and musicians hail from these parts, among them Salvador Dalí, Joan Miró, Felipe Pedrell, Pau (Pablo) Casals, Josep Carreras, Montserrat Caballé, and Pablo Picasso—born Pablo Ruiz Picazo in Málaga, but gained fame and a new spelling of his surname in Barcelona. Museums, galleries, a phenomenal opera house and theaters highlight these artists' work. The pull of tradition endures, for talent emerges of late from studios and street corners.

Barna, the gateway to Catalunya, boasting a significant intellectual and arts center, is economically sound, positioned for the future. Though more than twenty centuries old, Barcelona progresses, complex, robust.

Long live Catalunya and her beguiling capital, Barcelona.

SINGULAR, LYRICAL BARCELONA

Plane tree leaves the size of catchers' mitts scuttled across my Rambla path as I ambled down one-third its span. A peaceful stroll at first light, air surprisingly balmy for the season—but where was the pastiche, the ubiquitous buskers, steady buzz of mopeds, the flood of humanity? The desultory sign of life was muffled crowing of roosters behind shuttered stalls. Figures filed into an elegant church beneath a glazed green-tile roof and copper spires. This was baroque Església de Mare Déu Betlem. I took my place behind the queue of early-morning worshipers.

Cold as winter inside, gloomy but for candle-glow and an inkling of daylight penetrating windows of this hemmed-in church. Anarchist torching during the Civil War rendered this church gutted of superfluity, a circumstance yet unresolved. My kneeler of undressed oak with wide-open grain hurts my knees, but I linger painfully, silently, offering gratitude and petitions for a growing list of favors.

Sobbing.... From the corner of my eye, I see a middle-aged woman praying at a shrine. Her shadow fires up a candle, plinks a coin into a metal box, then the shadow shuffles away. After my own prayers, I find a beggar in the portal—a familiar accouterment in Spanish churches. I have nothing to give him but a nod and a smile. I spent all my coins yesterday on statuesque mimes in their outdoor office along La Rambla.

As I pace back to the hotel, La Rambla comes to life. A man in overalls guides a yellow machine atop great circular brushes, clearing debris from yesterday's sprees. With paste and broom, another fellow affixes a poster onto the side of a kiosk. People clad in business attire course the pedestrian mall. Dogs roam freely, sniffing the ground, anointing smooth, pale-gray bark of plane trees with pheromone calling cards. Roosters persevere in announcing a new day from their secured domain.

Uncle Chuck awaits me in the breakfast room. Beside usual buffet offerings, I find strange the rows of wine and liqueur bottles. *For breakfast?* But in this progressive, artistically driven city, why startle?

This year marks the one-hundred-and-fifty-year anniversary of Antoni Gaudí's birth. Here in Catalunya, they hail 2002 as *Any de Gaudí.* Awaiting us today is Sagrada Familia, Gaudí's copestone: an evolving emblem of his faith. Though begun in 1882, the architectural marvel is far from complete, albeit a stroke of sheer genius, a mind-numbing portrayal of Roman Catholic spirituality. I have admired this wonder in photographs, likening it to skyscraping termite hills, organic sculpture in mud.

A cabby with a Hadassah medal dangling from his rear-view mirror drives us through the *Modernisme* (Modernist) neighborhood of Eixample to the foot of the Sagrada Familia at Carrer de Mallorca 401.

We stand in shadows of towers and construction cranes. Tour buses spill Asians onto the street. Many people are drawn to a highly publicized national treasure, not to its essence; seeing it firsthand proffers bragging rights back home. But do casual tourists understand the temple's substance? Feel its power? Will a guided tour permit time and space for contemplation?

"Let's wait," Uncle Chuck advises, "for others to file inside. Meantime, we'll admire the edifice from over there."

He points to a park across the street, Plaça Gaudí. We head over, seeking camera angles. Here we see a young American male, a transient in grimy attire and backpack, making moves on an older Spanish man. *Click!* On an earthen courtyard, stringy-throated old Catalan men play a game of *bolos* (like French *boules*, played with metallic balls). A boxer fetches for his master. The dog leaps, nearly tripping me as he retrieves a stick. We wend our way, minding puddles, to a leafy, flowery fringe of emerald-green pond, a suitable foreground for the budding temple across the street.

"They've been building that for one hundred and twenty years," I mention, mesmerized by cranes swinging slowly amidst lofty spires.

"Bear in mind," Uncle Chuck says thoughtfully as I twist a polarizing filter onto my wide-angle lens, "the great cathedrals of the world evolved over centuries."

Masses of tourists move on, into the monument. Sidewalks and ticket booth clear. We mosey across the street for our own self-guided tour.

Was Gaudí madman or genius? A thin line, but I am convinced of Gaudí's genius. *Duende*? Gaudí epitomized it. Knowing new discoveries lurk around each corner, I want to spend an entire day here, admiring Gaudí's statement of melody and rhythm in an otherwise concrete quarter. I know also that Uncle Chuck will allow two hours, if that.

I have seen only one other cathedral in the course of construction—Our Lady of the Angels in Los Angeles, California. Hadn't the same effect, to say the least, as this Sagrada Familia, this embodiment of profound symbolism, evoking not only awe but also solemn reverence. Surprising, since the LA cathedral's architect is the famed José Rafael Moneo from Pamplona, Spain. From Rafael, I expected at least a parenthesis of *duende*. Contrasting Barcelona's basilica of the Sacred Family, the Cathedral of Our Lady of the Angels poses an unyielding sterile box; a waste, I've concluded, of US$195 million dollars. Modern it is, but where lies the symbolism? In the end, Our Lady of the Angels owes her uninspiring circumstance to hasty fabrication (just shy of five years), to a contemporary world devoid of genius, the result of mainstream American stoicism, the settling for less than extraordinary. On the other side, Los Angeles boasts an oddity known as Watts Towers, by Italian immigrant Simon Rodia, whose fanciful towers call to mind, in miniature, Gaudí's transcendent temple above me.

The termite hills of my imagination are eight of eventual twelve depictions of the Apostles. Inspired by needle-like spires of nearby

Montserrat, these bell towers rise hundreds of feet, each encasing a spiral of four hundred stone steps. Each spire, halfway up, bears the words *Sanctus, Sanctus, Sanctus*; closer to the top, *Gloria in Excelsis*, all crowned by veering geometric designs dazzling with Venetian glass mosaics.

Planned are four towers of even greater height, to represent the Evangelists, plus a seventeenth spire to symbolize the Virgin Mary. Another, at 568 feet, will terminate in a colossal crucifix, to signify Christ the Savior. When completed, the structure will include an exterior cloister, a fountain and a "purifying flame."

Dreamy façades are three: the Nativity, Passion and Glory.

This basilica, in the form of a Latin cross with five naves, a transept, an apse and ambulatory, continually evolves under guidance of architect Jordi Bonet, whose father worked directly with Gaudí. Construction continued after Gaudí's death, until interrupted in 1936 when shelling razed Gaudí's crypt and study together with his notes and designs, during the Spanish Civil War. The project resumed in 1952 and perseveres today, with completion estimated between 2050 and 2100. Had the improvisational Gaudí lived longer, Sagrada Familia would transition beyond what we see. The maestro worked from his head, never hesitating to revise or embellish his original notions.

On seeing photographs of Sagrada Familia, Louis Henry Sullivan, celebrated American architect, said of Gaudí's basilica, "This is the spiritual embodiment of what is concealed in stone itself." Salvador Dalí described Gaudí's work as "Terrifying, edible beauty." Dalí argued that the temple be left unfinished as a monument to Gaudí. On the other hand, George Orwell wished anarchists had destroyed the temple in 1936. At that time, Orwell described Gaudí's masterpiece as "something awful."

On the eastern façade, festoons of swirling plaster foliage cradle supple figures conjuring notions of Godliness. Here, the Sacred Family huddles in a grotto, a stable dripping with stalactite motif. Nearby, panes in blue, green and yellow pierce an evolving wall. Above us, a "cypress tree" spire bristles in ceramic with pure white doves encircling green botanicals. In Gaudí's vision, this tree symbolizes the stairway to heaven; the birds, an adoring congregation. Portals of the sculpture-encrusted façade exemplify Faith, Hope and Charity. Above the center portal sits a pure white angel strumming a harp, a portrayal of Love.

Behind the Nativity façade, we study the east transept and apse, rose and lancet windows, by far the most traditionally Gothic elements of this basilica.

These rigid features counterpose soft, muddy textures composing the greater part of the church.

We move to the inside, a shell open to the sky, alive with methodic engineers and masons. Above our heads soars a forest of angular, white fluted columns intersected with *Modernisme* medallions. Uncle Chuck heads toward an *ascensor* at the foot of one of the bell towers.

"To the top?" he asks me.

Behind a throng, it takes fifteen minutes to mount three shallow flights of steps. We now wait to board the lift, which will take us close to the top. To achieve the full height of this spire requires an additional negotiation of a steep spiral staircase.

This tower, pierced randomly as the others, presents bird's-eye views of Barcelona. Beyond neatly chamfered gridwork of El Eixample, a majestic church crests a distant rise: Temple Expiato del Sagrat Cor (Expiatory Temple of the Sacred Heart) on Tibidabo hill. A golden Christ figure with outstretched arms crowns that church, an austere custodian of the city. Now, winding our way upward, we peek through apertures to the Sagrada Familia's fabulist towers, twisted and studded in sun-kissed details. Shards of glass and ceramics blaze in scarlet, gold, white and gas-flame blue, elements, too, invested with symbolism: abstract episcopal iconography.

Having returned to the foundations, we set out to consider another façade. In striking contrast to softness of the Nativity scene, the Passion façade squares off in Cubist style: harsh, angular technique suggesting Christ's pain and desolation. We step about contemplating shadowy figures, noting mutant expressions as sun transforms the countenance of a weary, cubic Christ. We note, too, His aching wrists bound to a column. Aloft, encompassed by unflinching Roman soldiers, a faceless Veronica unfurls her veil branded with the sanguine impression of Christ's face. At the pinnacle, in like rugged style, He hangs from a crucifix. These riveting sculptures were begun in 1987 by Josep Maria Subirachs.

When this miracle of architecture is at last completed, plans include whitewashing, then studding with a pageant of colorful mosaics; my termite hills resembling then an enormous arrangement of tutti-frutti spires and domes.

"I believe I need a break to reflect on all this," I tell Uncle Chuck as we dodge a radar-deprived herd of expressionless Japanese tourists. We exit the site, making our way to a pedestrian mall just south of the basilica. Settled into sidewalk seating outside a café, we sip our favorite elixir. Magical spires of Sagrada Familia loom above us.

"I'm happy to have seen it," mentions Uncle Chuck, "but it's weird. Wonder if they'll ever finish it."

"Weird?" I ask. "It's an uncanny confirmation of faith. Unconventional I grant you, but when you consider the sheer genius, the sacred symbolism, it's mind-boggling."

Anglocentric Uncle Chuck requires more time for his impressions to settle. He cannot consider Gaudí's triumph "weird." He will reflect back one day, when I hope he will then grasp Gaudí's mysteries, his edifying invocations and the fervid dedication of a lonely soul, a man who never fell in love.

ANTONI PLÀCID GUILLEM GAUDÍ I CORNET
(1852-1926)

The firebrand Catalan architect Antoni Gaudí was born at Reus (some say in Riudoms near Reus), Catalunya, 25 June 1852 to coppersmith Francesc Gaudí i Serra and his wife Antonia Cornet i Bertran. In his youth, Antoni suffered a disease that paralyzed his legs. He first worked as a blacksmith's apprentice, then, at age seventeen, took classes from Eudald Puntí and studied at Barcelona's Escuela Provincial de Arquitectura (Provincial School of Architecture), graduating in 1878.

Antoni Gaudí's first commission came from the city of Barcelona: a street lamp design for Plaça Reial. Swayed by his nationalistic quest for a romantic medieval past, Gaudí incorporated elements of Gothic, Moorish and Art Nouveau into his wildly imaginative architecture. The visionary genius observed plant and animal forms and textures, inspiration for his whimsical, organic designs. Gaudí's work embodies space, polychrome, movement, parabolic arches and spirals. Likewise, Gaudí's artistic development was influenced by theories of French Neo-Gothic architect Violett-le-Duc and English-Victorian philosopher-scientist-poet-art-critic John Ruskin. Antoni Gaudí's first major commission came in 1888, by tile manufacturer Manuel Vicens i Montaner. The result: world-famous Casa Vicens on Carrer de les Carolines 24-26.

Antoni Gaudí did not marry, and biographers write that he did not fall in love. His foremost passion was architecture.

Gaudí's chief patron was industrialist Eusebi Güell i Bacigalupi. For Güell, Gaudí designed the Güell family's country estate, their Barcelona palace (Palau Güell), Pavellons Güell, Güell Cellars, Colònia Güell and a surrealistic development known as Parc Güell. Among Antoni Gaudí's other noteworthy accomplishments: Casa Batlló, Casa Milà (La Pedrera), Casa Calvet, Bellesguard Villa and Teresian College.

Gaudí's finest achievement remains the yet uncompleted Temple Expiatori de la Sagrada Família. A man of fervent, ascetic Catholicism, Gaudí devoted more than half his life to the evolving design and construction oversight of Barcelona's landmark temple. In 1866, the Spiritual Association of St. Joseph (the Josephines) conceived a Neo-Gothic plan for a church on this site, commissioning the project in 1881. In 1882, Francesc de Paula Villar i Lozano began construction, ceding the project to Antoni Gaudí, who took over in 1883. Moreover, Gaudí lived as a recluse on the site, begging public funding for construction. In his lifetime, Gaudí saw only portions of his powerful masterwork completed: the Neo-Gothic crypt, part of the apse, the Nativity façade (completed 1904) and one of the towers, that of St. Barnabas.

Antoni Gaudí's time was cut short when a tram ran him over on 7 June 1926. The revolutionary architect went home to God three days later, just shy of age seventy-four, expiring in the pauper's ward of a public hospital. Gaudí lies buried in a crypt on the Gospel side of the altar in his beloved Sagrada Família. He believed he would not live to see the completion of his temple, but predicted that St. Joseph would finish the work.

> Everywhere else, death is an end. Death comes, and they draw the curtains. Not in Spain. In Spain they open them. Many Spaniards live indoors until the day they die and are taken out into the sunlight. A dead man in Spain is more alive as a dead man than anyplace else in the world. His profile wounds like a barber's razor.
> —Federico García Lorca

FROM WHIMSY TO CLASSICAL TRADITION...

Conventional Uncle Chuck appreciated the next round of tours, when we worked our way back in time, visiting the Gothic Quarter, the historical center of Barcelona, and still more medieval wonders beyond in the fusty Ribera district.

Not far southeast of our lodging, the district Barri Gòtic sports remarkable Gothic architecture. Just off fashionable Vía Laietana rises Església Catedral de la Santa Creu, Barcelona's compact though inspiring cathedral crowning a sun-splashed square. Teeming with tourists, the square hosts an antiques market, a pair of mounted Mossos d'Esquadra (Catalunya's version of Guardia Civil) and buskers like those who enliven La Rambla. One, the most ingenious I've yet noted, is a man on stilts, his golden cassock flowing to the ground. From his back, crooked branches grow. His arms, resembling branches too, sway poetically. Fingernails are long, witch-like, the face painted in solar spectrum. He moves from the waist in slow measure as he surveys passersby. A tree, I conclude, from a haunted forest. This tree assuredly emits the *duende*.

Next, an angel greets with face and hands powdered white as flour, halo somewhat askew. He speaks thinly with a lisp, his gestures, Chaplinesque. At the foot of the steps, an emerald-green woman with Mister Spock ears speaks without voice as she reads from her old tome.

As we scale steps to the lacy, gray cathedral, we meet less creative sorts: beggars crouching, beseeching, moaning. Uncle Chuck moves on, evading their pleas. I linger on the steps admiring this Gothic jewel.

Dedicated to Santa Eulalia (Barcelona's patroness) and the Holy Cross, Barcelona's cathedral was begun in 1298 under Jaume II on the site of a Roman temple, an Islamic mosque and a former Romanesque church. Since then, it has been Barcelona's archbishopric center. The cathedral's Catalan-Gothic style waxed mostly between the fourteenth and fifteenth centuries, with a Neo-Gothic façade by Josep Mestres completed in 1889. The complex anterior impales the sky with three spires, the central one soaring above those abreast. Rising behind, a pair of octagonal towers add interest with bells suspended in iron cages.

I look up to a series of four telescoping lancet arches framing two doors divided by a *trumeau*. From this elegant *trumeau* springs an image of Christ the King, six Apostles flanking each side. As I crane my neck upward and trace with my eyes arched windows and one shaped as a six-pointed star, someone tugs at the hem of my trousers. Looking down, I see an old woman, squalid, in tatters. I proffer a coin and pass through.

Inside, racks of squat white candles greet—hundreds of them ablaze. From red glass canisters, the fiery spectacle warms a small sector of this dank vault of stone. I pause briefly, welcoming the warmth. Eyes adjusted, I peer into a chapel to the right of the entry. A priest in green-and-gold vestments leads prayers for a mournful congregation in the chapel of Sant Crist de Lepant. I respect the sign requesting visitors not interrupt the Mass, though, from a distance, I scan the room for the illustrious crucifix carried into battle against a Turkish army in days of old.[1]

I spot Uncle Chuck's figure in one of the aisles. He studies the riot of stained-glass windows at eighty-five-foot heights. I move past half of the twenty-eight side chapels, between slender pillars, to catch up with him.

"Now this is genius," he whispers.

I know he draws comparison to Sagrada Familia. How can he? The cathedral is remarkable, but its style and Gaudí's Modernist basilica are worlds apart, the cathedral so literal, easy to deduce.

I am particularly taken with the tomb of Santa Eulalia. Here she rests, ensconced in alabaster, in a crypt beneath the sanctuary of Capella de Sant Benet (St. Bernard). Her intricate urn, chiseled in a style known as "Pisa," rests on Corinthian pillars. Golden votive candles, each of them dark, encompass the casket topped with Virgin and Child amidst marble angels with gold-leafed wings.

Above, in the *capella*, we behold a marvel sculpted in marble, a sixteenth-century altar screen depicting the life and martyrdom of Santa Eulalia. Over the high altar dangles a cross in bronze by Frederic Marès (1976).

This cathedral is a palace of quiet contemplation in the midst of a city of three million. Lingering at a side chapel dedicated to Nuestra Señora de la Soledad, I allow the ambiance to sweep over me. The statue of Our Sorrowful Mother looks alive in soft candlelight. Nearby, an elderly Spanish woman dressed in black kneels with rosary beads.

Uncle Chuck meets me aside a tier of richly carved wooden choir stalls. I mention to him their intricate details, the calling to mind of organic contours in the Sagrada Familia. He discerns no connection.

"Here, at least," he says, "we have a roof over our heads."

"But this was begun six hundred years before the Sagrada Familia," I counter. "Remember what you said? These places take time to build."

Before leaving the cathedral, we stop at the back to contemplate an ancient font. Here, in 1493, six Caribbean Indians received the Sacrament of Baptism. They had accompanied Columbus back to Barcelona.

In Plaça de la Seu again, we round a corner, pausing to admire a touch of modernism in this Gothic square. The word BARCINO spreads before us in three-dimensional bronze, a sculpture by Joan Brossa.

Up a shadowy alley, beyond Capella de Santa Llùcia, we discover to our left an entrance to the old *claustro*, an intimate sanctuary from the hubbub of tourists, jackhammers and car horns. Stocked with a flock of snow-white geese, our cloister-haven is comely with pond and drizzling fountain. The geese enchant us as we amble under palms, magnolia and orange trees. Reputedly, these birds have Roman pedigrees. Though the story goes that thirteen geese are kept here—symbolizing the age of Eulalia at her martyrdom—I count only nine. We move to the rear of the cloister, discovering the fountain's finial to be a fine bronze casting of Sant Jordi (St. George) on horseback.

I learned years ago that Santiago (St. James) is the patron saint of Spain, Nuestra Señora del Pilar its patroness. Here, in Catalunya, a nationalistic populace acknowledges its own patrons: Sant Jordi and the Virgin of Montserrat.

From the cloister, we move alongside a series of medieval palaces: Casa dels Canonges, Casa del Degà, Casa de l'Ardiaca. One of these spans the dark alleyway with an elegant bridge of stone, pierced with ornate lancets.

"Shall we find that other church?" asks Uncle Chuck.

He speaks of Església de Santa Marià del Mar—in the words of our friend Monsignor Weber, "Barcelona's Lady of the Sea, the most beautiful church I have ever seen." And the monsignor has seen myriad churches in his tenured travels as ecclesial historian. "Don't leave Barcelona without seeing it," he exhorted.

Culled in a record fifty-four years (1329-1383) with stone from Montjuïc, this cathedral-like edifice consummated a vow by Jaume I to build a church for the Virgin of Sailors. Financed by local merchants, shipbuilders constructed the eminent temple in Catalan-Gothic style, its benefactors seeking to rival the cathedral's splendors. In my opinion—and Monsignor Weber's, as well—this church harmonizes in unity of style, no doubt an outcome of the brief span of time required for building it.

We cross back to Vía Laietana past a ruined splendor, Palau Reial Major with a puissant equestrian bronze of Ramón Berenguer III out front. Following our city plan, we cross over to locate Monsignor Weber's highly touted church on Passeig del Born 1.

Up the way, we note spray-painted graffiti on alley walls, separatist words like *Llibertat anarkos Valencia*. Deeper within the Ribera district, medieval storefronts purvey all from fine apparel to oriental baths and ultramodern bars to cozy restaurants. Across the street, traditional restaurants bulge to the rafters with mid-afternoon diners. Up the way, we pass hair salons, a pastry shop and boutiques chock-full of devotional articles. We peer through windows of an appliance store with Art Deco-revival refrigerators in hues of mint green, pink and turquoise. Dodging pariahs and tail-wagging pets, we roam in the thick of trucks and pedestrian traffic.

The sun cannot penetrate, for all hems in. Rustic façades straddle these constricted alleyways rising to four stories and higher, blocking all but noon's overhead rays. Unlike the sun-dappled square of the cathedral, this neighborhood feels eerie.

The grand church of Saint Mary of the Sea presents herself even before we reach Plaça de Santa Marià. A slit between towering walls of Carrer Argenteria, through which we pass, frames the church façade and its two octagonal campaniles of taupe-colored stone against burning blue sky. It is truly difficult to fully appreciate the church from close range, for this magnificent structure, as all others, wedges tightly between its neighbors.

We pass into the basilica's cavernous interior. Our eyes adjusted, we stand in awe, agreeing with the monsignor's accolades. Space is voluminous in this impeccably proportioned, time-honored temple. Wide expanses of vaulting float above three naves. A play of light floods through a garrison of lofty lancet windows. Straightaway, I am drawn to the altar, in front of which rises a lone marble statue of the Virgin of Sailors, a majestic Queen poised on her pedestal, overseeing comings and goings of centuries of worshipers and tourists. This Mary holds the Christ child for all to see; at her feet floats a fine model of a medieval sailing vessel.

Moving slowly past the Virgin, we gape at spacious vaulting, at a splendid rose window depicting Mary's coronation. We understand the effect of space as we note slender pillars carrying a sweeping expanse of ceiling.

In college, Uncle Chuck studied architecture. Old interests resurge as he stands here in awe.

"The cathedral is admirable," he whispers. "But this church is harmonious, so well balanced."

And he has a roof over his head....

With our aesthetic appetites on overdrive, we return to dim alleyways.

What's that? I don't believe my ears. *Ave Marie?* Drawn to Carrer Montcada, we find a handsome man bowing a cello, the notes resounding between acoustics of stone. A wave of emotions raises the hair on my neck. Uncle Chuck has *escalofríos*, too.

---

[1] The Battle of Lepanto (between Spaniards and Turks, 1571) endured for little more than an hour after Spanish troops carried onto the battlefield a crucifix and their faith in the prayers of Pius V to *Señor* Jesús Cristo (*Santo Cristo de Lepanto* in

Castilian, *Sant Crist de Lepant* in Catalan). The Spaniards defeated the Ottomans, sealing Spain's control of the Mediterranean, attributing this to miraculous intercession.

…NOW, FORWARD, TO THE AGE OF MODERNISM

Five adjoined medieval palaces provided room for a remarkable collection of Pablo Picasso's earlier work. Uncle Chuck reluctantly accompanied me to sample this fine repository. He was soon enthralled.

Still shivering with rapture, notes of *Ave Maria* coursing through our brains, we carry on along a dusky corridor near the textile museum (Museu Tèxtil de la Indumentària) to Museu Picasso at Carrer Montcada 15-23. Medieval mansions along this slim passageway have in common their graceful courtyards with arch-born staircases of stone and second-level galleries of slender columns. Uncle Chuck marvels at the aristocratic architecture, fine medieval arcades, stony textures of stately palaces, including those comprising the Picasso Museum: fourteenth to seventeenth century Palau Berenguer d'Aguilar, Baró de Castellet, Meca, Finestres, Casa Mauri. As a champion of naturalism, Uncle Chuck prefers the work of Pablo Picasso's formative years to the mature artist's avant-garde masterworks. The former tributes to Picasso's coming of age as an artist are mostly on the museum's ground level.

"These are lovely, but compared with his paradigms?" I argue.

My travel partner appreciates, however, Picasso's sober Realism, imitations of classic and impressionist masters and childhood sketches, studies of landscape, still life and portraits bringing their subjects to life. These are educational and I am happy to see Picasso's developmental work, particularly examples of his *Els Quatre Gats*, a suite produced locally. And his canvases from Paris: *La Nana* and *La Espera*. But I am spellbound, sampling Picasso's true genius trumpeting from walls of the upper level.

Upstairs hang *Les Demoiselles d'Avignon* (1907), paintings from Picasso's Blue Period (initiated here in Barcelona): *Los Desemparats* (The Abandoned, 1903), *El Foll* (The Madman) and portraits of his friend and personal secretary Jaume Sabartes. Visitors stand mere inches from *Senyora Canals* from Picasso's Rose Period (1905), seemingly interested more in the impasto or signature than in the overall compositions.

Walls carry more interpretations of Jaume Sabartes's likeness in varying techniques and medium. Sabartes initiated this museum, opened 1963, when he donated Picasso's works given him as gifts. The collection expanded to embody more than thirty-six hundred pieces including forty-two ceramics from 1947-65.

This spectacular museum is Barcelona's and Sabartes' tribute to genius, to a friend's contributions to a great city. Moreover, the collection is the largest body of Picasso's formative oeuvre.

Pablo Ruiz Picazo (1881-1973) lived in Barcelona from 1895-1904, training at Escola de Belles Arts de Barcelona as well as at art schools in Madrid and A Coruña. In Barcelona, Picasso served his artistic apprenticeship before he retreated for Paris.

> When I was a child, my mother said to me, "If you become a soldier,
> you'll be a general. If you become a monk, the Pope." Instead, I
> became a painter and wound up as Picasso.
> —Pablo Ruiz Picazo

I linger in rooms, scouring fifty-eight oil paintings: an exhaustive suite of color and rhythm, flat planes rendered in bold primary colors, delineated by tracery of black. This suite, bringing to mind fanciful stained glass, is the master's *Las Meninas* ("Maids of Honor," 1957) series, subversive variations on Diego Velázquez's 1656 masterwork of the same title. The style is Cubist, for which Picasso laid the basis. Forty-four portraits, primarily analytic studies of the *Infanta* Margarita (daughter of Felipe IV) mock Velázquez's static pose in the courtiers' pomp, even the dog's demeanor. In some of these paintings, I note the reflection of Picasso in a distant mirror. In others, his figure in a doorway, mimicking another technique used by Velázquez. Supplementing the forty-four portraits: nine of pigeons, three of landscapes, two free paraphrases.

I'm moved, too, by a grisly work called *Cavall Banyegat* (Gored Horse, 1917), reminding me of a later work, Picasso's riveting *Guernica* (1937) which I admired in Madrid's Centro de Arte Reina Sofía.

Uncle Chuck grows indifferent and cranky. I insist on viewing Picasso's etchings, a comprehensive ensemble from 1904-72. Uncle Chuck rests on a bench as I scrutinize the artworks. Among Picasso's engravings, I find those hatched with Don Quixote and bullfighting themes in straightforward, impromptu strokes of black. Virtual displays provide glimpses from Picasso's sketchbooks, those from his childhood, with caricatures of his instructors.

"You can always return," moans Uncle Chuck from his perch. "Maybe tomorrow, while I enjoy my siesta?"

Picasso would have found amusement in Uncle Chuck's indifference.

As the sky deepens, we drop in on crowded Café Zurich for a round of gin and to watch people watching people. Following a restful interlude, we hike back toward our hotel, pausing across the street to admire floodlit fountains on Plaça de Catalunya, a transportation hub where major streets converge. We barely noticed this plaza in daylight, La Rambla drawing us instead and repeatedly to the action. And at this time of year, the plaza's fountains are still until nightfall, when they come to fruition as spotlit, dancing jets and arcs of splashing foam. Statues of scantly clad Romans stand among us. Rosemary and roses of Castilla scent the air. In this classical setting, local youngsters hang out under a pendant crescent moon.

STRANGERS IN THE NIGHT

Dressed in dinner attire, we waited in our hotel lobby for an eight-thirty P.M. appointment. At eight-fifty, in sauntered two men in European-casual dress including tennis shoes. Ignacio, an attorney forty years of age, looked smart in ankle-length woolen coat with matching scarf to the floor, salt-and-pepper hair cropped short and spectacles fashionably small. Miguel, a designer in his mid-thirties, stood taller than Ignacio at six feet. "Long and black" described Miguel's coat as well as his glossy hair. While Ignacio would blend easily with any northern European group, Miguel characterized his Andalusian roots, his substantial brows framing soulful doe eyes against a background of olive complexion.

This evening, we will host the fellow responsible for our last-minute accommodations in this highly charged sector of town—a *Barcelones*. We invited him to choose the restaurant and bring a guest.

In unclouded English, Ignacio makes introductions. He also speaks *Català*, Castilian Spanish, French and Italian. Miguel is learning English. He smiles and nods, and though he understands us, he's too shy to speak.

"Enjoy Catalan cuisine?" asks Ignacio, urging us to call him "Nacho."

We explain that we have eaten mostly *tapas* since our arrival.

"Then we've chosen the ideal restaurant," he beams. "Come, follow us."

When discovering our guests had walked to the hotel, I suggest taking a cab to the restaurant. Air grows chilly, and I have read of crime in these parts.

"Why ride when you can walk?" Nacho queries, winding the long scarf around his neck. "Walking is good for us. I walk all the time. When I leave the city, I use my Vespa."

A scooter? Maybe I will spare Nacho my lawyer jokes.

Barcelona throbs with *el paseo* as we add our own footfall to sidewalks this brisk evening. As we walk through the night, we discuss Antoni Gaudí and zany Salvador Dalí. Uncle Chuck resigns to laughter when Nacho propounds his own apathy concerning the geniuses' works. Miguel and I disagree with these uninformed, biased opinions. After fifteen minutes, we arrive at Restaurant l'Olivé, Carrer de Balmes 47, Dreta de l'Eixample.

"Authentic Catalan cuisine," Nacho assures us.

With a deep bow and arm extended, Miguel allows us to pass before him.

At nine-thirty P.M., the austere, ultramodern restaurant sits vacant but for the help. Blond wood tones adorn the subtly lit space. Above each table, a single, minuscule halogen lamp focuses on a crimson anthurium.

A congenial host proffers a table with a view of the entire room. As our guests shed coats and scarves, we remove our ties and pocket them. Nacho wears drab grays. Miguel's sweater, overpowering the anthurium, glows in the most vivid shade of red I have ever seen.

With a menu the size of Eixample spread between them, Nacho holds a mini-conference with Miguel. They debate in Spanish, then select starter courses for the table. In a heartbeat, two waiters deliver armloads of plates, one with *pa amb tomàquet,* others with anchovies, raw *bacalao* (*bacalla,* in these parts), deep-fried *chipirones*, a range of dips and bread.

Nacho orders a bottle of Fransola (Catalan wine) and Catalan water from the steward.

"Please tell us about Catalan nationalism?" I inquire.

"It does not exist, in my mind," Nacho responds nonchalantly between bites of codfish.

By the look on Miguel's face, I wish he would speak up. I know he holds revelations I seek.

The men are impressed with my admiration of Junípero Serra. So, I venture, after a swig of light-bodied wine, "Are you Catholics?"

"Hell, no," Nacho fumes.

Again, Miguel looks puzzled.

As main plates arrive, Miguel speaks under his breath. Nacho recants his previous statement, "I am a lapsed Catholic. Miguel is Catholic, but rarely goes to Mass. Only funerals, weddings, Easter, Christmas."

"Please, tell me about *duende*," I say.

This gets a broad smile from Miguel. Nacho responds unfazed, "What artists have."

Miguel softly mumbles, *"Es el instinto...espíritu...orgullo...motivo...."* These are acceptable definitions.

Nacho fancies cod. He has eaten the lion's share of our *bacalla* appetizers. Now he orders a baked portion for entrée. Uncle Chuck and I admire monkfish and we cannot resist this restaurant's grilled version (*rapa la planxa*). Miguel has tuna (*llom de tonyina amb escalivada*). We swap tastes. Each bite: ¡*buen gusto!*

Ignacio and Miguel object to George W. Bush's administration, and they downright oppose war. Only Spanish politicians sided with America in the war against Iraq, they tell us; "real people" are opposed. I deflect, switching to the arts.

Nacho interprets for Miguel, who wants to know if we have seen Fundació Joan Miró. Uncle Chuck launches into a litany, stating his proclivity for realism and naturalism. I again change the subject, submitting, "Catalans surely are musical people. I believe music runs through their veins."

This gets a chuckle from both of our guests. Again, Miguel mumbles to Nacho, who in turn interprets, "An exaggeration. But we have a saying. When you pinch someone in the streets of Barcelona and he doesn't break out in song, then he is not Catalan."

The fellows are emblematic of their occupations. Nacho is bright, quick, a tad flippant with no discernable *duende*. Miguel is sensitive, warm, good-hearted, with *duende*. By now I believe the only thread we four share in common is our appreciation of good food.

At half past eleven, our plates are barren and we have polished off a second bottle of Fransola. The room now buzzes, packed with loquacious patrons. We sample desserts of cheesecake (*formatge de la casa*), mild cheese with marmalade (*formatge fresc i taronja amarga*) and dreamy *crema catalana*.

Uncle Chuck grows weary; maybe I do, as well. Our new friends champ for *madrugada* (taking on the wee hours by nightclubbing). We may have coffee to remain alert, but instead, bid Nacho and Miguel adieu before hailing a cab back to our quarters.

Viewpoints from Catalunya's Holiest Position

Pop quiz: Throughout Spain, how many statues of Black Virgins have shepherds discovered? Aware of two, I suspected there were more. One of those precious icons I viewed at the Monastery of Lluch in northern Mallorca. We found another, the most celebrated, in the basilica at Montserrat.

On this sun-kissed day, I am one of only nine on a Julià Tours coach headed out of Barcelona. Besides my trusty travel companion, there is across the aisle an elderly British-Filipino couple. Behind us sits a middle-aged American woman with Mediterranean features and seated opposite her, a young African-American couple. Our driver is an older man who speaks only *Català*. Joan (Catalan for Juan), a bright man in his thirties, is our multi-lingual guide. We pick up N-11, bound northwest toward Catalunya's holiest shrine.

On this side of Barcelona, we see ruins of brick textile mills and stone villages, testimony to an industry once prevalent in these parts. Midway on the excursion of thirty-eight kilometers, Joan speaks into his microphone, "See, over there," he gestures toward a rusticated bridge of redbrick, "Pont de Diablo, the Devil's Bridge. Is called this because Romans build it in one day."

The folkloric Roman span was destroyed, but replaced by the extant medieval bridge that fades into the background as our bus presses on.

On the distant horizon, "one hundred"—according to Joan—needle-like pinnacles come into view (highest elevation: 4,055 feet), an unrivaled profile magnified by banal surroundings of flat plains, a smattering of low hills. From this otherwise hackneyed topography looms mysterious, elephantine Montserrat, the folkloric Sleeping Dragon. Geologically speaking, these unusual peaks pushed skyward from a dried-up lake bed through tectonic activity in the Mesozoic period. Since then, Nature worked her magic, compressing calcareous sediment into conglomerate stone (quartz, limestone and slate), eroding exposed portions, creating fantastic forms. In my imagination, a cluster of outcroppings strike anthropomorphic: huddles of gigantic monks draped in pale beige cassocks. Now our windows yield the manifestation of Monestir de Montserrat.

As we draw closer, I fully expect our driver to pull over, for any shutterbugs on board. In books and videos, I have seen riveting shots made from this viewpoint: the monastery perched on the mountainside, cradled within a deep fold of the Sleeping Dragon. I now feast my eyes on its three-dimensionality, a vision of light on stone in rectilinear forms overshadowed by a breathtaking taupe-colored massif capped with natural spires that engendered the bell towers of Gaudí's Sagrada Familia. I long to photograph this site. Even the backdrop exhilarates—a clear lavender firmament. Alas, we negotiate switchbacks with no stops, zigzagging upward toward the monastery. I have mind to tell our hellbent driver we need to pull over so I can vomit....

EL MONESTIR I LA MORENETA DEL MONTSERRAT

In A.D. 880, according to legend—and Spain is rich with them—shepherds espied a particularly bright star above the massif known as Montserrat (Serrated Mountain). Accompanied by the bishop of Manresa, the band of shepherds followed a mysterious trail of light to its terminus on the side of the mountain, finding there a cave henceforth known as La Santa Cova, The Holy Cave. Inside, the shepherds and bishop discovered a polychrome wooden image of the Virgin. Blurred history blossomed to include St. Luke's having carved the statue, then conveyed here by St. Peter in A.D. 50. Centuries passed; then, through carbon dating, scientists determined the fabled icon to have originated in the twelfth century.

A religious community soon took root on this mountain, beginning as mere hermitages and shrines to the Holy Mother. In 1025, Abbott Oliba of Ripoll established the hermitage of Santa Marià, the seed of a Benedictine monastery. In the twelfth century, monks constructed a Romanesque church on the site. Inside they enthroned the statue of the Virgin.

By 1233, the monastery had grown to be one of the more important in Europe. A choir of boys was formed there, the first children's choir in Europe. Montserrat's library vaunted one of Europe's finest, housing more than 250,000 manuscripts. By 1409, Monestir de Montserrat had become a powerful abbey and the monastic community declared its independence from Rome.

In 1811, during Spain's War of Independence, Napoleón's men slaughtered Montserrat's populace and reduced the monastery largely to rubble. The venerated statue devotees hid off-site during the Napoleonic Wars and Spanish Civil War. Decades later, during the monastery's resurrection, devotees returned the statue to Montserrat.

The church was rebuilt 1830-1905, incorporating portions of original

Romanesque with a new façade in Neo-Baroque style by Venanci and Agapit Vallmitjana. Montserrat served as center for Catalan resistance in the early-twentieth century, a host for nationalist rallies behind Franco's back in the 1940s and 50s. Monks printed Bibles in *Català* on the monastery press.

Reconstruction of El Monestir de Montserrat pursued from 1942-1968. Building progresses with expanded quarters for pilgrims. His Holiness, John Paul II, visited in 1982.

In 1881, locals deemed *La Verge de Montserrat* (The Virgin of Montserrat) patroness of Catalunya. Montserrat continues to draw legions of tourists and pilgrims. The monastery is home to eighty Benedictine monks. Montserrat, with its Marian shrine, endures as a symbol of Catalan identity.

Joan draws attention to *El Camell*, a gigantic stone camel. Other natural shapes challenge the imagination, *La Mòmia* (The Mummy), *L'Escorpí* (The Scorpion), *La Cadireta d'Agulles* (The Little Chair). We also glimpse a lesser-known monastery, Santa Cecília, couched in a vale. Random sentinels of faith dot the landscape: chapels, shrines and scarcely discernable, abandoned caves, chasms—hovels of yesteryears' monks.

Having arrived in the coach lot, glimpsing the monastery, I note construction cranes, the buildings' lack of patina. But for sections of the church, doorways and remains of Gothic cloisters, all has been rebuilt since the nineteenth century. I shiver. Feels at least twenty degrees cooler than Barcelona. But what a location. What panoramas!

As we march in wide-eyed wonder behind Joan, youthful voices cry out. We look up, to a dormitory. Windows frame waving boys, members of La Escolania, the Montserrat Choir. We step up to Plaça de Santa Marià, a photographer's dream. Such majesty....

This monastery inspired the theme and setting for Richard Wagner's opera *Parsifal*,[1] we are told. The story goes that Montserrat's walls hid the Holy Grail, a legendary chalice now occupying Valencia's cathedral.

I stray, drawn to spectacles of immeasurable Llobregat valley. Captivated, snapping wide-angle pictures, I lose track of my group. Picking up my pace, I catch up with them in the basilica courtyard. At eleven A.M., Joan hands us site plans. The choir, he says, performs at one P.M.

"Please, return to the bus by half past one," he asks, then turns us loose.

Uncle Chuck and I pass up the gift shop, art museum and restaurants, hiking up part of Calvary Way and Path of the Monumental Rosary. Here we pause at bronze statues that symbolize *Pasos de la Cruz*. We gaze back to the monastery, to views stretching to Barcelona to the Mediterranean Sea to snow-dusted Pyrenees. We make out a chapel below, built around Santa Cova, the Holy Cave where shepherds discovered the precious Moreneta (The Dark One) in the ninth century.

What peace....

Above, *téléphérique* cars soar. I want to board one, or the funicular, to savor vistas from elevations higher still, but we head back to hear the choir. Keeping an eye on time, we note along our route more sculptures, memorials to secular people: one of Pablo Casals bowing his cello, another of poet Cinto Verdaguer.

Back at the basilica, the queue to the Moreneta no longer snakes twenty yards beyond the atrium. We file in place behind a gaggle of school children to make our pilgrimage. Creeping along the church's south corridor, we have plenty of time to peer into chapels lined with tombs, each with altar and fine statuary.

At last, we scale an alabaster staircase to the rear of the apse. Ahead we see pilgrims who have reached the holy image, pausing only briefly to pray and to press fingers to a protective glass case. They quickly move on, allowing the queue to pass through the *camarí* (small chapel). Now, as we step through a finely wrought alabaster portal, we have arrived.

I quiver.

In this *camarí* overlaid with Venetian mosaics, pulses an unearthly presence. Here, upon an argentine throne, the Black Virgin of Montserrat resides peacefully, staring solemnly, holding on her lap the Christ child, in her right hand, an orb. Centuries of candle soot have ebonized her face and hands. Gazing into her almond-shaped eyes, my fingertips pressed to the glass, I quickly offer a silent prayer.

I follow the others, Uncle Chuck behind me, down the Path of the Hail Mary, an exterior corridor along the north side of the basilica—dark but for hundreds of candles illuminating devotional portraits of *Nostra Senyora* in bright glazed tiles of lightening yellow, cobalt blue, forest green.

We head back to the basilica, passing under a façade encrusted with Christ and the Apostles. Pilgrims cram the space to standing room only. As we settle in, leaning against a wall, our eyes focus on the brightly lit chancel where a Benedictine conductor gently raises his arms. Now, like seraphim, fifty boys in black-and-white choir gowns discant the *"Virolai"* (the "Montserrat hymn"), their voices rising, now ebbing, in hair-raising harmony. Behind and above them, the Black Virgin and Child preside in the high altar. With a note still reverberating against walls of stone, the choir launches into liquid a cappella performance of *Salve Regina.*

Amen.

Nostra Senyora de Montserrat

Rosa d'abril	April rose
morena de la serra	brown one of the mountain
de Montserrat estel,	of Montserrat star,
il luminau la catalana	illuminate the Catalan
terra,	land,
guiau-nos cap al cel,	lead us to heaven,
guiau-nos cap al cel.	lead us to heaven.

—Cinto Verdaguer

[1] Wagner wrote *Parsifal* 1877-1881. The opera debuted in 1882.

SOMEWHERE, OVER THE RAINBOW

When booking Barcelona, we learned that our first choice, Hotel Colón, was fully reserved but for the last two days of our stay. For the first three, we settled for accommodations removed from the action. Then Ignacio stepped in to secure our lodging at Hotel Plaça Catalunya. After three days, we moved on to the Colón, that grand old hotel—and easily the best in Barna for the money—on a square facing the cathedral.

At six A.M., the city lies quiescent. I peer through the cool window. Black clouds cradle a waxing moon. Muffled cries of gulls recall our proximity to the seafront. I love Barcelona, resenting the hours spent sleeping here.

"Let's have a stroll on the waterfront," I say to a blanket-covered mound on the other bed.

"What time is it?" groans Uncle Chuck.

"A bit past six. Let's get going."

"I thought this was a vacation," he moans.

"Your life is a vacation," I tell him on my way to the shower.

When we hit the streets, a mantle hangs lowery over Barcelona. Back in the States, while packing, I had overlooked the detail of an umbrella. Uncle

Chuck had not forgotten his.

"You know the vagaries of Europe's weather," he says. "Besides, an umbrella doubles as a weapon," he sustains, slamming his closed umbrella against an open palm. Now jousting it about, "I've read how pickpockets come out of the woodwork in this city."

Across Vía Laietana, we weave through La Ribera in direction of the waterfront. We halt to admire Arc del Triomf, a *Mudéjar* triumphal arch of redbrick and green ceramic tiles from 1888. From Passeig de Picasso, we skirt verdant, statue-studded Parc de la Ciutadella, passing by the zoological park and Olympic Center. We reach the waterfront just as a rainy squall blows in from the sea. I duck under Uncle Chuck's umbrella until we reach a canopy of evergreens along the wide pedestrian Moll de la Fusta.

From the *moll*, we turn our attention to a gray horizon crosshatched with hundreds of yacht masts, with fishing tubs, mammoth cruise liners, and sightseeing vessels known as *Golondrinas*. We stand on the brink of Port Vell, *Barna's* commercial-leisure port and to the left, La Barceloneta, a fishing village centuries old.

On one side of Barcelona's ultramodern waterfront, twin office towers rise to five hundred and two feet. On another side, a novel pedestrian bridge presents an abstract sculpture of broken curvilinear spans. Beyond lie the Royal Yacht Club, a futuristic complex known as the World Trade Center, plus museums, Europe's largest aquarium, restaurants, bars, Maremàgnum shopping mall, even an IMAX cinema.

Afield from the hypermodernism of a quay-side jetty known as Moll d'Espanya, we glimpse peeks of an old citadel, an eighteenth-century castle built on flotsam of a 1640 fortress, squatting on the seaboard side of Montjuïc Hill ("Jewish Hill"); slopes, once a Jewish cemetery, giving the hill its name. As showers moderate to sprinkles, we step over to admire the finely spun façade of the old Llotja (commodity exchange).

Rain ceases and sun strikes first time this day. The air braces, fraught with brine.

"Look," says Uncle Chuck. He aims a finger toward a distant, familiar column, the perch of Columbus in bronze. Up there, the explorer-discoverer stands framed within an arc of glowing rainbow. I am energized, wanting now to explore waterfront museums, have a walk on one of the wharves and make a tour of the harbor on a *Golondrina*. The Columbus monument stands at the foot of La Rambla. We could have a stroll over there, as well. But Uncle Chuck reminds, "Let's find gifts."

If I Only Had a Brain

I resigned my camera equipment over to Uncle Chuck before the policemen took me away. The concierge at Hotel Colón explained that I likely needed a police report as proof for my insurance company. The policemen found it difficult to understand my pidgin Spanish. They spoke Català *so rapidly, I marginally made out what they tried to tell me. The concierge stepped in. There was an interpreter at the police station, he said.*

On a mission for gifts, we scour storefront windows along confined passageways, minding our steps around ladders. Above us, workmen in overalls drape swags of Christmas lights across alleys. Admiring shapes of twinkle-light candles, trees and bells, we soon find ourselves lost. Storefront windows evince tacky souvenirs, and there are tattoo parlors galore. We have wandered beyond where we want to be. Farther along, we discover an alley of intrigue; looks promising, but turns out to be a district of wholesale merchants. *Now, where are retail outlets for these fine goods?* Though tired, swooning with hunger after a frustrating interval, we manage to find suitable mementos: books, a scarf, devotional articles for friends and relations back home. Spotting an ice cream stand, a mere hole in the wall on an alley, I head over. Uncle Chuck plods behind methodically.

"Pistacho, por favor," I tell the blonde behind the foggy glass counter. A young man jams his body between Uncle Chuck and me, waving a ten-euro note in the vendor's face, demanding change. Busily scooping ice cream, the vendor asks this nervous euro-waver to wait. The fellow falls into me, then bolts away at bullet speed. I sense something awry. A glance to my camera bag reveals a vacant pocket where I kept my pouch of filters.

"Why did you have the pouch in an open compartment?" Uncle Chuck growls.

"Why didn't you use your umbrella, your weapon?" I counter. "Besides, the joke's on that thief. I'll bet he thought it was a wallet."

It all happened so quickly. Feeling violated, I lick my ice cream in a trance, convinced it would taste better if I still owned my camera filters.

"The value of those filters?" asks Uncle Chuck.

"Oh, three hundred dollars, maybe more."

"Expensive ice cream, young man."

Embarrassing, as I bounce along on a hard plastic seat in a police vehicle. Pedestrians, cabbies, other motorists leer at me. My journey through choked streets appears illimitable, but at last, we pull into a parking space. I follow my uniformed escorts into a police station where they leave me to register with a desk clerk. I give my name, nationality and birth date to the clerk. Another man ushers me to a window where a woman thrusts a clipboard at my chest.

I sit in a drafty waiting room, filling in blanks—on both sides of a lengthy questionnaire—in the company of Germans, Brits, French, Spanish out-of-towners. I feel blessed. Some of these people were robbed of passports, wallets or purses. One victim has a shiner, another, a fat lip, and a bandage across his nose. My *carterista* (pickpocket) at least did not assault.

I return to the window with my paperwork and hand it to a woman, my interpreter. She tells me to take a seat while she stamps then copies the document. On my way out, the clerk stops me. I must sign out before leaving. Now, will the policemen drive me back to the hotel?

"Imposible," the clerk states emphatically.

Auditing the streets for taxis, I see none, even at busy intersections. I walk on the wild side, through litter-strewn streets, alongside squalid tenements. From alleyways, black eyes leer from burkas and turbaned heads. *Where am I?* Heart racing, I glance warily over my shoulder.

Wait a minute. Cabs don't come to areas like this. Across the street, a clean-cut young man pushes a dolly. I approach him.

"¿Por favor, dónde está la Plaça de Catalunya i Plaça de Catedral?"

The man rattles off directions. His "straight ahead, to the right, to the left" give me the gist. After fifteen more footloose, anxious minutes, I reach the cathedral plaza, a landmark far safer than El Raval, the slum I escaped.

Cabezas i Cojones i Sesos, oh my!

Before we departed Barcelona, I was compelled again to drink in my fill of serendipitous La Rambla, that magical avenue reminding me of the golden-brick road to Oz. So what, if it wasn't Kansas nor even California? That storybook stretch bid a respite from headlines of terrorism, corporate corruption and threats of war. Though described as "the backbone," I considered La Rambla the heartbeat of Barcelona—my favorite district.

New characters stand amidst throngs coursing the center-way of La Rambla. A mustachioed man with face painted chestnut brown wears a sombrero and suit of the mariachi. The faux-Mexican throws down his hat and dances around it on a drum-shaped platform. As Californians, we consider this a hackneyed performance. Over there, we see a figure more engaging, a curvaceous woman with platinum face moving seductively behind sheer veils of indigo and teal. And there's the wild man perched in his tree. The gorillas perform an encore. Who is this rugged man in five-o'clock shadow, false eyelashes, painted lips, and stretch-wig awry—a transvestite flasher? The gap between this ridiculous man's trench coat and army boots reveals hirsute legs. If someone deposits a coin in his jar, will he open his coat?

Musicians are out in force. A folk singer with guitar performs Bob Dylan tunes in perfect English. Up ahead, a baritone accompanies a tenor. Now, an accordionist pulls and squeezes the melody, "Somewhere over the Rainbow." Across the way, a lanky fellow sways from side to side, growling "Spanish Eyes" through his saxophone.

The carnival theme persists, though static, at Museu de Cera (Wax Museum), a nineteenth-century building. On the roof, sculpted in wax, Superman is poised for takeoff. Back here on the mall, lime-green parrots call from cages, as do poultry, quail and grouse. Besides birds, we see rabbits, reptiles, chinchillas and rats.

Palau Güell and Palau de la Virreina endow this sector of La Rambla. And El Teatre del Liceu, Barcelona's esteemed opera house. I notice a mosaic set in the pavement, a whimsical addition to La Rambla made by Joan Miró in 1976. Flower stalls brim with kaleidoscopic color and across the street, another colorful sight: La Boqueria under a hangar-like roof of steel girders (Mercat de Sant Josep, *el mejor mercado de la ciudad*). This renowned farmers' market purveys comestibles for carnivore and vegetarian alike— and even for fanciers of offal. A regal manifestation of food glistens faultlessly arranged—a photographer's paradise.

We walk the aisles in wonderment, dazzled by a spectrum of impeccable produce exaggerated in fluorescent brilliance. Each of hundreds of unblemished tomatoes shines deep cadmium red. Banks of pears, grapes, artichokes and plums tempt marketers with their perfection. There's even a nut counter and peppers galore.

Merchants regard us photographers critically. As I frame a still life of hams and sausages, a butcher complains. I understand enough Spanish to decipher, "Tourists, they take nothing but photographs."

Gastronomes, restaurateurs, tourists and locals abound, ogling heaps of fragrant *setas*—mushrooms, the majority of them wild. Shoppers lean on marble-topped bars, munching steamed shrimp, crab and deep-fried *tapas.*

As we trek through aisle after aisle to the market's mid-section, air suddenly spikes familiar with iodine. Upon heaps of shaved ice, a battery of fish chills with scales shimmering white, blue and red. Plus pyramids of *percebes*, buckets of *navajas*, stacks of pink *gambas.*

"You've got to see this," I hear Uncle Chuck call from three stalls away.

He fumbles with his pocket camera, heading toward a meat counter. When I reach him, he frames sheep's heads (*cabezas del corderos*), then hog trotters (*patas de cerdo*), testicles (*cojones*) the size of my fist, veal brains (*sesos de ternera*) and meaty oxtails (*rabos del toros*). Though decapitated and skinned, the sheep's heads look back with doleful eyes.

"Let's have seafood," Uncle Chuck suggests.

As we await orders of crabmeat, shrimp and beer, my thoughts wander back to Sagrada Familia. Antoni Gaudí died in the vicinity of this market. Yes, near this remarkable emporium, he lay in a coma for three days at an obscure hospital before meeting his maker. I restrain myself, not bothering to mention this to Uncle Chuck; he does not have the *afición* for Gaudí.

We return to La Rambla where alleyways are plentiful, each lined with dozens of mopeds plus a serious Harley or two. I wish there were more time to explore each of the alleys. One, particularly arresting, retreats to stately Plaça Reial, a granite-paved square, an oasis of palms, fountain, coin and stamp shops all hemmed in by contiguous four-storied buildings swathed in pale butter yellow. Here, we step across lacy shadows of palm fronds to study Neo-Classical lampposts designed by Antoni Gaudí.

The crab and shrimp we ate at La Boqueria were mere appetizers. I'm still hungry. A shill working the sidewalk out front Restaurant-Bar Amatxu must have read my mind—or noted my drool—for she lures us inside for *tapas* (called *pinxos* here). Enterprising, this gorgeous saleswoman with soulful eyes. I agree to fall into her trap if she allows me to photograph her.

Uncle Chuck frowns warily at the food, mostly salads made with mayonnaise. I point out a thermometer imbedded in the glass case, a touchstone of properly kept food.

"But how long has this food been here?" he wonders.

"C'mon. Live dangerously," I laugh.

Uncle Chuck orders two *cervezas* as I consider the snacks. Let's see:

rations of *butifarra* (white sausage), octopus, gooseneck barnacles, anchovies and baby eels. For Uncle Chuck's sake, I forego mayonnaise-based dishes.

Between bites, we discuss local culture. Though physically a region of Spain, Catalunya, we agree, feels like another country. As the rest of Spain, there is an air of reverence for provenance manifested in architectural wonders so honorably preserved. As their fellow countrymen, Catalan people are proud, soulful and nocturnal. Yet, from what I sense, Catalans are more forward thinking than, for example, Andalusians. Throughout Spain, we have noted diverse variances in language, ethos and architecture. Here in Barcelona, we detect undertones of French influence. There is a lighter, gleeful mien, a dynamic fostering of art, music and literature. An adamant sense of nationalism permeates the air, notwithstanding Nacho's having shrugged it off. Others ardently express their pride as Catalans, as countrymen independent from Spain. I hope, one day, they shall be.

Català, a National Language

Català (Catalan) is one of Spain's four tongues, not a dialect, but a distinct Romance language, a hybrid of Latin. *Català* has standardized grammar and rich literary traditions, both written and oral. Though kings and dictators endeavored to suppress this language over the centuries, *Català* remains vital, spoken not only in Catalunya, but also in parts of France, Sardinia, Valencia and the Balearic Islands.

Before long, we shall quit Barcelona. In thin light of evening, I seek El Font de las Canaletes. Following tradition, ensuring my return, I sip from this legendary fountain as a sidewalk flautist plays "Stairway to Heaven."

Winding through streets, hotel bound, we pause at Plaça Sant Jaume, noting here the striking façade of Barcelona's *ajuntament*. Facing this town hall is the Generalitat (Catalan government palace), the entire edifice draped in canvas painted with Neo-Classical architectural designs. This draping happens regularly in Europe while a building undergoes renovation.

Deep in thought, I believe we'd need a month, maybe longer, to suitably absorb Barcelona's wonders.

Thumbing through notes, I check from my list each of the sites that I wanted to see in Barcelona. There are so many more, plus a number worthy of revisiting.

In true Spanish tradition, we graze through the day and land at Restaurant Farga for supper. The ground-floor *tapas* bar overflows with diners and tipplers; and five steps up, an empty restaurant. Here we settle in, enjoying a private dining experience until the room fills with a busload of American tourists.

Uncle Chuck and I share orders of succulent grilled *perdiz* and pork ribs, garden-fresh salads and a bottle of Viña Silvia. Each member of the boisterous tour group receives a small portion of what appears to be stew. Likely, their sightseeing in this charmed city will be equally abbreviated.

Near our hotel, on Plaça de la Seu, we exult in crisp, night air. The cathedral, a marvel of lacy luminescence, poses mightily against a moon-pierced, velvety-black sky. The party is in full swing, the square pulsing with diners, drinkers and music. Irresistible. We join the party, pulling up empty seats, warming up with snifters of cognac.

From the depths of his Catalan heart, a tenor belts out a poignant oratorio. Next, a guitarist plucks a classical number, spurring an older gentleman from his seat. The old man adeptly—albeit absurdly—prances across the plaza, balancing exaggerated movements with open umbrella. Laughter echoes through the square. Now, on a final note, the old man clinches up his umbrella and bows. Onlookers applaud fervidly.

O when the saints, come marching in...

As a Dixieland band conducts the twang of New Orleans from this open-air stage, we pay our *mozo. Barna*, as the rest of Spain, keeps late hours; we do not.

...O Lord, I want to be in that number....

aragón

1. Soria
2. Almazán
3. Zaragoza

ARAGÓN

SCENTING A TRAIL THROUGH CORDILLERA IBÉRICA

It was more or less a toss-and-turn night, attributable to "decaffeinated" coffee at Restaurant Farga, or the throbbing nocturne outside.

After three rounds of the cathedral's well-tuned bells peeling on the quarter-hour, we arose. Smitten with Barcelona, I resented leaving behind its myriad museums, symphony of architecture, minstrelsy air. The Fellini movie set, La Rambla, I would miss most of all. Beyond, new frontiers proposed, plus another engagement with Salamanca.

In a silvery Peugeot, we point west from Barcelona, aimed in direction of the old university town of Salamanca. I hope we will detour and pay our respects to more sites. Midway, we will overnight just south of Soria in the old garrison-town of Almazán.

Four pieces of luggage plus my camera bags we wedged into the trunk. If we'd accepted the car originally offered—a claustrophobic Ford hatchback—much of our gear would have been exposed to potential thieves. We headed back to the rental desk. After an hour of negotiation, then filling in more paperwork, we secured the Peugeot.

How easy to retreat from Barcelona's airport onto N-11. We expected more of an obstacle course with madding congestion, like Madrid's. We are instead pleasantly on our way, under bright, wind-whipped sky proffering temperature of twenty-one degrees Celsius. Before long, modern urbanscape blends to ruinous textile factories, sporadic farmsteads, prospects of the Cordillera Ibérica range. Now, views evolve to slumbering vineyards, pines, soils in nuances from bone white to ashy gray, from dun to pink and cinnamon. Dry-stone walls march along undulating terraces. Rows of almond trees grow neatly in green fields and an occasional slanted-roof shed dots the landscape.

Before we reach Lléida, traveling through a stretch of desert, gusts of wind whip cyclones of grit between the passes, across our path. As we cross over into Aragón, scenery shifts again, now to moonscaped, wind-eroded mesas in sandstone of golden pink. For kilometers ahead, these stomping grounds of Fernando II appear a wasteland gaunt and thirsty. Randomly, we spot a village abandoned in rubble.

Around one-thirty P.M., we pull into a *venta* at Candasnos. Sweet air carries the fragrance of corn. As far as the eye can see, this region waves in cornstalks bending away from the wind. Proceeding west on A-2, we pass under a concrete arch, the Greenwich Meridian.

Sky churns surly as we broach the fringes of Zaragoza. Above this old city soars a forest of glistening domes with cupolas, lanterns and slender minaret-style towers. I'm on the brink of pleading for a pullover when Uncle Chuck veers off the highway. We traverse a medieval bridge (Puente de Piedra) across the Río Ebro, into the city.

Two-thousand-year-old Zaragoza (population 620,000), Spain's fifth largest metropolis, capital of the province of Aragón and important religious center, draws pilgrims to an illustrious Marian shrine. In the time of Christ, a local *Celtiberian* settlement called *Salduba* was renamed *Cesaraugusta* by Roman conquerors. As did so much of Spain during Roman invasion, Zaragoza felt the effects of conquest, suffering through the Pax Romana. After Moorish invasion, Zaragoza served as a Hûdid[1] *taifa*.

Stately towers and domes that signaled us from the highway turn out to be La Pilarica, the baroque Basílica de Nuestra Señora del Pilar—a palatial temple of cocoa-hued stone built around a momentous pillar whereupon the Virgin appeared in A.D. 40 to St. James. Others say the Virgin appeared in the ninth century to St. James's incarnation as *Santiago Matamoros*.

We roam Zaragoza's plaza in awe, admiring the epical basilica designed by Francisco Herrera in 1677 and completed in the eighteenth century, its eleven towers and domes overlaid with mosaics. Modernistic pools, rippling fountains, bronze statues amidst arrayal of pink and red geraniums offset the old basilica in pleasant contrast.

Inside, we wander between white fluted columns, alongside wrought-iron tiers of blazing candles. Unlike votive candles we typically see in churches, these are tapers symbolizing, I believe, the Virgin's pillar.

We locate the illustrious marble pillar in opulent La Santa Capilla. Atop presides a Gothic statue of the Holy Mother: Virgin of the Pillar, patroness of the Hispanic world decked out in jewel-encrusted *manta* (mantle) of white and gold, a mantle they change each day. Pilgrims in a snaking queue wait reverently at the back of this shrine to kiss an exposed portion of the pillar.

To admire this basilica's beauty proves a neck-wrenching exercise. Francisco Goya applied frescoes—some of his earliest work within these domes. A zoom lens away, adoring marble angels hover amidst *potencias* (golden rays) and crosses. Below, an elderly priest awaits sinners in an antiquated, open confessional. He yawns. Little wonder; not a soul fesses up during our visit.

Oh, to linger, to soak up the significance of lovely Zaragoza, but Uncle Chuck has a mind to press on. So much more to see here under the sun now breaking through passing clouds.

"Not until I check that out," I call out, pointing, then moving on to an extremity of Plaza del Pilar.

Here stands hoary Iglesia de la Magdalena with leaning *Mudéjar* bell tower. Nearby, I spot a vestige of crumbling Roman wall. Opposite this end of the plaza, the *plateresque lonja* and *ayuntamiento* stand proudly behind an allegiance of snapping flags. Beyond the brick structures rises a *Mudéjar*-style *seo* (cathedral).

Pigeons are legion in this square, as many as I've seen in Venice's Piazza de San Marco. Stepping up to a vendor to buy popcorn for pigeons, I spot Uncle Chuck standing at the entrance to the underground parking lot. He points at his watch.

Our next jumping-off spot is Almazán, just an overnighter before we advance to Salamanca.

Views from N-122 diverge from arid on the north side to level vineyards vitalizing the south. As we roll along, terrain transitions to agricultural abundance.

Our car's air vents proffer the must of rotting apples. A truck spilled its load on the side of the road, thousands of yellow-red orbs simmering under intense sunlight.

Pewter clouds gather. The sun falls in the sky. Our drive is long, the geography hilly, curvaceous, on an approach cutting through aromatic pine forests. Though this province boasts more than two hundred castles and watchtowers, we spot not one from the road. Nevertheless, with Soria's history of invasion, blood of conquest surely watered its soils, running deep in the sap of these pines.

As we reach the crest of a hill, the sphere on the horizon blinds us until we cut down to southbound N-11, a poker-straight stretch of Roman road, the way in to Almazán straddled with more pine trees and stands of shimmery-yellow alders.

When we at last reach Almazán at six P.M., sunset strikes momentous, first pink, then orange, now aflame in scarlet. What a prospect as we weave through the tiny town! A pair of *campanarios* silhouette black against blood-red firmament; half-timbered medieval houses, stone bastions and towers flank our route. Below, on a bank of Río Duero, rolls a fine village green called Parque de la Arboleda.

Suddenly Uncle Chuck gives me a dressing down. "You're navigator," he says, "and it's your job to keep eyes peeled for the hotel."

Almazán is a small town; we'll find our hotel without a hitch. But we search without spotting even a sign.

Uncle Chuck pulls up to a *taberna*. We step inside, order gin and ask the bartender for directions to Hotel Husa Villa de Almazán. "Right down the street," he tells us. *How had we missed it in this town of fewer than six thousand inhabitants?*

The hotel is modern, maybe brand new. I open a window, but close it again. The air carries an odoriferous whiff of chicken or turkey manure. What a contrast from the streets of Barcelona....

THE FORTIFIED ONE

The name of this small villa founded by Abderramán II in 1088 on the Río Duero takes its roots from the Arabic meaning of *Almazán*: The Fortified One. The Arab stronghold fell shortly thereafter, in 1098, to Alfonso I de Aragón. By 1121, the town acceded under jurisdiction of the Bishopric of Sigüenza.

Thereafter, Almazán seesawed between the Aragonés Alfonso I and Castile's Alfonso VII. Under Castile, the villa's name was changed to *Plasencia*, but this designation did not endure.

By 1359, Almazán headquartered Pedro I El Cruel de Castilla. In that era, the villa hosted one of Spain's major *juderías* (Jewish settlements).

Among celebrated visitors to fortified Almazán were the Catholic Monarchs (1496) and Felipe II (1598), then Felipe V who took the town by force in 1707. The French captured Almazán in 1810, but Spanish troops under General Durán resisted, laying the stronghold to waste, banishing the French in 1813.

Remnants of Almazán's glory days endure, among them fortified, turreted walls with three restored gates: Puertas del Villa, Herreros, Mercado; and bastions, Palacio de Mendoza plus vague ruins of a castle. The small town hosts important ecclesial architecture: Iglesia San Vicente on foundations of a twelfth-century Romanesque church, Gothic Santa María de Calatañazor, seventeenth-century San Pedro; and the sixteenth-century octagonal Convento de Clarisas (Ermita de Jesús).

We pull up chairs in the hotel's modern bar. How pleasant it is, for a change, to enjoy martinis from fishbowl-sized brandy snifters.

Mere yards away, a Spanish family has gathered: mother, father and two boys. One of the cherubs, sporting lungs of steel, screams continuously at his brother in ear-shattering decibels. Squealing, the boys dart through the room, dodging tables, careening into chairs. Do the parents intervene? Hell no! As gin swimming pools soothe effects of our lengthy journey, they are moot in deadening blood-curdling screams. Over the din, I try to explain to Uncle Chuck that the Spanish tend to coddle their children.

"They do kids harm by not teaching them manners," Uncle Chuck snaps. "And at times like this, I agree with W.C. Fields's philosophy on children. Remember how he liked them? Well done...."

Meanwhile, the bipedal air-raid siren scoots through the room, fracturing our eardrums. We move to the lobby.

At eight P.M., the hotel's dining room opens. We file in, then right out again as we spot the parents with their brat pack. We drive through bantam Almazán, finding not a restaurant open. *Nada las taperías.*

I have always tried to keep an open mind, particularly during my travels. Spontaneity leads to marvelous adventure. But this is a first, bedding down on an empty stomach. So goes it for my grouchy compadre....

[1] *Hûdids* (431-540/1040-1146): one of the independent or *taifa* dynasties that rose to power with the collapse of *Umayyad* and *Amirid* rule in Islamic Spain. *Hûdids* ruled a large territory in the Ebro valley that included Zaragoza.

castilla y león otra vez

 1. Vallalodid
2. Peñafiel
3. Salamanca

CASTILLA Y LEÓN *OTRA VEZ*

A TEN-YEAR REUNION

Uncle Chuck's "carrot"—as he put it—for joining me in another dose of Spain was the promise of a return visit to Salamanca. When we dropped into that glorious city ten years ago, our visit was brief. "Just a tease," Uncle Chuck said. Soon, we would spend two days probing beyond Salamanca's sandstone surfaces.

I invoke *"reveille"* at four A.M.

"What time is it?" Uncle Chuck rasps.

When I answer, he tells me to go back to bed. I do, for a wakeful hour, then get up and hit the shower. Tomorrow I will meddle with his watch.

As Uncle Chuck moves through his snail-pace routine, I pad downstairs. The early-morning desk clerk will make my *café con leche*. As he fires up an espresso machine, I step over to a window, gazing out to blackness. Soon Uncle Chuck joins me for a continental breakfast.

We are on the road by 6:15 A.M. The sun has yet to greet the dawn and Almazán slumbers as we pull onto C-116—a mere country road—toward El Burgo de Osma/Aranda. Uncle Chuck prefers not to drive in the dark, whereas I favor driving without back-seat reproach. All considered and discussed, he negotiates curvy roads through gloom until 7:30 A.M. when twilight salutes and clarifies our way.

Aranda suggests a dull town of factories and tenements with no sign of life as we pass through. Just as we leave, a Guardia Civil officer gestures for us to pull over.

Ut-oh; were we speeding? A squad car sits parked on the shoulder. Uncle Chuck rolls down his window as two policemen approach. Dialogue in Spanglish commences and Uncle Chuck exits the car. One of the policemen hands a cellophane package to Uncle Chuck, who in turn tears the package open to discover a Breathalyzer. Uncle Chuck blows....

337

"¡Fuerte!" says one of the policemen.

Uncle Chuck blows harder. I reach for my camera, but decide it's best not to ruffle official feathers. Uncle Chuck passes the alcohol test and we head on.

Our windshield frames a sky in negative, a field of white swirled with blue. Now, the rising sun reflects rosy pink on underbellies of steely blue clouds.

"Look," I tell Uncle Chuck.

The village of Peñafiel scarcely rouses from slumber. Above the meeting point of three valleys, a Romanesque castle creeps along a ridge, a ghostly mirage veiled in powder-blue mist. On one hand, I'm surprised to have seen the castle, on the other, how could I miss thirty machicolated towers aped by a Castilian keep—even in its foggy shroud? Spanish troops took this aerie from Arabs in the eleventh century, and King Alfonso X once resided in the ominous pile so high above the village of Peñafiel.

Even Uncle Chuck is taken with the spectacle. He turns around and pulls into an alleyway. I hustle up cameras, then dash up an alley to stake out an ideal vantage point. On the way back to the car, I see the rushing Río Duero below. Thick fog hushes the current.

Back on N-122, we pass through the old capital (temporarily: 1600-1601) of Castilla y León-Valladolid, birthplace of Felipe II and Felipe IV, where Cristóbal Colón died as a recluse in 1506. All rushes by: sculpture museum (Museo Nacional de Escultura), cathedral, Iglesia de San Pablo, and Palacio Vivero where Fernando married Isabel in 1469. I would love to stop....

"If we stop on each of your whims, we will not reach Salamanca before nightfall," Uncle Chuck chides. "Valladolid looks like industrial glut to me."

Aha! The freeway has led us straight into Valladolid.

"How did this happen?" Uncle Chuck grouses.

He spots an on-ramp and guns back to the freeway, aimed southwest toward Salamanca.

Shit. I can't wait until Uncle Chuck turns eighty-five and no longer has a driver's license....

Pink clouds blush to translucent orange and then dissolve to fleecy white as a sky-in-negative unfolds to limpid blue firmament. A haze of bodegas, *fincas* and vineyards flash by as we proceed southwest toward Tordesilla. Now, we pass turpentine forests, meadows of munching sheep and lumbering cattle. Occasionally we spot modern sculpture of storks on nests atop poles. These must be cleverly disguised cellular transmitters.

At 10:45 A.M., we reach Salamanca, entering a city that contrasts the scenario we experienced ten years ago when entering from the south. Salamanca's northern end congests with boxy, modern structures on clogged streets with not an historical monument in sight.

SALAMANCA, A CHRONOLOGY: FROM ROMAN *SALMANTICA* TO UNESCO[1]-DESIGNATED WORLD HERITAGE SITE

Pre-Roman: Celtiberian settlement along the northern bank of Río Tormes.

B.C. 217: Hannibal conquered the local Iberian tribe and settled the area in B.C. 220, naming it *Salmantica* (also cited as *Elmantica* and *Helmantik*). The Roman settlement, a major commercial and communications center, became a major station between Mérida and Astorga.

A.D. 589: Salamanca became an Episcopal See.

A.D. Seventh to Ninth Centuries: Invaded repeatedly by Moors.

Eleventh Century: Alfonso VI expelled the Moors in 1085.

Mid-Twelfth Century: Construction of Catedral Vieja commenced 1140.

Early-Thirteenth Century: Alfonso IV de León founded Estudio Salmantino in 1215 (some say 1230); subsequently, Alfonso X converted this school into the University of Salamanca. Catedral Vieja completed.

Fifteenth to Sixteenth Centuries: Salamanca's Golden Era. Gothic-style university buildings erected on orders of Pope Luna, 1415-1433. Construction of Catedral Nueva commenced 1513 and Iglesia de San Esteban, 1524. University façade completed 1529. University reached a student population of ten thousand. Proclaimed by Pope Alexander IV and Alfonso the Wise one of the best four universities in the world, among Oxford, Paris and Bologna. Salamanca respected as one of Europe's major intellectual and religious centers. Home to fifty-four printing presses, eighty bookshops, fifteen monasteries and convents, nineteen hospitals, a number of churches, two cathedrals.

Seventeenth Century: Decline, worsened by flood of 1626.

Eighteenth Century: Resurgence of cultural pursuits. Plaza Mayor constructed 1729-1755 under orders of Felipe V. Lisbon. Earthquake of 1755 wreaked serious damage in the city.

Nineteenth Century: University in decline. 1808-1814 War of Independence (Peninsular War). Inquisition banned in 1812. The Duke of Wellington (Arthur Wellesley, 1769-1852) and his troops joined with the Spanish to defeat Napoleón, and triumphed at the 1814 Battle of Talavera, seeing the French out of Spain. The mid-nineteenth century marked the road to Salamanca's recovery.

Twentieth Century: University revived; again considered one of Europe's finest. Salamanca commissioned by UNESCO as World Heritage Site.

Twenty-First Century: Population one hundred sixty-six thousand (university students: forty-five thousand). One of Spain's most visited cities, its architecture considered the finest examples of *plateresque*/Spanish-Renaissance. Voted European City of Culture in 2002.

We booked at Hotel NH Palacio de Castellanos. But where is it? Enmeshed in honking traffic, we scan signs, glancing to hotel marquises. There's Castellanos III; maybe that's it. We stop to inquire. Wrong place: a dowdy residence-hotel. The kind desk clerk charts a course to our hotel with a yellow highlighter on a map.

Creeping through mire of commerce, we arrive at last in the old part of town. Now, to find parking.

"Over there," I tell Uncle Chuck.

A man waves us into a parking space.

"A ploy," Uncle Chuck grumbles. "He's not a parking attendant, just a bum trying to earn a couple of euros."

Nonetheless, we pull into the spot. Uncle Chuck charges forward toward the old town. I slip the fellow a coin. Next, to find our hotel.

This area looks comfortably familiar: beguiling alleyways and churches; but what's this? On Plaza Poeta Iglesias, mobs huddle about tables set in a tiny square just outside Plaza Mayor. Sightseers admire while judges grade *setas*: mushrooms of sundry size, shape and color. A fellow in natty suit must be the proud owner of this cluster of bright orange, polka-dotted specimens. Gingerly he sprays his mushrooms with a tiny misting canister.

Uncle Chuck, experiencing *déjà vu,* has moved ahead of me.

He smiles, pointing at a sign: Restaurante Casino de Salamanca, one and the same recommended to us ten years ago by an attorney we'd met at Plaza Mayor. For hours, we traveled from the region of Soria without a stop for sustenance. What a welcome sight, this reliably good restaurant.

Our *mozo* is the same as ten years ago, filled out a bit, his temples streaked with gray.

We nurse gin, awaiting orders of mushroom *croquetas* and fried *calamares* as scrumptious as we recall.

Our *mozo* directs us to Calle San Pablo and, given this advice, we drive straight to our hotel's underground car park.

Posh Hotel NH Palacio de Castellanos was a fifteenth-century palace. From outside, it smacks of mausoleum, but inside it is superbly restored and formal from spacious, pillar-flanked lobby, a former interior courtyard, to a smart-looking bar. As we encounter often in our travels, a grand lobby belies sleeping quarters. Our room looks clean and handsomely furnished, though cramped and facing a back alleyway rather than busy San Pablo out front. And I do appreciate the close-up view of cathedral towers.

Downstairs again, and from the hotel's patio-terrace, a phenomenon turns our head: an ornate, three-tiered façade of the church of Convento de San Esteban (St. Stephen), one of four old convents in Salamanca. We cross the street and scale a steep flight of steps to the convent's esplanade.

CONVENTO DE SAN ESTEBAN

In this convent, Cristóbal Colón met with Dominican monks before events leading to his voyage to the Indies. Monks, first to take seriously the fifteenth-century discoverer's dreams, arranged his meeting with Isabel La Católica.

Designed by the monk Juan de Álava in the fourteenth century, Salamanca's Gothic church (273-feet long, 50-feet wide, 146-feet high at the transept) of St. Stephen was begun in 1524 and completed in 1610 with the addition of a three-tiered *plateresque* façade by Juan Antonio Ceroni. A tapestry in stone, the façade sets deeply recessed within a soaring arch dripping with pensile carvings. We see, over the door, a deep-relief scene of St. Stephen's martyrdom by stoning. The next level sports a crucified Christ by Cellini. We look even higher to an overlay of carved coats of arms of Cardinal Juan Alvarez de Toledo amidst stony gingerbread swirling with foliated forms verging on *plateresque* grotesque. Animals, skulls and freestanding human figures count among myriad details. Above all soars a *campanario* with single bronze bell.

A wing jutting from the northern side of this church flanks with pillars bearing a library above. Behind the church is a solemn, sixteenth-century cloistered loggia, a commingling of Gothic and Renaissance styles.

The single-aisle church enfolds a side chapel enclosed within each of the massive buttress. Baroque artist José de Churriguera designed the ninety-eight-foot-tall gilded baroque altar (1693). A painting of St. Stephen's martyrdom by Claudio Coello (1692) crowns the altar.

Sunrays refract upon the majestic old church in spun brown-sugar radiance. Our self-guided tour begins in the cloister.

A perfect, late-blooming rose anointed in hues of deep pink graces the center of Claustro del Rey (King's Cloister, 1544). Other roses shed petals amid clipped box hedges and slim cypress. We enjoy this blissful setting all to ourselves.

Although the nave is closed to the public, the choir loft provides a view of the church interior. From 140 feet above, our eyes focus on a high altar ornate in twisting columns entwined with grapevines. Details in the loft include elaborately carved choir stalls by Alfonso Balbás (seating capacity: 118), a mammoth, revolving hymnal stand, a semicircular painting of a battle scene with Dominican intercession from above and a small coffin pinned over a doorway.

We move on through town past Plaza de Colón with its handsome bronze statue of Christopher Columbus shaded by plane trees. Alongside this tiny square stands butterscotch-hued Torre de Clavero,[2] a slender, octagonal keep; a tower, all that remains of a fifteenth-century fortress. Stunning in details, the tower is pierced with eight sentry turrets overlaid with coats of arms and *Mudéjar* trelliswork. We make snapshots, then aim toward Plaza Mayor.

Nothing equals the effect of sun-kissed sandstone. This stone known locally as *villamayor* is rich in iron oxide, easily hewn when quarried, hard as marble when cured. Honey-gold stone, the fabric of old Salamanca, gleams against crystalline sky.

At the plaza, we snag a table and plunk into webbed chairs. Instantly, a *mozo* appears and takes our order for Coca-Cola®. Ten years ago, we viewed this magnificent square through milky gloom. Sun anoints *Salamantine* filigree in deep ocherous tones. Salamanca's square is smaller than Madrid's, but oh my. What this plaza lacks in size, it makes up for in elegant details. We kick back, whiling away time gazing from passing parades to rich sandstone details of the *ayuntamiento* and Royal Pavilion to flags billowing on the wind. Under a three-bell *campanario* and clock, the royal standard waves in fields of crimson and yellow. A provincial banner glistens in red, white and gold with icons of towers and lions. Other flags swell in breadths of royal blue, red and fuchsia.

Sky fades to pink, then deepens to indigo. As bells of nearby Iglesia de San Martín clunk the hour of seven, we stroll back to our hotel. Sweet fragrance entices. On the sidewalk, a raven-haired man in plaid flannel shirt stirs chestnuts over glowing embers in a Weber® kettle. The man's uni-brow resembles a crow in flight. With asbestos gloves, he scoops aromatic treats into newspaper cones.

We take dinner in Restaurante Trento, our hotel's dining room. We're in the mood for salad but find none listed on the menu. No problem; they will make one for us—a nest of ice-cold lettuce couched with tuna, spears of asparagus, slices of boiled egg, shredded beets and carrots. Delicious.

"I prefer dressing my own salad," Uncle Chuck remarks as he drizzles pale green olive oil and vinegar on his portion of crisp vegetables. "In the States, salads so often come dressed with your choice of a bottled concoction, most often too much of it."

Uncle Chuck opts for lamb chops. I pick the winner: loin of piglet larded with bacon, ringed with huge roasted buds of nutty garlic, sauced with prunes, figs and walnuts. Need I mention that we are the only diners? As we enjoy the room all to ourselves, we sup on delicious entrées between sips of crisp Marqués de Riscal Sauvignon Blanc. For dessert, we savor sweet, velvety flan.

"It's good to be back in Salamanca," Uncle Chuck says with his last sip of wine, "a city of Spanish history etched in beautiful stone."

[1] UNESCO: United Nations Education, Scientific and Cultural Organization; established 1945; headquartered in Paris, France, with field offices in other parts of the world.

[2] Torre de Clavero was named after the tower's former *clavero* (key-holder), a warden of the Order of Alcántara.

Voices and Visages of Salamanca

At midnight, I awoke to golden tones of operatic voice. For a moment, I thought I had dreamed my way back to Barcelona, but the improvisational libretto was real, floating up from the alley beneath our Salamanca cocoon. A passionate man sang baritone from the depths of his guts, another man countering in superb contralto. I propped myself up on an elbow, listening as the oratorio trailed through the alley.

"Did you enjoy the entertainment last night?" I ask Uncle Chuck.

"Say again?"

"The concert in the alley. Didn't you hear it?"

"I slept well, thank you. Didn't hear a thing."

On a mission to make portraits of *Salamancans,* my first subjects present as we step from our hotel: a flock of elderly nuns in habits, as one still sees in Spain. The nuns turn their faces away as I frame them, so we move on to the esplanade of San Esteban. Here stands a priest, handsome, youthful, with movie star looks, saucer-sized eyes and baby's complexion. After proudly posing for a photograph, this Spanish priest blesses me with a vertical, then horizontal wave of hand.

We proceed to Convento de las Dueñas; closed tight, as will be all else at this hour. We head for the riverbank.

From the riparian shores of Salamanca, four bridges span Río Tormes: Puente Sánchez Fabrés, Enrique Esteban (vehicular), del Pradillo and Romano (pedestrian). We head down to Paseo San Gregorio to check out the old Roman bridge.

Dating to the era of Emperor Trajan (first century A.D.), sturdy, stone-block Puente Romano retains fifteen of its original twenty-six arches; the 1626 flood swept away the others. The placid river passes through northern arches but grass grows thick and green beneath six arches on the southern bank. From this bridge, we marvel at Salamanca's golden cathedral towers and rooflines of red *tejas* repeated in vivid blue sheen of Río Tormes.

As we cross back into town, a wall of glass in blue, white and opalescent green presents a spectacle across the street. The sign says *Casa Lis Museo Modernista*—an Art Nouveau and Art Deco glass museum.

Off Plaza del Concilio de Trento in the cavernous shadows of Convento de San Esteban, we return to austere Convento de las Dueñas. *Doña* Juana Rodríguez Maldonado (wife of Don Juan Sánchez Sevillano, court singer for Juan II de Castilla) put aside funds for this Dominican convent in 1419. In the early 1500s, a convent was built on the site of the *Doña's* mansion. Designer Rodrigo Gil de Hontañón also carried out his father's work on Salamanca's Catedral Nueva. We crouch to pass through the door to a minuscule courtyard, then step inside the thick-stone-walled convent. An *anciana* sells us tickets. Alongside her cage, there's a sign. Resident nuns handcraft and sell *yemas* here.

We note evidence of Moorish influence in the interior details: *Mudéjar* tiles, keyhole-shaped portals, a pentagonal courtyard snuggled by a *plateresque,* arcaded quadrangle with elegant loggia. Four stubs of columns stand as legs of a pagan altar at the cloister's center and all around, an ambulatory of plinthed columns carries the loggia. Between the levels rests a stone lintel sculpted with medallions of saints.

I clamber up creaky wooden stairs to the loggia. Uncle Chuck lingers below, contemplating the garden. I call down to him. Though his legs ache from walking, the climb will be worth the effort. It's amazing up here!

The austere exterior of this convent belies its cloister. Unlike masculine San Esteban, this architecture flows more gracefully, pillars in the loggia hewn with surreal capitals twisting, erotica writhing. Torsos, arms and legs spring from fretwork; overhead, skulls, wings, tormented faces and gargoyles leer from a sculptural pageant of grotesquerie.

Uncle Chuck catches up with me as I study the details. We audit each anthropomorphic capital, then head out for lunch.

Midway between our hotel and Plaza Mayor, on the corner of San Pablo and Plaza del Peso, we find Restaurante Casa Paca. The menu entices, so does a smart interior. The door does not give way, but the *casa's* bar one door removed is open for business. We step inside for *tapas* and beer.

I hit the streets with my cameras while Uncle Chuck siestas. I spot a likely subject, a *niño* about seven years old, who's just laid his backpack and bicycle on the sidewalk. Now, he hops up onto a concrete riser of a fountain and washes his face, splashing his blue-black tresses with cold flowing water.

"*¿Foto okay?*" I ask him.

Droplets of water fall from his lips. His eyes ooze *duende*. His round face shines caramel-brown with features strikingly Moorish, maybe Gypsy.

"*¡No!*" he says firmly.

"*¿Oh, por favor, hombre?*" I plead.

"*Okay. Sí,*" he says demurely.

If what I see through the viewfinder materializes on paper, what a shot.

"*¡Gracias, muchas gracias, amigo!*" I tell the boy.

"*De nada,*" he sings, then puts his bike into upright position and wheels away, glancing over his shoulder at me.

I collect Uncle Chuck and we hike a steep lane to the highest elevation of old Salamanca, passing shops of antiques and devotional mementos. We watch cathedral towers growing larger from Plaza de Anaya. A band of young vagrants with a gaunt, black dog have claimed a spot on the steps of Catedral Nueva. One of them, a trim man with dusty blond dreadlocks, natters on a conga-style drum. Another fellow claps wooden sticks against stone steps and sings in what sounds to be Arabic. A greasy-haired woman frolics with impunity. The forlorn dog looks hungry.

Inside the voluminous cathedral, fierce resonance of drum, sticks and voice amplify hauntingly.

CATHEDRALS: SALAMANCA'S CROWNING GLORY

Catedral Vieja (Old Cathedral)

In 1140, the Church enlisted twenty-five tradesmen to construct a cathedral at Salamanca under architects Pedro Pérez, Pedro de Axis and Juan Franco. This working arrangement waived the craftsmen's paying tributes to the Church. A small—by Spanish standards—cathedral they built with Romanesque exterior and Gothic interior, completing the project in the thirteenth century.

This architectural masterpiece includes:

El Torre del Gallo (The Cock Tower), a Byzantine *cimborio* (lantern) crowning the center of the transept. This complex architectural marvel, a semi-spherical aspect in ribbed umbrella overlaid with fish-scale tiling set on a two-tiered drum raised upon four circular turrets pierced with arched windows, a Salamanca landmark, they call Cock Tower because of rooster-tail motifs decking the span of its ribs. Atop perches a cockerel weather vane.

Reredos: Fifty-three panels depicting the *Life of Christ* and scenes of the Virgin. Completed in 1445, attributed to Nocivas (Nicolás) Florentino—though more likely painted by Florentino's apprentices—this brilliantly vivid altar screen survives in gold- and jewel-toned luster. Above the reredos, vaulting details frescoed scenes of *The Last Judgement*, attributed also to Florentino. Set within the altarpiece, the **Virgin of the Vega**, patroness of Salamanca, is portrayed in a stunning twelfth-century, Byzantine-style wooden statue plated with bronze and gilt, her throne sheathed in Limoges enamel.

Additional important artworks include **thirteenth-century murals** (1262) by José Sánchez and a sixteenth-century *Mudéjar organ*.

The Old Cathedral embraces fine chapels. Among them:

• **Capilla de Anaya** from the thirteenth century, housing, behind finely wrought *plateresque rejas*, the fifteenth century alabaster sarcophagus of Diego de Anaya, Archbishop of Salamanca and Seville;

• **Capilla de Santa Bárbara** where graduate students of the University of Salamanca spent pre-examination nights and where they received their degrees. Here lies Bishop Juan Lucero. Students placed their feet upon the

face of Lucero's recumbent effigy for luck;
* **Capilla de Santa Catalina**: the original, a survivor of the Lisbon earthquake;
* **Capilla San Martín** with thirteenth-century frescoes by Antón Sánchez;
* **Capilla de Talavera** capped with exquisite *Mudéjar* dome, founded by Salamanca University professor Rodrigo Arias Maldonado de Talavera at the end of the fifteenth century.

Tombs array the Old Cathedral's corridors, including sepulchers topped off with recumbent figures of Fernando Alonso (illegitimate son of Alfonso IX de León), Sancho de Castilla, Gonzalo de Vivero and Salamanca's eminent bishops. Crypts of thirteenth- to fifteenth-century benefactors of the Church also rank among Catedral Vieja's illustrious tombs.

The old **chapter house**, now a museum, boasts works by Francisco and Fernando Gallego (artists native to Salamanca) and Juan of Flanders.

Catedral Nueva (New Cathedral)
Construction commenced 12 May 1513 at behest of Fernando II when the congregation outgrew Catedral Vieja. In 1513-1531, during a period when Gothic style had fallen out of favor, Juan Gil de Hontañón began this cathedral as designed, in the Gothic mode. Upon his death, Hontañón's son Rodrigo supervised the work from 1538-1577. Thereafter, construction commenced under the Churriguera brothers, then under Juan de Ribero in the sixteenth century.

Original plans included dual towers, but only one was completed before the devastating Lisbon earthquake of 1755. As architectural styles evolved, the Churrigueras and Ribero added Spanish *plateresque* and baroque ornaments to Catedral Nueva.

Noteworthy aspects include beautifully carved **choir stalls** by Juan Múgica, a **pipe organ** from 1715 by Pedro de Echevarría, **statues** by Luis de Morales and Salvador Carmona, **altarpieces** by the Churrigueras.

Among relics are those of San Tomás de Villanueva and San Juan de Sabaguán.

Inside Catedral Nueva, we squint through chalky-white majesty of lofty vaults to a forest of fluted pillars stretching to delicate quatrefoil ribbing. Above the nave, a splendorous dome lantern glows with lapis columns and a fresco of the Holy Spirit. Stone tombs under effigy lids bearing recumbent bishops in miters flank the aisles.

Pausing at each side chapel, we admire polychrome statuary. Candlelight illumines a chapel where a small crowd huddles near an altar. When they move on, I step up to see what all the fuss is about. A small, chased-silver casket with glass panels rests atop the altar; inside, a severed arm and hand in wretched posture. According to an embossed plaque on the casket, these mummified remains belonged to a woman named Sánchez, now beatified.

We paid no admission fee to view this newer cathedral. We buy tickets to enter the old one that leans against the new. As if the majesty behind us were not spectacular enough, what lies ahead astounds. As we step through the portal between the cathedrals' common wall and step down into Catedral Vieja, we glimpse medieval history frozen in stone, uncommon elegance in beige: ancient cracked pilasters, an austere dome and faded, mystical frescoes.

Drawn to the front of the cathedral, to the high altar's reredos, we relish vividly painted panels shining forth richly. As we study fifty-three panels, we hear part of a narrative as a man reads to his wife from a book. As he does so, the couple carefully scrutinizes each portrayal of Christ's life.

Through the transept we pass toward the chapels, inspecting tombs guarded behind stone lions. Niches glow with frescoes in hues of scarlet, indigo, green and gold.

Off the cloister, we find the chapels. I have read of an ancient custom relative to one of these *capillas*. Medieval university students of Salamanca believed that putting their feet upon the head of Bishop Juan Lucero's tomb endowed them with wisdom and good fortune. Near Lucero's tomb in the Chapel of Saint Barbara, I sit in the chair at his head, then place my feet upon the Plexiglas cover.

"Move over," says Uncle Chuck. "I can't be too wise or too lucky."

As we leave, passing through the portal of Catedral Nueva, the musical vagrants pack up their gear. As we descend the steps, the man with dreadlocks glares at my camera bag. *Another heist?* I clutch the bag to my body. Uncle Chuck plays interference, moving quickly between the shady fellow and me. The fellow moves by, spitting at the pavement with contempt.

"Human pigeons," Uncle Chuck mumbles.

We move on in shadows of the massive cathedral complex, pausing on Patio Chico (Little Patio). Here we drink in splendorous postcard views of honey-hued cathedral towers, spires and domes. Torre del Gallo soars above deep-green cypress against a crisp sky of cobalt.

It's too early for dinner, so we head for Plaza Mayor along with umpteen-thousand other people. The arcaded square of eighty-eight arches throbs with *el paseo*: local youth and *ancianos*, tourists and even a midget. Sandstone architecture glows in floodlight, vagabond musicians play drums in one corner and bagpipes in another. Between arches, stone medallions highlight Spanish sovereigns in relief; in eerie floodlight, these carved monarchs look real.

Though the evening chills, each of hundreds of alfresco tables is occupied. In the arcade, we find Berysa, the *taberna* where we met the attorney ten years hence. Our bar looks even more beguiling at night, but there is only one available stool. I insist Uncle Chuck take it. From a tempting display, we order fritters, a wedge of *tortilla a la española* and *ginebras*. I call to mind Castillo de Buen Amor. In this bar, a decade ago, we learned of the enchanting castle.

Three customers move on. I barely make myself comfy on a stool when a threesome, two older men and a lady, saunters in. The men take the only available seats. I rise, offering mine to the lady. She smiles, nods and accepts.

As we leave, Uncle Chucks remarks on the arrogance of Spanish machismo.

We return to Restaurante Casa Paca, where rich paneling glows golden brown under respectably ambient lighting.

We begin with piping-hot soup, *de vegetal* bobbing with cabbage for Uncle Chuck; for me, heady *rabo de toro*. Walls come to life with equestrian prints and sepia portraits. I ask our *mozo* about a particularly intriguing gent posing stoically through oval-framed, wavy glass.

"*Eez Señor Paca,*" the *mozo* volunteers, but then winks. "I tease you, *Señores.* We do not know who *eez* he."

Outside of Burgundy, France, I have not sampled wine more expressive than Castillo Ygay. We ordered a bottle of this Rioja *tinta*, a *gran reserva especial cosecha* 1994, elixir of angels and a vivid accompaniment to our entrées: Uncle Chuck's joint of piglet, my grilled chops of *cabrito*, each with a backdrop of grilled red *pimientos*.

For cappers, Uncle Chuck delights in milky rice pudding. I take my time with mouth-watering spoons-full of *leche frito* (fried milk) *al aroma de la canela* (with a whisper of cinnamon).

FROM BAROQUE REFINEMENT TO SPAIN'S EXTREMES

We could not embark for Extremadura before checking out Salamanca's essence: the historic universities. Uncle Chuck had the notion of extending our stay in Salamanca. Over breakfast, he'd asked where to find "one of those Internet cafés, to get in touch with Ana," our Spanish travel planner in Los Angeles, "to finagle our arrangements." I steered him clear of such notions, suggesting he would like Mérida as much as he did Salamanca.

Near the cathedrals, between bookstores and graffitied walls along Calle Líberos, we seek the old *universidad* of Salamanca. Neatly lettered in red ochre, this elegant graffiti extols names of famous alumni, a tradition hailing back to the Middle Ages when graduates' names emblazoned these walls, names including Miguel de Cervantes Saavedra. In those days, graffiti scribes used bulls' blood mixed with olive oil to paint the monikers.

Though founded by Alfonso IX de León in 1218, university buildings we see germinated under order of *El Papa* (Pope) Luna in 1415.

Our first stop: Patio de las Escuelas (Schools' Square), where we gape at the iconographic façade (1513-1525) of Escuelas Mayores (Major Schools). Behind this mind-numbing wall of tracery subjects of literature, music, medicine and law counted among the curricula. The intricately carved, butterscotch-colored façade cornered the market as the finest example of *plateresque* and Hispanicized Italianate. With our eyes, we trace basket-arched twin doors between two ornate buttresses amidst a sandstone forest of filigreed intertwine, seeking the fine portrait-medallion of the Catholic Monarchs, major benefactors of this university. Fernando and Isabel grasp a single scepter in symbolism of a unified Spain. Atop this handsome detail, two more registers badged with Spanish shield and crown; flanking these, escutcheons of Carlos I carved with eagles, portraits—including Pope Martín V, another of the schools' ministering angels—six framed within wreaths, four couched within *concha*-shaped niches. Scanning the façade, we identify—besides Venus and Hercules, *The Virtues* and angels, griffins and skulls—a frog said to symbolize "the posthumous punishment." And, as placing our feet upon the tomb of Bishop Lucero, having found this frog amidst a jungle of tracery, we are guaranteed luck and wisdom. Crowning this glory, a lacy balustrade terminates in decorative finials.

Salamanca's Plaza Mayor pales in comparison to this 1529 masterpiece of Spanish baroque carving, at least in consolidation of details. Even the lacy façade of San Esteban cannot hold a candle to this glory.

Behind us, an emphatic bronze of the university's most illustrious professor *Fray* Luis de León (1527-91) stands upon a concrete pedestal. Luis, born to *conversos* (Jews converted to Catholicism), ranks high on the scale as one of Spain's leading Renaissance scholars, theologians and humanists. An Augustinian brother and classical Latin scholar, *Fray* Luis also mastered Castilian lyrical poetry. He held chairs at the university, among them post of Professor of Sacred Scripture. Here *Fray* Luis studied, translated and taught Hebraic texts for which he was accused of heresy and arrested in 1572. Exonerated in 1576, he was released from prison in 1577 with the summons to be more cautious in his teaching. *Fray* Luis immediately resumed his post as professor. To his students—who expected to hear of his prison term—he began simply, *"Dicebamus hesterna die...."* (We said yesterday....), then picked up his lecture where he'd left off five years past; as if to say, "As I had been saying before I was rudely interrupted...." The man definitely had *duende*.

> ...wherever virtue exists in an eminent degree, it is persecuted.
> Few or none of the famous men that have lived escaped being calumniated by malice.
> —Miguel de Cervantes, *Hidalgo Don Quixote de La Mancha*

We step inside the Gothic university (1415-33), marveling at a central cloister, at classrooms, among them the hall where *Fray* Luis lectured, preserved as it was. How uncomfortably spartan the desks and benches look, roughly hewn like railroad ties, worm-eaten, deeply grained boards in deep umber, seven inches square, twelve-or-more feet in length. In the Middle Ages, students, including Miguel de Cervantes and Calderón la Barca, accustomed to sitting on the floor, considered these crude desks a luxury.

Among the lecture halls, we find those of Renaissance professors Miguel de Unamuno and Francisco de Vitoria, plus a fine museum brimming with vestments and medical models. Additional treasures include richly carved *Mudéjar* ceilings, Belgian tapestries and a portrait of Carlos IV by Francisco Goya.

Ascending an overly filigreed staircase beneath equally overdone star vaulting, we note foliated and hermetic scrollwork in a carved banister. Upstairs, we peer into an eighteenth-century library of sixty-two thousand rare books: sixteenth- to eighteenth-century volumes, 2,774 manuscripts and

483 incunabulae dating to the eleventh century. The impressive collection boasts eight hundred thousand monographs and sixteen thousand periodicals. Old World globes from France offset these impressive tomes stacked twelve deep; fourteen deep in the middle of each wall.

At the foot of the richly carved staircase, we discover a chapel. We pause here in company of *Fray* Luis's cremains, admiring a stunning, arched portrait of *The Assumption* framed in black-and-red marble with gilded touches.

Outside again, we look to the bronze of *Fray* Luis who gazes eruditely back at the façade, his right hand raised as if in a blessing gesture; in his left hand, a scroll.

We move across the patio and hang a left to the façade of early-sixteenth-century Escuelas Menores (Minor Schools), a prep school for university candidates.

A lovely façade, though little to compare with the one behind us. Striking characteristics of this school are two: an inner courtyard (A.D. 1428 rectangular patio), a grassy green oasis centerpieced with ancient well, flanked with squat granite columns bearing mixed-linear springers and arches topped with baroque balustrade. Inside a lecture hall, we contemplate a frescoed ceiling by Fernando Gallego entitled *The Salamanca Sky* swirling with signs of the zodiac. Curricula of Escuelas Menores included the trivium and quadrivium: minor and major liberal arts, so-called in those days— among them astrology.

We head back toward our hotel to collect luggage and car, but stop short when we see Casa de las Conchas. We viewed this early-sixteenth-century knight's mansion ten years ago from the outside only. Today, doors of its massive portal swing open. Stepping inside, we admire a stony courtyard and a well amidst pillars overlaid with heraldic crests and lions' heads bearing rings in their grinning mouths. Whereas exterior ashlars and scallop-shell studs were hewn from golden *Salamantine* sandstone, the interior is sheathed in grayish stone. Wings of this old *casa* harbor library, bookstore and art gallery, but our time runs short. We climb to the loggia for quick inspection of leering gargoyles, for outlooks across the street to dual baroque towers of the Clerecía (Pontifical Jesuit College, A.D. 1617).

Off to Extremadura, we soon roll across Puente Enrique Esteban, gazing to Puente Romano, to the vision called Salamanca upon an azure Río Tormes.

We cut right, onto Carretera de Madrid, then connect with E-803 South.

How disappointing, the views just outside this city of golden carved stone: automobile dealerships, commercial signs, gasoline stations hemming the madding vehicular congestion. Soon, traffic eases and fertile landscape rolls with agrarian fields and livestock. I pull out a map, studying the route ahead. At Uncle Chuck's warp speed, we will see delights only as they whiz by in the distance....

extremadura

Bay of Biscay

France

Pyrenees

Portugal

★ MADRID

Spain

Balearic Islands

Atlantic
Ocean

Mediterranean Sea

Africa

1. Plasencia
2. Cáceres
3. Mérida
4. Montánchez

5. Trujillo
6. Guadalupe
7. Zafra

EXTREMADURA

PLEASING TO BOTH GOD AND MAN

Before long, we would set down in Mérida, crossroads of Roman Extremadura. First, if I had my way, we would sample cities north.

As we penetrate the little-visited province of Extremadura, land of *conquistadores*, we feast on frighteningly beautiful vistas. James A. Michener described this frontiersy region in ways contrary to heavenly landscapes I see as hungry, parched desolation. Tellingly, since Michener's time, irrigation technology improved in Spain. I imagined this to be a dismal, unnerving place, though firsthand, Extremadura purveys rural sublimity. Gone is an aura of poverty and isolation that drove young *Extremeños* from their beloved families to Barcelona or to Germany to make a living. But, said Michener, these men always returned to Extremadura.

Wherever the eye lands roll pregnant fields and plats of wine slopes, acres of golden wheat and burgeoning orchards. Ecru sheep and black goats feast on blankets of silvery-green, dewy munificence, completing the breathtaking panorama.

For nearly an hour, we climb then descend a narrow, winding stretch of N-630 known as *La Ruta de la Plata* (The Silver Route), just us two and two lanes of the historic road, Roman Spain's circuit linking *Sevilla* and Salamanca. Extremadura, a wild corner of the earth, delineated Roman *Lusitania* long before *Mudéjar* castles dotted its hillsides, before flamenco, the bullfight and paella symbolized Spain. Gliding along, we feast on spectacles of misty ranges, Sierras de Gata and de Gredos. Straight ahead, downy clouds nestle within vales. We glide between slate walls, gnarled holm oak and mantles of chestnut, cherry and ash. Forests of cork oak trees stripped of their bark present spectacles of sleek, cinnamon-tinctured trunks.

Greenery slides down to a valley cradling Embalse de Santa Teresa, a silky-surfaced lake. From curvaceous shores, terrain unfolds to bright emerald dotted with cattle and sheep, *teitos* (stony sheds), *ermitas* (tiny chapels) in fields, on terraced slopes.

Extremadura's sky brightens to cornflower-blue backdrop strewn with fleecy clouds. At once, a heady aroma of meat curdles the air. We note the reason: ham-curing plants. Moreover, we see victims a-hoof: charcoal-gray porkers sharing their acorns and edible carpets with cattle and horses.

Again we climb, my eyes focusing on cobbled hillsides of moss-covered boulders, serpentine walls of slate, meadows of shaggy oaks. On the banks of Valle del Jerte far below, Plasencia presents her Roman spectacle, a multi-arched aqueduct dwarfing contemporaneous cityscape.

We pull in, traveling alongside the base of the aqueduct that stands stalwartly above a curve in silty Río Jerte.

"Coffee?" asks Uncle Chuck.

PLEASANT PLASENCIA

Settled by Berbers around the Roman military bastion *Mons Fragorum*, Plasencia later fell to Alfonso VIII (1180) who named it *Placeat Deo et Hominibus* (Pleasing to God and Man).

For the tourist, Plasencia (population 40,000) yields a *casco viejo* (old town), *judería* (Jewish quarter), museums, a double cathedral (1189 and 1498), historic palaces, a fine *parador* and a traditional Tuesday open-air market, a custom of more than eight centuries on arcaded Plaza Mayor.

Infused with espresso, we take to the streets. Though the sun now jockeys behind a bank of gray clouds, I must have photographs. We follow the aqueduct, pausing for snaps, then hike up a hill, following signs to Zona Monumental. Along the way, ramparts step with mysterious alleys; ahead, a fortress for me, a men's shop for Uncle Chuck and beyond, cathedrals, cultural center, Bishop's Palace.

"If we're going to make tracks to Mérida, let's grab a quick lunch," Uncle Chuck says after a sartorial browse.

We seek Plasencia's historic inn, sixteenth-century Convento de San Vicente Ferrer (Parador Nacional de Plasencia).

On the site of a mosque and synagogue, a Dominican convent was founded here under the Papal bull of Paul II, in the name of Saint Vincent Ferrer. Pinching through steep alleyways micro-millimeters wider than our car, we maneuver infeasible ninety-degree turns. Walls of bastions and tenements press in on us. The entire village appears buildings piled upon sagging buildings. Must be wash day; like a pageant of pastel flags, laundry waves from clotheslines above narrow streets.

Having arrived at the *parador's* hilltop post, we agree the obstacle course was worthwhile; and our car survived without a scratch. The convent looms above a cobbled courtyard of twisted, time-forgotten orange trees in fruit. Castle-like proportions and a compass of stone block relieve with swirling details: a broken pediment over worm-eaten doors, fluted columns crowned with Corinthian capitals, twiggy storks' nests. Oh, the old chapel's façade. To access the inn, we move catty-corner through plate-glass doors.

Deep inside the old convent, walls of delicate trefoil arches, massive stone staircase and balustrade echo the past. A central *claustro*, now glassed in, fosters a reflective sanctum away from the jam-packed, cataclysmic world below.

We rest in the bar, drinking *cervezas*, chowing down on chargrilled trout served by a lady in traditional costume of white blouse with short puffy sleeves, a black skirt embroidered with flowers in skeins of jewel tones.

"To Cáceres," I tell Uncle Chuck, who's concerned that he left too much tip money on the table.

"I won't drive strange roads after dark," he mentions in cadent tone.

My mind is made up. We shall visit Cáceres. That town is, after all, on the way to Mérida. When darkness falls, I could take over the driving.

Ahead, more pockets of eye-popping splendor: velvety-green, rolling pasture-land gouged with grassy arroyos. As in California, eucalyptus proliferates, as do *nopales* loaded with deep-pink *tunas*. I beg for a pullover when I spot an old man walking abreast with his gray, swayback donkey. *Nada fotos.*

We reach granite heights traversing bridges stretched across abysmal gorges. Again, I plead to stop, at a cliff falling away to Embalse de Alcántara, a far-flung lake feeding a fork in Río Tejo. A remarkable sight. Stubby ruins intrigue me: a Roman bridge with arches cut off at mid-Tejo. Do we stop? *Nada otra vez....*

"If we're going to see—however you pronounce it...."

"Cáceres. Accent on the *a*."

"Whatever. If we're going to look at it, we can't stop each time you spot a ruin," says Uncle Chuck. "Besides, there was no turnout back there."

Good thing my memory is retentive, though I want photographs, as well. And traffic is clear. Who needs a turnout?

MEDIEVAL ACOUSTICS

Shadows stretched longer, the light, the mood sublime, the setting, a medieval stage. But Uncle Chuck's watch ticked toward nightfall; I had to soak up as much of this splendorous village as his decree allowed.

All in Cáceres was shut tight for siesta. Nevertheless, I gave my camera a good workout on the streets, time warping back to the Middle Ages. Cáceres proposed a photographer's and history buff's paradise. Ahead stood Casa de las Veletas in tawny baroque façade, and La Casa del Sol[1] badged with fanciful escutcheon of the sun, a knight's helmet above. As I moved between crenellated wonders, my ears perked.

Thrum-m-m-m!

"Ayyyyyyyyyyyyyyyyyyyyyyyyy...."

A Gypsy, here in Cáceres? Finer guitar work I have not heard. Nor such lungs! My ears, my heart follow strums, gravelly voice, up a rise to the foot of Palacio Episcopal.

This can't be. He's too young.

Clear voice and strumming bounce between walls of Episcopal and Mayoralgo palaces, resonating into the old quarter. The spiky-haired boy, about thirteen, wears one hoop earring. He recognizes in my expressions *afición*, I'm sure. His music sends me to heaven.

"*¡Estupendo!*" I praise, "*¡Eso es! ¡Por Dios!*"

An open guitar case before him holds but three meager coins. I toss euro notes inside. Voice grows stronger, scorched, guitar work haunting.

I shout, "*¡Qué voz! ¡Tanto duende!*"

Accolades fuel his inflection, finger-work and wily smile.

At the blow of a final strum, I tell the boy, "*Gracias,* maestro." The boy beams. Now, more sites. Turning to leave, I come face to face with Uncle Chuck, who's been here all along, behind me. He, too, obliges the talented kid with money.

I propose a drink at the *parador*, on me, a reward for Uncle Chuck's flexibility. First, we will need to find—and photograph—Palacio de las Cigüeñas (Palace of the Storks), churches, maybe more.

As we weave through a labyrinth of medieval tours de force in stone, in shadows of towers between *plateresque* façades and heraldic crests, voice and magical strings carry on the air. Old Town, this *casco antiguo*, acoustically amazes. The boy knows this.

Again, I am lured to the boy's "stage." I find him there with his runt of a dog. The boy slaps the face of his guitar, hamming it up, breaking again into *voz afilá*. More euros; he earns them.

I meet Uncle Chuck in the sunny bar of the *parador*, converted fourteenth-century Palacio Torreorgaz.

"The crap that passes for entertainment on television these days," I mention to Uncle Chuck, shaking my head, "and that kid back there, with such talent…why hasn't he been discovered? He's gifted."

"Success would only spoil him," answers Uncle Chuck, who's finished his drink. "And you wouldn't have seen him in person, by sheer luck, if he were a star. Now, let's push on."

It took considerable time, trying Uncle Chuck's nerves, to locate the *zona monumental* here in Cáceres. But the way out is a breeze. Two turns and we coast along N-630, southbound for Mérida.

Had we blundered in deciding to use Mérida as our *Extremaduran* encampment? Surely, more wonders lie in wait at Cáceres.

Chivalrous Cáceres

Before the fourteenth century, Cáceres experienced its quota of strife, ushered in with Romans who conquered the local *Celtiberian* tribe. Barbarians drove out the Romans who were in turn conquered by Moors who named this settlement *Quazri*, from which *Cáceres* takes its name. Christian armies defeated the Moors by 1170, after which Cáceres became headquarters for Los Fratres de Cáceres, a brotherhood of knights of the Order of St. James. Alfonso IX vanquished the town in 1227, usurping the village for the Kingdom of León.

Thereafter, rival knights, including the families Ulloa, Ovando and Saavedra lived in Cáceres. At one time, three hundred knights inhabited Cáceres, warrior-lords who put up seigniorial mansions and palaces defended with puissant watchtowers. Isabel the Catholic, to keep peace in this warring town, ordered destruction of all but three of its defensive towers.

For the history-minded, Cáceres gives vent to a medieval treasury. More than forty points of historical interest include Almohad walls incorporating sections of Roman *murallas*, four important churches, thirteenth-century Torre de Carvajal and Gothic and Renaissance civic buildings dating from fourteenth to sixteenth centuries. The historic center deemed World Heritage Site—the first in Spain—by UNESCO in 1949 glows rich with fifteenth- to sixteenth-century palaces, ecclesial structures and museums. The medieval time warp stands fossilized in sandstone and granite melded with crude mortar, accoutered with heraldic crests, griffins and gargoyles. Among oddly named structures: Palacio de las Cigüeñas (Palace of the Storks) with one of the towers surviving Isabel's mandate, Casa de las Velatas (House of the Weather Vane) and Casa del Mono (House of the Monkey).

The sprawl of modern Cáceres at the foot of the historic district prospers from agricultural concerns. This city of eighty-five thousand is capital of the northern province of Extremadura, with Badajoz capital of the southern province. And here in Cáceres, Francisco Franco was proclaimed Head of State.

[1] Casa del Sol: Baronial home of the Solí family.

SPAIN'S MINIATURE ROME

As we advanced under a mantle of steely gray, Extremadura's plains spread infinitely before us. Halfway from Mérida, the sun struck, blessing scenery with a diagonal light show: cloud-bent rays over a distant teal-blue mountain range. As light blushed to pink, we glimpsed our next staging post on the horizon.

AUGUST MÉRIDA

In Western Europe, all roads led *from* Rome—and principally to Spain, with the first Roman settlements outside of Italy. Publio Carisio, under Emperor Octavian Augustus (Gaius Julius Caesar Octavianus, B.C. 63-A.D. 14, grand-nephew of Julius Caesar), founded one of these, *Emérita Augusta* (now called Mérida), in B.C. 15. The settlement's original intent: observation post and retirement villa for veteran legionnaires who conquered northern Iberians. But the colony grew by B.C. 25 into a thriving cultural, economic, political, military center. With two forums, Mérida ranked as an important colony of Imperial Rome's westernmost province, *Lusitania* (Spain) until Visigoths overcame the Roman colony in the fourth century. Nevertheless, Roman legions left in their wake a legacy in stone.

Modern-day Mérida, indeed an open-air museum of classical-Italian architecture, contends only Italy has more Roman ruins. Sensitively conserved monuments of *Emérita Augusta* include:

- **Teatro Romano:** A well-turned outdoor venue for dramatic arts, composed of granite and marble in dry-stone construction. This classical theater (B.C. 16-15) seats six thousand. On view and still used for Festival de Teatro Clásico de Mérida (the city's Summer Drama Festival) are stadium with stage, orchestra pit, graceful colonnade and statues. Behind the stage, a reconstruction of Roman gardens is used as an open-air lobby for intermission.
- **Anfiteatro Romano:** Though not rejuvenated as completely as the *teatro*, this ellipsoid arena (B.C. 8) echoes with cheers of yesteryears' sports fans. For here were staged, before fourteen-thousand goading spectators, *naumachiae* (mock sea battles) and gladiatorial combat replete with wild beasts and human sacrifice.
- **Hipódromo Romano:** Mostly unexcavated, this was once an arena for chariot races. On view: old carriage houses. Seating capacity of the circus: 30,000.
- **Puente de Guadiana:** This massive bridge, part of the Roman link between *Sevilla* and Salamanca, has eighty-one extant, though heavily restored, granite arches that span the one-half-mile fork of Rivers Guadiana and Albarregas.
- **Acueducto de los Milagros, Acueducto San Lázaro:** Soaring arches of redbrick and granite, these aqueducts conveyed water from two reservoirs to Roman, Visigothic, Moorish and even the modern populace until the mid-twentieth century.
- **Murallas Romana:** A portion of Roman walls on Calle Almendralejo between Calle Mausona and Calle Camili José Cela.
- **Muralla Árabe:** Vestiges of Moorish bastions between the bank of Río Guadiana and Avenida del Guadiana, vicinity of the *alcazaba*.
- **Templo de Diana:** Corinthian-styled, hemmed with fluted columns, this elegant temple (first to second centuries A.D.) was not dedicated to the goddess Diana, but to Rome's imperial cult.
- **Templo de Marte:** An *oratorio* (seventeenth century) built over ruins of a temple dedicated to Mars. Alongside stands **Basílica de Santa Eulalia**, a seventeenth-century church on a site reputed to be that where virgin-child-martyr Eulalia was burned to death in A.D. 304.
- **Casa del Anfiteatro, Casa del Mitreo:** Roman patrician villa and palace, each embracing fine examples of frescos and mosaics; the latter, a Roman sauna.

- **Columbarios:** Open-air Roman crypts, behind Casa del Mitreo, with carved portraits.
- **Arco de Trajano:** Believed to be the portico to a series of temples, this fifty-foot arch of granite was formerly clad with a skin of marble flagstones.
- **Parador Vía de la Plata:** Though this eighteenth-century Dominican monastery stands revitalized and fitted with modern accommodations, the roadhouse was built on the ruinous site of a temple dedicated to the *Pax Augusta*. The convoluted history of this locale included church, hospital and prison. A gallery in the *parador* sports Roman fragments found on-site.
- **Plaza de Toros:** Roads to machismo indeed led from Rome. Mérida's bullring built on rubble of the Roman *Mithraeum* (*Mitreo*) was a temple where bulls were ritualistically slaughtered. Bulls' blood, they believed, endowed Roman warriors with luck.
- **Museo Nacional de Arte Romano:** Of Mérida's Roman legacy, what you do not see in the open air, you will find on display in this enlightening museum: Roman foundations, statuary, busts, frescos, mosaics, oil lamps and coins. Designed by Rafael Moneo; opened 1986.

CRUMBS OF VISIGOTHIC MÉRIDA

- **Museo de Arte Visigótico:** A fine collection of Visigothic pilasters, baptismal fonts and tombstones housed in former Convento de Santa Clara.

Visigoths occupied Mérida, their bishopric after the fall of the Roman Empire in the fifth century A.D. In 713, Moors conquered the city, building here a citadel. Peculiarly, Mérida's aqueducts present themselves in Moorish versus Augustan characteristics, attributable to Moorish restoration and enrichments. The only structure of Islamic sway above ground in Mérida is a rectilinear fortress.

- **Alcazaba Árabe:** Overlooking the banks of Río Guadiana, this massive pile of granite and sandstone block was built over a Roman dike under dictum of 'Abd ar-Rahmân II in A.D. 835, incorporating Roman and Visigothic materials. *Almohades* bolstered the fortress with defensive towers. Inside is found a dungeon and a fine example of Roman cistern. Contemporary archaeologists discovered within this citadel foundations of a Roman villa.

Mérida, seized by Alfonso IX de León in 1230 and made Orden de Santiago, headquarters for the Knights of Santiago, declined thereafter. The city did not regain the importance held under Roman dominion; for hundreds of years, Mérida stood all but abandoned. By the 1920s, her population dwindled to a mere one thousand residents.

With more than sixty thousand inhabitants, Mérida, capital of Extremadura since 1983, hosts a modern rail hub and agricultural-industrial center (textiles, leather and cork). In 1993, UNESCO granted Mérida status of World Heritage Site. Into the twenty-first century, archaeologists continue mining here for history, wrestling artifacts from the mud while others work diligently to conserve Augustan attributes.

The other side of dusk, we penetrate Mérida, gliding past a fragmented aqueduct girded with storks' nests, then a modern bridge and now, a Roman bridge. We land at the eighteenth-century *convento-parador* (Parador Nacional de Mérida, Vía de la Plata) after a couple of passes. From a gated car park, we take in our semi-circular inn, a three-storied, whitewashed structure carrying a roof of mossy, undulating *tejas* and a pair of *campanarios*. And *Mozárab*-styled *Jardín de Antigüedades* (Garden of Antiquities): cedar topiaries amid Roman columns bordering a patio set with mosaics.

Across tiles designed with glazed Islamic stars in periwinkle, we step under a frame of stone antae and pediment. A fine bust of Augustus rests on the reception desk. Moving at Spanish pace, a plump, dewy man with Romanesque features checks us in. We roll our luggage through a labyrinth of vaulted corridors, seeking our quarters on the quiet side of the inn: guest rooms generously sized, ceilings spanned with exposed beams, skip-troweled plaster walls. We settle in and head back downstairs, discovering off corridors a Roman-style spa, a gallery of Roman and Visigothic relics, and the old chapel, now an elegant parlor.

The dining room opens for dinner at eight-thirty P.M. Shall we while away time in the *parador* bar? Or sample the night air of Mérida?

We strike out under an indigo sky. Just up the street, we see a bar called Aqua and step inside for gin on the rocks. Uncle Chuck clears his throat, changes his mind.

"No ginebra. Cerveza, por favor," he tells the barman.

The fellow used his fingers to place ice in our glasses, a major malfeasance in Uncle Chuck's codex of hygiene.

We sip beer and watch, listening to brassy rock music. Our bar fills with tattooed teens, all of them chain-smokers. Gasping for breath, we move on to Plaza de España, radiant in a pageant of floodlit, arced water, the centerpiece: a classically styled four-tiered fountain adorned with trumpeting cherubs. Above it all, a canopy of palms sways in cool night breeze. And abreast, a jam-packed plaza pulses with *el paseo* Mérida-style.

Unlike *fashionistas* on parade in Madrid, Seville and Barcelona, nocturnal revelers here look like blue-collar folk, casually dressed, with toddlers, and babies in strollers. They share this, their "family room," with us, with solicitous hawkers of chestnuts and lottery tickets. We see an open-air bar, a pizza vendor, teens rearing bicycles to wheelie-position amidst fat-chewing *viejos*.

On the way back to our *parador*, we pass under Arco de Trajano, a spectacle of massive granite blocks in lamplight. Under this simplistic arch, we note sockets that once held fast an overlay of marble. Above, cloud-filled heavens blur a silvery half-moon.

From our *parador's propuesta de menú,* we select *las patatas viajeras con zorongollo extremeño*: casserole of potatoes, codfish, egg and roasted peppers. Uncle Chuck continues with gazpacho *a la extremeña* and I, with *ajo blanco*. My garlic-almond soup resembles not the velvety elixir I enjoyed in Granada's *parador*, but instead a grainy, garlic-inflected, though delicious version.

As we sup beneath buttery-yellow vaulting of a refined dining room, we detect, between canned musical numbers, splattering rain on the terrace.

"Oh, dear God," I breathe, "please clear up by tomorrow."

"Remember our tour of Roman ruins in Gloucestershire?" Uncle Chuck asks. "It rained then, too."

Solomillo de cerdo Ibérico rostisado: grilled loin of pork with roasted salsa is scrumptious. I pass a slice to Uncle Chuck, who in turn swaps a piece of lamb and a bite of vegetable terrine. We split a bottle of local wine, Viña Santa Marina Tempranillo 1999, Mérida.

Swells of rain pummel steamy black windowpanes. We console in our *comedor* with cognac and superb *postres*: *higos de Almoharín rellenos* (chocolate-covered liqueur-injected figs). *¡Devino!*

THE RAIN IN SPAIN

I believed in the power of prayer. Each one, my Grandma Ruscin assured me as a child, the saints heard—and answered, though not always in the affirmative. In Mérida, Ciudad Romana, *I should have prayed to Jupiter.*

It's five A.M. What's that hissing? Uncle Chuck in the shower? Through balcony windows, I leer at gray, malevolent clouds. Below, rain ricochets from flagstones. Uncle Chuck snoozes.

Itching to explore this town's Roman excavations, I pray the clouds are merely passing over. But informs the desk clerk, a storm threatens.

"Rain they predict through tomorrow, maybe the day after, as well," he tells me nonchalantly.

Sure, he lives here. I have come all this way to see the sights, to photograph them. Besides, I understood this to be the driest region of Spain.

"Since when are weather reports accurate? It will clear up," Uncle Chuck suggests, "by midmorning or so. Meantime, let's get the car and drive out to another engaging town. When we return, it will be sunny here. Now, what's within reasonable range?"

"The book shows Zafra, to the south—nicknamed 'Little Seville,' according to this write-up."

With Uncle Chuck's umbrella and another borrowed from the forecaster/ desk clerk, we head south on E-803 toward Zafra before nine A.M.

"Why don't they standardize cars?" Uncle Chuck complains as he fools with stems and knobs on the steering column. "And while those geniuses are at it, they should make all toilets with a flusher in the same place."

It pours. Uncle Chuck cannot engage the windshield wipers. I ask that he keep eyes focused on the road. Meanwhile, I identify the appropriate knob. We carry on through dampness past groves of olives, vineyards, gentle plains of russet soil. We find "Little Seville" just beyond Los Santos de Maimona.

"Little," granted; "Seville," no way. Zafra, a nondescript town of fifteen thousand, does not in the least resemble Seville, the jewel of Andalucía. At least clouds have moved on, but the sky remains bleak and temperature cool. As we roll slowly by Zafra's main square, our eyes feast on details of a fine old church, sixteenth-century Gothic-Renaissance Iglesia de Nuestra Señora de Candelaria. Standing guard above: a castle, fifteenth-century Alcázar de los Duques de Feria, Zafra's *parador.*

"Cup of coffee?" I ask.

"Sure. I'll bet we find a cozy nook in the *parador.*"

This grand old fortress bears earmarkings of Spanish castle in crenated towers, hoary stonework set with heraldic crests and billowing flags. *Conquistador* Hernán Cortés was guest of honor here before his departure to the New World. A fortress-like exterior sequesters a palace with creamy-marble-lined courtyard-arcade accoutered with palm trees and yuccas. Juan de Herrera designed this aesthetically pleasing atrium in the sixteenth century. A dribbling fountain augments the elegance of a castle rising on foundations of a Moorish fortress.

A bar lies beyond the marble arcade under richly carved *artesonado* ceiling of darkened wood with nuances of faded scrollwork. We linger here with *churros con chocolate*, watching Spanish businessmen strike deals under a cloud of blue smoke.

I wonder of Zafra's additional historical offerings, but again it rains. We push on toward Trujillo.

¿BASTARDOS?

Years ago, I worked with a Mexican-American fellow proud of his Azteca *heritage. He frequently, vehemently alluded to Extremadura's Pizarro brothers and Hernán Cortés as* bastardos. *When this fellow visited Spain, he purposely avoided Extremadura, the cradle of New World* conquistadores.

I argued, insensitively—and regrettably—with my co-worker, suggesting to him, "Those conquerors were simply products of environment." In my mind, the sons of Extremadura exemplified the notion of conquest, having endured their own share of defeat. They carried in their veins the blood of their conquerors, particularly Romans and Moors. After having read grim portrayals of Extremadura—those "brutal landscapes"—I reconciled the conquerors' inherent marauding ways—principally longing to enrich their bleak, landlocked region with spoils of another empire. Surely, poverty armed their fervor.

Later, through research and travel, in gaining a sense of cultural sensitivity, I learned that Francisco Pizarro, pride of Extremadura— particularly Trujillo—was indeed a bastardo, *both literally and figuratively.*

CONQUISTADORES DE EXTREMADURA

Extremadura's heroes, the most notorious spawned in Trujillo, were fierce conquerors. Francisco de Orellana (1490-1546) charted the Amazon River and led the conquest of Ecuador. Diego García de Paredes (1466-1546), known as "Samson of Spain," Cervantes described as having defeated the entire French army. Hernán Cortés (1485-1547, born in Medellín) wiped out the Aztec Empire. Hernándo de Soto (1500-42, born at Jerez de los Caballeros) discovered the Mississippi. Also born in Jerez was Vasco Nuñez de Balboa (1475-1519), who opened the door for New World exploration when he discovered the Pacific Ocean. Most famous of all, the epitome of *conquistador* was Francisco Pizarro (1475-1541), the bastard, swineherd son of a minor nobleman of Trujillo, *Capitán* Gonzalo Pizarro. Francisco, a Knight of Santiago and former crewman of Balboa's voyage, went on with two of his brothers to pre-Colombian South America. There, he extinguished the bright flame of the Incan Empire. Besides his conquest of gold and silver, he married Princess Inés Yupanqui, sister of Atahualpa, the Inca emperor he outfoxed then slew.

These fearless men, as were their fellow countrymen who exploited the wealth of foreign empires, became known as *Los Indianos*, for spoils from the Indies made Spain great.

While *Extremeños* plundered wealth from the Americas, they branded their own names: Albuquerque, Mérida and Trujillo. And Hernándo de Soto and Cabeza de Vaca settled Santa Fe and Taos, New Mexico.

VA-ROOM!
Will we proceed on efficient N-630 to Cáceres, then cut across N-521 to Trujillo? Uncle Chuck wants not a thing more to do with Cáceres, though I dream of an encore by the *niño talento*, the boy who entertained us with brilliant guitar work and voice. And I look forward to a more thorough exploration of Cáceres's monumental zone. Just as I think this, we veer off N-630 onto a country lane with signposts to Trujillo.

Fortuitous choice. We cruise through Extremadura's eye-popping uplands, pausing as a shepherd with crook maneuvers his wooly flock across our path. Below us spreads abysmal Valle Río Guadiana, sparkling meadows stretching between slopes stepped with autumn-kissed grapevines. Moss- and lichen-tinged boulders jut from forested banks of ancient oak and beech. Horned cattle with bells at their throats nibble leaves from the oaks. In the distance, silhouettes of farmers bounce along on tractors.

Rural sublimity enlarges as we reach Montanchega, the Montánchez mountain range.

"Pull over!" I cry.

If ever heaven existed on earth, Montánchez is where it resides. Never has landscape moved me to this state of euphoria. Before us: a hill town crowned with an apparition of Moorish fortress eerily cloaked in fog—Montánchez, a jewel under firmament pierced with sapphire blue. Through gauzy vapor rises a church and bell tower; leaning *casas* spill gently along mist-enveloped slopes. Over there, a goatherd prances single-file through a field. I must photograph this epic scene, so I plead to turn back when Uncle Chuck, in true Uncle Chuck fashion, rounds a bend beyond my must-have view.

Triumph! We turn back. We are scarcely stopped when I lurch from the car, metering light as I pace back to the castle scene. Ah...room to breathe.

After a few bracketed shots, I return to where we shouldered the car. I cannot believe my nose. The air, so pristine, sweeter than sweet. Uncle Chuck roams across the road making his own shots. Maybe there is hope for him, after all.... I linger, drinking in cool humid ether. Through my lens, I frame rusticated farm buildings, dew-laden pastures.

As I survey scenery, a donkey appears. I approach him, but hesitate when two golden dogs warn with growls, their backs bristling. I freeze in my tracks, then relax when a friendly looking *Extremeño* saunters toward me from his hut.

"*Buenos días,*" the man sings out.

Maybe forty-or-so years old, this man is skinny, with faded bib overalls, a stubby beard of salt-and-pepper.

"*¿Foto okay?*" I venture sheepishly.

"*Sí. ¡Pero espera por favor un momento!*"

The fellow, munching a rangy baguette, calls off his dogs, breaks a chunk from the bread and offers this to the donkey. I make my shots, thank the kind man and shake his callused hand.

IT TAKES A VILLAGE

Nicknamed "Balcony of Extremadura," the garrison town of Montánchez was originally settled by Moors as a taifa *during the dynasty of Aftásidas de Badajoz. In 1166, Fernando II de León seized the Islamic stronghold, but the sultan Almánzar (Ya'qûb al-Mansûr) recovered it in 1196. Machinations ended when Alfonso IX made the next move, taking back Montánchez for León in 1230.*

Amidst a 3,180-foot peak of Sierra de Montánchez, villagers reap Elysian bounty from fertile, acidic earth that blesses the slopes and plains of this region. Produced here are chiefly grapes and hams, attributable to mild climate of this geographical center of Extremadura. Notable wine includes Ribera del Guadiana, Borba, Alarije, Cayetana and Pedro Ximénez. Montánchez is also known for corridas.

"Gracias, señor," I tell my driver as we careen up the country road. In thirty minutes, we spot the imposing town of Trujillo on a distant ledge of granite.

Soon we inch by slick storefronts amidst a glut of vehicles, through modern Trujillo (population nine thousand). Above rises the original town founded by Romans, captured by Moors, conquered in 1232 by Fernando III and home to palaces of *bastardos conquistadores*.

"Up that way," I say, noting *Parador Turismo* in brown lettering on a white placard. "An old convent, in the monumental zone."

As we breach *casco viejo*, we arrive in a medieval ghost town. Exactly as I have always imagined all of Spain to be, this ancient scene strikes masculine, ponderous, mysterious.... Trujillo reminds me of Santillana Del Mar in Cantabria, but even more uncorrupted.

Rustically elegant Plaza Mayor sits virtually deserted. For a change, we will not have to stake out a parking space. But the ghost town stirs as we pile out of our car. A stout driver arrives in horse-drawn surrey; so does a pair of policemen who ask us not to park in the square.

"Too good to be true," Uncle Chuck says as he turns the key.

"Better for photography," I think aloud, anticipating pristine shots.

We pull into a parking spot just off a pillared arcade alongside a hoary church, fifteenth-century Iglesia de San Martín—a pile of crude moss-encrusted stonework with lanky clock and bell towers. We hike steps to a parvis, then pay a bald woman to enter. We find an exercise in futility negotiating chilly aisles without stepping upon medieval tombstones. At the altar, I send up a prayer for the ticket seller. She has no eyebrows, no eyelashes—marks of radiation or chemotherapy.

Catty-corner, facing the stepped Renaissance square, stands an equestrian statue of Francisco Pizarro—conqueror of Peru, bastard son of a minor nobleman from Trujillo. Menacingly, the bronze-green figure on horseback sits proudly clad in brutish armor. From his cuspidate helmet flow two curvaceous feathers in static pose. With his left hand, he grips reins, in his right, a broadsword, ready again to conquer.

Awed by this rousing tribute to Pizarro, I remember my Mexican-American co-worker. Plainly, Pizarro is champion in these parts, but his legacy haunts me. *Duende* he characterized, to be sure. But I am convinced that he, as do toreros, embodied a sinister brand of *duende*. I question why Pizarro lies buried in the cathedral of Lima, Peru, not here in Trujillo. Remarkably, a twin statue of this Trujillo landmark stands in Lima. I wonder also about the Americans Charles Runse and Mary Harriman who sculpted this memorial in 1927.

We scan ornate façades of palaces to seigniorial mansions financed with spoils of Incan treasure. From a wide expanse of steps on the square, we plot our tour. Across the way, we see Palacio des Marqués de la Conquista commissioned by Francisco Pizarro's half-brother Hernándo. Just beyond stands Palacio de Justicia (in the sixteenth-century *ayuntamiento*) and palaces badged with crests of Orellana-Pizarro, del Marqués de Piedras Albas, de los Chaves. Close by is Palacio de los Duques de San Carlos. We step inside.

In a dank, vaulted atrium, we see a sign telling us in Spanish to pull the chain; a nun will escort us inside. No one answers.

"Siesta-time," Uncle Chuck says, glancing at his watch. "Everything's closed. Let's find a sandwich."

Neatly arranged *tapas* tease from glass cases at La Victoria Cafetería on the square.

"I'm *tapa*-ed out," says Uncle Chuck. "We ate so many *tapas* in Barcelona."

Menú del día brings vaporous casseroles of *caldereta de cordero*: lamb stew. Between bites, my eyes focus on Pizarro's statue. When sunlight breaks through clouds, I excuse myself for more photographs.

Uncle Chuck has eaten; now, it is naptime. I put on my debate cap, convincing him to stay longer, to see more of Trujillo's sights.

Trujillo hosts three noteworthy churches. We have visited San Martín and skip Iglesia de Santiago in favor of a Romanesque-Gothic wonder up the way. Gripping flagstones with our rubber-soled shoes, we trudge through arched passageways up one of the town's steep lanes to Iglesia de Santa María la Mayor, a thirteenth-century pile reconstructed in the fifteenth century, retaining its Romanesque bell tower. This gray mass is colossal, austere, but inside, Gothic heaven. Besides a *Who's Who* in Trujillo Society spelled out in slabs beneath our feet, we note stone pews of the Catholic Monarchs. I chill, considering Fernando and Isabel seated here during Mass while visiting Trujillo.

I spot a stairwell, access to the choir, to the bell tower. I clamber ahead. Uncle Chuck walks side aisles of the nave reading tomb inscriptions, names including *conquistador* Diego García de Paredes. That tomb induced Cervantes's musings on conquerors.

On approach to the choir, my footsteps echo throughout the confined case of blocky steps. Splendid, the outlook from up here: the altar, a fine stone balustrade, a blazing stained window of the Immaculate Heart of Mary against a field of cobalt blue. I pause to squint at Mary's heart pierced through with a dagger, girdled with a wreath of white flowers, crowned with orange flames. I move higher, pinching through formidable passageways of even narrower flights, my shoulders brushing against sides of the bell tower. Breathlessly, I reach the top and peer out to rolling fields of green.

BONG-G-G-G! The one-o'clock bell reverberates through my skull. I jump back into my skin, catch my breath, then make a slow descent to the nave.

"Shall we be off?" Uncle Chuck asks, wiping dust and cobwebs from my jacket.

"Let's relax with coffee at the *parador*," I suggest, "then we'll head back to Mérida for your nap."

Outside, we look up at Trujillo's crowning monument, a thirteenth-century Islamic fortress—a granite pile of heavy square towers rising on foundations of a Roman fortification. Black rooks circle overhead, an ominous spectacle. Under a sprinkle of rain, we move on to an old monastery, Convento de Santa Clara, Trujillo's *parador*.

James Michener mentioned in his masterwork *Iberia*, a building here, slated for conversion to *parador*. Not this convent, judging Michener's descriptions of a smaller building just off the plaza. The *convento-parador*, a massive construction of honey-tinctured stone, wraps around a Renaissance cloister. Three façades embody Tuscan pilasters and arched windows. Rain abridges our scrutiny. We step inside, alongside a huge Sanctus wheel in the atrium and follow a corridor to a bar in the old refectory.

Churches and convents of Trujillo, too, rose on booty and blood of New World conquest. All cultural sensitivity aside, I wish to stay here. I find Trujillo more intimate than Mérida and more proximate to Cáceres.

THE VATICAN OF SPAIN

We slept in, having partaken in excess the previous evening when our parador sponsored a Comida Romana (Roman Banquet) with plenty of wine to wash down cabrito asado (roast kid) and all the trimmings. Servers dressed in togas or off-the-shoulder gowns; floors and tabletops were sprinkled with rose petals; pots of smoldering herbs overpowered the air. And plucking of lyre, beating of drum entertained us in candlelight.

Silence…. No splattering rain. We will at last see Mérida's Roman ruins, I hope. I nurse a headache, maybe a hangover from one-glass-of-wine-too-many last night.

We take a late breakfast of *jamón ibérica, quesos* Casar and La Serena with crunchy rolls, charting our day, chewing strong coffee. Though rain doesn't threaten, Uncle Chuck decides we will see Guadalupe today, then devote all of tomorrow to Mérida.

Soon, we soak up more *Extremaduran* splendors from our car, traveling under muddy sky along E-90, picking up C-401 at Zorita. Along twisting passes, we gape at inordinately wild scenery: sheer granite clefts thrust skyward above forested hillsides, mountains sheathed with deep indigo cloud shadows, grasslands blanketed with mist.

As we climb, climb along switchbacks, I scan the landscape for a peek of Guadalupe's monastery. On approach, my eyes feast on an awe-inspiring phenomenon, the profile of a monastery cleaving to a slope. From a mountain-cloistered valley, she dominates a village-covered grade, the nucleus of a mountainous arena. I'm astonished when Uncle Chuck pulls into a turnout. I thought he was having a heart attack….

"Beat you to the punch," he laughs, grabbing his camera, then walks to the brink of a cliff. He snaps away. I enjoy a spiritual moment. I don't bother with my camera. Uncle Chuck's subjects will be silhouettes against a backlighted scene.

In moments, we arrive at flag-stoned Plaza de Santa María de Guadalupe. In this deserted town square, rewards are two: breathtaking monastery and startling peace. Not a soul stirs but for a stout mongrel dog with a bell on his collar. As for busloads of pilgrims, *nada*. Off-season travel does have its perks.

The monastery looms mightily from one end of the plaza, a fortified complex of battlements, turreted spires and pinnacles giving the impression of fairy-tale castle. Amidst square, stony towers spreads a flamboyant Gothic façade of swirling motif and fifteenth-century bronze-relief doors depicting *Lives of the Virgin and Christ*. Cobbled walls are relieved with arches semi-circular and pointed and a lacy rose window. At the monastery's foot, in the tranquil plaza, stands a fifteenth-century fountain where American Indians were baptized; behind us, a ceramic plaque with the words *Patrona de Extremadura, Reina de la Hispanidad* (Patroness of Extremadura, Queen of the Spanish World).

A Shrine to the Queen of *Hispanidad*

Another statue of the Virgin and Child discovered by a shepherd? That's the story in Guadalupe—and not only another statue, but also one carved by none other than St. Luke. The year was 1300. Alfonso IX de León learned of this statue's discovery and ordered a church built in Guadalupe to house the precious icon. When Alfonso invoked the Virgin's intercession to overcome the Moors in the Battle of Salado, he promised in return a monastery in her honor. Alfonso defeated the Moors on 24 October 1340 and kept true his vow. Soon thereafter, Hieronymite monks constructed and populated a monastery around the church.

Real Monasterio de Santa María de Guadalupe grew in size and importance, amplified with wealth from the Indies and richly endowed by popes and kings. Builders appended hospital, pharmacy, royal lodge, medical and grammar schools and the largest library in Spain.

In Guadalupe's school of medicine, students witnessed Spain's first human dissection (1402). To a fountain on the plaza, Columbus brought Caribbean natives in 1496 for christening—the first Indian baptisms in Spain.

Napoleón's troops sacked the monastery in 1808 and it was abandoned entirely in 1835. Since 1908, Franciscan friars re-energized the monastery's splendor and today Guadalupe rivals Santiago de Compostela as a pilgrimage site. Extant structures date from the fourteenth to fifteenth centuries, with sixteenth- and seventeenth-century additions. The small village of Guadalupe (population twenty-five hundred) employs artisans of copper smelting and craftwork, devotional items and ceramics.

Alongside bronze doors of Guadalupe's grand church, a sensitively fashioned, life-sized bronze statue stands tiptoed upon a stone.

"Christ," Uncle Chuck remarks.

"No. He wears a cassock with capuche bound with three-knotted cincture. St. Francis of Assisi, I believe."

"Explain, then, the wounds."

A hole in the cassock reveals a gash between ribs. The subject's hands and feet are likewise pierced.

"Francis had stigmata," I remind Uncle Chuck.

One of the massive bronze doors gives way. Inside, we are at once drawn to a hallowed scene behind a span of *rejas*. The focal piece of this opulent shrine is the statue of Virgin and Child residing in the high altar. We peer between bars to the distant icon. Only dark-brown faces and right hands are exposed, the figures swallowed up by sumptuous gowns of navy and gold. The Virgin wears a crown conceivably too large for her delicate head. Her free hand grasps a golden scepter.

The only sound is our own breathing as we offer prayers. We move on to the Chapter House, knowing museums are housed here, but a sign informs that tours commence in an hour. Biding our time, we cross the street to whitewashed Parador Zurbarán, the fifteenth-century hospital of San Juan Bautista and Colegio de Los Infantes.

The old hospital, part of Guadalupe's monastery, retains a *Mudéjar* look in a colonnaded orange-grove patio. We relax, enjoying luxurious serenity, then park in the bar and order cups of steaming hot tea.

Back at the Chapter House, we meet a half-dozen Spanish visitors. Our tour guide, a man about sixty with enormous, bushy eyebrows, leads us through a dim corridor, then swings open a door to an eye-catching *Mudéjar*-Gothic *claustro*. Here rise amidst roses, citrus and cedar, an exotic chapel and a two-storied cloister undulating with Islamic arches. Again, all is peaceful. The guide breaks my reverie. Our group, including Uncle Chuck, step into the refectory.

Behind glass panes hang dozens of richly embroidered vestments, plus an ancient wardrobe for the Black Virgin. Guadalupe's monks, between centuries fifteen and nineteen, created these elaborate garments.

Believing a cope is a cope is a cope, Uncle Chuck exhales, "My God, he's going to describe every stitch and bead...."

Señor Eyebrows follows suit in the next suite of chambers, describing ad nauseam a collection of one hundred antiphonaries, illuminated hymnals created between the fifteenth and nineteenth centuries. Though the tomes are exquisitely detailed and impressively conserved, neither of us wants to hear—in accelerated Spanish—each of our guide's windy impressions. To ease the doldrums, I step outside and again partake of the cloisters' engaging serenity. Uncle Chuck joins me, yawning, complaining that siesta-time draws nigh.

At last, our group quits the manuscript museum; we follow them into the church. Our guide calls the sacristy Spain's "Sistine Chapel." But unlike the frescoed Vatican, paintings by Francisco de Zurbarán (1598-1664) envelop this chamber; canvases portraying mainly monks, plus the *Life of St. Jerome* painted 1638-47.

From here, we shuffle to the *camarín*, the statue's shrine, a room more richly appointed than the *camarí* we saw at Montserrat. Jasper, gilt and marble adorn walls and ceiling. Here we see the statue close-up, details of the Holy Mother's gold-and-enamel throne, her extravagant wardrobe and crown. We are each allowed to kiss her, thus fulfilling our pilgrimage. Uncle Chuck's lips kiss the air, just millimeters from germs' way.

The sky blazes fiery with sunset as we wind back toward Mérida, passing old farmer couples on *el paseo*, walking astride along the shoulder.

Back at our *parador*, Uncle Chuck luxuriates in siesta while I settle into a nook in the bar. *Does anyone here have a private thought?* I struggle to reflect within the gossipy din.

Uncle Chuck approaches my corner, suggesting, "Hit the streets to see what we can find for dinner?"

It's sprinkling as we head out. Uncle Chuck carries his umbrella and I, one borrowed from the desk. Unexpectedly, a chilly gale whips through the streets and sprinkling rain cycles to sheets. Typhoon-force wind turns my umbrella inside out. We dash inside the closest shelter, Hotel Meliá Mérida.

In the grand lobby, we shake off rain, then settle onto sofas with our drenched trouser hems.

"But it doesn't rain this time of year in Extremadura," our cocktail waitress explains.

Meanwhile, skylights rattle under lashing rain and *CLUNK*—on a gust of wind, heavy plate-glass doors whip into the lobby followed by a sheet of rain. A porter scoots over to push them closed, forfeiting his stovepipe hat in the process. We head for the dining room.

Complementarios are tasty and French in proportions. Before each of us, our *mozo* places a saucer, on each, a porcelain Chinese soupspoon construed with minuscule shreds of *jamón ibérico*. Over these, our *mozo* ladles creamy tomato *coulis*.

More *complementarios* bring miniature nests of *frisée* lettuce cradling julienne pickled herring. Next: salads followed by chargrilled, bacon-wrapped *rape* sidled with tiny haystacks of deep-fried vegetables. An artistic chef sends from his kitchen each course on square translucent plates in vivid primary colors.

We polish off a bottle of Lar de Barros (*blanco*, Macabeo 2001) and skip dessert. Our *mozo* proffers hazelnut liqueur on the rocks. When we rave up the quality of food, its presentation, our waiter disappears, then returns from the kitchen with a strapping, handsome fellow, the talented chef, a Mallorcan who glows with each accolade.

At half-past ten, a young couple strides into our dining room. Thus far, we have had the room to ourselves.

No rain falls as we stroll through the damp chilly evening to our *parador*. Am I really going to have to explain this umbrella—this twisted mangle of spokes—at the desk? After all, it never rains in Extremadura.

RAINY ROMAN HOLIDAY

I stepped up to a tiny window on the corridor and parted sheer curtains. Had weather improved since I peered out from our room only moments before? No. Still gray, still raining like a monsoon. I could have reached out and touched birds on the roof. Taupe-colored mourning doves raised wings straight above their heads, then shook off droplets and preened with impunity. From campanario-girded nests, storks' heads bobbed. One of these handsome, black-and-white birds stood up, stretched his wings and made castanet clicks with his beak. He then hunkered down again in his twiggy nest.

Our last day in Extremadura and we had not yet seen the sights of Mérida. I determined to do so, rain or shine. After all, Extremadura's victors included more than Pizarro and company. Long before the Spanish conquistadores, Roman heroes lived in Spain: Trajan, Hadrian and Theodosius. Romans left their mark on Spain, particularly on Mérida.

Maps in Euro cities prove virtually useless, particularly for directionally challenged folks such as I. Uncle Chuck's a runner-up. In these towns, street signs present randomly, typically embedded as ceramic or bronze plaques, twelve-or-so-feet above the ground, in a corner building. Bidding to sight one of these signs while driving has proven infeasible. But even on foot, with city plan in hand, I am partial to wandering aimlessly; eventually, I find what I seek, sometimes a surprise. Case in point: shopping for an umbrella this morning, we come face to face, by accident, with stately Templo de Diana.

This temple resembles a Parthenon in miniature. Through chain-link fencing, we see a Doric-style portico and fluted piers capped with Corinthian capitals of finely chiseled acanthus leaves. We gaze upon a construction site, where conservators reassemble pieces of an ancient puzzle. Each slender column bears gaping wounds between segments piled one upon the other. Yet, even in its ruined state, this memorial to a Roman cult makes a graceful statement.

Rain picks up. Uncle Chuck insists on working our way back to the *parador*, to get the car and drive to the acropolis. When we arrive at the acropolis near the center of town, the rain has ceased.

The Temple of Diana was merely a tease when compared with Mérida's Roman theater, a two-storied stage of columns I have seen on television—a night-lit backdrop for the musician Yanni. I tally fifty-eight piers of blue-gray-whorled white marble. Carried above, delicately reconstructed entablatures of granite and marble chiseled in grapevine-motif friezes swirling between ribbed architrave and beaded cornice. Below, reproduction statues immodestly pose between columns at the back of the stage. One of these, Ceres, goddess of agriculture, stands rain-splattered upon a raised platform.

We stumble about in amazement, through puddles, amidst momentous details of an empire, then carry on to an adjacent amphitheater. Behind us stands a forum for comedy and tragedy, ahead, an arena for debauchery. Wind whistles between tiers of stone bleachers in this gigantic coliseum, calling to mind exhortations of fourteen-thousand bloodthirsty spectators and heart-rending screams of tortured beasts.

My skin crawls as we pass through a vomitory into the bowels of this stadium of barbarism. How did Romans—so artistically inclined, masters of engineering—take pleasure in distorted amusements? Imagine. Here, muscled gladiators tilted; lions tore limbs from criminals and slaves....

Squatting, I scoop up a lump of damp soil and roll it between my fingers. Gritty.... I have read they used sand to absorb the blood.

Relieved to move on, we slosh across a lawn, a recreation of Roman gardens behind the theater, a pleasant environment that served as a retreat for intermission in Roman times, these days for Yanni concerts. Our respite accelerates as the sky opens and rain lashes in torrents. We dash through, across the street, to sheltering Museo Nacional de Arte Romano.

We viewed reproduction statues behind the theater's stage. Here in the museum, originals bathe in spotlight. We move along gangplanks of red brick through arches replicating the height and conformation of Arco de Trajano. No camera flashes are allowed; hence, forasmuch as these collections, we commit them to memory. History lessons abound, the walls recounting Spain's Roman past in earth-toned mosaics of hunting scenes or floral designs. Glass cases harbor coins, jewelry and terra cotta oil lamps. Headless statues and fractured amphorae bank galleries. Dioramas enlighten us of Mérida's textured Roman past.

As we drive Avenida de Extremadura in direction of our *parador*, we see walls spray painted with political graffiti, including swastikas and English words: FUCK THE BASTARDS GAY HITLER! SK↑NS MERIDA and an *X*'d-over, smartly rendered Roman helmet. Up the road, we spot granite-and-red brick Basílica de Santa Eulalia. Parked, we step over for a closer look, pausing short of a porte-cochere—a shrine to Santa Eulalia at the site where pagans roasted her alive. The pint-sized temple brims with flowers and flickers in candlelight. With his back to us, a rumpled old man stands, seemingly in prayer.

"I don't believe this," Uncle Chuck exclaims.

With conviction, the man urinates on the shrine. He shakes, zips and turns to leave, then spits on the shrine.

"Maybe, in his mind, he put out the fire that killed Eulalia," I suggest.

"Maybe he's just a crazy old coot," Uncle Chuck counters.

As we thaw in the warmth of our *parador's comedor*, we sip soothing tomato soup floated with the staff of life and poached egg: *sopa de birondanjo con huevo escalfado*, a regional treat. We follow soup with braised sweetbreads and dessert of *badila*: a soupy version of *crème brûlée*.

ALWAYS CHASING RAINBOWS

When rain stopped, sunglow rendered a rainbow above the gray river, mimicking the arc of Puente Lusitania. Grabbing my camera, I trekked down to the riverbank.

> Under the arch of the sky,
> across the clear plain,
> she shoots the constant
> arrow of her river.

—Federico García Lorca

The rainbow fades, but, by the looks of these clouds, there should be one hell of a sunset. Hanging out, I pace along the bank, admiring the lazy Guadiana spanned by a squat Roman bridge in shadows of a robust *alcázar*. Down-river stretches a silvery ultramodern span, Puente Lusitania, designed by Spain's Santiago Calatrava.

At the foot of the bridge, auration of water hisses from a granite pedestal washed in jets of liquid white. No plaque enlightens of the fellow atop, though with laurel wreath and toga, he must be Octavian Augustus. Up the way, a bronze she-wolf suckles Remus and Romulus.

Falling, the sun swashes pink through deep blue clouds, then blinks orange, rendering Puente Lusitania a shimmering arc. Moments pass. Sky blackens above a blood-red horizon in sync with a bloom of street lamps along the Lusitania.

I devour the scene from my riverside bench, contemplating Michener's words: *Men always return to Extremadura.* When this man returns, I hope for no rain.

andalucía otra vez

ANDALUCÍA *OTRA VEZ*

Sunday was not a day of rest for us. We exhausted the better part of it on highways between Mérida and Córdoba. Once arrived at Córdoba, we spent an hour and a half tracking down our hotel. Before we left California, I had asked our travel planner Ana for maps to hotels she'd booked for us. None such existed. We really needed a map in Córdoba....

Under gray sky and mild drizzle, we say goodbye to Mérida, sailing past Roman splendors, savoring a last peek at one of the aqueducts and squat Roman bridge. Southbound on N-630, traffic lightens as we pass through Almendralejo and Villafranca de los Baños and pick up N-432 southeast near Zafra.

Sun obliges somewhat, lending grace to groves of olive trees, to freshly plowed fields. The city of Llerana, Extremadura's southeast gateway to Andalucía, fills my view plane. I am tempted to petition for a pullover. A tower, maybe an old minaret, soars above a hill cleaved with *casas*, the backdrop, deep indigo-blue mountains steaming in mist. Ninety kilometers west of Córdoba, another scene graces at Fuente Obejuna, a prim white village crowned with the ever-present church. Now, Bélmez tempts with its ruined watchtower. We pass wonder after bewitching wonder begging to greet my eye through camera lens, but even my restroom excuse does not work on born-to-be-wild Uncle Chuck. As always, he eagerly makes tracks.

At last, we pull over just east of Bélmez in a *venta* with not a monument or point of interest. The usual routine: restroom-sandwich-beer-fill-up-the-gas-tank-and-zoom!

En route to Córdoba, we hiss along a rain-splattered highway. Even I do not expect a pullover in this weather, though scenery just west of El Vacar strikes photogenic with a wonderfully ruined fortress atop a mesa. We ply on through landscapes etched with russet soil, pine forests, holm oaks and damp sheep. Now we descend mountainous switchbacks, winding our way toward Córdoba *Norte*.

Rain lets up as we enter the sprawling caliphate city of Córdoba from the north. Ana said we would find our hotel within striking distance of the old *mezquita* (*masjid* in Arabic, or Great Mosque) in the historic sector. But where is this *mezquita*? I see signs for the mosque, but Uncle Chuck insists we look for specific signs for Hotel El Conquistador. We creep through a network of honking traffic, inciting even more honking as we clumsily negotiate in our pursuit.

No signs of our hotel, so we pull over near Plaza de los Califas (Córdoba's bullring). Quizzing pedestrians proves futile, so we step into a pastry shop. When we mention the name of our hotel, a woman behind the counter shrugs. Up the street, we inquire at a battery store where, like a machine gun, a fellow inside rattles off incomprehensible directions. Next stop: a newsstand where a merchant suggests a visit to the police station. Policemen will know how to direct us.... Scrapping that option, we hike back to our car, then strike out through one-way streets, winding up on a tree-lined avenue, República Argentina. I see a Meliá hotel. Inside I ask the concierge for directions. By the elbow, the concierge ushers me outside where we exchange in Spanglish. "Make the loop *esouth*," he tells me, "then *torn* left, right, left, right...." Soon we will *espot* the *mezquita* and nearby, our hotel.

Esounds esimple....

Weaving through a confined tangle of streets, we find ourselves lost. We pull over. I ask an ice cream vendor for assistance. He points. We pull out in the direction of his finger. Now, we sit in a one-way alley fraught with taxicabs with no place to turn around. I query a cab driver. Surely, he will know. He exits his cab, grabs me by the shoulders and forcibly turns me around. He points left and then gestures right with a mettle that says, *Does everyone not know the Conquistador?* We slowly back out of the tight alley, then pursue our quest.

¡Estupendo! We see the *mezquita*, an enormous construction of tawny stone with towering bronze doors and Moorish embellishments. We follow the mosque's perimeter to a street called Magistral González Francés where the cabby said we would find our hotel. As we roll slowly amidst tourists on the hoof and Gypsies hawking sprays of rosemary, my eyes lock with a guitarist's who sits on the steps of the mosque. Spooky.... His eyes exude intuitiveness—*muy duende*.

At last, at a quarter till three, we reach the desk of our hotel. We pause only briefly in our Lilliputian quarters and then head down to the hotel's bar for much deserved martinis. The motif in this lounge mirrors arches and tracery of the neighboring mosque, but shiny and new.

I champ to see the mosque. We head over.

A CONFLUENCE OF ISLAM, *SEFARDI* AND CHRISTIANITY

The fabled city of Córdoba, marrow of the Iberian caliphate, stands on two banks of a sharp bend in Río Guadalquivir at the geographical center of Andalucía. Founded circa B.C. 169 by Roman magistrate Claudius Marcelus, this Iberian outpost of Rome (*Corduba*) was capital of *Hispanis Ulterior*—an illustrious colony, birthplace of rhetorician Lucius Annaeus Seneca the Elder (B.C. 55-A.D. 39), his son Lucius the Philosopher (B.C. 4-A.D. 65) and epic historian-poet Marcus Annaeus Lucan.

Visigoths, who introduced Christianity to the region of *Corduba*, ruled here from the sixth through eighth centuries. Córdoba reached its cultural and architectural zenith two centuries later, under Islamic dominance, when Córdoba served as the Iberian Peninsula's caliphal capital. During that Golden Age of Islam, Córdoba boasted one thousand mosques, a *madrasa* (university), libraries, six hundred public bathhouses, and twenty-eight suburbs with lighting in the streets—seven hundred years before Paris and London sported streetlights. In 1031, the powerful caliphate split into minor kingdoms known as *taifas*. Forty years hence, the kingdom of Seville absorbed the former caliphate of Córdoba.

Under Moorish dominion, Córdoba flourished as one of the Western world's greatest centers of art, culture and learning. Illustrious denizens included poets, scholars, doctors, physicians, philosophers and mystics— among them, a thinker considered the Aristotle of medieval Islamic culture: Averroës (Abûl Walid Muhammad ibn Achmed, ibn Muhammad ibn Roschd), a Moorish physician, astrologer and philosopher, 1126-1198. And Moses Maimónides (Abu Amran Musa/Moses bin Maimum, 1135-1204), the Sephardic philosopher.

LA MEZQUITA-CATEDRAL, A MUTE SENTINEL OF ISLAM

The *masjid jâmi'* (Friday mosque) is Córdoba's crowning jewel. The mosque's unequivocal state of preservation earned Córdoba status of World

Heritage Site by UNESCO. This *mezquita*, considered the center of the universe by those of Islamic faith, is an image of Paradise, a presence of the Divine. More than a sanctuary for worshipful ritual, the mosque furnished also a stead for decisions of war, peace and issues of law and culture.

Córdoba's massive *mezquita*, second in size only to the Great Mosque of Mecca, passed from Christian to Islamic hands, then back again to Christian. Moors erected the mosque over the Visigothic basilica of San Vicente in A.D. 786 at behest of an *Umayyad*[1] Berber-refugee and self-appointed *amîr* (emir) from Damascus, 'Abd ar-Rahmân I (Abû al-Mutarrif 'Abd ar-Rahmân bin Mu'âwiya), who arrived in Spain in 756. The mosque's evolution involved erection of a minaret in 848 under orders of 'Abd ar-Rahmân II. Al-Hakam II, son of 'Abd ar-Rahmân III, expanded the floor plan (961-76) and embellished the *mihrâb* with labor of imported artisans. Ya'qûb al-Mansûr appended another enlargement in 987. Caliphs saw this monumental construction as a means of demonstrating their power. At 570 by 450 feet, this fine mosque at Córdoba spared Islamic residents their *hajj*, the obligatory pilgrimage to Mecca.

The mosque consisted of eleven naves (nineteen after expansion) divided by nearly one thousand columns of granite, marble, jasper and onyx—later reduced to 850, to make room for the cathedral. Recycled from former Hellenic, Roman and Visigothic structures, columns and ornate capitals carry a two-level labyrinth of arches, the first made up of horseshoe arcs, the second, of superimposed semicircular forms. Voussoirs present a repetitive motif in pleasing arrayal of alternating red brick and ecru-colored stone.

The Islamic ablution courtyard, Patio de los Naranjos, occupies more than one-third of the mosque. Inaugural construction of this courtyard historians ascribe to 'Abd ar-Rahmân III. In days of the caliphs, palm trees grew here and at one of the patio's corners rose a 305-foot minaret, today supplanted by a bell tower. In the sixteenth century, Bishop Martín Fernández de Angulo entrusted Hernán Ruiz I with remodeling the courtyard. Orange trees replaced palms. Eighteenth-century Cordovans added olive trees and cypress.

The *mezquita* framed the center of Islamic worship in Córdoba. The *Umayyad* city of royal palaces (medina, or *madînat*), sited four miles distant and known as Madînat al-Zahrâ', was built 953-957 for 'Abd ar-Rahmân III, then sacked in 1013 by Berbers. Fortified Medina Azahara—named after the caliph's favorite wife Al-Zahrâ'—supplied Córdoba's avatar of Granada's Alhambra, incorporating pools of quicksilver, terraces, a bathhouse, an *alcázar*, mosque and gardens. Caliphal details included stucco Kufic relief, multi-lobed arches and filigreed capitals. A cadre of twenty thousand slaves served emirs and their concubines. Afterward, post-emirate marauders ransacked the medina's rich supply of marble, ebony and jasper, laying the complex to ruin. With complete reconstruction plans underway, archaeologists excavate the formerly sumptuous complex and an elaborately designed aqueduct.

Sephardim

Jews, having arrived in Spain at the time of Greek and Phoenician predominance, played an instrumental role in developing Córdoba, as they did in much of Spain. Sephardic Jews or Sephardim (*sefarad*, Hebrew for Spain) settled in Córdoba. Though Jews suffered under Visigothic rule, they prospered under a more tolerant *Umayyad* Caliphate. Jews dispersed at the end of the eleventh century to escape intolerance under *Almohad* rule. With the Reconquest, Jews were made to wear red or yellow patches of cloth identifying their religious persuasion. By 1492, Jews were forced to convert or be expelled under decree of the Catholic Monarchs.

Córdoba's medieval *judería* remains a legacy of Jewish occupation, as does the fourteenth-century *Mudéjar*-style *sinagoga*, Andalucía's only surviving synagogue and one of only three in Spain. Moses Maimónides, one of the foremost Jewish philosophers, was born at Córdoba.

Catholic Reconquest

Fernando III conquered Córdoba in 1236, toppling the caliphate crown. Not only did the Christian conquest supplement churches, convents, hospitals, palaces and seigniorial mansions to the Cordovan urbanscape, but also a cathedral—in the midst of the old Friday mosque. Alfonso X ordered construction of the cathedral chancel. The first Catholic Mass was celebrated there on 29 June 1236. Capilla de Villaviciosa and Capilla Real were completed in 1371. Under order of Bishop Alonso Manrique, work began on the Gothic transept and apse (1523-1547) of Catedral de Santa María: 180 feet long by 50 feet wide. Builders removed one hundred columns and arches from the center of the mosque, then constructed the nuclear cathedral with *Hispano*-Flemish vaults, arches, Renaissance cupolas, a baroque chancel vault and high altar. Local architects Hernán Ruiz I, II and III, and Juan de Ochoa successively directed the work. Christians transformed the minaret into a baroque belfry between the sixteenth and seventeenth centuries.

MODERN CÓRDOBA

Córdoba is capital of the province of Andalucía, hosting a population of three hundred thousand. Though Córdoba could thrive on tourism alone, its economy flourishes with the trades of silver-craft and leather-work.

We gain entry to the *mezquita* through Patio de los Naranjos through Puerta de Santa Catalina. Here, in wavering shadows of palms and the mighty Torre del Alminar, the bell-tower-minaret, spreads a formal patio akin to Seville's cathedral patio. Here Muslims cleansed themselves before entering the mosque. In the midst of orange trees, palms, cypress and olives, a fountain trickles gently into a basin—a whisper of calm in this tourist-infested courtyard.

Near Puerta del Perdón, the gate where penitents received pardon, we see a *taquilla*. With tickets in hand, we queue behind throngs of Japanese, German and Dutch tourists. Inching through sunlit majesty of ancient stone with red brick inlays, at last we step inside.

Through dimness, my eyes dart above to a delirious network of candy-striped voussoirs—waves of arches sprouting from a forest of columns. In awe, we slalom between hundreds of thirteen-foot piers of marble and jasper, gaping above to a labyrinth of leafy motif and scrolling, multi-lobed arches to side chapels filled with iconographic flourishes glimmering in gold. The elements numb in detail, in sheer numbers. In this dream-like environment, I soon lose track of Uncle Chuck.

Córdoba's *mezquita* overwhelms. With respect to its vast size and abundance of cultural offerings, it calls to mind the Louvre, where I found several days of exploration left me yet unsated.

Looking for Uncle Chuck, I am distracted, my eyes leading me between a corridor of columns beneath *artesonado* ceiling interlaced with multi-lobed arching to a niche glowing in liquid gold. This transmutation of stone and metal into light is the hallowed *mihrâb*. Architectural overseeing—and technical oversight—of this elaborate niche is attributed to Al-Hakam II. A *qibla* must face east toward Mecca—direction of Islamic prayer, but this one indeed faces south. Nonetheless, this *mihrâb* stuns with golden inlays, intricate mosaics, alabaster lozenges and swirling Kufic relief. I peer through wrought-iron gates to remnants of a *maqsûra* (caliph's enclosure) and overhead to a concave, rosette-shaped dome. My eyes scan details for the sacred stone in the *qibla*. The stone floor is impressed from thousands of pilgrim-penitents circling seven times on their knees. This hauntingly beautiful alcove once housed an original gilded copy of *al-Qur'ân* and an arm bone of Muhammad the Prophet. A miracle the Catholic Monarchs left this *mihrâb* intact. I wonder about the copy of the Koran, the relic of Muhammad....

Joining up with me, Uncle Chuck asks if I've seen the cathedral. Amazingly, I had circumnavigated around it, so I follow him now to the center of the mosque.

This holy structure, the Great Mosque of Córdoba, experts consider the most relevant Islamic monument in the West—a legacy of the Moors' passion for beauty. James Michener disparaged the cathedral within, though now that I see it firsthand, I am not alarmed in the least. For my taste, this grafting of Islamic, *Mudéjar* and Christian symbols and architecture works— at least from within. To construct the cathedral meant raising the roof, so from outside it decidedly conflicts with the Moorish design of overall structure. But from the interior, this *mezquita-catedral* unveils as less intrusive than does Palacio de Carlos V at La Alhambra. Although the same King Carlos gave permission to construct a cathedral within this mosque, when at last he inspected the completed work, he said remorsefully, "You have built here what you or anyone might have built anywhere else, but you have destroyed what was unique in the world."

The vaulted ceiling of Catedral de Santa María accomplishes what a cathedral intends—drawing eyes heavenward to a visual feast of friezes, ribbing and Italianate dome exquisitely constructed. From choir stalls to marble pulpits, these are the finest furnishings we have seen inside Europe's great cathedrals. Best of all, the high altar retains a stunning masterwork by Antonio Palomino.

This cathedral's precious relics include those of San Bartolomé and Santa Úrsula. The treasury houses a gigantic monstrance by German goldsmith Heinrich von Arfe, plus Spanish baroque processional crucifixes including one with an exquisitely carved Christ figure in creamy ivory.

Darker it grows inside as day grows long. In the heyday of this mosque, a vast wall facing the courtyard opened to the elements. Christians shored up the walls after the Reconquest. But in spite of all its changes over the past twelve hundred years and the overlay of Christian symbolism, Córdoba's *mezquita* is one of the world's premium architectural gems.

Weary, overwhelmed, we aim for the exit.

...Its beauty and elegance challenge any description.

—al-Idrisi, "Dreses," 1099-1166

We take dinner alone in our hotel's dining room. Our waiter brings complimentary glasses of smooth, amber Gran Barquero Amontillado. We feast on green salads, following with *cochifritos de la sierra* (stew), mutton for Uncle Chuck and kid for me. For dessert, we split an assortment of tarts: chocolate, pear, apple and almond.

Soon the naked moon finds us on Magistral González Francés facing the floodlit mosque. Familiarity I sense in its series of buttresses, crenellations and high-set windows—a large-scale version of a mission church at San Gabriel, California. There is good reason for this mimesis in architectural elements of *mezquita* and *Fray* Cruzado's Misión San Gabriel Arcángel de los Temblores. In 1772, a Franciscan friar from Alcarazejo, in the diocese of Córdoba, named *Fray* Antonio Cruzado, OFM (1724-1804) instructed his California Indian neophytes to build a church according to his sketch. *Fray* Cruzado had drafted from memory a landmark from his hometown, the *mezquita-catedral* of Córdoba.

We veer left on Cardenal Herreros, following the perimeter of the Great Mosque. Candles blaze above, eerily illuminating an image of the Virgin, the shrine of La Virgen de los Faroles (Virgin of the Lanterns). Our Lady resides behind *rejas* interspersed with votive lanterns fluttering amid bouquets of yellow and heliotrope daisies. Up the way, the bell tower glows majestically in ivory luminescence against blue-black sky. Above hangs a platinum moon.

[1] *Umayyad*: First Islamic dynasty of *khalifas* (caliphs), A.D. 660-750. These Arabic people who belonged to the *Quraysh* in Mecca—a North-Arabian tribe whom ruled Mecca in the early-seventh century, a member of which was Muhammad the Prophet—were nearly wiped out in 750 by an *Arabo*-Islamic dynasty, the *Abbasids*. 'Abd ar-Rahmân I escaped and founded a new dynasty at Córdoba (756-1031).

DIRTY DUENDE

The best flamenco in Córdoba was just steps away from Hotel Conquistador, so said our concierge. The first show would begin at half-past ten. That was pushing it for Uncle Chuck, but he agreed to accompany me to Tablao Flamenco El Cardenal.

At Calle Herreros, we turn left on Torrijos. Half a block down at number ten, we enter a nightclub through a courtyard between Palacio de Congresos y Exposiciones, site of former Iglesia de San Jacinto and Hospital de San Sebastián. We give our names to a man at a podium.

"You are expected upstairs," the man says with a welcoming gesture toward the staircase. "Another man will meet you there."

At the top of the stairs, we step into a slender hall with seating for more than one hundred spectators. White plaster swathes barren walls, heavy dark beams traverse the ceiling; at the front of the room, a large stage set back from a sandstone Romanesque arch.

A man ushers us to row nineteen, midway into the room. A half-dozen Americans and a couple of German-speaking guests number among us, but primarily Spaniards fill the space. Emblematic of these *tablaos flamencos*, a puny table suffices for our beverages.

The show was to begin at half-past ten. At a quarter till eleven, two *guitarristas* take the stage. Lights fade, the audience pipes down. Now we hear familiar warm-up: plucking, strumming and slapping of guitar bodies. A chubby *cantaor* appears and titillates us with soaring vocals as guitarists pick up the tempo. Another singer emerges, joining the other in soulful duet.

The musicians are skillful, yet I wonder if the setting need be more intimate to sense *duende*. If only I were closer the stage, nearer their hearts.

Crimson spotlights caress a black-haired, kohl-eyed beauty. Staccato of *palmas* and steady rhythm of strumming set her feet in motion. The woman frowns and whips red fringes into cyclonic frenzy. As she exits the stage, another dancer emerges, a woman who does not look Romany. She is long-stemmed, light-skinned, with auburn tresses pulled back from forehead and temples, fixed in a ponytail. Her Rubenesque form fills out a slinky, mint-green dress. She clutches a fan of orange, from her throat flows a sheer orange scarf and in her hair blooms a bright orange flower. At once, with unwavering tempo, this full-figured redhead beats the boards with her heels, snapping her fan opened then closed, at her side, above her head. Though gestures say angry, her eyes spell pride. What a beauty she is, but *duende* is impotent—even when she arches her back and hoists the open fan high above her pretty head, gracing us with delectable profile.

In my teens and early twenties, I saw, four times, the Ike and Tina Turner Review live on stage, in the Turners' "Proud Mary" period when Tina sported flowing red wigs and mini-dresses exposing her legendary legs practically up to her navel. Ike called their band The Kings of Rhythm. The Ikettes, a triumvirate of Tina wannabes, backed up Tina's earthy vocals. That was an era before PR gurus homogenized Tina's risqué persona for the masses. Back then, even Tina described her old R&B act as "rough." Downright rough, the steamy performance was more than suggestively sexual. When Tina crooned Otis Redding's "I've Been Loving You Too Long," she milked her audience with carnal innuendo, with lascivious microphone technique. Tina Turner embodied—besides monumental charisma—*duende*, a virtue this troupe at El Cardenal with their polished performance lacks.

Guess I'm fussier in my middle age, finding blasé this evening's show. Or have I at last fledged into a bona fide *aficionado de flamenco*?

I recall the "Tiny Tim" performer in Seville as the next set of dancers takes the stage. Three lithe, attractive women in matching gowns and hairdos sway flawlessly in synchronization like the Spanish Supremes.

Foremost of this evening's performance is a sexy *bailaor* with jet-black hair drawn back tautly from his long Modigliani-esque face, cinched at the back in long, corkscrew tendrils. Olive skin, black nipples show through his sheer shirt. Adonis buttocks bulge from fit-to-busting pants. I wonder why this man carries a bamboo cane. Nevertheless, I'm soon enrapt with his *zapateado*—not only with the rhythm of his talented feet, but with his emphatic cane-work. His prop augments the footwork. I've not seen this before.

"¡Estupendo! ¡Por Dios!"

I stand corrected about the show-stopper. Midway into the show, dancers exit the stage and a singer steps up to a microphone, calling to our attention an elderly couple seated near the front of the room.

Spotlights reveal an withered man practically toothless. His woman wears a red kerchief and long turquoise skirt of crinkly crepe-de-chine. From what I can grasp, this old man and woman are flamenco stars of a previous era. Spaniards in the audience applaud and shout fervently as *guitarristas* duel discordantly. Now the toothless man rasps, compelling his kerchiefed woman to frolic through the aisle. This lithe old woman brings the house down, topping Tina Turner's antics, lifting her skirt, flashing us with her bare privates! The Spaniards roar, some falling forward on their knees. We tourists are amazed.

"¡Mozo! ¡Más sangría, por favor!"

Shadows: Tri-cultural Layers of Ancient Córdoba

What a city, this Córdoba! Though wanting for Seville's polish, for Granada's sense of fairy-tale milieu—and at least a measure of Barcelona's vitality—Córdoba embodied a duende *that throbbed deeply within the fabric of her ancient stones. A rich pull of tradition hung heavy in the air. Reputedly, Cervantes wrote part of his* Hidalgo Don Quixote de La Mancha *novel here. And Córdoba was birthplace of the illustrious torero, Manolete (Manuel Rodríguez, 1917-1947). I rared to explore.*

Hmm…what taints my coffee? Cardamom? I enjoy my favorite elixir undefiled of ulterior flavors. Richly brewed coffee with milk, *solamente*, hits the spot for me, *por favor*. I cannot understand those who tolerate liqueur flavorings, cinnamon, or—pass the barf bag—powdered mixes called "cappuccino mist" and such. Hotel Conquistador's coffee tastes like perfume.

Lusting after a bona fide cup or two of *café con leche*, Uncle Chuck and I hit the streets, our radar trained on a caffeine shrine.

Just north of the mosque, we stroll up renowned Calleja de las Flores (Alley of the Flowers), a narrow lane defined with whitewashed buildings studded with hundreds of flowerpots. Must be a spectacle in summertime, but we see this time of year only vestigial blooms on rangy vines.

As we pass by, metal doors roll up. Shopkeepers heave buckets of water onto sidewalks, then broom last night's debris into the street. The minaret's lower set of bells roll a clamorous nine o'clock. In sync with my caffeine radar, we carry on to the old *judería* where we mount a flight of steps to Café-Bar Judá Leví from a plaza of the same name. Ah…real coffee—damned good coffee. Inside of twenty minutes, I knock back three cups. Uncle Chuck nurses his first. He's not too pleased when he pulls a three-inch-long black hair from his pastry.

Córdoba's old Barrio de la Judería (Jewish Quarter), just northwest of the mosque proposes a gauntlet of narrow, twisting alleyways of whitewash, brick-arched and wrought-iron-gated, tiled courtyards and squares. The route bulges with gift shops and jams with trucks, cars and mopeds. People stream in throngs, though only a couple of non-Spanish tourists animate the streets this off-season month of November. We find here mainly Moorish features, complexions of olive-tan, sleek hair of blue-black.

Racks of trinkets clutter sidewalks. Above our heads hangs a pageant of colorful signs painted or neon, soliciting tourist euros: TAX-FREE, REGALOS, PAELLADOR, CAMBIO, TABACOS, HELADOS, BOLSAS, OH LA LA PIZZA, RESTAURANTE-this, RESTAURANTE-that. Long silken scarves wave as pennants outside *tiendas*. Heavy smells of fried food penetrate the cool air.

As we squeeze through walls of tourists, glancing to windows banked with wares from tacky mementos to handcrafted *mantones* and mantillas, we detect flamenco-guitar strains and clicking *castañuelas*. I follow my ears to a shop. Oh...the music is recorded, but so fine.

Planning to cover the waterfront, we head back toward the mosque. We now hear live music from the *guitarrista* I saw on the way in yesterday. He sits in the same spot at the mosque, on the steps, under morning's gray sky. This balding man with auburn-dyed fringe and broom moustache, hazel *ojos del duende* (*duende*-esque eyes) is dressed in white Polo shirt and navy cardigan sweater under open gray sport coat. With long nails of his right hand, he scrubs a haunting refrain, maintaining eye contact with me. Following sensitive finger-work, I glance to the hole in his guitar; inside, a label printed in red: *C725 CARMEN*. Uncle Chuck moves on. Though longing to hear more, I prepare to leave, tossing euros into his receptacle. The guitarist nods, his eyes still locked with mine.

"Gracias, señor," he says with a sense of familiarity.

I know this man. Was it he I saw years ago playing guitar in a corner of Madrid's Plaza Mayor? Or had I known him in another lifetime?

I pull myself away. Catching up with Uncle Chuck, I speak of the guitarist's intuitive eyes.

"Terry, you love the guitar; you're enamored of flamenco. Maybe he senses that. But, more likely than not, he saw you as gullible."

Not true. He saw through me—a *duende* connection, I'm convinced.

We move past Palacio Episcopal and Puerta del Puente and cross Ronda de Isasa to the northern bank of the shallow, muddy Río Guadalquivir. Moldering foundations shoulder the span of heavily repaired Puente Romano. At the other side of the bridge stands an intriguing beige pile crowned with crenellations. We walk tightrope-style along a ludicrously narrow, ten-or-so-inch-wide sidewalk as cars and mopeds zoom by. The hoary edifice we approach turns out to be fourteenth-century Torre Fortaleza de la Calahorra.

To defend Córdoba's entrance from his brother Pedro I El Cruel, Enrique II de Trastámara, in 1369, ordered the tower built upon an *Almohad* bridgehead fortification. In the eighteenth century, the structure was used as a prison for Cordovan nobility, then in the nineteenth century as a school for women. The *torre* houses a fine museum, Museo Vivo de Al-Andalus/El Museo de las Tres Culturas/Fundación Roger Garaudy (Institute for Dialogue between Cultures).

Inside, a pretty docent gives us audio headsets dialed in to English, then turns us loose to tour eight rooms. With the aid of imagination, augmented by high-tech audio and lighting technique, we project back to an atmosphere of tenth-century Córdoba. One of these stony rooms is outfitted with ancient, fierce-looking surgical tools. Above, along a stone staircase, niches embrace musical instruments. Beyond, we are offered a further retrospective of tenth-century technology in working models depicting the elaborate water system of Córdoba. In still another room, we view exquisite scale ensamples of Granada's Alhambra and Córdoba's *mezquita*. Lights glow on and fade off in sync with liquid dialogue as water bubbles and flows through dioramic fountains and placid pools.

At the top of the tower, we peer through a sentry window, an outlook carrying us across the Roman bridge to the mosque-cathedral. But the best of the tour awaits downstairs—the eighth room in the scheme of our suggested route.

We take seats on wraparound benches against the dark chamber's perimeter. A spotlight glows from dim to bright, focusing on the face of Ibn 'al-Arabi, a bearded wax mannequin realistically crafted, dressed in period caftan, his head wrapped in white turban. Through headsets, we listen to 'Al-Arabi's philosophic ruminations on faith—in English. Light fades from Ibn 'al-Arabi, then focuses on Maimómides. I swear I see these men breathe.

We also hear transcendental reports from Averroës and Alfonso X. Each of these profound leaders of science, religious law and government concedes a fundamental canon, "Three religions, one God."

"Regarding Islam," one of the mannequins tells us, "Beauty invoking Divine Inspiration evokes a notion of what is to be Eternity."

I relax my thoughts on Spain's transmutation of cultures. The ancient words remind me that tolerance can exist within the Spiritual, Law, Order and Life. I wish all humanity felt deeply these notions.

> God speaks to us in many ways. Let us open our ears, our eyes and our hearts to receive the message.
>
> —*Luke 16:19-31*

The sky proffers not an inkling of sunshine as we negotiate the Roman bridge's puny curb back toward the old center of town. The majority of those afoot do not observe the practice of right-hand traffic, those coming at us averting their eyes, marching assertively as Spaniards do, exploiting a game of cat-and-mouse. Always the mouse, I step into the street, a mere breath away from passing vehicles, allowing the cats their coveted space. Funny, how pedestrians aim right at you, pretending not to see. Maybe I'll try this, or emulate Uncle Chuck's swinging-umbrella technique.

We pause mid-span, gazing at the rushing river below. Marshy banks and silty shoals peak above cold brown water purveying grazing ground to a plethora of waterfowl. We identify heron, a cormorant and a variety of ducks. Other birds: swallows, sparrows and rooks, the pervasive pigeons and doves flit and swoop through riparian scenery.

On the eastern side of the bridge, atop a stone railing, rises a shrine to San Rafael, patron saint of Córdoba. At Rafael's feet, an avalanche of candle wax flows between cellophane-wrapped bouquets of cut carnations in red and white. I hear a tale that candles have burned here since 1651 and, as residents pass San Rafael, they tip or remove their hats.

To the west, sinuous water skirts crude stony architecture of old Roman flour mills known as Molinos de la Albolafia. Córdoba's mills and overall water system embellished when 'Abd ar-Rahmân II ordered installation of a ponderous, chain-driven pump for purposes of conveying river water to palace gardens above. Isabel La Católica commanded the removal of the device because of its clamorous squawking.

A reconstruction of the pump's waterwheel looms on the northern bank of Río Guadalquivir. We step over to study details of this great aquatic Ferris wheel of weathered wooden spokes. We see, along the wheel's slatted circumference, terra-cotta vessels bound to the mechanism with leather straps—a primitive system for scooping water into the aqueduct. Six centuries ago this wheel's antecessor jangled the nerves of Queen Isabel.

We cross the street, following reconstructed Roman and Moorish walls to Alcázar de los Reyes Cristianos, the old fortified castle of the *Umayyads*. The *Umayyad* castle stood seminally where now stands the Episcopal Palace, home to Córdoba's Diocesan Museum. All that remains of the former Moorish castle are foundations and gardens; the present *alcázar* took shape under Spanish dominion by orders of Alfonso XI in 1327.

A fine statue of Fernando III greets us as we step inside a *Mudéjar*-Gothic pile of stone. I'm enthralled as these walls conjure up their storied history.

The Catholic Monarchs resided here while planning their conquest of Granada. Here Columbus once met with his king and queen. And Boabdil was clapped into this palace's dungeon in 1483.

Three Gothic towers grace this fortified palace: Torre de León (Lion), del Homenaje (Homage) and de la Inquisición. For three hundred years this monument served as a base for the Inquisition and as royal quarters for the Christian Kings.

Here lingers flotsam of Córdoba's *Umayyad* glory: a restored bathhouse and comely gardens. We step upon marble-paved terraces under livid sky, imagining settings more splendorous in sunshine. Though but a remnant of Moorish Córdoba, this setting is as Moorish as it gets. Fountains refresh. Narrow ponds ripple reflections of citrus, palms and aromatic cypress. Chubby carp undulate lazily through the pools. Fuchsia bougainvillea cascade from rustic stone walls. Yellow-daisy hedges and deep-green boxwood bank brief flights of steps between rectilinear patios. I find unconventional amidst this Moorish refinery: faded Roman frescoes, ancient stone cisterns, *concha*-shaped niches.

We move inside to the old chapel, an eighteenth-century sanctuary converted into a showy gallery of excavated Roman mosaics. I stare back at an exquisitely preserved, snake-headed Medusa with hypnotic eyes. Just beyond, in a corridor, we discover a magnificently chiseled Roman sarcophagus from the third century A.D.

Uncle Chuck grows weary. We head back to the Conquistador for lunch. Our paellas—*del mariscos* for Uncle Chuck, traditional *a la Valenciana* for me—call to mind bursts of yellow sunshine on this gloomy day. Look good they do, but quality and flavor underwhelms.

Leaving Uncle Chuck to snooze, I strike out under a spritz of rain with my umbrella and camera. Weather hasn't put a damper on the *coches caballos* (horse-drawn carriages for tourists), nor on floods of locals and sightseers who ramble through alleyways of Córdoba.

After another prowl through the awing *mezquita*, I head toward the river. Along the way, votive candles flutter within outdoor *Ave María* wall shrines. There's a Gypsy on each corner. Intrigued with one particular Gypsy-tourist encounter, I stop to watch. The ponytailed Gypsy appears well-to-do in her supple leather coat and expensive-looking shoes. A family of Spaniards wants a palm-reading discount for the entire family of four. Bantering jockeys until at last they strike a deal: the Gypsy will read four sets of palms for forty euros plus a pack of cigarettes. Each time I train my camera lens on the Gypsy's face, she turns her back to me. After ten patient minutes, I give up—and I have no cigarettes to proffer.

On the north shore of Río Guadalquivir, I pause in a tiny square to admire an old gate, a bulbous triumphal arch called Puerta del Puente (from the 1500s, era of Felipe II), the work of Hernán Ruiz, replacing antecedent Roman and Moorish gates. Above rises an obelisk aloft with another statue of San Rafael, El Triunfo de San Rafael hewn in rococo style by Miguel Verdiguier, a French artisan who settled in Córdoba in the eighteenth century.

At once, twilight blackens with thousands of open-mouthed swallows swirling above this old sector of town. As they swoop toward rooftops, the vision, the racket calls to mind Hitchcock's *The Birds*. As the mantle sky wings north, cacophony gives way sweetly to classical notes. Piping melodies for euros, two flautists, a man and woman, stand sheltered from sprinkling rain, beneath an overhang. Rain pelts, so I hightail back to the hotel.

As we sought a coffee emporium this morning, Uncle Chuck staked out places to eat.

"There's an intriguing restaurant just north of the mosque," he tells me. "Let's have a look at the menu."

We head over to El Caballo Rojo, a restaurant tucked up a brick-arched corridor-courtyard between walls corsaged with flowerpots of gangly, dormant geraniums. Uncle Chuck has good taste. According to posted accolades, this restaurant is a Cordovan institution and recipient of the National Gastronomy Award. Besides, the menu entices.

We are not surprised to discover the bar open but the restaurant dark until eight—quite early for Spain.

Our bartender is a bruiser. She pulls espresso-machine handles as though shifting gears on a Mack truck, swaggering with more machismo than John Wayne did. But she stirs a mean martini and conducts herself professionally. A fraternity of regulars, middle-aged to grizzled old men, lean on the bar (there are no stools), exchanging tales in raspy resonance. Under their feet, a hodgepodge of castoff olive pits, toothpicks, crumpled paper napkins and squashed cigarette butts litter the floor.

At eight o'clock, we ride a squeaking elevator to the first floor and step into a beautiful dining room softly lit, graced with linen-draped tables. Our host seats us across from an American couple speaking broken Spanish, pretending not to be American. To me, this pretension smacks of Southern California.

As we pore over menus that boast "Cuisine of Moorish and Sephardic origin," our waiter proffers stout glasses of sherry. Mmm, nice and dry, nutty. Next, he brings a plate of fried fish battered lightly, moist, cooked just so, not at all oily. Uncle Chuck doesn't care for wine this evening, so I order a demi-bottle of Rioja, Cune 1999.

We start with soup, gazpacho for Uncle Chuck, *ajo blanco* for me. Each time I savor this delectable, white garlic soup, it varies from versions previously sampled, this one grainy with pulverized almonds, reasonably spiked with garlic, dotted with white raisins and tart apple slices.

A fragrant slab of Argentine beef *entrecôte* is Uncle Chuck's choice for entrée. My *perdiz* is tender as a mother's love, tasting of the wild, veiled in flavorful *demi-glace*. Each of our plates includes a neat fan of au gratin-style potatoes. Uncle Chuck eats but a portion of his beef, finding it stringy, chewy.

The American couple, overhearing our conversation, lets down their guise, asking where we call home. We oblige, then ask them the same. I guessed right: Orange County, California.

For dessert, we luxuriate with bowls of gâteau-style rice pudding scented with zest of lemon and essence of cardamom nestled within wisps of whipped cream. Delicious; cardamom works here. And I'm relieved when my coffee arrives unadorned.

As we wind down our meal on this last day in Córdoba, I mention to Uncle Chuck, "Shame, we leave tomorrow. There's so much more to see here in Córdoba. The churches!" I read from my city plan: "Iglesia de San Agustín, de la Compañía, San Cayetano, San Francisco, San Hipólito, San Jacinto, San Lorenzo, San Magdalena, Santa Marina, San Miguel, San Nicolás de la Villa, San Pablo, San Pedro, Padres de Gracia, San Rafael, Santiago, de la Trinidad."

"You'd need a week, maybe a month to do justice to a city like this...the churches alone...."

"And museums. Museo Arqueológico Provincial, Bellas Artes, Hospital de Caridad [now a museum of fine art], Julio Romero de Torres, Taurino, y Zoco [bullfighting museum and flea market]...."

"And don't forget palaces. Let's see...Palacio de los Marqueses de Viana and Palacio de Marqués de la Fuensanta. More my speed."

"The *marqueses* of El Carpio owned a palace here, as well. Remember the village of El Carpio, where we dropped in for lunch last year on the way down to Seville?"

I plan already my next visit to Córdoba.

CAFÉ CON HUEVOS

We deserved to sleep in till half past eight, after a jam-packed agenda the past two days in Córdoba.

For breakfast, we strike out for Restaurante El Caballo Rojo. The shorthaired woman at the bar shifts her espresso machine into gear, grabs two saucers already plotted with sugar packets and spoons and slams them down in front of us on the marble bar. She swaggers over to the orange press and squeezes fresh juice for us. *Slam!* Pulpy liquid splashes over rims of the glasses. Uncle Chuck points at croissants behind a glass counter. Our butch *barista* snatches them with metal tongs and tosses them on plates.

"*Seis euros, por favor,*" she growls.

Good coffee. Sure beats the pants off the cardamom crap back at the hotel. And at El Caballo, breakfast costs half that of the Conquistador's.

Back in our Peugeot, we cross the Roman bridge, passing through Barrio de Miraflores, across Puente Calle Rinconada, then ease onto the *autovía.* Time wise, it's a cinch exiting Córdoba onto N-IV, especially when compared with our one-and-one-half-hour entrance the other day. But it's difficult, leaving behind unvisited sites. Worse yet, our next destination is Spain's "least interesting city," according to the books. Planning our trip, I considered Valencia for a stay-over, spurring protests from Uncle Chuck. We chose Albacete, capital of southern La Mancha.

"I'm not going to get mixed up in big-city traffic," he'd said. "Let's stay overnight west of Valencia, then shoot up to Barcelona in the morning. Besides, if we went to Valencia, you'd want more than an overnight stay."

As we accelerate past El Carpio, I wave to its old Moorish bastion rising mightily against an aluminum sky. Next, we catch a glimpse of another defensive tower crowning the textile town of Rus. Now, endless groves of olives rush by. Breaking from our queue behind a caravan of laggard trucks, we pull off at the blasé village of Villacarrillo for gas and restroom, but we see nothing suggestive of coffee or photo tableaux. Winding up mountainous N-IV, we travel past olives, olives and more olives. We stop at Arroyo del Ajanco, but there's not much here but for a sprinkling of dowdy *casas* and a couple of stores.

At Bailén, we cut onto N-322, proceeding northeast through Linares, toward Úbeda....

la mancha

1. Alcaraz
2. El Jardín
3. Albacete

LA MANCHA

Eighty-one kilometers (about fifty miles) from Albacete, I petitioned for a pullover when I spotted what looked to be a ruinous aqueduct on a crest one hill over from the precipitous village of Alcaraz.

"You don't really want to stop, do you?" Uncle Chuck moans.

I insist. Parked at the foot of the hill with the ruins, Uncle Chuck waits in the car as I pad through a stand of pines, then negotiate a steep grade. I wade through deep grasses, minding my grip on tiers of sheer rock. Up top, nearly breathless, I frame a moldering scene with my camera. Little more than crumbling stone walls and redbrick arches of a Berber castle fill my viewfinder; not an aqueduct, after all. Now, happy with this bit of information, plus a record of Moorish rubble, I head back to the car and appeal for a browse of this village's *plaza mayor*.

"But the books say it's fetching," I tell Uncle Chuck as he shakes his head.

Alcaraz, a practically forgotten hill town of fewer than two thousand inhabitants, thrived as a Muslim stronghold before the forces of Alfonso VIII de Castilla conquered it in 1213. Alcaraz earned the title of *Ciudad* in the sixteenth century when noteworthy Renaissance construction added beauty to the central plaza. Architectural survivors include the *ayuntamiento* and *lonja* with formal Renaissance towers. I must see them, photograph them.

As we approach the center of town, not a soul stirs in these compressed streets. We wangle our Peugeot between sagging buildings on a hill inclined treacherously steep. Uncle Chuck has all he can do to keep our car from slipping backwards. Near the top, we are trapped in a one-way alley with a police vehicle heading straight at us. Uncle Chuck puts the car in reverse. We slowly back out of the squad car's way. The policemen glare, wondering, no doubt, what in the hell we are doing in Alcaraz.

Ten minutes later, burning our clutch, we pinch through narrow streets called Calle de Monjas and Calle de Vicario.

"I can't take any more of this," Uncle Chuck snaps. "Screw your Renaissance buildings! We're getting the hell out of here."

I slump in my seat. At the foot of the hill, we pull into a lot of a restaurant called simply J.M.

Outdoors, it's gray, cold and wintry, the restaurant, fragrantly cozy. A pleasant woman, the owner, waits on us, insisting we have the *menú del día*, plates of green string beans dotted with cubes of ham. A bottle of *vino de la casa*, Covas Yermas (an Albacete appellation) proves an ideal match with this rustic fare. While Uncle Chuck enjoys a bowl of flan for dessert, I nurse a cup of espresso, gazing out to the ruins. On another hill stands a gigantic stone figure of Christ. Sun breaks from cloud cover, anointing Him with golden light.

Back on N-322, I am not eager to get to Albacete.

I can't believe it when Uncle Chuck pulls over as I ask to stop at a beguiling village named El Jardín.

"Just a picture, that's all," he warns. "And shoot it from the side of the road."

El Jardín looks eerie, a time warp of mostly abandoned, *teja*-clad adobe *casas* growing from a hillside. Alongside this stretch of N-322, roadside structures are fixed up as mercantiles or warehouses. I see not one person.

We roll eastward through flat agricultural terrain, approaching the southeastern region of Castilla-La Mancha. Before long, we reach a plateau of brick-veneered, post-1960s high-rise confusion known as Albacete, a traffic-glutted city that miraculously earned the moniker "New York of La Mancha." Not even close; believe me. *How does New York factor into "Spain's least interesting city"*...? Albacete (*Al Basite*, The Plain in Arabic) embodies a blue-collar, textile-agricultural municipality of one-hundred-and-sixty-thousand inhabitants. Renowned for cutlery from days of Moorish occupation, Albacete gained popularity as an agronomic center (chiefly wine and saffron) by the twentieth century.

Our modern hotel, Tryp Los Llanos, hosts a convention of Scandinavian farmers in bib overalls. *Gee, this is going to be an exhilarating stopover....*

"Bound to be interest here," Uncle Chuck consoles as we settle into our room.

From our balcony, we see across the street the leafy Parque Abelardo Sánchez with its Museo Provincial. We head over. The museum is closed, so we stroll through the park before dinner. I sigh. Albacete can't be in Spain, the Spain I adore.

Sueño Dulce

I dreamed my way back to Córdoba, to the old mezquita. *No domes floated above, no vaults rose in its midst. The roof lay flat, as it did before the Reconquest. Cloying redolence of cardamom hung in the cool air as I gazed to the minaret. No bells. All trees were palms and the north end of the mosque opened to the air. I saw worshipers inside on the floor, crouched forward in prayer.*

No tourists throng the lovely environment of the courtyard, only three men in Moorish dress cleansing their beards in a well. When they move on toward the mosque, I step up to the well. On its stony side have been chiseled words and numbers: *NEMRAC 527C.* As concentric rings on the water's surface acquiesce to mirror-like finish, I startle at the reflection staring back: a hydrous man in white Polo shirt and navy cardigan sweater under an open gray sport coat; his moustache, dyed auburn. He locks his piercing, hazel eyes with mine. In echoic resonance, this apparition says, "Hello, my friend. Good to see you again. What brings you this time to Córdoba?"

I answer, "Here I have come to find myself...."

epílogo

409

EPÍLOGO

On a return trip to California, the Muse struck. Over years, seeking duende *in Spain, I glimpsed it in eyes of Gypsies. I even sensed* duende *fleetingly at Valle de los Caídos. El Cid, Santa Teresa, Cervantes and* Fray Junípero Serra had duende. *Federico García Lorca manifested its epitome.* Duende *pulsed from the canvases of Goya and Picasso, amidst details of Gaudí's Fabulist constructions. Even paisanos engendered the virtue of* duende. *I was stung by its allure at La Alhambra. But doggedly I searched the entire while to discover at last that* duende *resided deep within me.*

Duende is swollen passion, an inner demon festering for extrication. *Duende* stings with bravura, naked truth and wantonness, plunging one's being into all one does. *Duende* embodies the essential quality of life, a deep love of living. What's more, *duende* is reciprocal—we recognize it transpicuously, like stigmata, in others who exude it.

Nevertheless, I feel at home in Spain, the outlet for my *afición*. Until my return, I carry *duende* in my heart.

¡Viva España! ¡Vive el duende!

> The *duende*, then, is a power, not a work. It is a struggle, not a thought. I have heard an old maestro of the guitar say, "The *duende* is not in the throat; the *duende* climbs up inside you, from the soles of the feet." Meaning this: it is not a question of ability, but of true, living style, of blood, of the most ancient culture, of spontaneous creation.
>
> —Federico García Lorca, 1922

BIBLIOGRAFÍA

BOOKS

Ángel, Miguel, and García Guinea. *Santillana y Altamira*. León, Spain: Editorial Everest, 1990.

Barrucand, Marianne, and Achim Bednorz. *Moorish Architecture in Andalusia*. London: Taschen, 1992.

Caracciolo, Marella, and Francesco Venturi. *Houses & Palaces of Majorca*. London: Tauris Parke Books, 1996.

Cervantes Saavedra, Miguel de. *Don Quixote. The Ingenious Gentleman of La Mancha*. Trans. John Ormsby. New York: The Heritage Press, 1950.

Cipriani, Christin, ed. *Fodor's Spain*. Toronto: Fodor's Travel Publications, 2001.

Edwards, Gwynne. *¡Flamenco!* New York: Thames & Hudson, 2000.

Font, Bartomeu Obrador, Ph.D. *Fr. Junípero Serra. Mallorca-Mexico-Sierra Gorda-Californias*. Palma de Mallorca: Comissió Cultura, 1992.

Geiger, Maynard, OFM, Ph.D. *Franciscan Missionaries in Hispanic California, 1769-1848. A Biographical Dictionary*. San Marino, CA: The Huntington Library, 1969.

————. (translated and annotated by). *Palóu's Life of Fray Junípero Serra*. Washington, D.C.: Academy of Franciscan History, 1955.

Gili, J. L., and Stephen Spender, trans. *Selected Poems of Federico García Lorca*. New York: Hogart Press, 1943.

Goldstein, Joyce. *Savoring Spain & Portugal*. San Francisco: Sunset Books, 2000.

Hemingway, Ernest. *For Whom the Bell Tolls*. New York: Simon & Schuster (Scribner Classics), (1940), 1960.

————. *The Sun Also Rises*. New York: Simon & Schuster (Scribner Classics), (1926), 1960.

Inman, Nick, ed. *Eyewitness Travel Guides, Spain*. New York: DK Publishing, Inc., 2000.

Insight Compact Guides. *Mallorca*. Munich: Apa Publications, 1996.

Kenny, Sarah Thérèse, ed. *Let's Go Barcelona*. New York: St. Martin's Press, 2002.

Levitas, Mitchel, ed. *Spain: The Best Travel Writing from The New York Times*. New York: Abbeville Publishing Group, 2000.

Lonely Planet. *Andalucía*. Victoria, Australia, 2001.

Lozoya, Marqués de. *Palacio Real de la Granja de San Ildefonso*. Madrid: Editorial Patrimonio Nacional, 1985.

Martínez, Luis Montriel and Alfredo J. Morales. *The Cathedral of Seville*. London: Scala Publishers, 1999.

Maurer, Christopher, ed. *In Search of Duende*. New York: Directions Publishing Company, 1998.

Michelin. *Green Guide to Spain*. Watford Herts, UK: Michelin Guides, 1998.

Michener, James A. *The Drifters*. New York: Fawcett Crest, 1982.

————. *Iberia*. New York: Fawcett Crest, 1982.

Miranda, Rufino. *Toledo: Its Art and Its History*. Toledo: Julio de la Cruz, 1997.

Moore, Dina Bowden. *Junípero Serra in His Native Isle*. Palma de Mallorca: Gráficas Miramar, 1976.

Morgado, Martin J. *Junípero Serra's Legacy*. Pacific Grove, CA: 1987.

Palóu, Francisco, OFM. *Relación Histórica de la Vida y Apostólicas Tareas del Venerable Padre Fray Junípero Serra*. Mexico City: Don Felipe de Júñiga y Ontiveros, 1787.

Partington, Helen, ed. *Insight Guide: Spain*. Maspeth, New York: Langenscheidt Publishers, Inc., 2000.

Pereda, Manuel de la Reguera. *Guide: Santillane on the Sea and Altamira*. Santander, Spain: Aldus Velarde, 1971.

Queralt, Maria Pilar. *Montserrat*. Barcelona, 2002.

Schreiner, Claus, ed. *Flamenco. Gypsy Dance and Music from Andalusia*. Portland: Amadeus Press, 2000.

Van Zandt, Eleanor. *The Life and Works of Antoni Gaudí*. Bath, UK: Kliczkowski Publisher, 1995.

Williams, John Alden, ed. *Islam*. New York: George Braziller, 1962.

INTERVIEWS

Alles, Jaime: Ronda, 2001.
Curchin, Leonard: Segovia, 2002.
Corbera, Ignacio: Barcelona, 2002.
Corriente, Diego: San Diego, CA, 2002-2003.
Lozano, Tom: Santa Barbara, CA, Albuquerque, NM, 2001-2003.
Montoya, Rima: Santa Barbara, CA, Albuquerque, NM, 2001-2002.
Vallbona, Dr. Carlos: Houston, TX, San Diego, CA, 1993-2003.
Vavra, Robert: Seville, 2002.

WEB SITES

www.alcavia.net
www.arqbcn.org
www.castillosdesoria.com
www.dipualba.es
www.encyclopedia.com
http://herso.freeservers.com
www.ideal.es
www.info-ab.uclm.es
www.inquisitivetraveler.com
www.interlinkbooks.com
www.LukeTravels.com
www.newadvent.org
www.planetware.com
www.reverso.net
www.rootsworld.com
www.sierrademontanchez.com
www.SocialChannel.com
www.spain.net
www.uwm.edu

GLOSARIO

(CM = CATALAN/*MALLORQUÍN*)

A

abierto: open

acueducto: aqueduct

adiós: goodbye

aeropuerto: airport

afición: passion; group of aficionados or fans

aficionado: devoted follower; one impassioned with or expert in a subject such as flamenco or bullfighting

agua: water

ahí: there

ajimeces: Moorish paired windows divided by a single slender column

ajo: garlic

ajo blanco: cold soup of garlic, cream and pulverized almonds

ajuntament: town hall (C/M)

alcachofas: artichokes

alcázar: fortress

almejas: clams

alemán/alemanes: German/s

almendra: almond

almendro: almond tree

alminar: minaret

Almohades: ancient tribe from the High Atlas range (Algeria, Morocco, Tunesia)

Almorávides: ancient Berber nomad tribe from the Sahara

almuerzo: lunch

al-Qur'ân: the Koran

alta cocina: haute cuisine; fine food prepared by highly skilled chefs

amar a Dios: "good day"; literally, "love God"

a mata caballo: breakneck speed; Uncle Chuck's method of driving *ambiente*: atmosphere, surroundings

amigo/a: friend

anciano/a: elderly (*adj*); elder (*n*)

anguila: eel

anís: liqueur made with aniseed

aperitivo: before-dinner drink; appetizer

archivo: archive

arco: arch

arroz: rice

atalaya: watchtower (mainland Spain)

auto da fe: public persecution of heretics, imposed by the Inquisition (literally, "act of faith")

autopista: toll highway

autovía: highway

avenida: avenue

avinguda: avenue (C/M)

¡ay!: a jaleo

ayuntamiento: town hall

azulejo: glazed wall tile, usually with a painted design motif

B

bacalao: codfish, usually dried

bahía: bay

ballo: slingshot

banco: bank

bandolero: bandit

Barcelonés: denizens of Barcelona

basílica: basilica, a church granted certain ceremonial rights

bienvenidos: welcome

billete: ticket

bistec (*biftec*) *de buey*: beefsteak

blanco/a: white

bocadillo: snack, sandwich

bodega: wine cellar, warehouse

bon any: good year (C/M)

bon dia: good day (C/M)

boquerones: small, anchovy-type fish (whitebait)

bosque: wood; forest

bóveda: architectural dome

buen viaje: bon voyage

buenas noches: good night

bueno/a: good

buenos días: good day

buenas tardes: good afternoon

buen gusto: good flavor; delicious

C

cabeza: head

cabrito: goat

café con leche: coffee with milk

café cantante: singing club

café en vaso sombra: coffee with milk in a glass

café solo: espresso

calamares: squid

caldo: broth

caldereta de peix: fish soup (C/M)

caliente: hot

calle: street, road

callos: tripe

caló: Spanish Gypsy language

camarín: niche for religious icon (C/M: *camarí*)

camarones: shrimps

cambio sentido: highway flyover, turn-around

Camino Real, El: "The Royal Road" linking New Spain's government headquarters in Mexico City with her American colonies, including California

campana: bell

campanario: pierced bell tower or wall

caña: draft beer

capella: chapel (C/M)

capilla: chapel

caracol: snail

carne: meat

carrer: street, road (C/M)

carreta: hay cart, wagon

carterista: pickpocket

casa: house, dwelling

casal: mansion (C/M)

casco viejo: old town

castaña: chestnut

castellan: chatelaine

castillo: castle

castrum: Roman fort

Católico/a: Catholic

catedral: cathedral

celebridad: celebrity

cena: dinner

cercanía: commuter train

cerdo: pork

cerrado: closed

cervecería: bar, public house

cerveza: beer

charlatanería: café chatter

churro: deep-fried pastry stick, usually eaten after dipping in thick hot chocolate

cigala: mantis shrimp

cimborio: architectural lantern

ciudad: city

claustro: cloister

cocina: kitchen

cojones: testicles; "balls," nerve

comedor: dining room

comida: food; lunch

complementario (*servicio complementario*): complimentary appetizer

con: with

conquistador: conqueror

convento: convent

converso: one who is converted

corazón: heart

cordero: lamb / *asado*: roast / *chuleta*: chop

corrida: bullfight

cortado: espresso infused with a splash of milk

costa: coast

420

costalero: one who carries a religious icon upon his shoulders during the fiesta parade

crema catalana: creamy dessert similar to *crème brûlée*

criadillas: bulls testicles

Cristo: Christ

cuánto es: how much?

cuenta, la: account, bill

cueva: cave

cuidado: beware; warning

D

del: of the (*de* + *el*)

de nada: you're welcome

depredador: predator

desayuno: breakfast

Déu: God (C/M)

digestivo: after-dinner drink, liqueur

dinero: money, currency

Dios: God

dulce: sweet

E

embalse: lake

emir (*amîr*): Muslim ruler, prince or commander

emirate: sultanate; kingdom of an emir

ensalada mixta or *variada*: mixed green salad

ermlta: hermitage

escalofríos: goose flesh, shivers

escuela: school

¡eso es!: a jaleo meaning "way to go (sing, dance)"

espárrago: asparagus

estación: station

estancia: ranch

estupendo: stupendous, marvelous

Extremeño/a: denizen of Extremadura

F

fabada: bean and sausage stew

fachada: façade

felag-mengu (*felah men encûn*): Arabic for "singing laborers" (origin of the word "flamenco")

feria: religious celebration

fideos/fideuà: noodles; paella-style dish prepared with noodles instead of rice

fiesta: public festival, fair

finca: farm, ranch

flan: caramel custard

flor: flower

forn: oven (C/M)

foto: photograph

fray: brother or friar

frigidarium: cold bath compartment of a public bathhouse

frito: fried

frits: Mallorcan casserole

fuente: fountain

fuerte: strong, hard, heavy

G

gaitero: bagpiper

galería: gallery; passage

gambas: large shrimp, prawns

gato: cat

gazpacho: cold soup of puréed tomato, onion, cucumber

ginebra: gin

Gitano/a: Gypsy

gordales: large portions (of food)

gracias: thank you

granja: farmhouse, collective farm

greixeras: Mallorcan casserole prepared with lard (C/M)

Guardia Civil: national policemen of Spain

H

hajj: obligatory (Islamic) pilgrimage to Mecca

harén: harem

hasta la vista: goodbye; see you

hasta luego: see you later

helado: ice cream

hermoso/a: handsome, beautiful

hígado: liver

hidalgo: nobleman; honorable

hielo: ice

hierba: liqueur made with any herb

hijo: son; child

Hispanidad: "Spanishness"

Hispanophile: one enamored of Spain, Spanish ethos and people

hola: hello

horchata: cold, almond-flavored soft drink

horno: oven

hórreo: raised granary constructed of granite and typical of the Spanish provinces of Galicia and Asturias

hoy: today

huevo: egg

I

iglesia: church

Isabeline: Romantic style of architecture (late Gothic, early *plateresque*)

J

jaleo: words of encouragement; rhythmic accentuation and spontaneous verbal comments

jamón: ham

jardín: garden

jarra: pitcher, jug

jerez: sherry

jubilado/a: retired person, senior citizen

judería: Jewish quarter

jugo (zumo) de naranja: orange juice

K

Kufic: Arabic inscription

L

lagar: wine press, vat

langosta: lobster

langostino: langoustine, crayfish, prawn, small lobster

lechón: suckling pig

leche: milk

leche frita: fried milk (custard)

libro de reclamaciones: complaint book

limpia: shoeshine

llonganisses: sausages (C/M)

lomo: pork chop

lonja: commodities exchange

lumbrera: skylight, vent; one who is erudite

luz: light

M

Madrileño/a: denizen of Madrid

madrugada: taking on the wee hours by nightclubbing

magistral (*iglesia*): magisterial church of which all of the clergymen require university masters of Doctrine

manta: mantle

mantilla: veil or scarf of lace worn over a *peineta* (comb); literally, "baby clothes"

mantón: shawl

Manueline: Late-Gothic style of architectural flourish inspired by sea ornamentation (developed in Portugal; late Gothic)

mar: sea

mariscos: seafood

marisquería: seafood restaurant

marginado: urban fringe, usually a ghetto

más: more

matador: torero who slays the bull

medina: Islamic or North African city

membrillo: quince preserves

mentidero: gossipy din

menú del día: daily menu

mercado: market

merienda: light, early-evening meal

mesa: table; plateau of flat tableland

meseta: plain

mesón: inn

mexuar: Islamic council chambers

mezquita: mosque

migas: hors d'œuvres coated in crumbs and deep-fried; literally, "crumbs"

mihrâb: prayer niche facing Mecca

milagro: miracle; charms left at altars for acts of favors and/or gratitude for intercessional favors granted

minbar: staircase-like pulpit in a mosque

mirador: bay window; viewpoint

molí: mill (C/M)

molino: mill

monasterio: monastery

montera: torero's hat

Mozárabe: "Arabized"; converted Spanish Catholic servants of the Muslims

mozo: waiter, porter, servant (literally, young man or young fellow)

muchacho: boy, lad

Mudéjar: Ibero-Islamic forms produced under Christian rule

muezzin: one who calls the Islamic faithful to prayer from the top of a minaret

muqarnas: hanging ceiling of honeycomb-style cells and carved stalactites of *Nasrid* interior architecture

murallas: curtain walls, defensive walls, ramparts

muchas: much, many

museo: museum

muy: very

N

naranja: orange (the fruit)

naranjo: orange tree

navajas: razor clams

niño/a: child

nuevo/a: new

O

obispo: bishop

ofrenda: offering, such as flowers to (the image of) a saint

ojo: eye

oliva: olive

olivo: olive tree

oricio: sea urchin

oro: gold

P

padre: father; title of priest

paella: Valencian dish of saffron-tinted rice and meat and/or seafood

palacete: small palace; seigniorial estate

palacio: palace

parador: roadhouse

paraguas: umbrella

parque: park

párroco: parish priest; (C/M: *rector*)

paseo: boulevard; walk, stroll

Paso de la Cruz: Way of the Cross

passeig: boulevard (C/M)

pastelería: bakery

patas de cerdo: pigs feet

patata: potato

pato: duck

pazo: feudal estate (*Gallego*)

peineta: comb

percebes: gooseneck barnacles

perdiz: partridge

pero: but

peseta: unit of Spanish currency before the euro

Petrense/a: denizen of Petra de Mallorca

picante: hot, peppery, highly seasoned

Picares: nibbles, snacks; also called *pinchos*

pimienta: pepper (the spice)

pimiento: pepper (the fruit)

pinchos a la brasa: shish kebobs

pisto: fried vegetable hash

plateresque: Spanish architectural decorative style of baroque

plata: silver

plato: plate, dish

plaza mayor: main public square

plaza de toros: bullring

pobre: poor; poor fellow

pollo: chicken / *a la parrila*: broiled

pont: bridge (C/M)

¡por Dios!: for God! (sometimes a *jaleo*)

por favor: please

postre: dessert

potencias: golden rays fashioned from metal or gilded wood; large halos encircling statues of saints or Christ

prat: meadow (C/M)

prohibido: prohibited, forbidden

propuesta de menú: menu proposal

puente: bridge

puerta: gate, doorway

puerto: port

púlpito: pulpit

pulpo: octopus

pundonor: refined sense of self respect; honor

Q

qibla: direction of Islamic prayer

qué: what?

queso: cheese

R

rabo del toro: tail of the bull

raciones: small portions (of food)

rambla: avenue; dry riverbed

rape: monkfish

raya: skate (ray fish)

real: royal

Reconquista: Christian conquest of those parts of Spain occupied by Moors

recuerdo: keepsake, souvenir; memory

reina: queen

rejas: wrought iron bars, grille

resaca: hangover

restaurante: restaurant

retablo: altarpiece, reredos

retiro: retreat (*n*)

revuelto: scrambled (usually eggs), mixed up

rey: king

ría: inlet from ocean or bay

riñon: kidney

río: river

Rioja: province of northern Spain, wine from that province

rodaballo: turbot

rojo: red

Romany: Gypsy, of the Gypsy; language of the Indian Gypsies

romería: pilgrimage

romero/a: pilgrim[1]; *romero*: rosemary[2]

S

salsa: sauce

santo/a: saint; holy

sardana: folk ring-dance of the Catalan people

seco/a: dry

seo: cathedral

sepia: cuttlefish

sesos: brains

setas: mushrooms

seu: cathedral (C/M)

sí: yes

sierra: mountain

solamente: only one

soledad: solitude

solomillo: veal filet

sol y sombra: sun and shade

sopa: soup

sudatorium: sweat room of a public bathhouse

sueño: dream

supermercado: supermarket

sûq: oriental bazaar

T

taberna: tavern

tablao: stage

taifa: petty Islamic dynasty

talaia: watchtower (C/M)

tapas: bite-sized snacks

tapería: tapas bar

taquilla: booking office, ticket office, box office

taurino: bullfighting; the business of bullfighting

teito: a shed made of stone (*Gallego*)

teja: half-cylindrical roofing tile of fired orange clay

ternera: veal

terraza: terrace

tienda: shop, boutique

tinto: red (wine)

tío: uncle

tocino de cielo: custard dessert (literally, "bacon of heaven")

Toledano/a: denizen of Toledo

torero: professional bullfighter

torno: a revolving counter, turnstile

toro: bull

torre: tower

tortilla: omelet

tortilla a la española: casserole of potatoes, onion and egg, usually served room-temperature

tragador/a: glutton

traje de luces: torero's satin "suit of lights"

trampa: swindle; illegal card game

Transverberation: ecclesial term given to the Holy Spirit's piercing of St. Teresa de Ávila's heart *tren*: train

trona: pulpit

trucha: trout

tumbet: Mallorcan stew (C/M)

V

vaya con Dios: "go with God"

vega: valley

venganza: vengeance, revenge; retaliation

verduras: vegetables

vieiras: scallop meat

viejo/a: old (*adj*); old one (*nm/f*)

venta: selling; a roadside store

Vera Crucis: True Cross

Vía Crucis: Way of the Cross

vino: wine

virgen: virgin

viva/e: to burst out cheering

viva yo: "good for me"

Y

yemas: candy made of and resembling egg yolks

Z

zona monumental: monumental zone; historic section of town

INDICE DE NOMBRES

I

N

O

EL AUTOR

Terry Ruscin's *Mission Memoirs* (Sunbelt Publications, 1999), a coffee-table book on the historic California missions and Spain's impact on Alta California, was recipient of the coveted Benjamin Franklin Award, was honored as "Art Book of the Year" by *San Diego Magazine* and was one of only twenty-eight titles included in Rounce & Coffin Club's 2000 Western Books Exhibition. Photographic images by Terry Ruscin are included in Jerome Tupa's and Holly Witchey's book *An Uncommon Mission* (Welcome Enterprises, 1999).

Ruscin's *Taste for Travel* (1stBooks Library, 2003), embodies a trilogy of gastronomic adventures in England, France and Italy.

Terry Ruscin, a retired advertising executive, lives in Hendersonville, North Carolina, and is editor for *¡Siempre Adelante!*, an international newsletter to promote the Cause of Blessed Junípero Serra's canonization.

A seasoned, independent traveler, Ruscin has found pleasure in Western Europe for more than three decades. For *Los Duendes*, he drew on copious research notes and interviews.

If you would like to share *Los Duendes* with family and friends, it is easy to order through your local bookstores, directly through the publisher (www.publishamerica.com) or through www.Amazon.com.

Watch for Terry Ruscin's next book:

DINING AND WHINING
Conservative Viewpoints on Eating versus Dining

Printed in the United States
31900LVS00002B/18